GHALIB

Mirza Asadullah Khan Ghalib 1797–1869. On the paper he holds are the following words:
*I am the renowned Ghalib; do not ask of my name and fame. I am both Asadullah and Asa-
dullah's man.* That is, my name is Asadullah, and my allegiance is to Asadullah, 'The Lion
of God'—a title of Ali, cousin and son-in-law of the Prophet Muhammad, and the object
of Ghalib's special reverence.

❀ GHALIB ❀
1797-1869

VOLUME I: LIFE AND LETTERS

translated and edited by
RALPH RUSSELL
and
KHURSHIDUL ISLAM

HARVARD UNIVERSITY PRESS
CAMBRIDGE   MASSACHUSETTS
1969

FIRST PUBLISHED IN 1969

UNESCO COLLECTION OF REPRESENTATIVE WORKS
INDIAN SERIES

This work has been accepted in the Indian translation series of the United
Nations Educational, Scientific and Cultural Organization (UNESCO). It was
recommended for publication by the Committee on Far Eastern Literature set
up to advise Unesco in this field by the International Council for Philosophy
and Humanistic Studies, and by the National Academy of Letters of India
(Sahitya Akademi).

PRINTED IN GREAT BRITAIN

✸ Contents ✸

✵ Introduction ✵

The modern literatures of the Indian sub-continent are comparatively young, and though there are in many of them figures who have for two centuries and more been recognized within their own language-communities as great writers, few of them have yet become widely known outside them even as names. The few that have are generally those who are so enthusiastically admired by the people in whose language they wrote that this very enthusiasm arouses the curiosity of others. In Urdu there have been two such writers—Iqbal and Ghalib. Their fascination for Urdu speakers is amply attested by the fact that these two—and, as yet, these two alone—have in the last few decades each become the subject of a whole literature of research, criticism and appreciation, and both have inspired attempts by Urdu speakers to win for them a wider audience through translations and studies in English. Iqbal's fortunes have prospered beyond this point, and there now exists a number of studies and translations in English, aimed at, and likely to appeal to, a world audience, and affording access to anyone who can read English to a widely representative range of his work; and translation and studies are also available in other European languages. This has not yet happened with Ghalib. Studies and translations in English of varying merit do indeed exist, but these are either not aimed at, or are not for one reason or another likely to appeal widely to, an audience outside the sub-continent. We hope that the present work may do so. We have for many years believed that if once the barrier of language could be satisfactorily surmounted and Ghalib's prose and verse made available to a world audience, his work would win him a place in world literature which historical circumstance has hitherto denied him; and it is this belief which has inspired us to undertake the present work.

Its plan, stated in general terms, is to present in translation a representative selection of his prose and verse set against a portrait of the man and his age. The present volume, devoted to Ghalib's life and letters, is the first of two. In a second volume we shall attempt the far more difficult task of presenting his poetry. To speak in more detail, we have attempted wherever possible in the volume now before the reader to let the story of Ghalib's life emerge from his own words; but this can become the predominant method only from the early eighteen-fifties, when the steady flow of Urdu letters which was to last nearly twenty years begins. For the earlier years we have drawn mainly upon the *Memoir of Ghalib* written by Ghalib's friend and younger contemporary Hali—a book which is in its own right a classic of Urdu literature. But this could not

A*

supply all the materials necessary to our purpose, and we have supplemented Hali's account with material from other writers and with writing of our own. In the earlier chapters such supplementary writing amounts to a substantial part of the whole, but the proportion decreases sharply from the point where Ghalib's letters and other writings largely suffice to tell their own story. We have deliberately chosen not to put into separate compartments the different kinds of materials of which the book is composed. Where anything that Ghalib or Hali says requires elaboration if it is to be fully intelligible to the general reader in the English-speaking world, we have supplied it at once in the main text, believing that the general reader does not like having to refer to footnotes more than is absolutely necessary, and likes still less having to turn the pages and seek elsewhere for what he wants to know there and then. On the other hand we know that there are those who, so to speak, like to take their author neat, even where this impairs their awareness of exactly what is going on. For their benefit we have tried as far as possible to separate text from comment sufficiently clearly to enable them to do without the latter if they wish to try. Little more remains to be said. Naturally enough, Muslim names occur frequently throughout the book, and since these often cause confusion to those who are not familiar with them, we have thought it best to give a note about them at the outset. (In the same note we have dealt with our treatment of the problem of transliteration.) For those who may wish to refresh their memories of the thread of the narrative from time to time we have provided a chronology of Ghalib's life, and a note on the letters and some of Ghalib's correspondents follows the main text. For the benefit of our fellow-scholars (to whom we address ourselves briefly in the next paragraph) we then give full notes and references relating to what we have written. And finally we provide an annotated index—i.e. one in which we have, for example, under the entry for Alai, prefaced the list of page references by a brief account of who Alai was; the index also includes Urdu words used in the main text, which are given and explained at the point where alphabetical sequence places them. A single section containing all these things has seemed to us more convenient for the reader than a whole series of items—glossary, biographical notes, index and so on—supplementing the main text. Whatever else is provided is listed in the table of contents and calls for no comment here.

A book of this kind is, naturally, not intended primarily for those who can read Ghalib in the original, and still less for Ghalib scholars. All the same, we hope that it will not be devoid of interest even to them, and therefore add here a few remarks addressed primarily to them. We would first draw their attention to the way in which we have chosen to arrange our materials. Hali's biographical sketch of Ghalib is largely anecdotal, and the many incidents which it relates are not for the most part placed in any sort of historical order. Similarly the published collections of Ghalib's letters have always been arranged in such a way as to give all the letters to, say, Majruh, in a single block, all those to Tufta in another, and so on. We have chosen instead to follow a more strictly historical order throughout, rearranging Hali's materials and taking Ghalib's letters (with occasional exceptions) in order of date, regardless of the correspondent to whom they were written. (Here we have made full use of the valuable—and often underrated—work of Ghulam Rasul Mihr, accepting his dating without question except in a very few cases where there seemed to be strong grounds for modifying his conclusions. We have likewise accepted the dating given by Afaq Husain in his collection *Nadirat i Ghalib*.) We are convinced that this chronological arrangement yields a clearer picture than the traditional arrangement can give, and we look forward to the day when editors of the Urdu and Persian texts of the letters will adopt the same principle. Our aim has been to include in our selection everything of significant interest in Ghalib's published Persian and Urdu prose writings, excluding only those elements in them—for example, the detailed discussions of the sins of the Indian lexicographers of Persian—which are meaningful only to those who possess specialised knowledge. To this end we have, between us, read all the relevant writings of Ghalib. Much of the material has been studied by both of us, but Ralph Russell is responsible for the final selection from Ghulam Rasul Mihr's *Khutut i Ghalib*—the most comprehensive collection of Ghalib's Urdu letters so far—while Khurshidul Islam has made the selections from *Nadirat i Ghalib* (the letters of 1848-59 to Nabi Bakhsh Haqir), from *Makatib i Ghalib* (the letters to the Nawwabs of Rampur), and from the Persian materials (of which *Mihr i Nimroz*, *Dastambu*, and the Persian letters in *Panj Ahang* are the most important). The English translation is primarily Ralph Russell's work, but the text was finalised only after thorough checking by Khurshidul Islam, after which discussion and consultation with him resulted in numerous modifications.

As we have already said, for the material on Ghalib's life our main source, after Ghalib's own writings, has been Hali's *Yadgar i Ghalib*. But we have made full use of the work of subsequent scholars and biographers, notably Ghulam Rasul Mihr's *Ghalib*, Malik Ram's *Zikr i Ghalib*, (4th, revised edition) and *Talamiza i Ghalib*, and Shaikh Muhammad Ikram's books. To the last-named author's *Hayat i Ghalib* we owe a special debt. It is in our view the best short biography that has appeared in recent years, and certainly the one best suited to our present purpose. The author's arrangement of his material is, in general, admirable, particularly for the period to 1857, and up to that point we have not only adopted the arrangement as the basis for our own, but also drawn heavily upon the factual material which the book contains.

But it is not only he to whom we have a debt to acknowledge. One or other of us (in some cases both of us) has had occasion at various stages in our work to meet or correspond also with Ghulam Rasul Mihr, Imtiyaz Ali Arshi, Malik Ram and Afaq Husain. We found them all very ready to help us, and we gladly take this opportunity to express our sincere gratitude to them all and also to the Raza Library, Rampur. We are especially grateful to Malik Ram for his detailed criticisms of our manuscript, and particularly of the first half of the book; we must add that he is in no way responsible for any errors which it may still contain, and would not necessarily agree with all of our judgements.

It remains to add a word about the notes and references section to which brief reference was made earlier. Since the main text is intended primarily for the general reader, we have not encumbered it with numbers indicating the detailed notes and references intended for the scholar. (Such numbers as are to be found in the main text indicate the few footnotes which we have felt it necessary to include on the pages where these numbers occur.) The scholar reading through the main text will generally know where a note is called for, and if, whenever he feels that a note or reference is needed, he will turn to the section which follows the main text, he will find, we hope, that we do not disappoint him.

We are under no illusion that our work represents anything approaching the last word, even on the limited ground which we have covered. In the first place, fresh materials are still being discovered. As we write these lines we are aware that a small but important collection of Ghalib's Persian letters which has quite recently come to light is being included by Imtiyaz Ali Arshi in an edition of the Persian letters which he is preparing; and it is in our view entirely probable that other letters may yet be discovered in years to come. Secondly, Ghalib's prose works have been, in general, very inadequately edited. Imtiyaz Ali Arshi is perhaps the only editor who has fully responded to the demands which Ghalib's greatness surely makes of his editors, and who has produced work distinguished both by a very high degree of textual accuracy and by scholarly and adequate annotation; and Arshi's work extends only to a relatively small proportion of Ghalib's letters. Even Ghulam Rasul Mihr, whose notes are valuable, has failed to achieve a satisfactory standard of textual accuracy. We are therefore, for the moment, obliged to operate with inaccurate and inadequately annotated texts. Thirdly, without undervaluing the work done by the scholars whom we have named above, it is still true to say that there is still considerable scope for the more detailed study of Ghalib's many associates and of the nature of his relationship with each of them. Only when all these deficiencies are made good will it be possible to produce work of definitive accuracy and to fill some of the gaps that must certainly be present in any work based upon the materials currently available.

Finally, we are well aware that mistakes are inevitable in any work of this length, no matter how much effort one makes to eliminate them. To any reader who will take the trouble to draw our attention to them, or indeed to any passage which arouses his doubts, we shall be duly grateful; for this will help us to improve the quality of our work and so to serve more adequately both Ghalib and the new audience of readers to whom we seek to introduce him.

RALPH RUSSELL
KHURSHIDUL ISLAM

Note on Muslim Names and their Pronunciation and Transliteration

Before we begin to mention names it will be as well to give some approximate indication of how they are to be pronounced—approximate, because the average reader will not be aspiring to complete accuracy and this could in any case not be imparted without lengthy and detailed descriptions which considerations of space do not allow. The main points to note concern the vowel sounds. These are much less numerous than in English, but also do not in most cases correspond completely to English sounds. However, the following are approximate equivalents:

'a' is like the 'a' in 'attire'
'ā' is like the 'a' in 'father'
'i' is like the 'i' in 'him'
'ī' is like the 'ee' in 'keen'
'u' is like the 'u' in 'put'
'ū' is like the 'u' in 'rule'
'e' is like the 'ay' in 'day'
'o' is like the 'o' in 'hole'
'ai' is like the 'a' in 'hat'
'au' is something like 'awe'

For the consonants the reader may use the sounds that the English letters indicate, though there are, in fact, substantial differences between the consonant systems of the two languages.

For the benefit of readers who are acquainted with Urdu or its script we have used accurate transliteration in the bibliography, in the notes and references where appropriate, and in the index.[1] Elsewhere, bearing in mind that all but the expert reader are apt to be intimidated by words dressed in their full panoply of diacriticals, we have confined ourselves to marking such long vowels as seemed necessary—for example, to distinguish Hāmid from Hamīd. Place names fairly widely known in traditional English dress have been

[1] We have followed with very minor modifications the system adopted by Platts in his dictionary (John T. Platts, *Dictionary of Urdu and Classical Hindi,* Oxford University Press, Fifth Impression, 1930) except that we have used the more usual *gh* where he uses *g*.

left in their familiar attire—e.g. Meerut instead of the correct Mīrath and Oudh instead of Avadh.

Hali begins his life of Ghalib with the words: 'Mirza Asadullah Khan Ghalib, known familiarly as Mirza Nosha, holder of the titles Najm ud Daula, Dabir ul Mulk, Asadullah Khan Bahadur, Nizam Jang, poetically named Ghalib in Persian and Asad in Urdu, was born in Agra on the night of the 8th of Rajab, 1212 AH.' Thus 'Ghalib' is only one element in a whole string of names and titles. In Ghalib's case the string is longer than in most, but the names of most of the men that occur in this book are quite long enough to make most readers feel, as an eminent British historian of India did, that 'the length of these Muhammadan names is terrible'. In this book we have done our best to state the names in a form that the reader will find it possible to cope with, and we shall explain presently how this has been done. But we should first describe the different elements that go to make up a Muslim name, and what these elements signify.

Besides their length, Muslim names have another feature that adds to the reader's difficulty. He is used to names made up of one or more forenames and a surname. But these concepts are unknown in Muslim society (except to those members of it who have had occasion to travel to countries where for official purposes they have been obliged to pick on one of their names and use it as a surname). In some families there is indeed a tradition of conferring upon a son the last element of the father's name; the noble Loharu family, to whom Ghalib was related by marriage, is a case in point. In this family the names end in 'ud Din Ahmad Khan'—Amīn ud Din Ahmad Khan, Ziya ud Din Ahmad Khan, and so on. But this is the exception rather than the rule, and there is often nothing in the names to show that fathers, sons and brothers are related. For example, in the present volume, one of Ghalib's correspondents is named Nabi Bakhsh; his sons' names are Abdul Latif and Nasīr ud Din. Another is named Mir Mahdi; his brother is named Mir Sarfaraz Husain. Incidentally, the same is true of Hindu names. Ghalib's best Hindu friend was named Hargopal; his son's name was Pitambar Singh.

Muslim names may be regarded as composed of three essential elements—prefixed styles of address (similar to our 'Doctor', 'Professor', 'The Reverend' and so on, but much more numerous than these), personal names (quite often consisting of a single word), and suffixed styles indicating ancestry, or local connections, or other things. Some examples of each will be given below. The use of the word 'Sahib' also calls for some comment. It is often said that it corresponds to the English 'Mr'; but the correspondence is only a partial one, for the use of 'Sahib' suffixed to the name or style of the person addressed or referred to is appropriate not only in relationships of a rather formal kind, but also to familiar and informal relationships. For a lady the word 'Begam' is similarly used, sometimes prefixed, but more often suffixed, to the personal name.

Among the prefixed styles, Mirza (Ghalib's own style), Mir, Sayyid, Hakim, Qazi and Munshi occur commonly in this volume. Mirza is the style appropriate to a man of Mughal (or Turkish) descent. Mir generally implies that the man so addressed is a Sayyid, that is, one who claims direct descent from the Prophet Muhammad through his daughter Fatima; and Sayyid itself is a common pre-fixed style of address. Hakim means one who is qualified to practise the traditional Greek system of medicine, which was inherited and modified by the Arabs and transmitted by them throughout the Islamic world. Qazi is one who dispenses Muslim law, conducts marriages and so on. Munshi has the root meaning of writer, or secretary, but as a title implies a person of somewhat higher conse-quence in the old Mughal administration. Maulvi and Maulana also occasionally occur. The first describes a man well-versed in Islamic learning, while the second, which literally means 'our master' has a similar, though perhaps less precise, connotation. Ghalib some-times humorously confers these and other titles upon his corres-pondents' children. Any of these styles, with 'Sahib' suffixed, may be commonly used in address or reference without any element of the person's name being attached. Hali in his book nearly always refers to Ghalib simply as 'Mirza'. Where a man is addressed as 'Hakim Sahib', or 'Qazi Sahib' or 'Munshi Sahib', it does not always imply that he himself follows the profession in question; it may merely mean that one or more of his forebears did so. Among titles of men more exalted than these the most common is 'Nawwab', to which the English 'Lord' is an approximate equivalent. Its holder may be nothing more than a big landlord, or he may be the ruler of a vast province, for the root meaning of the title is some-thing like 'one who exercises delegated powers', and an Emperor might entrust a man with powers over either a very small or a very large area.

The prefixed style is followed by the personal name. In Ghalib's case this is Asadullah. Like all Muslim names, this is meaningful. It means 'Lion of God', and was a title of Ali, the cousin and son-in-law of the Prophet. Ghalib quite often plays upon the literal meanings of his name and the names of his correspondents in his letters to them.

The personal name is generally followed by one or more suffixed styles. In Ghalib's case these begin with 'Khan', a style which may indicate one of two things; it shows either that its holder is a man of Afghan or Pathan stock, or else that he (or one of his ancestors) has been granted the title of Khan by some ruling power. 'Khan' is not a very exalted title. 'Khan Bahadur'—a title which Ghalib bore —is a grade above it. Other suffixed styles denote ancestry, either physical or spiritual. Yet others indicate a family connection with some famous place (for if it is not famous a man will not generally advertise his connection with it). One of Ghalib's correspondents is Safir Bilgrami. Safir is the personal name, and 'Bilgrami' means 'of Bilgram', a small township in the neighbourhood of Lucknow famous for its tradition of learning and scholarship. But generally the most significant of these suffixed styles is that of which 'Ghalib' is itself an example. 'Ghalib' is a takhallus—that is, an assumed, single-word name under which a poet writes his poetry. Every poet had to have one, for there are classical forms of Urdu poetry which require that the poet introduce his takhallus into the final couplet. And since in Ghalib's day almost every cultured man in Muslim society was a poet of sorts, there are not many of his friends who do not have a takhallus after their personal names.

Finally, some men have a familiar name by which their friends address them informally. Ghalib's was 'Mirza Nosha', and it was, incidentally, one which he very much disliked. One of his friends, Zulfaqar ud Din Haidar Khan was familiarly known as Husain Mirza.

In this book we have generally used the poetic pen-name alone in referring to Ghalib's many friends and acquaintances. Our first aim in doing so was to lighten the burden upon the reader's memory, for the single name is more easily remembered than a whole string of names, and in a society where poets abounded every man's takhallus was of necessity a reasonably distinctive one. But poets were (and are) in any case quite commonly referred to by their takhallus alone, or by their takhallus prefixed with some polite form of address—e.g. Mirza Ghalib, or Maulana Hali. Where this was not possible we have used the shortest acceptable form—e.g. Husain Mirza instead of Zulfaqar ud Din Haidar Khan.

All the same there are some for whom such conveniently short names are not available, and in such cases there was no alternative to using the longer and more difficult ones. Besides which Ghalib's own practice is sometimes confusing, for he uses more than one style in referring to people—e.g. Husain Ali Khan as well as Husain Ali, and Shihab ud Din Khan as well as Shihab ud Din Ahmad Khan. If in such cases the reader loses his bearings he can turn to the index for help.

Chronology of Ghalib's Life

(based mainly on Ikram)

1797	December 27th	Ghalib born in Agra.
1802		Ghalib's father dies. His uncle takes charge of him.
1803		British defeat the Marathas, occupy Delhi and establish virtual control of the Mughal Emperor.
1806		Ghalib's uncle dies. About the same time Ghalib starts writing Urdu verse.
1807-8		He begins writing Persian verse.
1810		Married to Umrao Begam, daughter of Ilahi Bakhsh Maruf. Shortly afterwards he moves to Delhi. Study under Abdus Samad during these years.
before 1822		A love affair.
1821		He compiles his first collection of Urdu verse.
1822		He starts writing almost entirely in Persian, and so continues for about thirty years.
1826		A year of misfortunes. His brother Yusuf goes mad. His father-in-law dies. He is pressed by creditors. Difficulties and disputes arise over his share in the hereditary pension originally granted by the British to his uncle.
1827		He leaves Delhi to go to Calcutta to pursue his pension claim. On the way, he stays for several months in Lucknow.
	June 27th	He leaves Lucknow.
1828	February 20th	He reaches Calcutta. The disputes over Persian usage. He compiles a selection of his Persian and Urdu verse and entitles it *Gul i Rana*.
1829	September	He leaves Calcutta.
	November 29th	He arrives back in Delhi. He prepares a revised collection of his Urdu verse.

1831	January 27th	His pension claim is finally rejected, and his share confirmed at Rs. 62 As. 8 a month.
1835	March 22nd	William Fraser, Resident of Delhi, murdered at the instigation of Ghalib's adversary Shams ud Din.
	October 3rd	Shams ud Din publicly hanged.
1837		Bahadur Shah Zafar becomes Emperor. Ghalib completes compilation of his collection of Persian verse.
1841		Police raid Ghalib's house. He is fined Rs. 100 on a gambling charge.
1842		He renounces a chance of employment as a teacher of Persian at Delhi College.
1847		He is imprisoned on a charge of keeping a gaming-house. Of all his friends, only Shefta stands by him.
		On his release he gains access to the Mughal Court.
1850		He is commissioned by Bahadur Shah, on Hakim Ahsanullah Khan's recommendation, to write a history in Persian prose of the Mughal dynasty; he is granted a stipend of Rs. 600 a year. He resumes writing verse in Urdu.
		He takes to Urdu as the usual medium of his letter-writing.
1851	December	Ghalib's prothalamion, Zauq's reply, and Ghalib's apology.
1852		Death of Arif, the nephew of Ghalib's wife. Ghalib adopts Arif's two boys, Bāqir Ali and Husain Ali as his 'grandsons'.
1854		British decisions to curtail Mughal powers still further when the present Emperor dies. Ghalib writes to Queen Victoria asking for a stipend in recognition of his standing as a poet.
		He is made *ustād* of the heir-apparent, at Rs. 400 a year.
		At about the same time he is granted Rs. 500 a year by Vajid Ali Shah, King of Oudh.
	October 16th	Zauq, the Emperor's *ustād*, dies. Ghalib is made *ustād* in his place.
1856		The British annex the state of Oudh.

1857	January	Ghalib receives a reply from London which encourages him to hope.
	February 5th	The ruler of Rampur becomes Ghalib's *shāgird*. Ghalib sends him a copy of his collected Urdu verse.
	May	The 'Mutiny' breaks out. Rebel sepoys occupy Delhi. The Emperor, under pressure, puts himself at their head. Ghalib is 'inwardly estranged, but outwardly friendly.' He begins his Persian diary *Dastambu* in which he recounts his experiences.
	September 14th	British assault on Delhi begins. Ghalib's street protected by Sikh soldiers.
	September 20th	British re-establish full control in Delhi. Mass expulsion of the Indian population.
	September 30th	Ghalib hears of British soldiers breaking into his brother Yusuf's house.
	October 5th	Ghalib questioned by Col. Burn.
	October 19th	Ghalib gets news of his brother Yusuf's death.
1858	January 1st	Hindu inhabitants of Delhi allowed to return to the city.
	March	Ghalib petitions the British for the re-issue of his pension.
	April	He hears that Shefta has been sentenced to seven years imprisonment, and Maikash hanged.
	August 1st	*Dastambu* completed.
	October	*Dastambu* printed, and copies presented to the Queen and the British authorities.
	November 1st	The Queen's proclamation of amnesty; transfer of the Government of India from the East India Company to the Crown.
1859	early months	Ghalib writes *Qāte i Burhan*, his attack upon Indian lexicographers of Persian.
	January	Shefta is released on appeal. Ghalib travels to Meerut to visit him.
	March	Ghalib paid Rs. 100 grant in aid pending the settlement of his pension claim.
	June	Ghalib under suspicion of complicity in the 1857 revolt because of an inscription he is alleged to have composed for the King's coinage.

	July	The Nawwab of Rampur grants him a stipend of Rs. 100 a month.
	November	Muslims now allowed to re-settle in Delhi.
1860	January	General return of Delhi Muslims' properties.
	January 19th	Ghalib leaves Delhi for Rampur in response to the Nawwab's invitation.
	March 14th	He leaves Rampur for Delhi.
	March 25th	He arrives back in Delhi.
	April	The British authorities order the re-issue of Ghalib's pension.
1862	March	*Qāte i Burhan* published.
late 1862		The beginning of Ghalib's long illness, which continues intermittently for two years.
1863	March	The British restore Ghalib's former court honours.
1865	April	The Nawwab of Rampur, Yusuf Ali Khan, dies, and is succeeded by Kalb i Ali Khan. The new Nawwab continues Ghalib's monthly stipend.
	October	Ghalib visits Rampur for the celebrations of the Nawwab's accession.
1866	January	Mishaps on the return journey from Rampur. He reaches Delhi on January 8th.
	April	He writes of his failing health.
	September	He prepares a selection from his Persian and Urdu verse for the Nawwab of Rampur.
1867-69		Ghalib's requests to Rampur for financial help —for allowances for his 'grandsons', for help towards the expenses of Husain Ali's proposed marriage, and for money to clear off his debts before he dies—meet with little or no response.
1867	December-March 1868	Ghalib takes a critic of *Qāte i Burhan* to court for defamation, but is obliged to settle out of court. Anonymous letters of these months.
1868	October 27th	*Ud i Hindi*, the first published collection of Ghalib's letters, appears.
1869	February 15th	Ghalib dies.
	March 6th	*Urdu i Mualla*, a larger collection of Ghalib's letters, is published.

❀ Chapter 1 ❀

Family Background;
Boyhood and Youth in Agra

Ghalib's ancestors were of Turkish stock and came from Transoxiana—
'beyond the river' as the Islamic world called it. But his grandfather emigrated
to India in the eighteenth century to seek his fortune at the court of the Mughal
emperor, and in India, at Agra, Ghalib was born on December 27, 1797. He has
himself given an account of his family background in one of his letters, but in
terms which become fully meaningful only if one knows something of the
period of Indian history to which it relates.

When Ghalib was born the Mughal Empire was dying, and indeed it was
already in full decline at the time when his grandfather came to India. A century
before that it had been one of the most splendid empires known to world
history. Its territory had included all of northern India and had extended far
south into the peninsula. Its wealth and splendour were known throughout the
civilized world, and its internal stability was ensured by the general prosperity
of its subjects. Its capital, Delhi, was, in Percival Spear's words, '. . . a great and
imperial city . . . with anything between one and two million inhabitants. It was
the largest and most renowned city, not only of India, but of all the East, from
Constantinople to Canton. Its court was brilliant, its mosques and colleges
numerous, and its literary and artistic fame as high as its political renown.' The
Empire's achievement was above all the work of Akbar, the greatest of the
Mughal Emperors, who died in 1605 after a reign of nearly fifty years; but
during the century which spans the reigns of his successors, Jahangir, Shahjahan, and Aurangzeb, its splendour was maintained, and it drew to India in
these years men of talent and ambition from all over the Islamic world, who
saw that it was here that their abilities would find their fullest scope.

But this period comes to an end with Aurangzeb's death in 1707, and from
that time the decline is catastrophically rapid. The multiplicity of factors which
contributed to it makes the story a complex one. The first great blow was struck
by the Marathas, a people inhabiting the territory of the present-day state of
Maharashtra, whose struggle to throw off the Mughal yoke is perhaps the first
which clearly indicates the character of the sub-continent as a land of many
nationalities. The development of Maratha nationhood had already become
fully evident by the sixteenth century, and the subsequent emergence of a great
political and military leader in the person of Shivaji gave it a political cohesion
which had hitherto been lacking. From small beginnings Shivaji initiated the
struggle for Maratha independence, and so successful was he that by the second

half of the Emperor Aurangzeb's reign the imperial armies were engaged in an unceasing and ultimately fruitless struggle to reduce the Marathas to subjection. Aurangzeb's death left them in virtual control of their own national territories, and they then turned their attention increasingly to the plunder and domination of the territories around them. By 1720 they were raiding far into northern India, and in the course of time they aimed to establish their ascendancy throughout the sub-continent. Meanwhile the Empire was itself disintegrating, weakened by fierce successive struggles for the throne between rival claimants, and by the virtual secession of its provinces to form independent states under hereditary dynasties of great nobles whom the centre was no longer able to control. By the mid-century the six provinces of the peninsula—the Deccan— had, in effect, seceded from the Empire to form what was to become the princely state of Hyderabad. To the East, in Bengal, the British East India Company had become the real ruler. West of Bengal lay the province of Oudh, by now, in all but name, the hereditary, independent dominion of its Governors. Between it and Delhi were a number of smaller dominions, while all the regions south-west, west, and north-west of the capital were either dominated by the Marathas or ruled by independent powers. The Emperor's own territory was increasingly restricted to a relatively small region centred on Delhi, and even within this region the real power was not his, but that of dominant groups of nobles who one after the other controlled the emperor until overthrown by more powerful adversaries. Yet Delhi remained a key centre of political development, for all the different powers in the land alike owed formal allegiance to the emperor and alike derived from him their title to power. For this reason the ever-shifting balance of forces brought repeated invasion and despoliation to Delhi, as contending forces fought for the control of the capital and of the emperor's person. In this struggle forces external to India were also engaged. From the north-west came the invasion of the Persian King Nādir Shah, who in 1739 crushingly defeated the emperor's army, occupied Delhi, and returned home only after systematically despoiling the capital of all its accumulated treasure. After Nadir Shah's death, Ahmad Shah Abdali, the successor to the Afghan part of his kingdom, continued his policy, and from 1748 to 1761 invaded India repeatedly. By 1760 Afghans pressing down from the north-west and Marathas pushing up from the south came into collision, and in 1761 the two armies met in full force at Panipat. The Marathas were so decisively defeated that for ten years they were unable to assert themselves again; yet it was not they but the Afghans who were henceforth to drop out of the contest for the control of Delhi. For while Abdali, beset by growing troubles at home and faced with the sustained rebellion of the Sikhs of the Panjab, was too pre-occupied to intervene, the Marathas recouped their strength and by 1771 had once again established their ascendancy. Only the British remained as serious rivals. But British strength was growing. To the control of Bengal, firmly established by the battle of Plassey in 1757, they had in 1765 added that of Oudh, defeating its ruler in battle and imposing a treaty which in effect made him their vassal. As their power continued to increase a contest with the Marathas became inevitable, and in 1803 the issue was settled by the Marathas' defeat and the establishment of a British supremacy which was to last for nearly a hundred and fifty years.

This is the background which alone makes intelligible to the modern reader Ghalib's letter of February 15, 1867, in which he briefly describes the history of his family fortunes:

'I am of Seljuk, Turkish stock. My grandfather [father's father] came to India from beyond the river [Transoxiana] in Shah Alam's time.[1] The Empire was already weakened, and he took service with Shah Alam with a command of only fifty horse . . ., receiving a fertile estate sufficient to provide for his own livelihood and for the upkeep of his troop. But after his death this was lost in the anarchy of those times. My father Abdullah Beg Khan Bahadur went to Lucknow, and entered the service of Nawwab Asaf ud Daula.[2] After a short time he went to Hyderabad and took service with Nawwab Nizam Ali Khan.[3] There he had the command of a force of three hundred cavalry. He stayed there for several years, until he lost his appointment as the result of internal dissensions there. He then decided to move right away to Alwar, where he took service with Rao Raja Bakhtawar Singh [the ruler of Alwar]. There he was killed in some battle. His brother, my uncle, Nasrullah Beg Khan Bahadur was in the Marathas' service as Governor of Agra, and it was he who took charge of me. In 1803 when the action with General Lake[4] took place, the Governorship became a Commissionership, and an Englishman was made Commissioner. My uncle was ordered by General Lake to raise a force of cavalry, and became commander[5] of a force of four hundred. His personal salary was one thousand seven hundred rupees and he was granted in addition, for the duration of his life, land which brought in a hundred to a hundred and fifty thousand rupees. He had not held this position for much more than a year when he died suddenly. The cavalry force was disbanded and the grant of land replaced by a monetary allowance. This allowance I still receive. I was five years old when my father died, and eight years old when my uncle died. . . .'

The background which this letter outlines is one of the most important factors in Ghalib's development. His ancestors belonged to a medieval world, where a noble entered the service of a more powerful overlord to whom he pledged his allegiance and his service in war in return for the wealth and rank appropriate to his position. But his grandfather migrated to India in a period when the

---

[1] The Emperor Shah Alam came to the throne in 1759 and died in 1806.

[2] Ruler of Oudh, and nominally Wazir of the Empire from 1775 to 1797. Lucknow was his capital.

[3] Ruler of Hyderabad State from 1762 to 1803.

[4] Lord Lake commanded the British forces which defeated the Marathas in 1803 and replaced them as the controllers of the Emperor Shah Alam, the masters of Delhi and Agra, and the dominant power in Northern India.

[5] Ghalib uses the English word 'brigadier'.

centres of power were for ever shifting and when one's allegiance must shift with them if one was to survive; when, therefore, no commitment to any superior could be much more than provisional, and to engage one's loyalties too deeply was to court disaster. Ghalib's own account makes this clear, if only by implication, and if in his childhood he could not yet understand fully all the implications of the repeated changes of allegiance in his family history, they were nevertheless a part of his heritage, and his own life was to show their influence.

Ghalib's father had married into one of the most distinguished families of Agra. He had never set up house on his own, but had made his home with his wife's parents, and his own children—Ghalib, his brother Yusuf, and a sister known as Choti Khanam ('Little Lady')—grew up there—that is, in the house of their mother's parents. Little is known of the family except that its wealth and its influence were considerable; and occasional references in Ghalib's own writings show that he grew up in conditions where every kind of material comfort was assured to him. Proper provision was also made for his education, and he acquired the subjects traditionally taught to the sons of aristocratic Muslim families—Persian, a little Arabic, the elements of logic, philosophy, medicine, and so on. It was in Persian that his progress was most marked, and by the age of eleven, according to his own account, he was already writing Persian poetry. He had, he says, begun writing Urdu verse some years earlier, and Hali quotes an account which supports this claim:

'Munshi Bihari Lal Mushtaq says that there was a gentleman named Kanhayya Lal, who was a resident of Agra and a contemporary of Ghalib's. On one occasion when he visited Ghalib in Delhi he asked him in the course of conversation whether he remembered the masnavi[1] he had written in the days when he used to fly his kite in Agra. Ghalib said he did not. Lala Sahib then said, "It is an Urdu masnavi and I have a copy of it." Accordingly he brought it and gave it to Ghalib, who read it with great pleasure. At the end he had put into the mouth of the kite the verse of some classical Persian poet:

> My friend has tied a string around my neck
> And leads me everywhere it pleases him.

Lala Sahib used to say that Ghalib was eight or nine years old when he wrote this poem.'

Kite-flying was a popular sport with adults as well as children, and Ghalib recalled in later years how it had ranked with chess as one of his favourite pastimes in his early youth. It was often played as a contest. The kite-strings were treated with powdered glass, and the object of the game was to fly your kite so that its string sawed through that of your opponent. Elsewhere he admits

---

[1] A poem in rhymed couplets.

indirectly to less innocent pastimes, speaking in vague poetic terms of a love of wine, woman and song—a love of which other contemporary writers speak more directly, if in suitably delicate terms. In his society these things were a graver offence against conventional morality than they are in ours, for the drinking of wine is specifically forbidden by Islam, and the purdah (parda) system—that most drastic form of segregation of the sexes—left association with courtesans as virtually the only way in which a man could freely enjoy the company of women. On the other hand, society always tolerates a good deal in those who have wealth and social status, and Ghalib's society was no exception to this rule. An early marriage in 1810, when he was thirteen and his bride eleven, does not seem to have inhibited these enjoyments in any way.

He did not spend all his time on them. Some of it he devoted to pursuing his enthusiasm for Persian, in which he continued to show a most remarkable promise. In this he was very greatly helped by a man named Abdus Samad, a Persian who had emigrated from his own country and come to Agra when Ghalib had already acquired a grounding in the language, and under whom he now studied for two years. Ghalib enjoyed the inestimable advantage that his teacher had Persian as his mother tongue. Such a qualification was by now extremely rare in India, and Ghalib might well feel proud of the distinction which he enjoyed. It no doubt played its part in giving added impetus to his poetic ambitions, and his prowess here was sufficiently marked for him to be mentioned in contemporary accounts by the time he was in his teens. Thus when a year or two after his marriage he left Agra permanently to live in Delhi, he was already something of a public figure.

By Urdu standards we are fortunate to know as much as we do about Ghalib's early life, and yet there is much more one would wish to know in order to determine how early influences shaped his character and outlook. As it is one can only surmise, seeking in his boyhood experience the sources of the qualities which we find in the mature man. This it is necessary to do, for the little direct evidence that we have leaves important aspects of him unexplained.

Ghalib's own later memories of his boyhood and youth in Agra (for even after he moved to Delhi, he often made prolonged visits there) were, all in all, pleasant ones, as his writings show. True, there are passages in which he expresses regret for the sensuous pastimes of his youth, but these are largely conventional, and the most that we can legitimately deduce from them is that he regretted the amount of time he spent in such pleasures rather than the pleasures themselves. It is when one studies his early work—work written while he still lived in Agra—that one realizes that there must have been other experiences that affected him profoundly and received expression in his early verse. For his early work is clearly that of one who knows the meaning of mental and emotional distress and has been forced by his experience to think deeply on the problems of life. To understand it, we are compelled to think of experiences which Ghalib himself preferred to forget. We must recall that he

was left fatherless at the age of five, and lived through the rest of his boyhood
dependent upon the kindness of others. He must have learned that his father
was a man who had never succeeded in making his own way in life, remaining
in the last resort dependent upon his wife's parents. In Indo-Muslim society,
the position of the wife of such a husband, living in her parents' house, was
not an enviable one. That of a young widow was even less so; and the fact that
she and her children lived as dependents of a family higher in the social scale
than her husband had been did not make things any easier. A sensitive and
intelligent child such as Ghalib clearly was must have felt all these things
keenly; and this sort of situation was prolonged by his being married, at the
early age of thirteen, into one of the aristocratic families of Delhi, a family
which, like his maternal grandfather's, was much wealthier and much more
socially distinguished than his own. Given the aristocratic values of the society
he lived in, it is more than likely that those upon whom he was dependent
regarded him (perhaps even without being conscious of it) as an inferior class
of being. Ghalib himself knew no other values; indeed, he was to cling to them
throughout his life—and he must have felt at one and the same time both a
secret sense that their attitude towards him was justified and a resentment that
it should be so.

It is safe to say that these less pleasurable experiences combined with the
enjoyable ones of which he speaks to form important aspects of his character
which continued unchanged throughout his life. When in his teens he left
Agra permanently to go to live in Delhi, he was a man who had experienced
and enjoyed without any strong sense of guilt the pleasures which life can offer,
including the pleasure of using the intellectual and poetic talent which he knew
he possessed. A sense of the instability of relationships in the world to which
his family belonged perhaps enhanced his sense that all that life can give is to be
treasured and enjoyed to the utmost while it lasts, while at the same time it
made him cautious of looking too far ahead, or of committing himself un-
reservedly to any one love for fear of too deep an involvement which might
ultimately bring him to grief. This ability to hold himself a little aloof must
have been strengthened by his boyhood experience of living *in* a family (and
one which was a microcosm of aristocratic society) and yet never quite being a
fully integrated part *of* it. This, together with his intellectual sharpness, produced a quality of ironic scepticism, and a sense of humour which both enhanced
his capacity to enjoy life and armed him against its more bitter experiences.
Finally this same early experience produced what is the most noticeable flaw in
his character, while at the same time it spurred him to develop his poetic talent
to the full. He had felt keenly that others had regarded him as inferior to themselves—all the more keenly because he himself accepted as valid the yardsticks
—birth, wealth, profession, rank, and social and political influence—with
which they measured him, and knew that he could not compete in these fields.
He reacted with a jealous assertion of his worth, and for all one's sympathy with
him, one cannot help smiling at some of the ways in which he did so. Thus, he

always took an inordinate pride in his ancestry. Hali's words well reflect his feeling on this point:

'References to his family, its origin and its worth occur frequently in Ghalib's own writings. His ancestors were Aibak Turks, who traced their pedigree back to Tur, the son of Faridun [a legendary king of ancient Persia]. When the Kayyanis conquered all Iran and Turan, and the power and majesty of the Turanis departed from this world, the line of Tur was for a long time stripped of its dominion and its wealth. But the sword never fell from its hand, for among the Turks it was an age-old tradition that when a man died, the son inherited only his sword, and the rest of his property and wealth and home went to the daughter. At length, after many years, during the period of Islam, by the power of this same sword the Turks restored their fallen fortunes, and in the Seljuk dynasty the foundation of a mighty empire was laid. For several centuries it ruled over all Iran and Turan, and over Syria and Rum (i.e. Asia Minor), until at last after many years the Seljuks' empire came to an end, and their sons were scattered and dispersed abroad. One of them was Tarsam Khan, a man of noble birth, who made his home in Samarkand. And it was from this Tarsam Khan that Ghalib's grandfather . . . was descended.'

Ghalib, in his best Persian prose style, writes that it was this illustrious fore-bear who, 'descending like a torrent from the heights into the depths below, left Samarkand and came to India'. His inordinate pride that 'his ancestors for a hundred generations had been soldiers' recurs again and again in his life, and it was this pride which made him throughout his life live in the style appropriate to a distinguished noble, regardless of the fact that he rarely had the necessary resources to maintain this style of living.

His second assertion of his worth was made in the field of Persian—traditionally for several centuries the language of culture of the whole Islamic world. True, his mother tongue was not Persian, and his ancestors were not Persians but Turks. But he had been taught by a Persian, and his natural aptitude had enabled him to show a prowess which was indeed wholly exceptional. Moreover he took as his models only those poets who had Persian as their mother tongue, treating with contempt most Indian writers and scholars of the language. His contempt was in some measure justified, but there is a quality of exaggeration about it which springs from an awareness of his own exceptional talent and an over-anxious desire to force this upon the attention of others. This same awareness of his own talent is perhaps mainly responsible for his view, which he held almost to the end of his days, that Persian was *par excellence* the language of literature, and that Urdu, by contrast, was an inferior medium for poetry and no medium at all for prose. Even his own Urdu poetry he regarded, or professed to regard, as of little or no significance, and whenever it came under attack he tended to reply by an aggressive assertion of his excellence in Persian—thus shifting his ground to a field where he knew that his critics could not easily follow him.

But if in his pride of ancestry and his claims for his Persian work there is sometimes a false and exaggerated note, in his third claim he is on the firmest of firm ground. He rests his final claim to men's esteem on his poetry, and here his claim is justified to the full. He does not hide the fact that a yearning to excel was one of the driving forces which made him strive for perfection as a poet. In the poetic prose of his Persian letters he writes,

'Alas for my fate! born to be struck down by misfortune and to see my granaries reduced to ashes! I had not the means to ride to war like my ancestors . . . nor the capacity to excel in knowledge and ability like Avicenna and the wise men of old. I said to myself, "Be a darwesh and live a life of freedom". But the love of poetry which I had brought with me from eternity assailed me and won my soul, saying, "To polish the mirror and show in it the face of meaning—this too is a mighty work. The command of armies and the mastery of learning is not for you. Give up the thought of being a darwesh, and set your face in the path of poetry". Willy nilly I did so, and launched my ship upon the illusory sea of verse. My pen became my banner, and the broken arrows of my ancestors became my pens.'

Because he 'brought the love of poetry with him from eternity', in the course of time he accomplished this 'mighty work' and knew that he had accomplished it. As he did so he became convinced that he would never win the universal recognition from his contemporaries which his achievement merited, and he reacted to this realization in ways which are not always admirable. But he was confident that posterity would recognize his full worth:

> Today none buys my verse's wine, that it may grow in age
> To make the senses reel in many a drinker yet to come.
> My star rose highest in the firmament before my birth:
> My poetry will win the world's acclaim when I am gone.

His confidence has proved to be well-founded.

❈ Chapter 2 ❈

Delhi and Calcutta, c.1810–29

Ghalib made Delhi his permanent home within a year or two of his marriage, but for some years he continued to spend long periods in Agra, and there are letters of his which show with what affection he still thought of it long after it had ceased to be his home. Thus he writes to his friend Ziya ud Din Ahmad Khan, who is visiting Agra:

'Twin soul of mine, may Agra's air and water, distilled from hapless Ghalib's sighs and tears, rejoice your heart. Though we are far apart, yet the power of thought of my far-ranging mind has brought our oneness to the point where distance dares not to draw near. Granted that you have gone on a far journey and that the thought is near to you that you are far from me; and yet while you yet stay in the city of my birth, then truly we are near to one another. And I rejoice because my love that sees afar has sent my eyes and heart with you upon this journey, that I too, held in this place of exile [Delhi], may pay due tribute of joy at the sight of the city of my birth. Let no man look upon Agra as of slight account, but as he passes through her roads call on God's preserving and protecting power to hold her in its keeping. For she . . . was once the playground of my love-distracted heart. There was a time when in her soil only the mandrake grew, and, save the heart, her trees would bear no other fruit, and the drunken breeze of morning ranged through her gardens to lift up and to bear away men's hearts so that the drunkard longed no longer for his morning draught, so that the pious bent his mind no more to prayer. To every grain of dust of that land in flower my body sends its message of love, and on every leaf in those fair gardens my soul calls benedictions to rain down.

'I think of your good fortune, and . . . my eye is on the road to see when you will write, and weeps to see no letter ever comes to tell me how the stone horse[1] received my greeting and how the river's ripples made reply.'

All the same, as the years passed, his ties with his birthplace gradually weakened and he came to regard himself as a Delhi man. With only one prolonged absence, he was to spend the rest of his life there.

At the time he settled there the city was just emerging, after a century of incessant troubles, into a period of peace. From 1739 to 1803 it had been repeatedly fought over, beseiged, fought in and plundered—by Persians, Afghans, Marathas, and by rival aspirants for power within the imperial

[1] A famous monument in Agra.

nobility itself. Much of it was ruined and deserted. Its population had fallen from the nearly two million of Aurangzeb's day to well under a tenth of that figure. Percival Spear has described how a traveller approaching it '. . . in the sixties of the eighteenth century would . . . observe not only the deserted tombs and ruined gardens which are to be seen today, but also miles of decaying suburbs, the relics of other Delhis which had been abandoned during the troubles of the mid-century.' It was no longer a great centre of literature. One by one practically all of its poets had left it and moved to less troubled centres farther East, above all to Lucknow, the capital of the British client state of Oudh. But 1803 brought a change. With the British triumph over the Marathas, Delhi and the Empire passed into the hands of a power far stronger than it had known for nearly a century. No rival from without could effectively challenge its control, and no force from within could effectively oppose its will. Lawlessness and brigandage were methodically suppressed, and life and property in the city and on the roads leading to and from it were once more secure.

In the half-century of internal peace that followed, Delhi experienced something like a renaissance, a flowering of literature and learning to which men of the next generation such as Hali looked back nostalgically. Hali begins his preface to his life of Ghalib by evoking this memory,

'In the thirteenth century of the Muslim era[1] when the decline of the Muslims had already entered its most extreme phase, and, along with their wealth, renown and political power, their great achievements in the arts and sciences had also departed from them, by some good fortune there gathered in the capital, Delhi, a band of men so talented that their meetings and assemblies recall those of the days of Akbar and Shahjahan. . . . In the days when I first came to Delhi autumn had already come to this garden—some of these men had left Delhi, and others had departed this world. Yet even among those who remained were men whom I shall always feel pride at having seen, men whose like it seems that the soil of Delhi, and indeed of all India, will not produce again. For the mould in which they were formed has changed, and the breezes in which they grew and flowered have veered round. . . .'

Characteristically, the Delhi renaissance expressed itself largely in religious forms, for here as in medieval Europe, religion still concerned itself with every aspect of man's existence and prescribed the norms of his social and political behaviour no less than those of his private life. Religious learning was the one major department of intellectual life which had not declined in the city even in its darkest days. Indeed, the family of Shah Waliullah, one of the most important thinkers in the history of Indian Islam, 'had made the plundered capital the centre of the theological sciences' in the latter half of the eighteenth century. He can be regarded as the founder of the radical reforming trend in modern Indian Islam, and from his time dates a long drawn out conflict between the

---

[1] Corresponding roughly to the nineteenth century of the Christian era.

traditionalists in religion and the radical reformers who, like the Protestants of the European Reformation, thought of themselves as reviving the original purity of their faith. This conflict was raging vigorously in Delhi when Ghalib settled there. Along with the flourishing of religious controversy went the development of the studies necessary to it and traditionally associatsd with it— above all, Arabic and Persian. In the early nineteenth century Delhi was a famous centre of these studies, attracting students from as far afield as Balkh and Bukhara (in Central Asia). The period also produced its great hakims, practitioners of the traditional system of medicine inherited from the Greeks and developed and transmitted by the Arabs throughout the Islamic world. Their names are cited by Urdu writers alongside those of other prominent learned men of this period.

Urdu too received a new impetus. Shah Waliullah's son, Shah Rafi ud Din, produced in 1803 an Urdu translation of the Quran, a significant event not only in the history of religious movements, but also in the history of modern Urdu prose, of which it was a pioneer work. The drain of poetic talent to Lucknow ceased, and Delhi again became the centre of a group of distinguished poets, of whom Ghalib was one. This revival of poetry owed a great deal to the en- couragement of the Mughal court which, deprived of all far-reaching political powers, turned more and more to cultural interests. It patronised Urdu poetry as its predecessors, before the decline of the Empire, had patronised Persian. Indeed, it was an important patron of learning in general; the great royal libraries were well cared for, and there is evidence that they were available not only to the court but to Delhi scholars and students in general. In addition there were fine manuscript libraries in the private possession of individual nobles.

British ascendancy at this juncture did more than provide the security within which this intellectual flowering could take place. The British in India were still at the stage where their rule operated as far as possible through the old Mughal forms. Persian was still the official language; the educational system, the administration of justice, and indeed the administration in general were largely along the traditional lines. Many of the leading intellectual figures among the Muslims held important posts in the judiciary. The British officials themselves were men who were thoroughly at home in the Mughal setting. Many of them knew Persian well and had a genuine enthusiasm for it. They mixed freely, and were often on friendly and intimate terms with the Mughal aristocracy. There were even some who tried their hand at composing Persian and Urdu poetry. Through them their Indian acquaintances came into contact with western ways of thought too, and learned something of the material and intellectual achieve- ment of Europe; and the general atmosphere of intellectual activity in Delhi led also to a widespread interest in western-style education. It was during these years that Delhi College was established. Here, alongside the traditional Arabic and Persian studies of Mughal India, western studies were also provided for, and some of the prominent Muslim divines of the day encouraged Muslims to take an interest in them. It is highly significant that many of the great Urdu writers and leaders of Muslim thought in the second half of the nineteenth century were men who had been connected with Delhi College in their youth. In short, Mughal culture and English culture met in these fifty years on terms of mutual respect. This situation was ended by the upheaval of 1857 and is only now, a century later, again being generally restored. Sleeman, one of the outstanding British officials of the period, and one who served continuously for forty-five years in the country, bore impressive testimony to the enthusiasm of the Indian Muslims for learning, and to the high standards which they attained:

'Perhaps there are few communities in the world among whom education is more generally diffused than among Muhammadans in India. He who holds an office worth twenty rupees a month commonly gives his sons an education equal to that of a prime minister. They learn, through the medium of the Arabic and Persian languages, what young men in our colleges learn through those of the Greek and Latin—that is, grammar, rhetoric and logic. After his seven years of study, the young Muhammadan binds his turban upon a head almost as well filled with the things which appertain to these branches of knowledge as the young man raw from Oxford . . . and, what is much to his advantage in India, the languages in which he has learnt what he knows are those which he most requires through life.'

Sleeman goes on to describe some of the Arabic and Persian classics—works by Ghazali, Tusi, and Sadi—which the Indian Muslim most commonly studied, and concludes, 'These works . . . are the great "Pierian spring" of moral instruction from which the Muhammadan delights to "drink deep" from infancy to old age; and a better spring it would be difficult to find in the works of any other three men.' This last comment is typical of the sincere respect for oriental learning which characterized the best British officials of the day. Sleeman himself was, we are told, well-versed in Arabic, Persian, and Urdu, and he is not untypical in this respect.

It is not difficult to imagine how congenial this setting was to one of Ghalib's background and attainments. He took his place among the Delhi aristocracy, meeting them on equal terms and living in the same style as they did. 'He jealously maintained his sense of self respect,' writes Hali, 'and always kept up the style he considered appropriate to his position. . . . He would never go out except in a palanquin or an open sedan chair. He never called upon those nobles who did not visit him, and never failed to return the visits of those who did.' He was fully involved also in the intellectual life of the city, dominated at this time by the religious controversies between the traditionalists and the radical, militant followers of Sayyid Ahmad Barelavi and Shah Ismail.[1] These

---

[1] Often called Wahhabis because of their resemblance to the similar movement in contemporary Arabia. But the Indian movement was in fact of independent origin.

controversies were not by any means confined to theologians; all educated Muslims were affected by them and, in general terms, allegiance would be given to one side or the other. Ghalib's own position was characteristically different. His closest personal friend during this period was Fazl i Haq, the main protagonist of the traditionalists and a man whose erudition, particularly in Persian, combined with his integrity and moral courage to win Ghalib's respect and affection. Yet Ghalib did not allow his admiration for the man to dominate his own judgements. Hali writes,

'Maulana Fazl i Haq was a very close friend of Ghalib, whom he regarded as an extremely accomplished Persian poet. Since he was a vigorous opponent of the Wahhabis, he pressed Ghalib strongly to write a masnavi in Persian attacking their teachings, and dealing in particular detail with the question of the impossibility of a peer of the Seal of the Prophets.[1] Maulana Ismail's . . .opinion on this question was that a peer of the Seal of the Prophets was . . . impossible because this would negative his finality in the line of prophets, not because God did not possess the power to create his peer. Maulana Fazl i Haq, on the contrary, held that the creation of a peer of the Seal of the Prophets was beyond God's power, just as it is beyond His power to create His own peer. Fazl i Haq's request to Ghalib was for a poem in Persian expressing this opinion. Ghalib first objected that it was difficult to discuss learned questions of this kind in verse, but Fazl i Haq brushed this objection aside, and Ghalib had no alternative but to write a masnavi. . . . When he recited it to Fazl i Haq, he praised it extremely highly and said, "Even if I had been as practised a Persian poet as you are, I could never have expressed these things so well." But he was extremely annoyed that on the question of the peer of the Seal of the Prophets Ghalib had expressed an opinion somewhat at variance with his own. Ghalib had not written in so many words that God had the power to create the peer of the Seal of the Prophets, but had made the point in another way by saying that in this present world there cannot be more than one Seal of the Prophets, but that God has the power to create another world just like this one, and to bring into being in it a peer of the Seal of the Prophets who would be the Seal of the Prophets for that other world.'

Hali then quotes the verses in question, ending with one which says that in one world there cannot be two Seals of the Prophets, but there could be a hundred thousand worlds and a hundred thousand Seals. He goes on,

'When Ghalib first brought the masnavi he had written to Maulana [Fazl i Haq], he had concluded the discussion of the question with this line. The

---

[1] Muslims hold that the Prophet Muhammad was the last of the prophets sent by God for the guidance of mankind, and that since God revealed to him all the knowledge that humanity needs to guide it in the right path till the end of the world, no more prophets will be sent. He is therefore called the Seal of the Prophets.

B

Maulana had said, "What nonsense is this you have written? You say that there could be numbers of worlds and numbers of Seals of the Prophets. Not so! If God were to create a hundred thousand worlds there would still be only one Seal of the Prophets. Cut out this point altogether from the masnavi and write what I tell you." Ghalib had no quarrel with the Wahhabis, and owed no allegiance to their opponents. All he wanted to do was to fulfil his friend's request. He therefore immediately did as he had told him, leaving the former verses as they stood, but adding others . . . [which had the effect of rejecting their argument and expressing Fazl i Haq's view]. Maulana Fazl i Haq had fully explained his view on this question to Ghalib and thoroughly impressed it upon him, and Ghalib had himself wanted to express this view in his poem. But just as anything crooked becomes straight when it is passed through a pipe, so Ghalib's regard for the right straightened out this involved view, and without wishing to support the Wahhabis it was what he felt to be correct that his pen willy-nilly wrote down. Whatever he wrote after that was done at Maulana Fazl i Haq's command and has nothing to do with Ghalib's real opinion.'

Hali's incidental comment that Ghalib held no brief for either party in the dispute is a pertinent one, for he was no ardent protagonist of any religious point of view. But what must quite certainly have appealed to him in Wahhabi doctrine was the insistence that the long and respectable pedigree of a particular doctrine did not necessarily guarantee its correctness, that human fallibility was as evident in former days as now, and that a man must use his own judgement to decide on the correctness or otherwise of an accepted belief. In the fields of thought which did interest him passionately—as religious controversy did not—these were his own life-long convictions. Above all they emerge clearly and repeatedly in his recurring polemics on Persian usage and the evaluation of the Persian poets of the past. His whole temperament drove him to reject any idea of the absolute finality of anything that had happened in the past, and no doubt this underlay his almost unconscious divergence from Fazl i Haq's view in Hali's anecdote.

The same independence, the same reluctance to involve himself deeply in religion, and indeed a certain cheerful irreverence towards it is evident in an anecdote of an encounter with his father-in-law, Ilahi Bakhsh Maruf. Maruf was not only his elder; his family was one of the most distinguished among the Delhi aristocracy, and in addition Maruf himself was both a poet of established reputation and a deeply religious man whose fame for piety and religious insight brought many to seek his spiritual guidance. But Ghalib was not unduly overawed by these considerations. Hali writes,

'Ilahi Bakhsh Maruf . . . used to accept people as his disciples, and when their numbers swelled sufficiently he would get copies made of his line of spiritual descent through all the principals of his order, and distribute copies to each of them. On one occasion he gave Ghalib a copy of this pedigree and told him to make a further copy. But in the copy he made he wrote alternate names only, including the first and third, but omitting the second and fourth, and so on. When he had finished, he took the original, together with his "copy" back to Maruf. When he looked at it he was extremely angry and asked him, "What is this you have done?" Ghalib replied, "Sir, think nothing of it. The pedigree is really a ladder on which one climbs to God. If you knock out alternate rungs, it merely means that one must put a little more spring into one's step; but one can climb it just the same." This reply angered Maruf even more, and he tore up what Ghalib had written and had another copy made by someone else. And in this way Ghalib rid himself of this chore for good.'

We have no detailed knowledge of the evolution of Ghalib's views on religion. He came of Sunni stock, but at some stage of his life became a Shia,[1] or if not actually a Shia, one closely sympathetic to Shia beliefs. But we do not know of any period of his life when he could have been described, in the conventional sense of the words, as a religious man. He seems to have accepted sincerely enough the main tenets of Islam, and equally, for all practical purposes, to have accepted them alone. As Hali puts it:

'From all the duties of worship and the enjoined practices of Islam he took only two—a belief that God is one and is immanent in all things, and a love for the Prophet and his family. And this alone he considered sufficient for salvation.'

Hali might have added that Ghalib's attitude to God Himself was not always one of reverential respect. Thus he himself relates:

'He was lying on his bed at night looking up at the sky. He was struck by the apparent chaos in the distribution of the stars and said, "There is no rhyme or reason in anything the self-willed do. Just look at the stars—scattered in complete disorder. No proportion, no system, no sense, no pattern. But their King has absolute power, and no one can breathe a word against Him!" '

Open and implied criticism of God is common both in his poetry and his prose. He shared the view, expressed by Persian and Urdu poets long before him, that man is a helpless puppet in God's hands, who cannot perform a single act of his own volition, and yet is unfairly accused by God of being free, and hence accountable to Him for his sins. Such sentiments are usually (but not always) expressed humorously in Ghalib's writings, but something deeper lies beneath the humour.

When Ghalib permitted himself to think of the God of Islam in these terms

---

[1] The two major communities of Muslims. Shias, who are greatly outnumbered by the Sunnis, differ from them mainly in rejecting the legitimacy of Muhammad's first three successors (caliphs) and accepting only that of Ali and his descendants.

it is not surprising that he should have rejected Islam's more irksome restrictions, at any rate where he himself was concerned. Thus he had always liked wine, which is not permitted to a true Muslim; but far from attempting to conceal his liking for it, he openly sang its praises, recognizing at the same time, without any evasion, that he was breaking the laws of Islam in so doing. His drinking is usually treated humorously in his verse, and many anecdotes show that this generally was his attitude. He would not be drawn into serious discussions about it, and could rarely resist the temptation to make fun of people who tried to lecture him. Hali quotes one such instance.

'A man, in Ghalib's presence, strongly condemned wine-drinking, and said that the prayers of the wine-bibber are never granted. "My friend," said Ghalib, "if a man has wine, what else does he *need* to pray for?" '

Not that he generally drank to excess.

'He used to take a little wine at bed-time, but he never drank more than the amount that he had prescribed for himself. The key of the box in which he kept his bottles of wine was entrusted to his steward, who had strict instructions that if . . . ever he contemplated drinking more than the fixed amount, he was on no account to agree or to hand over the key. It quite often happened that he would demand the key, and if he was a little drunk, would scold the steward for not giving it to him. But the steward had his master's welfare at heart and would never let him have it. He not only limited his drinking to quite a small quantity; he also diluted his wine with two or three parts of rose water.'

It seems that he found wine a stimulus to writing poetry. Hali says,

'He often used to compose his verses at night, under the influence of wine. When he had worked out a complete verse he would tie a knot in his sash, and there would be as many as eight to ten knots by the time he retired to bed. In the morning he would recall them, with no other aid to his memory, and would write them down. . . . He wrote a pleasant and attractive hand . . . in the style that most Persians use, and though his letters were well formed, he wrote quickly and continuously.'

Just as he never observed the prohibition on wine, so also he never kept the fast of Ramzan,[1] when for a whole month between the hours of dawn and dusk the true Muslim may not eat or drink or smoke or indulge in any other form of physical pleasure. To the orthodox Muslim, fasting is one of the five basic duties of his faith. Hali tells a story of how Ghalib was once visited during

[1] We give the word as it is spoken in Urdu. The Arabs call it Ramadan.

Ramzan by a pious Sunni maulvi who was apparently unaware of Ghalib's non-conformity in this respect.

'It was the middle of the afternoon, and Ghalib told his servant to bring him a drink of water. The maulvi sahib was astonished and said, "What sir? Are you not keeping the fast?" Ghalib replied, "I am a Sunni; I break the fast two hours before sunset." '

This is a joke at the maulvi's expense. Needless to say, the Sunnis and Shias alike fast throughout the hours of daylight. But Shias are in some respects more meticulous in the religious restrictions they impose upon themselves, and they do in fact break their fast later than the Sunnis.

Hali relates another incident that happened one year when the month of Ramzan fell during the hot season.[1]

'The room in which Ghalib spent his day was over the main gateway of the house, and leading off it to one side was another little room, small and dark, and with a doorway so low that one had to stoop right down to go through it. In this room there was a carpet laid on the floor, and in the hot season, when the hot wind was blowing, Ghalib usually spent the day there from ten in the morning until four in the afternoon. One day during the hot season, when it was the month of Ramzan, Maulana Azurda [a friend of Ghalib, renowned as a mufti (expounder of Islamic law), a scholar and a poet of Persian] came to visit him when the sun was at its hottest. Ghalib was sitting in this little room with a companion playing backgammon. . . . Azurda went in, and when he saw him playing backgammon during Ramzan said, "I have read in the Traditions[2] that during Ramzan Satan is held prisoner; but what I see today makes me doubt the authenticity of this Tradition." "Respected sir," Ghalib replied, "the Tradition is completely authentic. But I should perhaps inform you that the place where he is held prisoner is this very room!" '

In general he would not allow his religion or the lack of it to become a cause of friction in any of his personal relationships with men whom he liked and respected, and he evaded making it an issue either by refusing to be serious or else by saying whatever he thought the other wanted to hear.

Yet despite his avowed unorthodoxy he felt himself to be a part of the Muslim community. Hali writes:

'Although he paid very little regard to the outward observances of Islam, whenever he heard of any misfortune befalling the Muslims it grieved him

---

[1] The Muslim calendar is lunar, and over the years Ramzan therefore moves through the whole range of the solar year.

[2] The Hadith (in Urdu, pronounced 'hadis'), accounts of the words and actions of the Prophet in different situations, which, after the Quran, serve to guide the true Muslim in his own life.

deeply. One day in my presence when he was lamenting some such occurrence, he said, "I have none of the hallmarks of a Muslim; why is it that every humiliation that the Muslims suffer pains and grieves me so much?" '

Despite his free and easy attitude towards religious observances he shared the interest, general among the cultured Muslims of his day in religious controversy. For him, perhaps, a good deal of its appeal lay in the opportunities for intellectual exercise which it offered. His friend and fellow-poet Shefta told Hali how quickly Ghalib could grasp even the most abstruse argument:

'I was reading a Persian tract of Shah Waliullah[1] on some exceedingly abstruse questions, and had come to a passage which I simply could not grasp when Ghalib chanced to call. I showed him the passage in question. He thought for a moment and then explained the point of it so well and lucidly that I do not think Shah Waliullah himself could have done it better.'

Hali says that Ghalib often studied books on these themes. His intellectual grasp was aided by a remarkable memory, which so long as his faculties were unimpaired made it unnecessary for him ever to buy a book.

'He never—or practically never—bought a book. There was a man whose trade it was to bring round books from the booksellers and hire them out on loan. Ghalib always used to get his books on loan from him, returning them when he had finished reading them. Any striking idea or point of substance that he read in a book engraved itself upon his memory, and he never forgot it.'

These years in Delhi, and above all his close friendship with Fazl i Haq, brought about an important advance in his development as a poet. His keen intellect, his prowess in Persian and his determination to win himself a distinctive place as a poet had led him to write—whether in Persian or in Urdu—in a highly original, but exceedingly difficult style. Hali quotes one of his early Urdu verses in illustration:

> Heedlessness kept us far removed from self-oblivion's joy—and yet
> The eyebrow of each nail we pared could signal us to understand.

He explains that the verse means something like this: 'We should have known what joy it is to devote oneself so completely (to God) that all consciousness of one's own identity is destroyed. Thus when we pare our nails we feel pleasure as a result, though the paring (which is part of the nail and hence part of us) passes into oblivion. And this paring itself is shaped like an eyebrow, the function of which, as we know, is by its movement to convey a situation to us.'

---

[1] Cf. p. 30–31 above.

Elsewhere he writes:

'Not only were his ideas strange; his language was equally so. He regularly used Persian constructions . . . in his Urdu verse, and many of his lines were such that by changing a single word one could turn them into Persian. Some of his modes of expression were his own invention, unparalleled by anything that had gone before either in Urdu or in Persian. For instance, there is a line in his Urdu diwan:

> The dove is but a pinch of dust,
>   the nightingale a coloured form:
> O lamentation, what is there that shows
>   the burning of their hearts?

[In the stock imagery of the Persian and Urdu ghazal,[1] the dove, who sings for love of the cypress, and the nightingale, who sings for love of the rose, are the symbols of the lover, consumed with grief because his beloved is indifferent to him.] I myself asked Ghalib the meaning of this verse. He replied, "Substitute 'Save' for 'O', and the meaning will be clear." The meaning is that the dove is no more than a pinch of dust and the nightingale no more than the elements arranged in a certain form. Their song alone is evidence of the burning of their hearts—i.e. of their being in love. Obviously, the way in which Ghalib has used the word 'O' in this context is an innovation of his own. Someone who had the meaning of the verse explained to him said, "If he had *said* 'Save' instead of 'O' . . . the meaning would have been clear"—and this is perfectly true; but Ghalib always did his best to keep clear of the beaten track and as far as he could, avoided ordinary forms of expression; and he was therefore less concerned to make his verse readily intelligible than to express it in an original and striking way.'

Not surprisingly, Ghalib's verse came under heavy criticism from the start. During his Agra period he paid little attention to his critics, putting them down as ignoramuses incapable of understanding serious poetry; but he could hardly maintain this attitude when he found that in Delhi too such criticism of him was general. Much of it was conveyed to him through the characteristically Urdu institution of the mushaira. A mushaira was a gathering of poets, usually called together at the invitation of some prominent patron of literature, where each would recite his latest compositions. The proceedings were governed by well-known conventions, but within the conventional forms both appreciation and criticism could be frankly expressed—and in more than one way.

'I have heard,' writes Hali, 'that the poets of Delhi would come to mushairas where Ghalib was present and recite ghazals which sounded very fine and impressive but were really quite meaningless, as though to tell Ghalib in this

---

[1] Lyric poem.

way that this was the kind of poetry *he* wrote.' Azad[1] relates how on one occasion Hakim Agha Jan Aish, a well-known Delhi wit, recited these lines at a mushaira at which Ghalib was present:

> What is the point of writing verse which only you can understand?
> A poet feels the thrill of joy when others too can understand;
> We understand the verse of Mir, we understand what Mirza wrote;
> But Ghalib's verse!—Save he and God, we know not who can understand!

Other conveyed their criticism more privately.

'On one occasion Maulvi Abdul Qādir of Rampur said to Ghalib, "There is one of your Urdu verses which I cannot understand," and there and then made up this verse and recited it to him:

> First take the essence of the rose
>   out of the eggs of buffaloes—
> And other drugs are there; take those
>   out of the eggs of buffaloes.

Ghalib was very much taken aback and said, "This verse is certainly not mine, I assure you." But Maulvi Abdul Qādir kept up the joke and said, "I have read it myself in your diwan[2]; if you have a copy here I can show it you here and now." At length Ghalib realized that this was an indirect way of criticizing him and telling him that verses of this kind could be found in his diwan.'

Ghalib would have resisted such criticism longer had not Fazl i Haq criticised him in the same way. Fazl i Haq was a man whom Ghalib both loved and respected. He regarded him as one of the very small number of his contemporaries who had a real command over his beloved Persian and a capacity to appreciate real poetry. Equally, Fazl i Haq felt all these things about Ghalib too. Hali sums up:

'Since Ghalib was basically a very sane man, he learned his lesson from the objections of his critics, and gradually came onto the right path. In addition, as Ghalib's relationship with Fazl i Haq became more and more intimate, he began to dissuade him more and more from writing verses of this kind, so much so that [when Ghalib compiled his Urdu diwan] he discarded at Fazl i Haq's suggestion practically two-thirds of all the Urdu he had written.'

Thenceforth, without surrendering any of his originality, he was to express what he had to say in more intelligible form.

Hali's testimony to the great esteem in which Ghalib held Fazl i Haq is borne out by Ghalib's Persian letters. He once wrote to him:

---

[1] A contemporary of Hali.   [2] Collection of lyrical verse.

'During these last days I formed the desire to compose a few verses in the manner of Urfi[1] on the oneness of God. Now, when the effort of my poetic power has reached the point where I have excelled both Urfi and myself, I am constrained to lay these verses before one whose true appreciation of verse can sustain a hundred such as me and a hundred thousand such as Urfi, and can indicate to each one of us his station [in Persian poetry].'

The controversies around his poetry do not seem for the most part to have been at all acrimonious, for Ghalib was a popular figure in Delhi. Hali writes that he was, in appearance and temperament alike, an attractive man.

'Delhi people who had seen Ghalib in his youth have told me that he was generally regarded as one of the most handsome men in the city, and even in his old age, when I met him for the first time, one could easily see what a handsome man he had been. . . . Tall and broadly built, and with powerful limbs, he looked even then like a newcomer from Turan.'

Many years later Ghalib himself recalls his youthful appearance in a letter to a friend:

'I am noticeably tall . . . and [in former days] my complexion was [unusually] fair, and people of discrimination used to praise it. . . . In this uncouth city [Delhi] everybody wears a sort of uniform. Mullahs, junk-dealers, hookah-menders, washermen, water-carriers, inn-keepers, weavers, greengrocers—all of them wear their hair long and grow a beard. The day your humble servant grew a beard, he had *his* hair shaved. But, God save us! What am I prattling about?'

This well illustrates his aversion to following the common herd, an aversion which made him go out of his way to be different, not only in his poetry, but also, says Hali, 'in his ways, his dress, his diet, and his style of living'. He was a man to whom people quickly felt attracted.

'There was a sincere welcome for all who came to see him, so that anyone who had once met him always wanted to keep up the acquaintance. He was always delighted to see his friends, and felt their joys and their troubles as his own. That is why he had innumerable friends, of every community and creed. . . .'

He had a great reputation as an amusing conversationalist, and this too drew people to him.

'In Delhi some people use the word *rath* [a sort of carriage] as feminine, while

---

[1] A classical Persian poet.

others make it masculine. Somebody said to Ghalib, "You tell us, sir; is *rath* feminine or masculine?" Ghalib replied, "My friend, look at it this way: when the passengers are women it should be feminine; and when they are men it should be masculine." [1]

He was all his life extremely fond of mangoes, but

'one of his closest friends Hakim Razi ud Din Khan did not share this taste. One day he and Ghalib were sitting in the verandah of Ghalib's house when a man passed by in the lane driving a donkey. There were some mango skins lying in the road, but the donkey just sniffed at them and passed on. "You see?" said Razi ud Din, "even donkeys don't eat mangoes." "Of course!" said Ghalib, "*donkeys* don't eat them." Shefta used to relate how on one occasion Ghalib, Fazl i Haq and other friends were discussing mangoes. Everybody was expressing his opinion on what qualities a good mango ought to have. When everyone else had spoken Fazl i Haq said to Ghalib, "Why don't you give us your opinion?" "My friend," said Ghalib, "in my view there are only two essential points about mangoes: they should be sweet, and they should be plentiful." '

One evening a friend came to visit him. When after a short stay he rose to go, Ghalib himself picked up the candle and accompanied him to the edge of the carpet so that he could see to put on his shoes. His guest said, 'You should not have troubled, I could have seen to put on my shoes myself.' 'Oh,' said Ghalib, 'I didn't bring the candle so that you could see to put on your shoes, but to make sure you didn't go off in mine.'

In short, Ghalib was well liked and had many friends; a number of them were British, some of whom held important positions in the British administration.

There are events of these years of which one would like to know a good deal more. One such was a love affair which influenced him deeply. Such things are not spoken of in Muslim society, but Ghalib was an exceptionally frank man, and three times in his life he wrote of this experience. The most specific detail comes latest, in a letter, undated, but perhaps written in 1860, in which he says that the girl was a domni—a singing and dancing girl—and that she died suddenly. 'It is forty years or more since it happened,' he writes, 'and although I long ago abandoned such things and left the field once and for all, there are times even now when the memory of her charming ways comes back to me and I shall not forget her death as long as I live.' A moving poem written at the time she died is included in his collected verse, and a Persian letter to Muzaffar Husain Khan, who, it seems, had suffered a similar loss, tells both of the grief he felt and of the resolve which he afterwards made.

[1] He himself used it as masculine in the singular and feminine in the plural. Cf. p. 294.

'In the days of my youth,' he writes, 'when the blackness of my deeds outdid the blackness of my hair, and my head held the tumult of the love of fair-faced women, Fate poured into my cup too the poison of this pain, and as the bier of my beloved was borne along the road, the dust rose from the road of that fortitude which was my essence. In the brightness of broad day I sat on sack-cloth and clad myself in black in mourning for my mistress, and in the black nights, in the solitude of sorrow, I was the moth that flew to the flame of her burnt-out candle. She was the partner of my bed, whom at the time of parting my jealous heart could not consign even to God's keeping. What pain that her lovely body should be consigned to dust! So beautiful she was that for fear of the evil eye of the narcissus, I could not take her to walk with me in the garden. What outrage that her corpse should be borne to the burial ground! When the fowler's prey has broken from his broken snare, what does he know of peace? And when the flower falls from the flower-gatherer's grasp ... how can joy come near him? When the beloved one gives herself to her lover—what though an age of toil and torment go before—only a lover knows the measure of the love and kind compassion it betokens. A thousand praises to those loyal beloveds who make in measure more than due, restitution for the lovers' hearts their glance has stolen, and give their very lives in love for them!

'Yet with all this, though grief at a beloved's death tears at the soul and the pain of parting for ever crushes the heart, the truth is that to true men truth brings no pain; and amid this tearing of the soul and this crushing of the heart we must strive to ponder: Where is the balm than can banish this distress? Who has the strength that can twist the wrist of death? In God's name! A man must not rove far into the valley of these parching, pestilential winds and must, amid the sorrow that melts the soul, set out to learn the lesson of fortitude. You who have eyes to see, think upon this: that all the capital of those who venture all for love ... is this one heart, lost now to the supple waist of their beloved, caught now and fettered in the ringlets of her curling locks. But where has a dead body the suppleness of waist to make the heart leap from its place? And where the curling ringlets to catch the soul in their toils? I fear lest this unlawful grief throw dust into the clear eye of the soul or slowly ripen till it bear the fruit of the heart's death. The nightingale, notorious for love, pours forth his melody for every rose that blooms, and the moth to whose great passion all men point, gives his wings to the flame of every candle that makes radiant her face. Truly, the candles radiant in the assembly are many, and roses bloom in the garden abundantly. Why should the moth grieve when one candle dies? When one rose fades and falls why should the nightingale lament? A man should let the world of colour and fragrance win his heart, not bind it in the shackles of one love. Better that in the assembly of desire he draw afresh from within himself the harmonies of happiness, and draw into his embrace some enchanting beauty who may restore his lost heart to its place and once more steal it away.'

Apart from this, the first period of Ghalib's life in Delhi seems to have been a happy one, until in a single year a series of heavy blows befell him. In 1826 his only brother Mirza Yusuf went mad (and was to remain so for the rest of his life); his father-in-law died; and he found himself for the first time in severe financial difficulties, with creditors pressing him hard to pay debts which he could not possibly meet.

In general it is not difficult to see why Ghalib should have found himself heavily in debt. He moved in the highest circles of Delhi society, and his pride would not allow him to live in an appreciably different style, even though he lacked the resources to support it. But the full details of the situation are obscure. In his boyhood and early youth it seems likely that he had had all he wanted from his mother's parents, and he may have continued to fall back on their resources to some extent during his early years in Delhi. But at some stage this source dried up—when and why we do not know—and this left him in the last resort dependent upon a wealthy and influential noble named Ahmad Bakhsh. Ghalib's family had in fact owed its livelihood to him since Ghalib was six years old, when his uncle Nasrullah Beg, who had been in the service of the Marathas, lost everything by their defeat at the hands of the British in 1803. Ahmad Bakhsh was at that time

'. . . the agent of the Alwar Raja in his dealings with Lord Lake and the British. He so favourably impressed both the Raja and the British that he was granted the district of Loharu [some 100 miles west of Delhi] in hereditary rent-free tenure by the one and the principality of Firozpur [about 60 miles south of Delhi] by the other.'

He was thus a man of considerable influence, and out of regard for the obligations of kinship (for his sister was the wife of Nasrullah Beg) he now used it to get Nasrullah Beg taken into the service of the British and provided with adequate means of livelihood on the sort of scale he had previously enjoyed. And it was Ahmad Bakhsh again who, when Nasrullah Beg died in 1806, intervened with the British authorities to provide indirectly for his dependants. Nasrullah Beg's grants had been, as Ghalib himself tells us in the letter already quoted (p. 23), for the duration of his own life only; but Ahmad Bakhsh now persuaded the British to make an arrangement whereby he was excused his payment of Rs. 25,000 a year to them on condition that he made provision for Nasrullah Beg's dependants and maintained a force of fifty cavalry to be made available to the British in case of need. A month later he got their authorization to reduce by half—from Rs. 10,000 to Rs. 5,000—the amount allotted to the support of Nasrullah Beg's dependants. Ghalib's share under this arrangement amounted to Rs. 750 a year. In all probability Ahmad Bakhsh also contributed indirectly to Ghalib's support in another way. Ilahi Bakhsh Maruf, to whose daughter Ghalib was married, was Ahmad Bakhsh's younger brother. Ghalib almost certainly drew some of his financial support from his father-in-law, and it is likely that Maruf in turn may have been able to draw from time to time on the greater resources of his elder brother. It is also possible that Ahmad Bakhsh himself may have helped Ghalib financially by gifts of money over and above the annual Rs. 750 which he was obliged under his agreement with the British to pay him. Thus Ahmad Bakhsh was the key to Ghalib's financial security.

For many years all went well, and it is more than likely that so long as money was coming in, Ghalib did not bother to enquire where it all came from and how much of it was his by legal right. But in the closing years of his life Ahmad Bakhsh took steps to provide for his sons' position after his death, and these measures, in the long run, spelt trouble for Ghalib. Ahmad Bakhsh had two wives; by the first he had a son named Shams ud Din, while by the second he had two sons, Amīn ud Din and Ziya ud Din. (Amīn ud Din was one of Ghalib's closest friends.) In 1822, with the consent both of the Raja of Alwar and of the British, he declared his eldest son Shams ud Din his heir. This settlement naturally displeased the two younger sons (the more so because their mother was an aristocrat, while Shams ud Din's mother was a common Mewati woman), and in 1825, at his father's wish, Shams ud Din assigned Loharu as a provision for them. In the following year he took over from his father, and in 1827 Ahmad Bakhsh died. The two younger sons were still very much dissatisfied with the position, and the feud between them and Shams ud Din intensified. It lasted for years, with both sides appealing repeatedly to the British authorities, who gave successive decisions, supporting now one side and now the other. Ghalib's Rs. 750 a year was throughout payable by Shams ud Din; the fact that he was a close friend of Amīn ud Din would have been quite enough to ensure that Shams ud Din paid Ghalib no more than he was obliged to, and seems in fact to have prompted him to pay him less than was due to him, and that too only at irregular intervals.

All this compelled Ghalib, perhaps for the first time, to examine his legal rights in the matter. To what extent he was already aware of them we do not know. He seems to have known the general tenor of the May, 1806 agreement between Ahmad Bakhsh and the British, but not perhaps that of June 1806, which reduced by half Ahmad Bakhsh's liability to Nasrullah Beg's dependants. At all events, in the legal proceedings he now initiated he challenged the validity of the document of June, 1806, declaring it to be a forgery.

After a fruitless visit to Firozpur, where Shams ud Din kept him hanging about, treating him with courtesy, but clearly prepared to concede him nothing, Ghalib decided to appeal in person to the British supreme authorities in Calcutta. He set out from Delhi in the spring of 1827, and was away for nearly three years, the greater part of which was spent in the British capital waiting for his case to be decided.

In the experience of these two years, the question of his 'pension' as Ghalib always called it, is of relatively minor significance, and may be cleared out of the way at once. Shams ud Din, his half-brothers, and Ghalib all had influential friends among the British on whose support they could count, and Ghalib had perfectly good reasons for hoping for a successful outcome. But as Hali writes,

'In the end he achieved nothing. The Government made enquiries about Ghalib's case from Sir John Malcolm, Governor of Bombay. (He had been Lord Lake's secretary, and documents relating to pensions and grants of land had been conferred in his presence.) He reported that Ghalib's claim was unfounded, and sent in a detailed account, which went completely against Ghalib's, of the fixing of the manner and the amount of the pension payable from Firozpur. When Ghalib's hopes from this quarter were disappointed, he appealed to England, but there too without result.'

The date of the Governor-General's rejection of Ghalib's claim was January 27, 1831, and throughout his life he never received more than the Rs. 750 a year laid down in the document of June, 1806.

But if Ghalib did not achieve the purpose for which he set out for Calcutta in 1827, he gained greatly in other ways. The experience of so long and arduous a journey was itself a new and interesting one for him. Large parts of the journey were over unmetalled roads; part of the way he travelled by river; and the final stage, from Banaras (Benares) to Calcutta, he did on horseback. The journey brought him in personal contact with men of letters in all the important centres along his route, and he continued to maintain this contact by letter in the years to come. He first broke his journey for any considerable length of time at Lucknow, where he stayed for several months. From the 1770s it had virtually replaced Delhi as the centre of Mughal intellectual life, and a second generation of Urdu poets and of Persian and Arabic scholars was now flourishing there. Its leading Urdu poet Nasikh now became Ghalib's personal friend, and an appreciable part of Ghalib's early verse shows his influence. Hali writes:

'When Ghalib left Delhi on his journey to Calcutta he had not at first intended to stop anywhere on the way. But influential people in Lucknow had long wanted him to visit the city, and when he reached Kanpur (Cawnpore) he decided to do so. In those days Nasīr ud Din Haidar was king [of Oudh] and Raushan ud Daula his Deputy.[1] Ghalib was given an excellent reception in Lucknow, and was highly spoken of to Raushan ud Daula. In the midst of his troubles he had not been able to compose an ode [in Raushan ud Daula's praise], but he had written a prose encomium . . . for presentation to him. However, Ghalib had stipulated that in his audience with the Deputy two conditions should be observed, and these were not accepted. The first was that the Deputy should greet him with due honour, and the second that he should be excused from making the customary gift. Because of this he was not granted audience, and left for Calcutta without presenting his encomium.'

[1] Hali's memory is at fault here. Ghazi ud Din Haidar was still reigning at the time, and Motamid ud Daula Agha Mir was his chief minister. (Cf. Ikram, p. 71 ff.) Ghalib's dealings were with the latter's deputy, Subhan Ali Khan Kanboh. Ghazi ud Din Haidar died about four months after Ghalib had left to continue his journey to Calcutta.

Hali's account is not correct in every detail, but its overall picture is quite accurate.

Ghalib had hoped to be granted an audience by the King, and to receive enough from him to defray a substantial part of the expense of his journey to Calcutta. Although his hopes in this respect were disappointed, he stayed on in Lucknow for several months, and his Persian letters show how many contacts he made there. Some of these were to serve him in good stead later on.

In October he went on his way, passing through Banda, Allahabad and Banaras, and finally reaching Calcutta on February 20, 1828—near enough a whole year after he had set out from Delhi. Banaras particularly enchanted him, and he wrote a Persian poem in its praise which he entitled *The Lamp of the Temple* in allusion to its fame as a holy city of the Hindus. More than thirty years later he still remembered it with pleasure, writing on February 12, 1861 to his friend Sayyah:

'What praise is too high for Banaras? Where else is there a city to equal it? The days of my youth were almost over when I went there. Had I been young in those days I would have settled down there and never come back this way.'

Calcutta too, he liked. He admired the greenery everywhere, and, less understandably, seemed even to have liked its climate. During his stay there he became involved—for the first time in his life, but by no means the last—in an acrimonious public dispute with Indian scholars of Persian, who were at that time no less numerous in Calcutta than in other centres of Mughal culture. The incident began at a mushaira where poets, Ghalib among them, had gathered to recite their verse. When Ghalib recited his Persian poem, objections were raised to the language of some of his lines, and these were supported by reference to the authority of Qatīl, an eighteenth-century Indian poet and lexicographer of Persian who was generally acknowledged by Indian scholars of Ghalib's day as a great authority. Hali writes,

'But except for Amir Khusrau[1] Ghalib did not hold any Indian poet of Persian in esteem. In one of his letters he writes, "Among the Indians, except for Khusrau of Delhi there is no established master. Faizi's[2] poetry is all right in parts." For this reason he considered men like Qatīl and Waqif of no account whatever. At the mention of Qatīl's name he turned up his nose and said, "I do not accept the word of Dilwali Singh, the Khatri[3] of Faridabad; only the work of Persians can be accepted as authoritative." (Mirza Qatīl was a convert to Islam. Before his conversion his name had been Dilwali Singh, a Khatri from Faridabad, in Delhi district. After he became a Muslim he went to Lucknow, where he was very highly regarded.) This answer raised a storm among his opponents, and he was inundated with objections.'

---

[1] A famous Persian poet of thirteenth-century Delhi.
[2] A famous poet of the reign of Akbar (1556-1605).   [3] The name of a Hindu caste.

Although plenty of others in Calcutta took his side in the dispute he thought it politic to retreat before the storm, and wrote a poem entitled *An Adverse Wind*, in which he attempted to placate his opponents while at the same time maintaining (albeit apologetically) his original stand. His reasons for seeking peace were probably largely diplomatic ones, for among those who had sided against him in this dispute were influential men whose support could be valuable to him in fighting his case for his 'pension'. He might have known beforehand that to provoke this kind of dispute would land him in trouble, but his enthusiasm for Persian and his conviction of the rightness of his standards of judgement where Persian was concerned made it impossible for him to hold back. Now and throughout his life his zeal in his own defence led him into exaggerations; but his position was basically sound, and it is significant that during the Calcutta controversy he was supported by a Persian, an envoy of the Persian prince Kamran who was in Calcutta at the time.

This incident was not his only distasteful experience in Calcutta, and as time went on and he made no discernible progress in his case, he sometimes wrote bitterly of the place. One of his short Persian poems gives an imaginary dialogue between himself and an unnamed adviser:

> I said to him, 'So tell me, then, what is Calcutta like?'
> He said, 'You cannot find its like in all the seven climes.'
> I said, 'What calling would a man do best to follow here?'
> He said, 'There is no calling you can follow free from fear.'
> I said, 'Then tell me, what course would you recommend to me?'
> He said, 'The course of giving up all thought of poetry.'
> I said at last, 'It is in search of justice I have come.'
> He said, 'Then run away! Why beat your head against a stone?'

But his subsequent recollections of Calcutta were often pleasant. In a Persian letter written after his return to Delhi he says,

'One should be grateful that such a city exists. Where else in the world is there a city so refreshing? To sit in the dust of Calcutta is better than to grace the throne of another dominion. By God, had I not been a family man, with regard for the honour of my wife and children, I would have cut myself free and made my way there. There I would have lived till I died, in that heavenly city, free from all cares. How delightful are its cool breezes, and how pleasant is its water! How excellent are its pure wines and its ripe fruits!

> If all the fruits of Paradise lay there outspread before you
> The mangoes of Calcutta still would haunt your memory!'

Ghalib's love of mangoes alone would have made Calcutta dear to him. There are numberless anecdotes on this point, relating to all periods of his life. Hali writes,

'He was extremely fond of mangoes. When they were in season his friends far and wide would send him the finest fruits; and there were some of his friends of whom he himself was always demanding them. In his Persian letters there is one, written, I think, during the period of his stay in Calcutta to the trustee of the Imambara[1] at Hooghly asking him for mangoes. In it he writes, "In some measure I am a slave to my belly, and in some degree I am weak. I seek an adornment for my table and a comfort for my soul; and wise men know that in the mango they may find both these things. The people of Calcutta say that Hooghly is the kingdom of mangoes—yes, roses from the rose-garden, and mangoes from Hooghly. From you, generosity; from me, gratitude! It is the hope of my eager heart that without fail twice or thrice before the season ends you may remember me. And my greed cries out that so little will not be enough to content your humble servant." '

In a short Urdu poem, which the strait-laced Hali does not quote, it is other pleasant recollections which are given more prominence.

> Ah me, my friend! The mention of Calcutta's name
> Has loosed a shaft that pierces to my very soul.
> Its greenery and verdure take away your breath;
> Its women's charms are such that none escapes them whole.
> Their glances pierce the armour of the stoutest breast;
> What heart withstands the blandishments of forms so fair?
> All freshness and all sweetness are its luscious fruits;
> Its mellow wines are pleasing beyond all compare.

Pleasant memories of mangoes and of pretty women were not Calcutta's only gifts to him. The city was the British capital, a modern city which had grown up under British rule on a site where before their coming there had been only three small villages. English influence, English ways, and English material progress were more evident there than anywhere else in India, and Ghalib's lively intelligence and the strong element of modernity in him which had long since been evident cannot have failed to feed on all these things. He knew neither English nor Bengali, but he had Muslim friends who had been resident there for some time, and Persian was in those days still a medium through which he could converse with appreciable numbers of Muslims, Bengalis, and Englishmen alike. Ram Mohan Roy, the first great intellectual figure in modern Indian history to take up and propagate with enthusiasm much of the outlook of modern Europe, had already made an impact in Calcutta, and *Mirat ul Akhbar* ('Mirror of News'), the Persian newspaper which he published, was only one of several which were current in Calcutta at the time. Ghalib's Persian letters speak of a number of them. At that time there were no newspapers in Delhi or anywhere else in northern India, and some years were yet to pass before the printing press made its appearance there. Ghalib formed during this

[1] A building where in the Muslim month of Muharram the martyrdom of Husain is mourned.

period the habit of reading newspapers which remained with him for the rest of his life. From it he gained a range of general knowledge and a widening of his intellectual horizons which his contemporaries in Delhi could not yet attain. Thus his nearly two years' sojourn in Calcutta must have still further strengthened his appreciation of the new which his own temperament and the atmosphere of Delhi in the early days of British rule had already made a part of him.

❧ Chapter 3 ❧

Delhi, 1829–47

Ghalib arrived back in Delhi on November 29, 1829, with none of his financial difficulties solved; and when fourteen months later the Governor-General rejected his claims absolutely, it was clear that no certain prospect of solving them remained.

It is more than likely that by this time Ghalib had long since resigned himself to the prospect of defeat. At some earlier stage he had written in anger and disgust to Siraj ud Din Ahmad:

'A report on my case has been sent up to a higher court. And, God save me, what a report!—a report involved and involuted as a Negro's curling hair, a report full of tumult and disorder as a lover's distracted heart, a report to encompass the murder of a world of hopes and longings, a report to call forth a decree to dash my honour in the dust.'

And at a later stage, when the case was under the consideration of the Governor-General, Lord Bentinck, he wrote again:

'My heart, which is a mirror of the secrets of the unseen, holds no hope; and when I look upon the blemishes in this government's laws and reflect upon the long vicissitudes my case has undergone, then if, let us say, my execution were ordered it would cause me no surprise, and if on the other hand one half of so and so's estates be awarded to me, that would not surprise me either. True justice is not to be had, and one must greet whatever happens with, "Be it so".'

Ghalib's debts at this time amounted to more than Rs. 40,000—that is to nearly sixty times the amount of his regular annual income. But the anxieties which this caused him were only a part of his misfortunes. His adversary Shams ud Din was both influential and popular in Delhi society, and Ghalib's failure to win his case against him gave many people a good deal of satisfaction. He says in one of his letters that he became an object "of ridicule to all and of censure to some", and for a time he kept very much to himself and avoided the society of others. Within a few years he was subjected to further humiliation when two of his creditors grew tired of waiting and took him to court. The court ordered him to pay Rs. 5,000 or go to jail. He had no means of paying, but fortunately for him, prominent men were treated with special consideration in the Delhi of those days, and were safe from arrest so long as they kept to their own houses. Ghalib's period of 'imprisonment' amounted therefore to no more than house-arrest. All the same, the indignity would have rankled deeply even with men far less touchy about their honour than Ghalib was, and he writes bitterly to his Lucknow friend and fellow-poet Nasikh, who had written to ask him for news of what was happening. The letter is in Persian, but he writes with a feeling and spontaneity which for the most part leaves him no time to produce the elaborate prose which his Persian letters generally exemplify:

'Four months have passed since I retired to my corner and closed the gates of access on friend and stranger alike. I am not in prison, but I eat and sleep as any prisoner does, and may I be branded as an infidel if in these few days I have not suffered torture and distress more than twofold the torment that the infidel suffers in a hundred years in Hell. Urfi has said:

> The bitter fragrance of the poison Fate poured in my cup
> Has burnt to ash the heart that could have felt hope and despair.

The first spark that fired the harvest of my hope and fortitude was that two of my creditors, in accordance with the rules of the English courts, obtained a decree against me. The rule is that I must either pay the sum named in the decree or hand myself over to the confining bonds of prison. And king and beggar in such case are alike. True, a distinguished man gains this much, that the court's men may not come to his house to take him. So long as he does not venture out to pass along the street he cannot be taken. Since I had no means to pay the money, regard for my honour compelled me willy nilly to seclusion, and to forgo the pleasure of riding out. And to this day the strong bond of my self-regard binds my exhausted hands and feet and makes them still.'

The letter goes on to speak of a still more painful experience that befell him while he was still undergoing this 'imprisonment'. On March 22, 1835, William Fraser, the British Resident of Delhi, was shot dead. Ghalib was closely involved in two ways. First, he knew Fraser personally, and was genuinely attached to him. Though the details of their relationship are not known, it is easy to see on what it was based. Fraser was, like Ghalib, a proud and independent man, impatient of convention and filled with intellectual curiosity. 'He lived as a solitary among his colleagues, saying that they had no rational conversation. But when he met the botanist Jacqemment, he travelled two days' journey out of his way to enjoy his company.' Jacquemment described him as 'an excellent man with great originality of thought, a metaphysician to boot....' In marked contrast with his lack of interest in his British colleagues was his easy intimacy with the aristocratic families of Delhi, an intimacy based on an insight into and respect for their culture. An Indian contemporary tells us that he possessed a substantial library of Persian and Arabic books. All these things must have won him Ghalib's sincere regard. But the two men were also connected by a further tie, for Fraser had espoused the cause of Ghalib's friends Amīn ud Din and Ziya ud Din against their kinsman Shams ud Din. The tone in which Ghalib continues his letter to Nasikh is therefore understandable:

'While I dwelt in this same seclusion and distress, a cruel, ruthless man who knew not the fear of God—may he dwell in eternal torment—in the blackness of the night killed with a musket's shot William Fraser Sahib Bahadur, the Resident of Delhi and unhappy Ghalib's kindly benefactor. My heart felt afresh the grief of a father's death. My soul was shaken within me; a mighty sorrow seized in its grip all my power of thought and burned to ashes the granary of my content and scraped from the page of my spirit all trace of the writing of hope. As chance would have it, far-sighted men saw signs that did not err, and on their foundation [Karim Khan] a horseman in the service of the Lord of Firozpur [Shams ud Din] was seized on a charge of the murder of that officer of lofty rank and noble qualities. The Magistrate of the City already knew me and felt the bond of mutual regard. In the seclusion I have spoken of, when like the owl I flew by night alone, from time to time I went to him at night to pass an hour or two in pleasant converse. When this event took place he made me his partner to pry into the mystery, until at last the crime was brought home to the Lord of Firozpur, and on the Government's command he was made prisoner, along with others who were close to him, and a force of police was sent to his estate. The men of Delhi knew that he and I were at odds, and now all assailed me and laid at my door the seizure of that man of black ingratitude and killer of a just ruler. That is, the men of Delhi, high and low, have spread abroad the slander that Shams ud Din Khan is innocent, and Fathullah Beg Khan and Asadullah Khan [Ghalib] have out of their abundant malice caught the authorities in a web of lies they have woven, drawn them from the path of right, and plunged poor Shams ud Din into disaster. And in all this the best of it is this, that Fathullah Beg Khan is himself the uncle's son of the Lord of Firozpur. In short the stage is come when the slanderers of Delhi repeat their constant curses upon me. At first my heart felt only the grief of William Fraser Sahib's death; but now that the man who killed him is identified, and the slanderers of the city loathe and shun me, I raise my voice each morning in prayer to that God who strikes down the oppressor and succours the oppressed, and call on Him to speed the day when that ruthless, overweening man shall pay the penalty and be hurled from the heights to the gallows' degradation. And I know that my desire will prevail and my prayer will find acceptance. . . . Within a month the outcome will be settled. . . .'

Things did indeed come to an issue soon after. Investigations showed that Karim Khan, the actual murderer, had acted on the direct instructions of Shams ud Din, and on October 3, 1835, both of them were publicly hanged. In a further letter to Nasikh, Ghalib tells him of this outcome:

'If I am late in sending you this letter do not conclude my affection for you fades. What could I do? For my resolve was set upon a mighty task and my eyes upon a lofty aim, until the turmoil was stilled and each one met the end he merited. The ruler of Mewat [Shams ud Din], like Karim Khan his man, was hanged by the neck and sent into oblivion:

The day must come when every man reaps what he sowed.'

He goes on to say that the Firozpur estate and all its appendages had been confiscated, but that a full and final settlement had not yet been made. When it was, he hoped to gain by it:

'My eyes still wait to see the token of my triumph. To speak more plainly, what the Lord of Firozpur used to pay me was less than was my due; and if the government pays no more than that sum, I shall not rest content.'

Meanwhile he had more immediate difficulties to face. His first letter had not spoken too strongly of the strength of feeling in Delhi over the Fraser murder, and if his love for Fraser made him feel a fierce satisfaction at Shams ud Din's execution, many of his fellow-citizens of Delhi felt differently. Among Shams ud Din's numerous well-wishers there were many who believed him to be innocent and suspected his enemies—and Ghalib among them—of having conspired to get him hanged. The strength of popular feeling may be gauged from the fact that for some years Shams ud Din's tomb was a place of pilgrimage, and that in the 'Mutiny'—twenty-two years later—the insurgents completely destroyed Fraser's tomb, while leaving those of other prominent British officials unmolested.

A letter written about the same time to Mir Azam Ali, who taught in a Muslim seminary in Agra, reflects the same bitterness and distress as his letters to Nasikh, and is of special interest because in it he reviews the whole course of his life since he left Agra for Delhi many years earlier. He writes:

'[Your letter] recalled to my mind that the world in former days held a city that I called my birthplace and men I called my friends. Your asking after me was like a dagger, thrust into the very vitals of my mind; and now you may see and wonder at the blood that drips from my lamenting lay. The years of separation which you, my master, reckon at sixteen years and I who write this letter deem to be not less than twenty, have been the sharp point of a knife scraping the writing of all peace and happiness from the page of my heart. When I first came to Delhi, my goblet held still the lees of the wine of heedlessness, and some few days of my life were given up to seek the satisfaction of my sensuous desires. I wandered erring in these ways until my drunken head was reeling, and, lost to myself, my feet strayed from the tavern floor and stumbled in the pit. I rose, with my whole body bruised and broken, and with dust upon my head and face. From one side came the onset of my brother's madness, and on the other rose the angry outcry of my creditors; such turmoil came upon me that my breath lost the way to my lips and my sight the way to the windows of my eyes, and the world lit by the shining lamps of heaven was darkened in my sight. I sewed my lips against speech and closed my eyes to the sight of myself, and set myself to live with my grief through world upon world of ruin and disaster. . . . Lamenting the injustice of the age I pressed my breast against the edge of the sharp sword and reached Calcutta. Those who held sway there strengthened my spirit with kindness and compassion, bringing me hope that the road that lay blocked before me would be opened up. And the desire to go out into the wilderness and die, which had brought me out of Delhi, departed from me; and the yearning for the temples of the god of fire and for the taverns of Shiraz[1] which tugged at my heart, calling me to Persia, left my soul. Two years I dwelt in that place of radiance, as though it were a shrine and I in constant attendance there. When the Governor-General prepared to go to Hindustan,[2] I hastened before him to Delhi. But the times turned against me, and the building I was building fell to ruin. Six years have passed since then, and I have thrown to the winds all thought that I might prosper. I give up my heart to the high hope of sudden death and keep to my corner, closing the doors of access on friend and stranger alike.

If in the midst of this grief and sorrow of which I have told you but a part, my letters cease and words fail me and my pen and voice write and speak no more, and I forget the august elders of the city of my birth, then in the realms of justice I go innocent. But what of those who hold high rank in the land of love and loyalty, and care not for those who lie in distant parts, and do not even seek to know whether they live or die? If I should speak of them, then would the steed of grievance course side by side with the steed of speech. If in this field I should contest with you, how will you score against me? And if you ignore so weak an adversary, what answer will you render to God, Who is not weak? None of my countrymen has helped me bear my grief, and I must think that in this world I *have* no country.'

He goes on to reject bitterly and emphatically a suggestion that he should come to Agra to plead his case before a court about to assemble there. For the man under whose authority it meets 'is that same self-willed, callous man whose dagger of oppression struck me down, and whose black glances darkened my days. Grant me, O God, that he too suffer loss, and the things that he has made my eyes to see, Fate may compel him too to look upon!'

In all these hardships Ghalib seems to have found his main consolation in writing, and he comforts himself with the idea that his greatness as a poet

---

[1] The ancient religion of Persia was Zoroastrianism. Shiraz was the city of Hafiz, the great classical lyric poet of Persia.

[2] In the more restricted sense of the central region of the northern plains.

necessarily means misfortunes without end. One of his poems of this period contains the lines:

> I asked the Mind Supreme why Destiny
> Decreed for me life-long captivity.
> It said, 'Ill-starred one, are you then a crow,
> Caught in the snare only to be set free?
> You are nightingale, held in a cage
> So that the age may hear your melody'.

A Persian letter written some years later to his friend Haqir amplifies the same thought.

'Words cannot tell of hapless Ghalib's failures. One might say that he has no God to care for him. And intellect bears witness and observation argues that cutting and wounding alone makes beauty and excellence shine forth. That the beauty of the cypress may appear, men cut and wound it. That the wine may be worthy to be passed round, they press and strain it. Until the reed be cut and shaped it cannot be a pen; until the sheet of paper be cut and reduced to pages it cannot be the bearer of a letter. Assuredly in this great workshop of creation and destruction He must needs create in order to destroy, and must needs destroy in order to create. He made me out of earth, and then exalted me to the skies. For some years He had regard for my exalted station; and then He hurled me down to earth, and that too with such force that my whole form made its imprint in the earth—and such an imprint that no knife can scrape this imprint from it. One would think that these accidents of creation and destruction bore me away from the world and brought to it in my place a broken man, a man so broken that death and life, laughter and weeping seem the same to him. O God, grant that this form that made its imprint on the earth and this imprint on the earth that this form made, may soon be removed from the face of the earth and consigned to the bosom of the earth.'

It was during these years that he first compiled the volume of his selected Urdu verse, discarding much of his earlier work as has already been described. He also gathered together his Persian verse and prose, and wrote many new Persian ghazals at this time. The Persian prose collection was probably compiled by about 1840 (though it was not printed until 1849), and is in five sections, of which the third and the fifth are the most interesting. In the third section Ghalib quotes selected lines from his Persian verse and instances appropriate contexts where they might be quoted in letter-writing; in the fifth he assembles his Persian letters to his friends. These include letters to many of the most famous names in the literature and scholarship of the nineteenth-century Muslim India, and show how well-established Ghalib's reputation was. It is worth stressing that these letters were written with the most elaborate care—as is clear from the some of those already quoted—and Ghalib regarded them as much as any other of his Persian prose writings, as models of literary composition on which he could pride himself. They cover a number of years, and most of them are either undated, or dated with insufficient precision to be placed accurately. Moreover in the published text of Ghalib's collected Persian prose the publishers supplemented them in 1875 with any other Persian letters they could find, without indicating at what point in the text these later additions begin. From internal evidence it is clear that the letters go back at least to the time when he was contemplating his journey to Calcutta, and a number of them were written during that journey. They vary greatly in mood, so that while some are intensely serious, others are equally light-hearted; and though as a general rule Ghalib composes them with the utmost care, he does not sacrifice warmth and spontaneity of feeling. In one he stresses that letter-writing should be like conversation:

'God is my witness that as I write this letter of humble service to you the desire to be with you so wells up within me that it leaves no room for the formal styles and titles of address. For I want to write to you in every way as though I were talking to you; and this means that many a time my words stray from the point, and I take no thought of what comes first and what comes last, and I write on and on without care for the length at which I write. Lost to myself, I let the reins fall from my hand, and am carried along over the ups and downs as I pass through the valley of conversation.'

To another correspondent he writes,

'Praise be to God that I was born a straightforward and a truthful man. My tongue speaks out all that my heart holds. If I have sinned against the religion of love and loyalty, then I deserve the torment of punishment; and if I be thought worthy of forgiveness, then I deserve the good tidings that my fault is pardoned.'

He often jokes with his correspondents. One letter is addressed to a man named Alif Beg, to whom a son had been born in his old age, and who had written to Ghalib asking him to suggest a name for the boy. Ghalib's answer plays upon the technicalities of the Urdu alphabet associated with the letter *alif* and the sign *hamza*. *Alif* is a simple vertical line, while *hamza* has a zig-zag shape. Both represent the same phonetic value, and both happen also to be used as personal names.[1] He writes:

'Kind of face and kind in grace, greetings! The tree of hope has borne fruit out of season, that is, a son has been born to you in your old age. Congratulations on so happy and auspicious an event! You wrote . . . to me to name the new-born babe. . . . Know then, I did not have to undertake the toil of thought. A

[1] The spelling of Hamza differs from that of hamza, but in Urdu the pronunciation is identical.

name flashed on my mind; my mind despatched a poem to my tongue; and my tongue entrusts the poem to the pen. May the Lord prosper him whom I name with this auspicious name! And may he be a loyal son to you, and in your lifetime live to be your age, and live for years and years when you are gone! This is the poem:

> A child is born to Alif in old age,
> A perfectly entrancing little son.
> I name him Hamza, for, as all men know,
> An Alif bent with age turns into one!

Your old associates speak often of you. Some day you should take the road towards this wilderness too.'

He writes to Rae Chajmal Khatri from somewhere on the way to Calcutta:

'Congratulations on becoming the agent of Zeb un Nisa Begam—and may this prove the prelude to further advancements in the future. If only you had told me what salary you were receiving I should have known in what measure to congratulate you.'

He goes on to speak of the marriage, which had just been celebrated, of Chajmal Khatri's son Jawahir Singh.

'The occasion requires both that I congratulate you and demand that you congratulate me.[1] May He Who grants increase of life and wealth grant us both to see the day when we may act the hosts at the wedding party of Jawahir Singh's sons. A diverting idea has just occurred to me—and you are not to treat it lightly! This joyous gathering took place in my absence. Well then, I should not be deprived of my share in the festivities. You should put aside the money to entertain me. If I live to return to Delhi I'll get the entertainment; if not, you'll get the money.

You say that So-and-so leads the philosopher's life and conducts his affairs as one who knows the ways of the world. Despite my sorrows I had to laugh, and let fall the reins of self-restraint from my hands. Don't you know? It's not the way of a philosopher to ride out on fleet horses with serving-men running before him, and to adorn his body with all manner of raiment, and to fill his belly with all manner of choice foods and to let his lust lead him into every excess and so soil his head with the dust of evil-doing; nor do such things become the man who seeks after the truth. . . .'

A letter to the same man, also written during the journey to Calcutta, introduces to him a man who is going to Delhi and who may need his help:

---

[1] i.e. Jawahir Singh is like a son to me too, and if you are to be congratulated on his marriage, so also am I.

'I write to introduce to you Mirza Amjad Ali Khan Sahib, a man of excellent qualities. This letter will bring him the honour and the pleasure of meeting you. He is a scion of the nobility of this city, and one who has suffered at the hands of fate; and his journey, like that of him who writes these lines, is occasioned by circumstance. He desired of me that I write a letter to some one of my acquaintances in my home city [Delhi], that it might be the means of his introduction to them. I who humour the every whim of my friends and feel without displeasure the indifference of my acquaintances, am at a loss to know to whom I should write; for I fear lest he to whom I shall write should fail to give first place to the duties of kindness and hospitality and so lay on me the burden of all manner of shame. In the event, I saw no other course before me than to write to you, in whom all the courtesy and kindness of the city is assembled. So he comes to you, alone and far from his homeland; and he must receive at your hands all that this condition merits, for you too have a friend who is far from his homeland. I do not say 'Do this' and 'Do that'; but this I know, that you will treat him with all the marks of consideration that the situation demands. I need not write more.'

Some of the best letters are to his Calcutta friend Siraj ud Din Ahmad, a man whom he was to describe many years later as one of the two best friends he had ever had. For years after his return to Delhi, Ghalib continued writing to him. One letter begins with a rebuke to him for not having written:

'You whose command Ghalib obeys, and in whose service Ghalib is bound and to whom Ghalib turns in reverence, were it not that a great grief possesses my heart, I and my heart alone could tell what new paths of complaint against you we would have opened up, and for what quarrels we would have laid the foundations. It is your gain that I am hapless and helpless. Otherwise, had I the resolve and the strength, I would have grappled with you and fought till your clothes were all torn and my face and head were cut and bruised. Fear God! Ponder well and judge justly: our relations have come to this, that ages pass and not a letter comes to show that you remember me!

I have said that I am bound by the need to lay a new grief before you. What room for complaint is there in a soul that grieves? The few lines I have written had no place on this page, but I wrote them because my reason told me—and writhed in pain to tell me—that perhaps my friend, who is unacquainted with the ways of friendship, might think that I am pleased with him and, so thinking, might neglect to atone for the wrong that he has done me.

The real reason why I write this letter is this. The home of my dear brother Nawwab Amīn ud Din Ahmad Khan Bahadur, son of Fakhr ud Daula Dilawar ul Mulk, Nawwab Ahmad Bakhsh Khan Bahadur, Rustam i Jang, suffered destruction in that same floodtide of misfortune that sank my ship. And I have done violence to the rights of loyal love, that in this journey I failed to bear him company.

My house lies all in darkness: I am its burnt-out candle;
In shame I hide my blackened face even from my own eyes.[1]

Judge of my haplessness and helplessness from this, that I harden my heart and
let Amīn ud Din Ahmad Khan go on his journey alone. If for this crime he
who passes judgement in the cause of love should pin me to the ground and draw
his ruthless sword to spill my blood, it would not be more than I deserve. And
the worst is this, that the more I speak of this, and the more I wax eloquent in
apology, the more my sense of shame and of unworthiness increases.

But yes, let Siraj ud Din Ahmad arise to make atonement, so that I may shed
this burden of grief and wipe the grime of shame from my face—in short, let
him gird his loins to entertain the traveller and lighten his troubles, resolved
to see himself as Amīn ud Din Khan's old friend, and to show him such sympathy and consideration that he, though beset by troubles and far from his
home, may forget the disgraced Asadullah [Ghalib] and look upon you in his
place.

My worthy brother (whom God preserve) has been told that when he
reaches Calcutta and meets you there he will think to himself, "See, Asadullah
has reached Calcutta before me!"

Were I to write more, it would be contrived, and contrivance is a thing from
which I flee.'

Siraj ud Din was evidently interested in getting subscribers in Delhi to a
newspaper called *Aina i Sikandar* ('The Mirror of Alexander'). (In Persian
legend, Alexander the Great set up a huge mirror in Alexandria in which he
could see all that was happening in Europe and so be forewarned of anything
that was being plotted there against him.) He approached Ghalib to help him,
and Ghalib replied:

'My friend, the sight of *Aina i Sikandar* brought lustre to my eyes, and its pure
style threaded pearls upon the string of my gaze. Its reports are well-written,
its news succinct: the points it makes are pleasing to the mind, and the eye
rejoices to read all that it writes. With all my heart and soul I obey your command, and intend to make every effort to secure the circulation of its pages.
The people of this city feel strong dissatisfaction at the inaccuracy of the news
that appears in *Jam i Jahan-numa*. ['The Cup that shows the World'—a
reference to a legendary cup of the Persian Emperor Jamshed, into which he
had only to look to see what was happening in all parts of the world.] It happens
but rarely that the news which the editor of *Jam i Jahan-numa* publishes this
week is not declared false next week by this very same editor. One week he
threads upon the string of writing this pearl, that before winter comes [the
British] will declare war upon the ruler of Lahore; and two weeks later he writes
that this news proved to be false. One week he gives the news that the mosque

---

[1] The verse is Ghalib's own.

in Agra Fort and the Taj Mahal mausoleum have been sold for such-and-such a sum. Again two weeks later he writes that the authorities of the Council have declared this sale invalid.

Anyway . . . Mubariz ud Daula Hisam ud Din Haidar Khan Bahadur and Fakhr ud Daula Amīn ud Din Khan Bahadur have seen the paper, and have decided not to subscribe. Hereafter I shall write and tell you what other prominent men of the city have to say.'

Another letter concerns the death in Calcutta of a common friend, Mirza Ahmad Beg.

'He used to say, "I shall be coming to Delhi," but, unkind man that he was, he forgot his promise and turned into another road, urging his camel swiftly on towards another goal. And, granted that he cared nothing for his friends, why did he not take thought for his little children, that he withdrew his protecting shade from over their heads? Alas for the friendlessness of his friends! and woe for the fatherlessness of his children!'

He goes on to speak of the dangers that beset the children—for even the eldest son is no more than a boy—and concludes,

'At all events, what is needed now is a trustee, a man who is both prudent and who respects their rights, who will come to their help and comfort them in their fatherless state. . . . I know what they must feel, for I was myself a child when I lost my father. By God I tell you that the care of these poor children is a prime duty, a binding duty, upon you and Mirza Abul Qāsim Khan. You must keep their helplessness ever before your gaze and never be heedless of them. . . . "God sees to it that they who do good shall not fail of their reward." '

On another occasion he writes of the resignation from his post and departure from Delhi of his old friend Fazl i Haq. Exactly what happened is not clear from the letter, but it appears that Fazl i Haq, who held a post in the Delhi courts, was unjustly put in a position where he felt that the only honourable course was to resign. Ghalib writes bluntly and indignantly about it.

'Be it known that the ineptitude of the authorities who do not know men's worth, has come to the pitch where that man of unparalleled learning . . . Maulvi Hāfiz Muhammad Fazl i Haq has resigned [his post] and so released himself from shame and degradation. Take Maulvi Fazl i Haq's knowledge and learning and wisdom and character and reduce them all a hundredfold; then measure this hundredth part of them against this post in the civil courts; the post would even then be less than these qualities merited. To be brief, after his resignation Nawwab Faiz Muhammad Khan appointed a monthly sum of Rs. 500 for my master's [i.e. Fazl i Haq's] expenses and sent for him. The day

Maulvi Fazl i Haq left Delhi I cannot describe what the people of the city felt. The heir apparent to the throne of Delhi . . . Mirza Abu Zafar Bahadur sent for him to bid him farewell. He took a shawl from his own personal apparel and laid it upon his shoulders, and the tears came to his eyes as he said, "As often as you say 'I am leaving', I think that there is nothing I can do but bear it patiently. But All-Knowing God knows with what infinite effort I bring the words of farewell from my heart to my tongue." These were the words of the heir apparent; and what a distracted Ghalib wants of you is that you should write in shining words the news of Maulvi Fazl i Haq's leaving Delhi and of the heir apparent's grief and of the sorrow in the hearts of the people of the city, and put it into print in *Aina i Sikandar* and so put me in debt to your kindness.'

One of the last letters to Siraj ud Din in the published collection is evidently in answer to a request that Ghalib should send his verses for him to see. Ghalib replies:

'Now that I am involved in all manner of struggles with myself, it is no easy matter to write verse. I am a man who, had the age granted him but some small measure of ease, would by the force of my imaginative power have wrested the prize from the grasp of the masters of the art. In a word, whatever in the way of poetry shall come to my lips, despite all the misery I feel, shall be committed to the pen and so be brought before your attentive gaze.'

If writing consoled Ghalib, it did not feed him, and his financial position was as acute as ever. The one gain he could register was that after the execution of Shams ud Din, the Firozpur estates were confiscated and Loharu given into the possession of Amīn ud Din, while Ghalib's own 'pension' of sixty-two rupees eight annas a month became payable by the British authorities in Delhi. To know that he would now get his pension regularly was something; but the pension itself was quite inadequate to his needs. In 1837 an English tradesman named Macpherson obtained a court order requiring Ghalib to pay him Rs. 250, and on this occasion he was taken by surprise while away from his home and actually arrested. Only the intervention of Amīn ud Din, who generously paid out Rs. 400 in settlement of the whole debt together with the interest due, saved him from imprisonment. But if he badly needed extra income, he would not seek it in any way he thought derogatory to his honour. In this way he missed an opportunity in January 1842 of a professorship in Persian at Delhi College. Hali relates what happened:

'In 1842, when Delhi College was reorganized on new principles, Mr Thomason, Secretary of the Government of India, who later became Lieutenant-Governor of the North-Western Provinces, came to Delhi to interview the candidates. A teacher of Arabic had already been appointed at a salary of Rs. 100, and Mr

Thomason wished to make a parallel appointment for Persian. The names of Ghalib, Momin Khan and Maulvi Imam Bakhsh had been suggested to him, and Ghalib was the first to be called for interview. When he arrived in his palanquin . . . Mr Thomason was informed, and at once sent for him. But Ghalib got out of the palanquin and stood there waiting for the Secretary to come out and extend him the customary welcome. When some considerable time had passed and Mr Thomason had found out why Ghalib did not appear, he came out personally and explained that a formal welcome was appropriate when he attended the Governor's durbar, but not in the present case, when he came as a candidate for employment. Ghalib replied, "I contemplated taking a government appointment in the expectation that this would bring me greater honours than I now receive, not a reduction in those already accorded me." The Secretary replied, "I am bound by regulations." "Then I hope that you will excuse me," Ghalib said, and came away.'

It was more in accord with the traditions he knew to take the course open to every poet or scholar of established reputation and seek the patronage of a ruler wealthy enough to provide for his support. Modern opinion too readily assumes that such a relationship necessarily implies subservience of the poet to his patron; but this was certainly not the case. In Mughal society the patronage of learning and letters was one of the accepted social functions of the nobility, and the established poet could look to receive patronage simply because he *was* an established poet; occasional panegyrics of his patron and odes on special occasions would be expected of him, but this was by no means the most important basis of the relationship, and the poet saw nothing injurious to his self-respect in it, any more than the great noble saw anything dishonourable in his allegiance to his overlord. Ghalib was of all people the least likely to fawn upon a patron, though he readily accepted the composition of panegyrics as a recognized part of the unwritten contract between them. He had made his debut in this line some years ago, when in 1827 he had composed an ode to the ruler of Oudh, hoping to receive in return a substantial contribution to the expenses of his journey to Calcutta. It is significant that in it he had written

> I pledge my faith, and swear I never fawned on kings;
> Our independent pride was handed down to us.
> We too give bounty, and I need to feel no shame
> To come now asking bounty from the bounteous.

This always remained his attitude. But if his independence of spirit was admirable, he was often to find that his diplomatic skill left something to be desired. This became most evident in his attempts to gain favour with the Mughal King—the nearest and most obvious target for a Delhi poet. When Ghalib made his first approaches in 1834 Akbar Shah II was King, and his son Zafar the heir-apparent. But Ghalib knew that the King was anxious to get another son, Salīm, recognized as his successor, and was negotiating with the

British to this end. Ghalib calculated that his own interests lay in the same direction, for Zafar had already made Zauq, a rival poet of Ghalib's, his ustad; and in an ode to Akbar Shah he therefore went out of his way to sing the praises of Salīm as well. As things turned out, this was a blunder. The British refused to agree to Zafar's supersession, and only three years later Akbar died and Zafar became King under the name of Bahadur Shah. It may be imagined that he did not look too kindly on Ghalib, and for years together he failed to gain entry to the Court, despite a number of odes which he composed in praise of the new king. Nor did his efforts elsewhere meet with much success. Many years later he was to recall the continuing failure of his efforts to gain the patronage of the Oudh court. In a letter to his friend Tufta dated August 19, 1861, he speaks of one of his odes and continues:

'I sent this ode, through Munshi Muhammad Hasan, to [the Prime Minister] Raushan ud Daula, and through Raushan ud Daula it was presented to [King] Nasīr ud Din Haidar [1827-37]. The very day it was presented, the King gave order for Rs. 5000 to be sent to me, but my intermediary—i.e. Munshi Muhammad Hasan—did not inform me of this. When the late Muzaffar ud Daula came from Lucknow he told me this secret, adding, "For God's sake don't mention my name to Munshi Muhammad Hasan." All I could do was to write to . . . Nasikh asking him to find out what had happened to my ode and write to me. He wrote in reply, "You were granted five thousand rupees, of which Raushan ud Daula helped himself to three thousand. He gave the remaining two thousand to Munshi Muhammad Hasan and told him to send you as much of it as he thought fit. Has he not sent you anything yet? If not, write and tell me." I wrote back that I had not even received five rupees. He replied, "Now you should write me a letter to the effect that you have sent an ode in praise of the King and have been informed that it was presented to him, but do not know what was granted you in reward. I will have your letter to me read to the King, and see that the man disgorges your money and sends it to you." Well, my friend, I wrote the letter and posted if off. Two days later the news reached Delhi that Nasīr ud Din Haidar had died. So, I ask you, what could I or Nasikh do now?'

Another intermediary in a later reign was to serve him equally badly. He recalls the whole story in an undated letter to Shafaq, placed by Mihr between one of June, 1862 and one of February, 1864:

'Let me tell you a story. In the early days of Amjad Ali Shah's reign[1] there was a man with whom I was slightly acquainted. I don't know where he came from,

---

[1] Amjad Ali Shah was King of Oudh from 1842-47. However, as Mihr points out, Ghalib in fact means Ghazi ud Din Haidar, 1814-27.

but he had come to Agra at some time and had once been a tahsildar[1] somewhere; he had a plausible tongue and could use his wits, and he had come to
Agra to get some sort of a job. But he never managed this. He came to see me
once or twice, and then disappeared God knows where. Meanwhile I moved
to Delhi. It must have been near enough twenty years later, in Amjad Ali
Shah's reign, when out of the blue the mail brought me a letter from him. In
those days my mind was alert and my memory sound, and I realized that it was
this same gentleman. He began his letter with this line of verse:

> I thank my fortune, and I thank the age

and went on, "Since we last met I have spent twenty years wandering from
place to place. I got employment at Jaipur, but I left it after two years, and
since then have been to all sorts of places and done all sorts of things. Now I've
reached Lucknow. I've met the Wazir, and he is most kind to me. Through
him, I have entered the King's service. The King has bestowed on me the titles
of 'Khan' and 'Bahadur' and entered my name on the roll of his courtiers. My
stipend has not yet been fixed. I have aroused the Wazir's interest in you, and
if you write an ode to His Majesty and a petition or letter (as you think fit)
to the Wazir and send it to me, I am sure that the King will send for you. . . ."
I had only recently written an ode to Amjad Ali Shah . . . but was at a loss to
think whom I should send it to for presentation. Anyway I put my trust in God
and sent it off. A mere acknowledgement came, and then a fortnight later, a
letter came: "The ode has been presented to the Wazir, who has read it with
great pleasure and has promised to present it in due form to the King. Now I
would ask you to get Miyan Badr ud Din . . . to engrave a seal for me showing
my name and title, and send it to me. It should be a square silver seal, and the
engraving should be in a bold script." Your humble servant fulfilled this
commission and sent the ring off. I received an acknowledgement, and with it
the good news that my ode had been presented to the King. Then for the next
two months I heard nothing. I sent a letter, and it was returned to me with the
explanation from the postal authorities that the addressee was not there. A
long time later I discovered that the gentleman had indeed gained access to the
Wazir and waited upon him, but that he had never been taken into the King's
employment or been granted a title. He had tricked me into getting the seal
with the title engraved and had gone off to Murshidabad. When he left, the
Wazir had made him a present of two hundred rupees.'

It may have been, in part, his financial straits which made Ghalib indulge all
the more a fondness for gambling, and this was now to involve him in one of
the most distressing experiences of his life. The full circumstances of the
incident, which occurred in 1847, are somewhat obscure, and there are several

---

[1] The chief revenue officer of a tahsil—a small area consisting usually of a small country
town and its neighbouring villages.

C

conflicting accounts of it. It appears that Ghalib had always enjoyed gambling, though he had not habitually played for high stakes. It was his misfortune that he was now living in a period when the authorities seem to have felt that gambling had assumed the proportions of a serious social evil in Delhi society, and were determined to stamp it out by the most drastic legal penalties. He had already felt the effects of this policy six years earlier, when his house had been raided and he had been fined Rs. 100; but he now seems to have thought that he had meanwhile acquired influential friends in the British administration on a sufficient scale to protect him from any drastic consequences even if he were caught. He was soon undeceived. This time when his house was raided he was arrested, brought to trial, and given a heavy sentence. A contemporary newspaper reported: 'Mirza Sahib has been sentenced to a fine of Rs. 200 and six months' imprisonment with hard labour; in the event of failure to pay the fine, the period of imprisonment will be extended, while on payment of Rs. 50 over and above the Rs. 200 he may be excused the hard labour.' This sentence was upheld in higher courts. This was an unexpected and terribly heavy blow to Ghalib, not least because he could not understand how his influential contacts had failed to protect him. Hali writes:

'Ghalib has himself given a brief account of this incident in a Persian letter, which I give here in translation: "The Chief of Police was my enemy, and the Magistrate did not know me. . . . Although the Magistrate has authority over the Chief of Police, he behaved, where I was concerned, as though the Chief of Police had authority over him, and issued the order for my imprisonment. The Session Judge was my friend; he had always treated me with friendship and kindness, and in most companies where we met, had behaved quite informally with me; yet he too acted now as though he did not know me. An appeal was made to the higher court, but my case was not heeded and the sentence was upheld. . . ." '

The heavy sentence seems to have created a great stir in Delhi, and a good deal of indignation. The newspaper report already quoted continues:

'When it is borne in mind that Mirza Sahib has long been a sick man on a strict diet . . . we are obliged to say that the distress and the hard labour will be beyond his strength to endure, so much so that his very life may be endangered. . . . It is contrary to all justice that, for a very ordinary crime, a talented nobleman, whom the public honours and respects profoundly, should have to pay a penalty so drastic that it may well cost him his life.'

So great was the concern at Ghalib's arrest that the King, who entertained no very warm feelings towards him, was induced to write to the authorities requesting his release; but he received the reply that this was a matter for the courts, and the administration could not intervene.

Accordingly Ghalib began to serve his prison sentence, and if he had felt deeply humilitated by his 'imprisonment' in his home twelve years earlier, it can be imagined what his feelings were now. The hardships of prison life[1] were not all that was in store for him; even more painful to him was the effect of his sentence on his friends and relations. All except one held aloof from him, apparently thinking it discreditable to continue association with one who was now a convict serving a prison sentence. Two of Ghalib's closest friends from his earliest years in Delhi had been Fazl i Haq and Amīn ud Din, who was now Lord of Loharu. Fazl i Haq was no longer in Delhi; Amīn ud Din, who had not only been Ghalib's friend but was related to him by marriage, became openly hostile, and when an Agra newspaper mentioned in a report that he was Ghalib's kinsman, he went to the extent of having it made clear in a subsequent issue that the relationship was one by marriage only. His brother Ziya ud Din's conduct was no better. The one exception was Ghalib's fellow-noble and fellow-poet Shefta, whom Ghalib had come to know well later than the others, after his return from Calcutta, and who now did all he possibly could to relieve Ghalib's distress.

Nawwab Mustafa Khan Shefta was nine years younger than Ghalib, having been born in Delhi in 1806. His background was strikingly similar to Ghalib's, except that his ancestors had migrated to India not from Turkestan but from Kohat, in the borderlands of Afghanistan, and were related to the family which early in the eighteenth century established the small principality of Farruk-habad in what is now western Uttar Pradesh. His father served in the Maratha armies as the commander of a regiment, and when the conflict with the British under Lord Lake developed, he used his diplomatic skill to bring about a peaceful settlement between Lord Lake and his own commander. The British rewarded him in 1813 with estates bringing in three hundred thousand rupees a year. This grant was for the duration of his own life, and he provided for his descendants the following year by buying the estate of Jahangirabad in the Meerut district, then being auctioned by the British because the former owner had failed to pay them the revenue due on it. On his death the British resumed possession of the estates they had granted him, but in recognition of his past services appointed a stipend of Rs. 20,000 a year to his successors.

Shefta grew up in Delhi, and received a thorough education in Persian and Arabic. In his youth he lived in the usual style of the young Delhi aristocrat; wine and women formed part of his regular pleasures, and his liaison with a stylish, wealthy and cultured courtesan named Ramju was well-known. But he later turned to religion and gave up these things. In this connection the story is told that he visited Ghalib one day during the cold season when Ghalib was drinking wine. Ghalib invited him to join him. 'I have given it up,' said Shefta. 'What?' said Ghalib, 'Even in winter?' In 1839 he set out on the pilgrimage to Mecca, and after an adventurous journey during which he was shipwrecked, ultimately returned to Delhi in 1841.

[1] Though he did not have to eat prison food. His food was sent to him from his home.

Though no such reform had taken place in Ghalib, Shefta's regard for him was unchanged. Poetry was the great bond between them and each had the highest opinion of the other's work. Ghalib once wrote to him:

'Envy of Talib[1] and pride of Ghalib, greeting. My heart was still full of my ode ... though it had travelled from the heart to the tongue and from the tongue to the world beyond, it was yet in my heart. But when I read the ghazal that you sent me, my ode was both banished from my heart and lowered in my eyes. A fine ghazal! A ghazal to gladden the heart! Though I am one whose language is unworthy and whose tongue falters, yet if I should write a separate ode of praise to every one of its verses, that were fitting. . . . And whose tongue can praise its last couplet? . . . I envy you that final couplet. Live on for ever and ever, for you are the life and soul of poetry!'

Mihr writes:

'Hali used to say that as soon as Shefta heard the news of what had happened, he at once took steps to see everyone in authority he could think of, and made continuous efforts to get Ghalib released. Then came the trial and the appeal. Shefta paid all the expenses out of his own pocket. All the time Ghalib was in prison he went to visit him regularly every other day. He used to tell people, "My deep regard for Ghalib was never based upon his sobriety or his piety, but on his greatness as a poet. Today he is accused of gambling, but that he drinks wine has always been known. Why should it make any difference in my regard for him that he has been charged and sent to prison? His poetic talent is the same today as ever it was." '

Ghalib felt a gratitude to him as intense as the bitterness he felt for the friends who had turned their backs on him, and both feelings find expression in a long poem which he wrote in prison:[2]

> Here within prison walls confined I tune the lute
>   of poetry
> That sorrow bursting from my heart, transmuted
>   into melody,
> May sing a song to draw forth blood—that even
>   from captivity
> I may work wonders in the world, and build a
>   tavern for the free.
> Thus shall I labour hard; hard labour consorts
>   with imprisonment
> Bonds shall no longer choke my voice, and I
>   will sing my heart's lament.

---

[1] A classical Persian poet.   [2] It is considerably abridged in the translation that follows.

Old friends, you must not incommode yourselves to
        come and visit me,
And knock upon my door—I cannot open it as
        formerly.
Imprisoned thieves are now my friends, and bow
        to my supremacy.
I still their clamour, telling them, 'Outside there
        is no loyalty.'
    The sentence passed upon me, true, is not for
        all eternity,
    But from the world I look no more for joy
        that makes man truly free.

The candle's flame with equal ease puts darkness
        everywhere to flight
But better that it burn for kings, filling their
        palaces with light.
Ghalib is precious frankincense; if he must burn,
        then it were right
To burn him in a costly censer, symbol of a
        prince's might.
    Alas that he lies here where never comes
        the cooling breeze of morn—
    Only the burning, searing wind that scorches
        even the desert thorn.

But prison warders, prison guards, assemble here,
        for I am come.
Open the gates to welcome me as I draw near, for
        I am come.
Friends, prisoners in your narrow cells, be of good
        cheer, for I am come.
A poet's words, a poet's wisdom you shall hear,
        for I am come.
    When friends and kinsmen all have turned away
        from me in my disgrace
    Why should I not find comfort here from strangers,
        captive in this place?

It was no policeman sent me here, no magistrate, no
        power of earth—
This suffering, this imprisonment, was written in my
        fate at birth.
And what of that? One noble man, Mustafa Khan,
        despite this dearth
Of noble men, asks after me, and makes me see my own
        true worth.

He is God's mercy, God's compassion, sent in
human form for me
And if I die I shall not grieve, knowing that
he will mourn for me.

Friends, in this garden of the world I am a weed;
if I should die
You need not grieve; its cypresses and fragrant flowers
are you, not I.
But if you lack the heart to love, still you can raise
your voice on high;
I lay this poem before you now; its meed of praise do
not deny.
You will not think of me, I know, in one another's
company
But still, where men recite their verse, surely
you will remember me.

Ghalib did not serve his full sentence, and, so far as is known, did not have
to perform hard labour—means were presumably found to pay the Rs. 250—but
he did serve three whole months in jail. Then, in circumstances which are now
quite obscure, and which he himself declared he did not understand, he was
released. The letter quoted by Hali says as much, and continues by describing
Ghalib's feelings about the whole affair:

'Then for some unknown reason when half my term had expired, the Magistrate
took pity on me and wrote a report to the higher court recommending my
release, and the order for my release was handed down. . . . Because I believe
that all that happens, happens by God's will—and there is no fighting against
His will—I hold myself free from any stigma in what has happened and resign
myself to accept all that the future may bring. Yet to entertain a desire is not to
contravene the law of submission to Him, and it is my desire no longer to stay
in this world, and if I must stay, then not to stay in India. There is Rum; there
is Egypt; there is Iran; there is Baghdad. But these too I pass by. The Kaba
itself is the sanctuary of the free, and the threshold of the Prophet,[1] who is
God's blessing to all the worlds, is the resting place of His devotees. I await
the day when I shall gain release from this bondage of wretchedness, which
wears away my soul more than the bondage I have undergone could do, and
shall set my face towards the wilderness, not caring where I go. This, then,
is what I have suffered, and this is what I desire.'

[1] Medina, where Muhammad is buried.

Chapter 4

Ghalib and the Mughal Court, 1847–57

His imprisonment is a milestone in Ghalib's life; and the same year of 1847 is memorable also because it marks the beginning at long last of his connection with the Mughal Court. He was befriended by Nasīr ud Din (generally known by his nickname of Kale Shah, or Miyan Kale Sahib), whom the King had accepted as his murshid, or spiritual guide. On his release from jail Kale Shah put a house at his disposal, where he was able to live rent-free, and it was through his influence that Ghalib at length gained audience with the King. Ghalib joked about his obligation to Kale Shah, whose nickname means roughly 'the Black Saint'. Hali writes: 'One day he was sitting with Miyan Kale when an acquaintance called to congratulate him on his release from prison. "Release? Who's been released?" said Ghalib, "I've come out of the white man's prison into the black man's prison".' Thanks to Miyan Kale Ghalib now had access to the King, but for another three years no permanent connection was established. Then in 1850, the King's physician, Hakim Ahsanullah Khan, who was an admirer of Ghalib's Persian writing, secured for him a commission to write in Persian prose the history of the Mughal dynasty. For this service he was to receive a stipend of Rs. 600 a year. Thus at the age of fifty-two he began to receive, for the first time in his life, a regular income over and above his 'pension'. At the same time the King conferred upon him a ceremonial robe, and the titles Najm ud Daula, Dabir ul mulk, Nizam Jang ('Star of the Realm, Scribe of the State, Marshal of War'). This was only a beginning. For the next few years a measure of good fortune continued to come his way. In 1854 he was chosen as the ustad of the heir-apparent, Mirza Fakhr ud Din. Ikram comments: 'The heir-apparent had taken the widow of Shams ud Din, Ghalib's ancient enemy, into his harem. Clearly, Ghalib's literary fame must have been very firmly established for the heir-apparent to overlook Ghalib's enmity to Nawwab Shams ud Din and make him his ustad.' Ghalib was to receive as ustad a stipend of Rs. 400 a year. In the same year (or perhaps a little earlier) he reaped the reward of his panegyrics of the Kings of Oudh, and Wājid Ali Shah, the last king, directed that he should be paid a stipend of Rs. 500 a year. In 1854, too, Zauq died, and Ghalib, perhaps only because no other poet of comparable standing was now left in Delhi, was appointed to succeed him as the King's ustad. Thus at the end of 1854 his financial position was better than it had been for many years. Besides his pension of Rs. 750 a year he was getting Rs. 600 from the King, Rs. 400 from the heir-apparent, and Rs. 500 from the King of Oudh.

If these years mark a certain turn in Ghalib's fortunes, they are also important for another reason. These were the years in which Ghalib, for the most part, gave up writing his letters in Persian and changed over to Urdu instead. Substantial numbers of these Urdu letters have been preserved, so much so that from this point onwards they begin to become the most important source for the story of his life, and it will be increasingly possible to tell that story in his own words. Hali believes that it was his appointment to the task of writing the history of the Mughal dynasty that marked the turning point. He writes:

'It seems that up to 1850 Ghalib always conducted his correspondence in Persian; but when in that year he received the appointment to write the history of the Mughal dynasty and became wholly engrossed in writing *Mihr i Nimroz*,[1] he must, out of necessity, have been driven to do his letter-writing in Urdu. He used to compose his Persian prose works, and most of his Persian letters too, with the utmost labour, and one sees in them, somewhat more than in his verse even, the working of his imaginative and poetic powers. Thus when all his effort was directed to the writing of *Mihr i Nimroz*, it must have been a burden to him to continue writing his letters in Persian, and that too in his own characteristic style. We must infer, therefore, that from 1850 onwards he began writing them in Urdu. . . .'

Hali's general inference is probably correct, though as we shall see, there are on the one hand a number of Urdu letters written as early as 1848, and, on the other, at least a few Persian ones which were written after 1850.

The letters show that the enhanced status and the improved financial position which these years brought did not make Ghalib by any means completely happy. In the first place the bitter and humiliating experiences of 1847 continued to affect him deeply. As late as January 1850 he writes to Haqir:

'My kind and compassionate and generous friend and benefactor, I owe you a reply to your letter. But what am I to do? Heavy grief and sadness is always with me. I no longer wish to live in this city; and the difficulties and obstacles in the way are such that I cannot leave it. In brief, my misery and sorrow is such that only the hope of death keeps me alive.

> He who lives on because he hopes to die
> *His* hopelessness is something to be seen.'

Secondly, though money was important to Ghalib, other things were much more important to him—nor, for that matter, was the money, welcome though it must have been, enough to solve his financial difficulties. These continued to oppress him, and it oppressed him still more to think that the King whose patronage he had at last won—and not only the King—was incapable of

---

[1] The name which Ghalib gave to the first part of his history—cf. below.

assessing him at his true worth. Being the man he is, he makes this perfectly clear in the preamble to the history he is writing for him. He begins with eloquent praise to Kale Shah, to whose kindness after his release from prison he owed so much.

'I am his neighbour, and the dwellers in the skies lie in my shadow, and so long as I sit in the dust of his threshold, the angels envy me my high estate and I am the apple of the eye and the joy of the heart of the shining stars, and the moon and the heavenly bodies lie at my feet.'

But he goes on to speak of his listlessness of spirit, and of the general unawareness of his talent that has reduced him to his present state.

'In my body, made of dust, there is no life, as there is no life in the whirling dust-storm that provides a brief spectacle for men's eyes. Perhaps I am the painted picture of the nightingale of the garden; the fragrance from the rose inspires no melody to burst forth from its heart. Or I am the verdure on the tempered sword, which cannot bend before the blowing of the drunken wind. The bond that linked my heart with joy was broken long ago, and the blood still drips unceasingly from my heart. How strong that bond must have been! And with what force it must have been broken! One night I said to my frenzied heart—a heart more wise than I: "Grant me the power to speak, and I will go into the presence of that King whose court and its wondrous works rank with the garden of Iram, and will say, 'I am the mirror of secrets, and should be made to shine; I am the creator of poetry and should be cherished.' " It said "O foolish one, these were words for another occasion; the time for them has passed. Now if you still have words to say, say, 'I am bruised and need balm for my wounds; I am dead and need life to revive me.' "

'. . . I cannot feel too great a pride in my happy fate, that I have a master such as you to direct my labours; and as I would lay down my life for you I swear that you too must feel pride in the great kindness of fortune, that you possess a slave like Ghalib, whose song has all the power of fire. Turn your attention to me as my skill demands, and you will treasure me as the apple of your eye and open your heart for me to enter in. They say that in the days of —[the Emperor Shahjahan], by that open-hearted sovereign's command [the poet] Kalim was time and time again weighed against silver and gold and pearls and rubies. I desire that you command men of discernment to flinch not from the toil and effort, and to weigh my poetry—not many times, but just once— against Kalim's verse.

> Look not upon me slightingly: though I
>   am dust beneath your feet
> Men honour this your capital because I
>   dwell in it.

c*

See my perfection, look upon my skill; see how despite the rage that wears away my life, despite the distress that drains away my strength, my rich imaginative power cherishes the muse of poetry and my eloquence surrounds her with all the delights that her heart could wish. I dwelt long with the Source of all Bounty, and drew constantly upon His store; and I excel the poets that came before me because I dwelt longer in His splendid abode. For I was sent down into the world after twelve hundred years,[1] and Sadi and Khusrau appeared after six hundred and fifty. And why talk of the poets of the Emperor Akbar's day? My presence bears witness that your age excels his. . . .

'And now the age makes new demands of me—me, who have drunk wine my whole life through, and felt its heady exaltation and in that exaltation have spoken nothing but poetry, and if my steps have strayed into the paths of prose, have walked there too with the same drunken gait; now—at this time, when my heart is cleft in twain and my imaginative power destroyed, and my senses and perceptions dulled, and my mind as though no longer in being and my body broken because my soul is sick, and my soul in disarray because of my body's pain and if I set myself to write no more than a page, then before it is completed and I turn the leaf, the joints of my fingers have stiffened and the pen falls from them, and my blood is burnt to nothing in my veins, and my sight in my eyes, and my breath on my lips and my marrow in my bones—even so the age demands of me that I tune the lute of narrative, that it may judge of the quality of the melody I play and put my style of playing to the test.'

We can follow the progress of his work in the letters to Haqir. Its final form differed from that which he had originally planned. He describes the general plan thus:

'I have named the work *Partawistan* (The Land of Radiance) and divided it into two volumes. The first volume begins with the creation of the world[2] and goes up to Humayun [i.e. to 1556]; I have entitled it *Mihr i Nimroz* (The Sun at Midday). The second volume will begin with . . . Akbar and go up to the reign of His Majesty the present King, and will be entitled *Mah i Nimmah* (the Moon at Mid-month).'

Mihr i Nimroz was completed quite quickly, although, as we shall see, a stage came when Ghalib had to re-write the first part of it. His stipend for writing it was payable half-yearly in arrears, and as the first half-year came to an end he seems to have been anxious to be able to produce tangible evidence that he had really earned it. This is clear from a letter which he wrote to Haqir on January 2, 1851; and the same letter makes it clear that he had little other motive impelling him to write, for the task was one which did not inspire him. He writes:

[1] i.e. in the thirteenth century of the Muslim era.
[2] This describes the final form. Cf. below.

'Well, my friend, I've completed the account of the Emperor Babur [died 1530] ... the first six months—July to December, 1850—are up. Let me see when I get my first six months' pay. If after I receive it my salary is henceforth made payable monthly then, of course, I'll go on writing. Otherwise I'll bid this job goodbye. I haven't yet sent this account of Babur to His Majesty. I finished the manuscript yesterday, and it is being written out in fair. When the fair copy is ready I shall present it, and at the same time apply to have my salary paid monthly. The six months were nearly up; that is why I concentrated on completing the manuscript. And that is why I have not had time to write to you. God save me, what a life! ... The pen is never out of my hand.'

Ghalib put forward his request for monthly payments in a poem which is included in his collected Urdu verse. It ends with a couplet which he was to use later repeatedly in addressing other patrons:

> May you live on another thousand years
> And every year have fifty thousand days!

If the writing of *Mihr i Nimroz* gave him any pleasure at all, it was simply the pleasure of exercising his command of Persian prose, and this was a pleasure which he wished to share with Haqir, of whose literary judgement he had an exceedingly high opinion. Thus the same letter makes it clear that he had a copy of whatever he wrote specially made to be posted to Haqir: 'Write and tell me where the instalment I sent you ends. Write out the last sentence or the last verse—whichever it is—so that I can get the rest copied out from that point and send it to you.' More than once in subsequent months he stressed—in the words of a letter of August 4, 1851—'Rest assured, until what I write reaches you and you read it, I myself don't feel any pleasure in it.'

In another three months he had reached the end of Humayun's reign—that is, the point at which he had planned to bring the first volume to a close. On March 28, 1851, he writes: 'I've completed the account of ... Humayun; ... now I shall start on Akbar.' But in fact he never managed to get further. On September 6, 1851 he wrote:

'What have I to tell you about the history? I have only got as far as the end of Humayun's reign, and haven't even begun to write about the Emperor Akbar. My friend, this thing is a headache to me, and I can't cope with it. So I've left it as it is. I've found a copyist who writes a beautiful hand and copies accurately, and have given the manuscript to him. ...'

However, his labours even on the first volume were not yet over. He later wrote to Haqir (April 10, 1853): 'Let me explain what happened. When I got as far as Humayun, by way of excuse—though what I said was no more than the truth—I told the Hakim Sahib [Ahsanullah Khan] that I could not manage the selection of the materials. I asked him to make the selection of relevant materials from the historical texts, get a draft written out in Urdu, and send it to me. I would put it into Persian and deliver it to him. He agreed to this, and sent me a draft beginning with the creation of the universe and of Adam. Now I had, in effect, to write a new book. [Ghalib had started his history with Timur (Tamerlane) the ancestor of the Mughal kings.] I prefaced it with a short introduction, and began to write in a quite distinctive style. The draft he had sent me covered the period from Adam to Chingiz Khan ['Jengis Khan']. I wrote after my own fashion and handed over my manuscript to him. From the month of Ramzan up to the present day—that is, for the last ten months—the drafts have stopped coming. What I have written must amount to sixty-four pages. Two or three times I have pressed for more drafts, but I have always had the same answer—"It's Ramzan"; then "People are busy with the Id celebrations"; and so on. I thought, "What does it matter to me? Why should I ask to be given hard labour?"—and I stopped asking them. Hakim Sahib [Ahsanullah Khan] must have got the sixty-four pages I have written, but I'm not going to ask for them back. Why should I? Let them be, and good riddance to them. What have *I* to do when not even the foundation has been laid?'

He had already had occasion some months earlier to avow quite bluntly his lack both of interest and of competence in history. A Brahmin friend of Haqir had apparently approached him to consult Ghalib on some point relating to the history of a particular locality in which he was interested. On November 19, 1851, he had replied:

'I am so much a stranger to history and geometry and arithmetic that I don't even understand them. Employees of the royal offices write out in Urdu the material I need for the book and send it to me. I put it into Persian and hand it in. I don't possess a single book; my only acquisition is that I can write verse and prose according to my lights. I am no historian:

> I have not read the stories of Sikandar and Dara
> The tales of love and loyalty are all my stock in trade.'

(The verse is a much-quoted Persian couplet. Sikandar and Dara are the Persian names of Alexander the Great and Darius respectively.)

It is characteristic of Ghalib that even so he had taken pains to do what he could to help his questioner. He explains at some length why the question does not fall within the scope of the kind of history he is writing, and how little help is to be expected from the inadequate stock of books in the royal libraries. Then, after explaining his own incompetence in the words already quoted, he continues:

'I have a brother [actually a relative by marriage] Nawwab Ziya ud Din Ahmad

Khan, son of the late Nawwab Ahmad Bakhsh Khan. He is my shagird in prose and verse. Now he has developed a taste for history, and has acquired an unparalleled knowledge and mastery of the subject. I asked him to investigate the point, so that I could send you something in reply, but he told me that nothing would be found in any book except *Ain i Akbari*—and he has read every book on the subject and carries its gist in his head. So that is how I am placed; this is what he, in whom I have full confidence, tells me; and that is the state of affairs in the royal libraries. Express to him my humble service, and my regret.'

Mihr i Nimroz was ultimately printed and published in 1854, on the initiative of the heir-apparent, who in the same year made Ghalib his ustad. Ghalib wrote to Haqir on September 15, 1854:

'This time I didn't write a paneygyric ode at Id, but finished and presented a volume of the history. . . . In short, *Mihr i Nimroz* has been completed and presented to His Majesty. Now, if I live long enough, I shall write *Mah i Nimmah*. I have been presented with the King's letter of pleasure—that is, with a document expressing the royal praise and pleasure. I try to look upon it as the equivalent of a robe of honour and an estate. . . . Well, I must be thankful for my connection with the King. I cannot boast of anyone who appreciates my worth. As the *dom* said, "When a man understands me, he is my slave; and when he doesn't I am *his* slave." [The *doms* are a Hindu caste of male singers and dancers, hired by wealthy men on occasions for celebration. The *dom* whom Ghalib quotes means that he can command his own price from the man who really appreciates his art; otherwise he is helpless, and must be content with what he can get.]

> Life lies upon you like a yoke upon your neck, Bedil,
> And, willy-nilly, you must live it; what else can you do?'

In the event it seems probable that *Mah i Nimmah* was never written, or, if written, was never published.

This letter makes it clear that by presenting *Mihr i Nimroz* to the King he escaped the chore of writing an ode in his praise. Repeated references in his letters to Haqir show that the writing of such poems at Id and on other occasions for rejoicing—which would be expected of him as a poet in the King's service—became ever more distasteful to him. The following year (June 23, 1855) he wrote to Haqir: 'This Id I didn't even contemplate writing an ode; in fact not even a qata or rubai. I composed two or three couplets on the spot and recited them and I didn't even keep a copy of them.' And three months later, on September 24, 1855, he wrote again:

'I've left off writing odes; and why do I say "left off"? The fact is that I *can't* write them. I've been writing a qata or a rubai for the two Ids [Id ul Fitr, which follows the Ramzan fast, and Baqar Id, which falls forty days later] and presenting them. On this occasion Hakim Sahib [Ahsanullah Khan] insisted strongly, saying that these were no Id offerings at all—no better than the couple of couplets which schoolboys write to give to their teacher as an Id offering. There was nothing else for it but to write these forty or so couplets in masnavi style and present them.'

These remarks come in the course of a letter replying to an enquiry from Haqir. It seems that Haqir had heard of this masnavi and had written to complain that, contrary to his usual custom, Ghalib had not sent him a copy. Ghalib replied:

'My lord and master, do you *understand* what you are writing about, or do you just come forward to complain? . . . You may put me on oath, and I will swear to it that I never entered these verses in my diwan. It's nothing; so why should I send it to you? I am sorry that you have no inkling of my plight. If you could see me you would know that

> I no more have the heart on which
> I used to pride myself.

I do not draw breath without thinking of the last breath that I shall ever draw. I am already sixty years old.[1] How much longer have I to live? I have written ten to twelve thousand couplets in Persian and Urdu—ghazals, odes, qatas and rubais. How much longer can I go on writing? Through bad times and good, I have passed my days the best way I could. And now the thought of death occupies me; what will death be like? And what shall I have to face after death?

> I lived my life waiting for death
>   to come,
> And, dead, I still must see what
>   else I face.

If I didn't send you these verses it was only because I was depressed. Had I included them in my diwan I could not have failed to send them. But when I didn't include them, what point was there in sending them to you?'

In his next letter, of October 3, 1855, he adds the comment, 'I only wrote the Id masnavi to save money; because if I hadn't presented that I would have had to make an offering of three or four rupees.'

Where poetry was concerned his relations with the King had from the start been of a somewhat ambiguous kind. A delicate situation which arose in December 1851 well illustrates the sort of problems which they posed. In that

---

[1] In fact, he was not quite 58.

month Ghalib wrote a prothalamion on the occasion of the forthcoming
marriage of the King's youngest son, Mirza Jawan Bakht. Azad relates the
story in detail; but Azad was the loyal shagird of Ghalib's rival Zauq, and,
consciously or unconsciously, he suppresses things which it is important to
know if we are to see the incident in its true perspective. Fortunately we
possess Ghalib's own (albeit less circumstantial) account of the early stages,
and this throws additional light on the affair. Azad says:

'Nawwab Zinat Mahal [one of the King's wives] was a great favourite with the
King, and although her son Jawan Bakht was younger than many of his other
children, the King was trying to get him recognized as his heir. On the occasion
of this marriage, the most elaborate preparations were made, and Ghalib composed this prothalamion and laid it before His Majesty. [Azad then gives the
full text of the poem, but the only significant lines are the last, in which he
makes the poetic boast:

> As one who knows the worth of poetry—and not as
> Ghalib's partisan—I say
> If you would write a prothalamion, read this of
> his and try to know the way].

When this last couplet was read out to him it occurred to His Majesty that it
implied a hit at him, as though to say,

"No one else can write a prothalamion like this, and since you have made
Shaikh Ibrahim Zauq your ustad and Poet Laureate, this shows that you do
not 'know the worth of poetry' and are merely Zauq's 'partisan'." Accordingly, that same day, when Zauq presented himself as usual, the King handed
him the prothalamion and asked him to read it. Zauq did so and the King then
said, "Ustad, you too compose a prothalamion". "Very good, Sire," replied
Zauq. "Write it now," said the King, "and consider well the last verse." Zauq
sat down there and then, and wrote this prothalamion. [The full text follows;
the last verse is:

> Take this to those who claim that they are poets;
> Stand and recite it to them, and then say:
> This is a poet's prothalamion:
> If you would write one too, this is the way.]'

In Ghalib's account there are significant differences. First, it appears from it
that the prothalamion was a command performance, written at the King's
virtual order or, more precisely, at the order of the Queen, conveyed through
the King, and that even the final rhyme (which Ghalib did not approve) was
laid down for him. In the elaborate prose style which he usually prescribed for
himself when he wrote in Persian, he wrote (in a letter to Shafaq):

'I have long ceased to tune the lute of Urdu verse. True, to gain the good will of that Sovereign before whom Solomon is a simple scribe, I from time to time untimely pour out the strains of Urdu song. And especially at the command of that Queen before whom Bilqis bends in worship, I bent my mind to the writing of rekhta[1] in this unreasonable rhyme. Perchance I may in the concluding couplet have cried the drunken cry of poetic drunkenness. One [Zauq] whom the fancy possesses that he possesses a perfection he does not possess, presumed that it was he of whom I spoke. In the concluding couplet of a poem he struck a note accordingly and stood in the stance of combat, and thought that thus my challenge had been checked. But I, drunk still with the lees left in the glass in which my pen had once distilled the wine of

The verse on which you pride yourself is verse I should feel shame to own—[2]

did not deign to turn towards him, deeming sheer disdain sheer proof of my distinction.'

There follows the passage already quoted in chapter one,[3] in which he laments the fate that barred the paths to martial prowess and to learning and to the wandering life of a darwesh and made him a poet; and he goes on:

'And either in this age there is none with eyes to see, or else there are such, but they will not glance my way. And surely that is why, in the deep darkness of my days, none knows and none acknowledges the wonder of my work. And now in these last days when my teeth are gone and my ears are slow to hear and my hair is white and the wrinkles line my face and my hands tremble and my foot is in the stirrup,[4] what is left of the tumults that once raged in my heart? I break my daily bread and taste the tortures of approaching death—and that is all. What shall I reap tomorrow of all I have sown today?'

It seems clear that when Ghalib wrote this letter he did not yet know that Zauq's rejoinder to his original poem had been written at the King's instance and that it was the King's displeasure as much as Zauq's that it expressed. However, he soon realized the true position, for, to continue in the words of Azad's narrative,

'Zauq's poem was at once given to the singers who attended on the King and by evening it was being sung in every by-lane of the capital. The very next day it appeared in the newspapers. Ghalib was not slow in understanding these things. He presented the following poem to the King:

An Apology

I write these lines to lay the facts before you
And not to boast my sterling quality.

[1] An old term for Urdu.　　　[2] Cf. p. 82 below.　　　[3] Cf. p. 28 above.
[4] i.e. ready to make my last journey—that is, to die.

For centuries my ancestors were soldiers
My standing does not rest on poetry.

Broad-minded, I would live at peace with all men
Friendly with all, with none at enmity.

That I am Zafar's slave is ample honour—
Though without wealth or rank or dignity.

Could I presume to cross the royal tutor?
I could not think of such temerity!

The King's all-seeing eye knows truth from falsehood:
I need no oath to pledge my honesty.

I make no claims to be an Urdu poet:
My object was to please Your Majesty.

I wrote the poem at the royal order—
To tell the truth, out of necessity.

Nothing that I expressed in the last couplet
Intended any breach of amity.

I taunted none—or let my face be blackened!
I am not prone to such insanity!

My fortunes may be ill: not so my nature;
Thank God, I pass my days contentedly

God is my witness, Ghalib is no liar;
I set great store by my integrity.'

The poem seems to have satisfied the King and allayed his displeasure, but it is in fact far from being a mere apology. As in so much of Urdu poetry, there are other meanings besides the surface one, and many of them are not complimentary either to the King or to his ustad. They emerge already in the second couplet where he says, in effect, 'I am a noble, whose ancestors have for generations followed the noble profession of arms; and as such I would have my place in society even if I had never written poetry',—and he *implies* that this is a claim that Zauq certainly cannot make. It was common knowledge that Zauq was a man of humble birth, and only his poetry had won him social status. The seventh and eighth couplets imply that a really great poet says what he has to say in Persian, *the* language of Muslim culture, and that which all the really great Mughal emperors had patronized; if their latter-day successors choose instead to patronise Urdu, so that in order to please them a poet must write in this inferior medium, that, of course, is another matter. These

two reactions—to vaunt his ancestry, and to exalt Persian at the expense of
Urdu—are, as we have seen, typical of Ghalib when he is under attack, and
they do not command much sympathy from a modern reader. But the tone of
the poem as a whole is admirable; his assertions of his own position in the
third, eleventh, and twelfth couplets are sincere and dignified, while the implied
irony of the fourth and fifth hit hard at the King and his tutor in a way which
delights us because we feel that they are getting what they deserve. In particular
the piling up of the words 'wealth' and 'rank' and 'dignity' reminds us forcibly
that it was in the King's power to bestow all these things, and that he had chosen
to bestow them on much lesser men than Ghalib. Finally, the last couplet, with
its emphatic assertion that he is a man of his word, ostensibly rounds off the
poem; but it inevitably suggests comparison with the last couplet of the
original prothalamion and could well be interpreted as a re-assertion that what
he had written there was no more than the plain truth. It is difficult to think
that the King did not see these possible implications, but there was nothing the
poem overtly said to which he could take exception—indeed, it is precisely in
the lines that hit hardest that the surface meaning is unexceptionably meek—
and he would be forced to accept it at its face value.

Ghalib's high-brow claim that Urdu was not really a fit medium for poetry
reflects a feeling which possessed him more strongly at some times than at
others. One result of his ties with the King in these last years before the revolt
of 1857 was an increase in his output of Urdu verse. Hali comments:

'It is important to emphasise here that Ghalib did not regard Urdu poetry as
his field. For him it was a diversion; he would write an occasional ghazal
sometimes because he himself felt like it, sometimes at the request of his friends,
and sometimes in fulfilment of the commands of the King or the heir-apparent.
That is why in his Urdu diwan there is no significant number of poems in any
form other than the ghazal. In a letter to Munshi Nabi Bakhsh [Haqir] . . . he
writes, "My friend, you praise my ghazal, and I am ashamed of it. These are
not ghazals, but things I write to earn my bread. The Persian odes that I pride
myself upon, nobody enjoys. My sole hope of appreciation now arises when
His Majesty the Shadow of God takes it into his head to issue his command,
saying, 'My friend, it is some time since you brought me a present'—i.e. a
new Urdu poem. So willy-nilly occasion arises when I compose a ghazal and
bring it to court." ' . . . He did not look upon the ability to write Urdu poetry
as an accomplishment; in fact he thought it beneath him. Thus he writes in
lines generally said to have been addressed to Zauq:[1]

> Look at my Persian; there you see the full range of
> my artistry

---

[1] Ghalib's own words quoted on p. 80 above leave little or no doubt that what was 'generally
said' of these lines was quite correct.

> And leave aside my Urdu verse, for there is nothing
> there of me.
> I tell you truth, for I am one must tell the truth
> when all is done,
> The verse on which you pride yourself is verse I
> should feel shame to own.

Yet since most of his contemporaries were men of cultivated taste and quick to discern poetic merit, in his Urdu poetry too he was concerned to maintain the same pre-eminence as in Persian, and he gave all his attention and all his efforts to writing it.'

Hali's estimate is on the whole a sound one. There were indeed some verses which were written simply as a necessary chore, as the letters already quoted make clear. But other letters to Haqir show that during these same years he produced Urdu verse of which he felt proud, even where it was at the King's instance that he wrote. Where he was pleased with the results he praised them with an engaging lack of reserve, and demanded that Haqir praise them equally highly; and, indeed, some of his very best ghazals are the product of these years. Early in 1851—probably between April and June—he writes:

'You should know that when I attend upon the King he usually asks me to bring him Urdu verse. Well, I wouldn't recite any of my old ghazals. I compose a new one and bring that. To-day at midday I wrote a ghazal which I shall take and recite to him tomorrow or the day after. I'm writing it out, and send it to you too. Judge it truly: if Urdu verse can rise to the height where it can cast a spell or work a miracle, will this, or will this not, be its form?'

He then appends not one ghazal, but two. The second is still one of his best-loved.

In May or June 1852, he writes, enclosing another, now famous, ghazal: 'My friend, in God's name, give my ghazal its due of praise. If this is Urdu poetry, what was that Mir and Mirza wrote? And if that was Urdu poetry, then what is this?' In other words, My verse is in another class from that of Mir and Mirza (the colloquial names for Mir and Sauda, the two greatest Urdu poets of the eighteenth century)—so much so that you cannot call their work and mine by the same name. He goes on: 'This is how I came to write it. A gentleman—one of the Mughal princes—brought this zamin with him from Lucknow [zamin is a technical term in Urdu poetics: it is a prescription for a ghazal in which metre, rhyme and end-rhyme are all laid down]. His Majesty himself composed a ghazal on it, and commanded me to write one too; and I fulfilled his command.'

From a letter of somewhere between April 10 and 23, 1853, it appears that that the King could, on occasion, issue such commands fairly frequently. Ghalib writes: 'The King has given instructions for a mushaira to be held at the Fort. It is held twice a month, on the 15th and the 29th. His Majesty prescribes one *zamin* for Persian and one for Urdu'. He then states what these were for 'the last mushaira, held on the 30th Jamadi us Sani' and continues: 'I wrote one ghazal in Persian and one in Urdu on the prescribed pattern, and another in Urdu on the same pattern, but incorporating something different. I'm writing out all three for you. Read them, and show them to friend Tufta too.' Once again, one of the three ghazals is one of his very best.

The following year the King's old ustad Zauq died and Ghalib was appointed in his place—an appointment that was probably reluctantly made and reluctantly accepted. In the forties and early fifties Zauq, Momin, and Ghalib were the only poets of outstanding reputation in Delhi, and Momin had died in 1852, two years before Zauq. Thus the King could hardly avoid choosing Ghalib as Zauq's successor. He did so knowing perfectly well the poor opinion of Zauq as a poet which Ghalib held. Hali writes of how Ghalib felt about his new duties:

'In 1271 AH [AD 1854] when Shaikh Ibrahim Zauq died, the duty of correcting the King's verses fell to Ghalib, but it seems that he discharged this duty with an unwilling heart. The late Nāzir[1] Husain Mirza used to relate how he and Ghalib were sitting in the Hall of General Audience one day when a footman came to tell Ghalib that His Majesty was asking for his ghazals. Ghalib told him to wait, and turning to his own servant said, "In the palanquin you'll find some papers wrapped in a cloth, Bring them here." The servant brought them at once, and Ghalib opened the package, and took out eight or nine sheets of paper, each with one or two half-verses written on it. He called for pen and ink and started to write ghazals, each beginning with one of these half-lines. He completed eight or nine as he sat there, and handed them over to the footman. According to Nāzir Husain Mirza, it took him no longer to write all these ghazals than it takes a practised ustad to read through a few ghazals and make occasional corrections. When the footman had gone off with them, he turned to Nāzir Husain Mirza and said, "Now I am free; for the first time for ages all His Majesty's occasional commands have been fulfilled."[2] Whatever Ghalib wrote in his own style—whether in verse or in prose—cost him a great deal of effort and concentration, as he himself tells us more than once in his writings. But whenever he did not need to write in his own style, he could compose with very little effort.'

The fact that the kind of poetry which both Zauq and his royal pupil admired could be churned out without effort in this way constituted the whole basis of Ghalib's poor opinion of it, and it was this fundamental difference in their view

---

[1] Nāzir is a title, and indicates that he was Steward to the Royal Household. For a fuller account of him cf. pp. 206–8.

[2] The clear implication is that some of Zafar's poems were not in fact his own work but that of his ustad. A similar tradition is current about Zauq.

of poetry which was, in great measure, responsible for the uneasiness of their relationship, an uneasiness evidenced, among other things, by the fact that Ghalib never received the title of Malik ush Shuara ('King of Poets'—i.e. Poet Laureate) which he might legitimately have expected, and that the new appointment was not accompanied by any increase in his stipend. Much of Zauq's and Zafar's verse is polished, but much of it lacks depth, and Ghalib was strict in these matters. He could neither admire nor pretend to admire verses which he thought mediocre. Hali writes:

'In our society it is the general rule that when a man recites his verse, every line—good or bad—is greeted with cries of approval, and no one distinguishes between a good line and a bad one. Ghalib's way was quite the opposite of this. No matter how revered and respected a poet might be, until he heard a line that he really liked he never on any account expressed appreciation. Towards the end of his life he became completely deaf, but this was not the case in earlier years. One had to raise one's voice in speaking or reciting to him, but if this was done he could hear perfectly well. Yet until he heard a verse that really appealed to him he would remain quite unmoved. Some of his contemporaries were offended by this attitude, and that is why they found fault with Ghalib's poetry; but although Ghalib was by temperament one who did not like to quarrel with anybody, he never deviated from his practice in this respect.'

Hali goes on to make it clear that there was no motive of jealousy behind this:

'Yet to any verse that did move him, he gave praise that was almost extravagant—not because he wanted to please anyone, but because his own love of poetry compelled him to praise it. His rivalry with Zauq is well-known. Yet one day when Ghalib was absorbed in a game of chess, the late Munshi Ghulam Ali Khan recited this verse of Zauq to someone else who was present:

> Tired of all this, we look to death for our release
> But what if even after death we find no peace?

He used to say: "The moment Ghalib caught some snatch of this he at once left his game and asked me, 'What was that verse you recited?' I recited it again. 'Whose verse is it?' he said. I told him it was Zauq's. He was astonished, and made me recite it again and again, savouring it every time I did so." You may see in his Urdu letters that he speaks of this verse repeatedly, and wherever he quotes examples of good verses, this one is always included. In the same way, when he heard this verse of Momin's:

> I seem to feel that you are by my side
> When all are gone and I am quite alone

he praised it highly and said, "I wish Momin Khan would take my whole
diwan and give me this one verse in exchange." This verse too he has quoted
in many of his letters. . . .'

Hali's evaluation of Ghalib's stand in these matters is borne out by other evidence. His judgement of a verse was not influenced one way or another by his
opinion of the man who wrote it, whether as a man or as a poet. For Zauq he
seems to have had no great liking in either capacity. On his death he writes
respectfully enough of him to Haqir: 'The latest news here is that friend Zauq
is dead. . . . The truth is that the man was unique in his own way and in this
age a poet to be thankful for.' But a well-attested tradition says that his first
reaction to the news of Zauq's death was to express his satisfaction that 'the
man who spoke in the language of a lodging-house keeper' was no more. It is
noticeable that his opinion of Momin as a poet, expressed also in a letter to
Haqir of May 21, 1852 shortly after Momin's death, had been given in similarly
vague and non-committal words: 'He wrote well in his own way. A man of a
fertile and inventive turn of mind.' But this is preceded by warm praise for
Momin as a man:

'You must have heard that Momin Khan is dead. It is ten days since he died.
Just see, my friend, one after the other our children die; one after the other
people of our own age die; the caravan moves off, and we ourselves are waiting
with one foot in the stirrup. Momin Khan was of the same age as I, and was a
good friend too. We got to know each other forty-two or forty-three years
ago when we were no more than fourteen or fifteen years old, and in all these
years there was never the slightest bad feeling of any kind between us. And,
my good sir, you'd be hard put to it to find even an enemy of forty years'
standing, let alone a friend.'

   Because he knew that much of the poetry that he would hear there was
worthless, it was with mixed feelings that he went to mushairas. Some of his
Persian letters describe his experiences at them. Thus he writes to Majruh:

'The King's command came, bringing joy to those that dwelt near and good
tidings to those who dwelt afar; and the Chamberlain of his Court directed
the poets to the Hall of the Royal Steward, saying that on Friday February 25th
they should come to that auspicious abode and ply one another with the wine-
cups of poetry. A band of the princes of Babur's line and a few of the capital's
men of distinction gathered together, and so great a throng assembled that every
space was filled, and you would have said that body merged with body. First
of all the Prince of Poets, Shaikh Muhammad Ibrahim Zauq plucked the string
and recited a ghazal of the King in a voice so sweet that Venus descended
from the sky to listen. Then that prince who possesses Yusuf's beauty . . .
Mirza Khizar Sultan Bahadur, recited a . . . ghazal in such wise that you would

think that the Pleiades had sprinkled the carpet with their stars. Then the melody of the verses of Mirza Haidar Shikoh and Mirza Nur ud Din and Mirza Āli Bakht Āli rose on high, and then Ghalib . . . who was seated at the side of Mirza Āli, recited his ten couplets. Then a stripling named Mahvi, one of those who drink the wine of Sahbai's tavern [i.e. a shagird of Sahbai's] tuned his intoxicated lay. And Mirza Haji Shuhrat presented to the ears of us seated in the assembly a poem of some seventy couplets. [A ghazal should be a *short* poem.] I, on the pretext of easing a physical need, rose from the gathering and took the road to my abode of sorrow. The doors of the shops stood open and and the lamps were still burning, and clearly the hour of midnight had not yet passed. . . . I sat and took wine. As the next morning drew to a close I made my way to the Auspicious Fort. The four princes whose names the tongue of my pen has already spoken revived the melodies of the night, and I again recited my ghazal. Friends told me that the whole night had passed in these diversions and the assembly had dispersed as the white light of morning began to appear. They say that as the gathering drew to a close the Prince of Poets [Zauq] recited two ghazals of his own. . . .'

Ghalib's ironical tone, the purely conventional praises, and the absence of any reference to the content of the ghazals recited, including his own, speak for themselves.

On other occasions he found himself pleasantly surprised. He writes to Shefta:

'On Friday, as night fell, the poets held their assembly. I had not composed a ghazal, and, ashamed to go empty-handed I sat with head bowed, and the thought of going to the gathering was far from my mind. But . . . Nawwab Ziya ud Din Khan, whom God preserve, sent two angels to stand over me—Zain ul Abidin Khan Arif and Ghulan Husain Khan Mahv. These two insistent, stubborn men came as evening fell to my lonely cell of solitude riding on an elephant; and loading me on it just as a man loads a tiger he has killed in the hunt, they bore me off to the gathering. There the sight of my exalted master. . . . Maulvi Muhammad Sadr ud Din Bahadur [Azurda] made up for all the sorrow I had suffered on the way . . . and I too raised my voice in melody and recited. . . .'

In other letters to Shefta he speaks slightingly of poets who wrote only in Urdu: 'Those who make verse in Urdu were there in plenty to recite their great long ghazals, and it was past midnight when I got back home and lay myself down to sleep.' And, in another letter:

'A man had been sent to ask . . . Azurda to come. He came late, but come he did, bringing radiance to my heart and voice to my tongue. I had written an ode . . . but I was thinking to take the manuscript back with me, like a rejected petition, and not to vex the hearts of the poets of Urdu. But . . . Azurda's coming put me in good heart and gave my tongue leave to sing.'

Even those who knew him well did not always understand his attitude in these matters. As a man whose literary reputation now stood very high, many a would-be poet sought the honour of becoming his shagird, while other writers would approach him to write forewords to their works. His generous nature made it difficult for him to refuse these requests, while on the other hand his integrity as a writer would not allow him to express any greater measure of praise than he sincerely felt. This latter trait put his forewords into a class on their own. The standard foreword of his day was an elaborate piece of ornate Persian prose full of exaggerated praise for the book and its author. Hali remarks:

'Obviously only a very few books really deserve high praise. Ghalib would not refuse the requests made of him, but he wrote his foreword in a fashion which would please the author without doing violence to the truth. He would begin with describing the author's good qualities, or his character, or the sincerity of his love and affection; or else he would write of other interesting . . . topics which had some relevance to the book; and these things would occupy the greater part of the foreward. Then he would add a few pertinent sentences about the work in question which contained points of substance, and at the same time would be enough to satisfy the author. But . . . it did sometimes happen that people complained to him that he had been rather niggardly in his praise.'

This happened in the case of Ghalib's friend Hargopal Tufta. Tufta was a devotee of Persian poetry, and had himself been writing it for a number of years, with Ghalib as his ustad. By 1848 he had a volume ready for publication, and Ghalib wrote an introduction to it at his request. A letter from Ghalib to Haqir on May 25, 1855 recalls what Tufta's reaction had been:

'On one occasion I wrote an introduction to please him, and the reward I got was that he got cross with me and wrote to me saying that what I had written "ridiculed him with seeming praise". I wrote back, "My friend, you are not my rival, not my enemy. You are my friend, and you call yourself my shagird. Curses upon that friend who would ridicule his friend with seeming praise, and a thousand curses upon that ustad who feels a rivalry with his shagird and so ridicules him." That shamed him somewhat, and he calmed down.'

Ghalib was quite capable of writing to Tufta in these terms, but if he did, the letter has not survived. We do have another letter, written with more restraint in May 1848:

'I received your letter, and though it did not please me, at any rate it did not displease me either. Anyway, you may continue to think of me—unworthy and despised of men though I am—as your well-wisher. What can I do? I cannot change my ways. I cannot write the way the Indian writers of Persian do, and start talking all sorts of nonsense like a hired panegyrist. Look at my odes and you will see how long the preamble is and how relatively short the panegyric proper. My prose is the same. Look at my foreword to Nawwab Mustafa Khan's [i.e. Shefta's] tazkira to see how much praise you find in it. Look at my introduction to Mirza Rahim ud Din Bahadur Haya's diwan. Take the foreword I wrote, at Mr John Jacob's request, to the Diwan of Hāfiz—you will see that apart from one couplet of verse in which I have mentioned his name and praised him, all the rest is taken up with quite different themes. I swear by God that if I had been writing a foreword to the diwan of some prince or nobleman I would not have praised him so highly as I have praised you. If you knew me and my ways you would have counted what I wrote as ample praise. Anyway, in short, I have taken out the sentence I wrote about you and written another in its place, just to please you. It is clear to me that you don't think these things out for yourself, but allow yourself to be misguided by other gentlemen, most of whom, I expect, will regard my verse and prose as worthless. And why? Because their ears are not accustomed to its sound. Well, you can't expect people who rank Qatīl as a good writer to appreciate the real worth of prose and poetry.'

A few years later Tufta had a second volume of verse ready, and asked Ghalib for another foreword. He replied:

'It's easier for you to write a diwan than it is for me to write the introduction or foreword. . . . If you're as keen as all that, go on writing verse, but wait a while and see. Otherwise you will have this second diwan printed now and start worrying about producing a third. It'll only take you another three or four years, but how am I to go on writing forewords? Wait till this diwan is as long as the first. Try your hand for a while at the ode and the rubai, and whatever you get together in this way over the next three or four years can be added to your second diwan.'

The letter to Haqir just quoted shows that this reply again incurred Tufta's displeasure:

'He's cross with me. He commanded me to write an introduction. I replied, "Sir, you will write a diwan every year. How long am I to go on writing introductions?" Since then he hasn't written to me. I won't write to him either; I'll wait and see when he favours me with another letter. My friend, is it an easy matter to write an introduction? It's a heart-breaking task. To write prose is just as hard as to write verse. How can I do it in this heat? What can I write? . . .

By your life I swear to you, it's not that I grudge him the introduction; it's simply that I no longer have the energy. God knows how I survive. Id, Baqar Id, Nauroz—it's all of two to three years since I stopped writing odes for these occasions. I write simply to let you know that my refusal is justified and his anger out of place. I wanted you to know. . . .'

Haqir must have gone and reasoned with Tufta—or perhaps Tufta was not as cross with him as Ghalib thought. Anyway in his next letter to Haqir he writes:

'Well, my friend! This is a diverting state of affairs! You urge me not to upset Tufta, when I was all along afraid that he'd stopped writing to me because he was upset with me. In the end I wrote to you about it. You found an appropriate way to let him know, and then he wrote to me. And so two days ago I replied to his letter. Thanks to your kindness my fears have been allayed, and my mind is at ease. Now what is there left, that you commend him to me? By God, I look upon Tufta as a son, and I feel proud that God has given me a son so talented. As for the introduction, you do not realize the plight I am in. . . . I am sure that you and he will both accept my apology and excuse me. God has excused me prayers and fasting: cannot you and Tufta excuse me the introduction?'

Tufta, so far as we know, was then content to accept the situation.

In at least one famous case Ghalib was to find that in attempting to please an author and to express his own views at the same time, he had bitten off more than he could chew. In the early 1850s he was approached by Sayyid Ahmad Khan, later to become Sir Sayyid Ahmad Khan, and the outstanding leader of the Indian Muslim community in the last three decades of the century. Sayyid Ahmad Khan had just completed the task of editing *Ain i Akbari*, the work in which Abul Fazl, the minister of Akbar, the greatest of the Mughal emperors (1556-1605), describes in detail Akbar's system of administration. Hali writes:

'Prominent men in Delhi had written prose introductions to the work, and Ghalib wrote one in verse. . . . He was very attached to Sir Sayyid, and was on intimate terms with him and his family. But he was not an admirer of Abul Fazl's style; he thought the system of administration which *Ain i Akbari* describes beneath all comparison with those of modern times; and, as he himself admitted, he felt no interest in history. Hence he regarded the editing of *Ain i Akbari* as a pointless task . . . and could not restrain himself from saying so in his introduction.'

Not surprisingly, Sayyid Ahmad Khan did not include Ghalib's introduction along with the others when the book was published, 'for the introduction found fault with *Ain i Akbari*, and far from praising the excellent work which

Sir Sayyid had done, expressed the view that it was valueless.' In consequence relations between the two men remained strained for a number of years.

The same considerations which influenced him in his writing his introductions governed also his conduct as an ustad. He readily accepted requests from poets to correct their verse, and despite the volume of work this involved, he gave it his most careful attention. His attitude was the same towards those who aspired to write Persian prose. One of these was Haqir's son Abdul Latif. When Haqir wrote saying that Abdul Latif wanted to submit his Persian prose to Ghalib but felt diffident about asking if he might, Ghalib replied on April 23, 1853:

'Abdul Latif is my life, my soul, my son. Who are you to come forward to plead his case and negotiate for him? Who ever forbade him to send me his work? And who forbids him now? Verse, prose, anything he likes he can send to me. He must not press me to return it. I'll look at it in my own good time and then return it to you. This shyness he feels will be the death of me. When Abdus Salam [Abdul Latif's child] was born I wrote to congratulate him; his honour the Munshi Sahib, that is, our young friend Abdul Latif, did not reply; in the end you wrote to say, "My friend, he's shy. He doesn't know what to write to you in reply." And now there's this matter of his sending his prose for me to correct. Is this too something that his honour feels shy about? God save us!'

And when even after this Abdul Latif still hung back, it was Ghalib who on his own initiative sent him, through Haqir, repeated reminders. Thus he writes two months later, on June 22, 1853:

'Munshi Abdul Latif Sahib has made up his mind and then stopped short. Why doesn't he send his prose? Is it that he sees my letters in Urdu and imagines that I've forgotten how to write Persian prose? Give him my blessing, and tell him that I'm eager to see what he's written.'

Months later, on March 27, 1854, he is still telling him the same thing.

From a letter of October 18, 1855 it seems that he was even prepared to correct the verses of poets whom he did not even know, for he writes to his friend Shafaq, who, it seems, had proposed to forward such verses to him, 'I shall be waiting now for the other gentlemen's ghazals to arrive. Would you please be kind enough to write, along with the takhallus of each of them, his name and a few particulars about him?' Tufta, whose output was prolific, apologized on one occasion for sending him so many verses to correct. Ghalib replied on June 18, 1852:

'Listen, my good sir. You know that the late Zainul Abidin Khan was my son,[1]

---

[1] Actually, his wife's nephew. For Ghalib's relationship with him, and his adoption of his two sons after his death, see pp. 104 below.

and that now both his children, my grandsons, have come to live with me, and that they plague me every minute of the day, and I put up with it. God is my witness that you are a son to me. Hence the products of your inspiration are my spiritual grandsons. When I do not lose patience with these, my physical grandsons, who do not let me have my dinner in peace, who walk with their bare feet all over my bed, upset water here, and raise clouds of dust there—how can my spiritual grandsons, who do none of these things, upset me? Post them off at once for me to look at I promise you I'll post them back to you at once. May God Almighty grant long life to your children—the children of this external world—and give them wealth and prosperity, and may He preserve you to look after them. And on your spiritual children, the products of your inspiration, may He bestow increase of fame and the gift of men's approval. . . .'

At the same time he expected those who accepted him as their ustad to be ready to take his forthright criticism. He writes in an undated letter to Tufta (about mid-1853), quoting a Persian half-line which he had submitted for Ghalib's comment. The line, literally translated, means: 'Whether the rose, or the lily, or the dog-rose, or the eglantine, do not make.' Ghalib comments,

'The "do not make" should complete the meaning. It is not superfluous; the trouble is that whether you leave the half-line in Persian or translate it into Urdu, it has no sense or meaning . . . "Do not make"—"Do not on any account make". Do not make what? Only when you yourself reply, "Do not make mention, sir" will anyone *know* what; otherwise no one could ever discover that you mean "Do not make mention". And what's more, even if you tell me, "I mean 'do not make mention',," then how does your honour establish a connection between the "mention" and the "rose" and "lily" and "dog-rose" and "eglantine"? You'll reply, "I have, not 'mention', it's true, but 'speech' in the preceding half-line". But you can drag your "speech" with ropes and chains, and it still won't connect with these four words. Do what you like . . . but you won't get your line to make sense. It's absolutely meaning-less.'

A few months later (January 13, 1854) he begins another letter:

'Your word "*did-mast*" is a new invention. *I* understand what you mean, but you may depend on it, no one else will. This is what they mean when they say "The meaning is in the mind of the speaker". . . . In all these verses there is nothing wrong—and nothing of interest.'

In Urdu and Persian poetics immense importance was attached to precedent. An apprentice-poet whose ustad criticized some expression in his verse would, if he could, justify himself by producing a precedent from the verse of a classical poet. Ghalib's attitude in these matters is characteristic of him. He had objected to Tufta's use of a double plural, and Tufta, in reply, had produced a precedent from the poet Saib. Ghalib wrote again, quoting a well-known Persian verse:

'To find fault with our elders is a fault'

and continuing: 'My dear friend, in such instances we should not find fault with the verse of the classical writers; but we should not follow them either. Your humble servant will not tolerate a double plural; nor will he say anything against the great Saib.' Elsewhere he writes:

'*Be-pir* is a word coined by Indians of Turkish descent. When I forbid my pupils to use it even in Urdu verse, how can I permit you to do so in Persian? Mirza Jalal Asir (peace be upon him) is a free agent, and the usage of his verse is authoritative. Who am I to say that a word which he has used is wrong? But I am surprised, *very* surprised, that a Persian of noble family should have used such a word. *Be-pir* is not authentic Persian, even though Asir is as much a master of his language as Zahuri.'

And on occasion he could be even more emphatic. In a letter of mid-1853 he writes:

'In this couplet [which he has just quoted] Hazin [a classical Persian poet] has written one "hanoz" too many; it is superfluous and absurd, and you cannot regard it as a precedent to be followed. It is a plain blunder, a fault, a flaw. Why should we imitate it? Hazin was only human, but if the couplet were the angel Gabriel's you are not to regard it as an authority, and are not to imitate it.'

One of the tasks of the angel Gabriel, in Muslim belief, has been to convey the words of God to the prophets sent to mankind; he is therefore associated with divine eloquence.

Ghalib encouraged the same independence of judgement in his friends and shagirds. Thus he wrote in a Persian letter to Hisam ud Din Haidar Khan:

'The rhythmic speech which men call poetry finds a different place in each man's heart and presents a different aspect to each man's eyes. Men who make poetry all pluck the strings with a different touch and from each instrument bring forth a different melody. Pay no heed to what others see and feel, and bend all your efforts to increase your own perception.'

At the same time he had definite views as to which poets and writers repaid attentive study—and he included himself in their number. In a Persian letter to Nawwab Ali Bahadur he writes of how the secrets of poetry are to be learned:

'If you seek to find these secrets and desire to know the frets of this lute then keep before your eyes, of the Urdu poets, the verse of Mir and Mirza [Mir and Sauda] and, of the legion of the poets of Persian, the poetry of Saib, Urfi, Naziri and Hazin. Keep them before your eyes—but not in such wise that the black lines on the page do not travel from your eyes to your heart. Bend all your efforts to this end, that you may come to know the essence of each word, and that the range of meanings may come beneath your gaze, and that you may know true coin from counterfeit.

'If *Panj Ahang* had not been my own work I would have said that the wise approve it as a model of Persian writing. In it there are deep and subtle points expressed, and in its pages is abundance of beautiful phrases and sweet and fair words.

'I speak the truth in hope that men will credit it. . . . For the writing of Urdu verse I have long felt no inclination. I write in Persian, but since it is the pleasure of His Majesty the Shadow of God that I should from time to time bring verse of this kind as a gift into his exalted presence, I perforce write now and then in Urdu too. Thus I enclose in this letter of humble submission a few recent ghazals . . . which I have copied out. Be pleased to study them, and set your heart on winning for your pen this style of writing, and for your song this kind of melody.'

Nothing delighted him more than meeting a man whose love of poetry and discriminating judgement matched his own. This was above all the basis of his warm feelings for Haqir, as one can see from the remarkable Persian letter which he wrote to Tufta after they first met:

'In these days when night descends on the darkling day of my life—and how dark must be the night of him whose day has been so dark!—I sat in the darkness of sorrow and solitude, at war within myself. My tortured heart that burns with grief to look upon my solitude, is the one poor lamp that lights the black abode in which I dwell. But God's compassion sent a man to me who brought balm for my bruises and the comfort of his comradeship to quell my pain, and set a thousand stars to shine in the dark night of my soul. Truly his eloquence has lighted a candle, a candle by whose shining light I see shine out the lustre of the pearls of poetry my lips have spoken, when in the thronging darkness of misfortune's night their lustre had lain hidden from my eyes. O Tufta, you whose verse roves in new realms, singing new melodies, this wise man without peer, Munshi Nabi Bakhsh [Haqir] is a gleaming gem of a man in whom great God has made the talent of man manifest and given insight of the soul in high degree. For though I am poet and know poetry, until I met this venerable man I did not understand what understanding is or what it means to be well-versed in verse. The tale is told that when the Great Creator bestowed beauty upon men He made two halves; and one half He bestowed on Yusuf and the other half He sprinkled over all mankind. What wonder if when He gave out the power to value poetry and know its meaning, in this same way He took two portions? One He apportioned to this man of many virtues; the other was the portion of the others. Tell the revolving heavens not to turn for me, and leave my destinies to sleep unheeding; for I have found a friend the joy of whose comradeship frees me from all fear of the age's enmity and this is a wealth which leaves me no complaint against the world.'

We have seen that he had a similar opinion of, among others, Fazl i Haq and Shefta.

Ghalib sometimes had occasion to make it clear to his shagirds that to accept him as their ustad meant, in his view, to accept his corrections, though he did not mind these being questioned before they were finally adopted. There are letters in which he makes these points explicit. Thus in a letter to Tufta dated February 19, 1852, he asks him to give a message to their mutual friend Rind, who, like Tufta, used to send his verses to Ghalib for correction: 'I corrected his verses within a week of receiving them, adding my comments and advice, as I always do. . . . Tell him to read carefully what I have written at the end, and make it his permanent guide. It is not something to be glanced through and then forgotten.' A month later, on March 22, 1852, he insists to Tufta himself that the corrections he makes are not made lightly, and should be accepted—though he puts the matter in the nicest possible way:

'I recall that I had taken your half-line [here he quotes it] and re-fashioned it into this rhymed couplet [here he quotes it]. In this form it appealed to me so much that I was tempted not to let you have it back but to use it as the first verse of a ghazal of my own. But then I felt I must not begrudge it you, and I sent it to you. Your lordship didn't choose to study it. You had been drinking when you wrote to me, and you must have been in the same condition when you went through the corrected verse. Now you are to delete the half-line you have written and let my couplet stand. It's a good one. . . . My friend, when I correct your verses, read the corrections carefully, so that the labour I spend on them is not wasted.'

In mid-1853 he writes:

'Study carefully what I write and see that you understand it. It doesn't annoy me when you raise questions or return to them again; on the contrary, I feel pleased. But I grant you I don't like it when you keep on about "*besh*" and "*beshtar*", because that amounts to a clear reproach to me. When I write an expression myself why should I forbid you to write it?'

We do not know what exactly Tufta's query on this point was. But we do know that he was not to be put off by Ghalib's words. In the very next letter Ghalib complains: 'There you go again! You're determined to wrangle with me over this *"besh"* and *"beshtar"* business.' And in the letter after that: 'There you go! You've again dragged up this *"besh"* and *"beshtar"* business in your letter.' Despite which there is no change in Ghalib's at once forthright and friendly tone.

It is noteworthy that he did not attempt to impose his own style on his shagirds. In a letter to Haqir dated September 3, 1853, he singles out one couplet from a ghazal Haqir had sent him for correction and begins his letter: 'My friend, who wrote this verse? [He then quotes it.] Yes, who else? It could only be one of mine or one of my brother's [i.e. yours]. By God, what a verse! It has a distinctive quality that not everyone is master of.' On October 6, 1853 he speaks of the same ghazal again:

'One of its couplets was in my style, as I wrote to you. And all the rest of the couplets are good, without any fault or unevenness. Had there been room for correction I would not have overlooked it. My relationship with you isn't such that I would flatter you. I look upon your verse as my verse, your skill as my skill, your faults as my faults. Now look at the ghazal. I cancelled one or two couplets, and in the opening couplet and one other, made some verbal changes. The verses that I marked with *swad*[1] are very good, and you're to be congratulated on them. And the ones I have left unmarked are just good.'

He goes on to praise a piece of someone's Persian prose which Haqir had sent him to correct, calling it, characteristically, 'the equal of Zuhuri's *Sih Nasar*, and half the equal of [his own] *Panj Ahang*.' He then details some of its good points and goes on,

'I am obliged and grateful to you, because thanks to your kindness I have had the opportunity to see it. . . . I am one who pays good writing its due, and wishes writers well. Where there is room for correction I do not shirk it. Beyond that, I am not the kind of man who interferes with writing which has no fault or defect in it. Return these pages to their owner and give him my greeting; and show him these lines I have written.'

Elsewhere he states his attitude towards criticism. It seems that some acquaintance of Tufta's had criticized his verse, even after Ghalib's corrections had been incorporated. Ghalib tells him:

'Although his objection is absurd and the question he raises a pointless one, it would not become us to refuse to reply or to discuss it. His objection to your verse is really a criticism of me, since I had seen and approved it. I am not concerned with whether he accepts this or not. I am satisfied that our verse is essentially sound and true, and anyone who knows the language will under-

---

[1] The first letter of *sahih* ('correct') and the sign regularly used by an ustad to show that a verse needs no correction.

stand it. If out of ignorance or perversity they don't understand it, well, so be it. It's not our job to improve and instruct all humanity. Education and instruction are for our friends, and not for others. I don't need to remind you how often I have told you: See to it that *you* aren't in the wrong, and never mind if other people are. Today your verse is such that no one can pick holes in it.'

The ustad-shagird relationship between Ghalib and the King was, of course, of a different order. When Tufta and others made him their ustad they did so freely, and he accepted freely, whereas in the present case it was because neither could see any other course open that the King had made, and Ghalib had accepted, the appointment. In the circumstances he seems to have limited himself to such corrections as he felt the King would be likely to accept without reluctance. Each knew perfectly well that the other did not greatly admire his verse. Ghalib used to complain to Shefta of the King's inability to appreciate what he wrote. 'One day,' writes Hali, 'he went straight to Shefta's house after leaving the Fort. "Today His Majesty was pleased to show his appreciation of me," he said bitterly. "I had presented an ode of congratulation on the occasion of Id, and when I had recited it to him he graciously said, 'Mirza, you recite excellently'." ' Ghalib did indeed 'recite excellently', but this was hardly the kind of praise the occasion called for. Moreover the effectiveness of his recitation was generally acknowledged. Hali describes one occasion when he himself had heard him:

'His style of reciting his verse, especially in mushairas, was most moving and effective. I myself only heard him once at a mushaira, a few years before the Mutiny, when mushairas used to be held in the Hall of General Audience. His turn came at the very end, so that it was already morning when he rose to recite. "Gentlemen," he said, "I too must sing my lament." Then he recited, first an Urdu ghazal, and then one in Persian . . . in a voice so full of feeling that his voice alone seemed to be saying that in this whole assembly he sought in vain for one who knew his worth. . . .'

It was not only because the two men were ill-matched as poets that Ghalib's relationship with the King was a somewhat uneasy one. As a member of the nobility, a great writer, and from 1854, as the King's ustad (and hence in this sphere his formally-acknowledged superior) he took it for granted that he could treat the King with considerable freedom, and he did so, employing only the minimum of formality. For the same reasons he often found his duties as a courtier irksome. We have seen how often he evaded his unwritten moral obligation to present odes on formal occasions, and in this matter it seems that the King, to his credit, did not specifically insist, as he might have done, on his producing them. But where on occasion His Majesty saw fit to command his courtiers, they could hardly disobey, whatever their own inclinations might be. Ghalib wrote of such an occasion to Haqir on December 9, 1856:

D

'His Majesty has for the last twenty days or so been holding court every day. I go between eight and nine and return at twelve, and the call to midday prayer comes either while I am still having my lunch or as I wash my hands after it. All the courtiers are in the same position. I expect that some of them eat before they go, but I can't manage it. All this was bad enough. And the day before yesterday the King in his kindness commanded me, saying, "There is kite-flying every evening on the sand by the riverside. You must come to Salimgarh [the northern extremity of the Red Fort] too." In short, I go in the morning, return at noon, have my lunch, rest a couple of hours, go again, and get back as the lamps are lighted. My friend, I swear by your head, I lie down to sleep at night as exhausted as a labourer. It's four days since your letter came, and only today have I been able to get time to write to you. And that too only because instead of resting after lunch I have written this letter to you.'

Hali tells a number of stories which show how freely Ghalib behaved with his royal master.

'One day . . . Bahadur Shah, accompanied by Ghalib and a number of other courtiers, was walking in the Hayat Bakhsh or the Mahtab Garden. The mango trees of every variety were laden with fruit, but the fruit of these gardens was reserved exclusively for the King and his queens and members of the royal family. Ghalib looked at the mangoes repeatedly, and with great concentration. The King asked him, "Mirza, what are you looking at so attentively?" Ghalib replied with joined hands, "My Lord and Guide, some ancient poet has written:

> Upon the top of every fruit is written clear
> and legibly:
> 'This is the property of A, the son of B, the
> son of C.'

and I am looking to see whether any of these bears my name and those of my father and grandfather." The King smiled and the same day had a big basket of the finest mangoes sent to him.'

Equally characteristic of Ghalib was the freedom with which he joked about religion both in conversation with the King and in poems addressed to him, though the King was, in the main, religiously orthodox. However, we have to distinguish here between Ghalib writing in his official capacity and Ghalib speaking his own mind. As a poet and writer in the King's employ it was the King's religious views which he was sometimes required to express. Hali writes:

'On one occasion the King fell seriously ill. At the time Mirza Haidar Shikoh [a member of a branch of the Mughal royal family long settled in Lucknow] . . .

had come to Delhi on a visit from Lucknow and was staying as the King's guest. He was an Asna Ashari [a Shia sect], and when nothing seemed to bring the King any relief, healing dust[1] was administered to him at Mirza Haidar Shikoh's instance, after which the King recovered. Mirza Haidar Shikoh had made a vow that if the King recovered he would make an offering of a standard at the shrine of Hazrat Abbas in Lucknow. [Abbas was the cousin and standard bearer of Husain, the grandson of the Prophet, at the fatal battle of Karbala.] When he returned to Lucknow he wrote to the King to say that the fulfilment of his vow was beyond his financial means, and requesting the King's help. The King had money sent to him and the offering of the standard was made with great pomp and ceremony, in the presence of the whole royal family of Oudh and all the most prominent nobles and divines. . . .

'This incident gave rise to a general rumour that the King had become a Shia, a rumour which caused him much pain. . . . Hakim Ahsanullah Khan had a number of pamphlets published to counter the rumour and . . . proclamations were posted . . . in the markets and byways. On the King's order Ghalib too wrote a masnavi in Persian . . . in which the King was cleared of the charge of having turned Shia. Ghalib expressed nothing of his own views in the poem, but simply put into Persian verse whatever Hakim Ahsanullah Khan told him. When the poem reached Lucknow, the leading Shia divine[2] enquired from Ghalib whether the views which it expressed about the Shia religion and Mirza Haidar Shikoh were his own. He wrote in reply, "I am in the King's employ and carry out whatever order he gives me. You may attribute the contents of the poem to the King and Hakim Ahsanullah Khan and the words to me." '

Ikram adds further details:

'In 1853–4, when the rumour went round that Bahadur Shah had become a Shia, the leading Muslim divines in Delhi warned him that if this rumour were correct they would exclude his name from the Friday sermons and the Id address. To refute the rumour, Bahadur Shah had Ghalib write a Persian masnavi. After this the King wrote a book . . . [in vindication of Sunni beliefs], to which Ghalib wrote an eloquent and forceful foreword. . . .'

It is worth noting in passing that this foreword was written in Urdu, and Ghalib, with his usual bluntness, makes clear in the course of it that this medium was not his own choice. 'When this work was completed,' he writes, 'the command came from His Majesty . . . that the servant of his court Asadullah should show his graceful submission in writing a foreword, contenting himself to adorn his eloquence with the adornment of the Urdu tongue . . . The fulfilment of this command is incumbent upon me. . . .'

---

[1] Dust brought from Karbala, the scene of the martyrdom of Husain, and believed to have miraculously curative properties.

[2] *Mujtahid ul asar*—a title officially conferred by the Lucknow Kings on the leading Shia divine.

In point of fact, says Hali,

'Ghalib's real religion was "enmity towards none", but he inclined towards Shia beliefs and held . . . [Ali], after the Prophet of God, to be pre-eminent. On one occasion . . . Bahadur Shah said in the presence of his court, "I hear that Mirza Asadullah Khan Ghalib is of the Shia persuasion." Ghalib was informed of this and wrote a number of rubais which he presented to the King. I remember one of these . . . and quote it here. [In prose translation the verse reads:] "Men who are deeply hostile to me call me 'heretic' [i.e. Shia] and 'atheist'. How can one who is a Sufi be an atheist? And how can one who hails from 'Beyond the River' be a Shia?" The gulf that exists between atheism and Sufism is clear: the atheist denies even the existence of God, while to the Sufi all that exists is God, and all else is nothing. So how can a Sufi be an atheist? The point of the fourth line is that the people of "Beyond the River", i.e. of Turkestan, are proverbial for their Sunni bigotry . . . and since Ghalib's ancestors came from "Beyond the River" he asks how a man from "Beyond the River" can be a heretic or a Shia.'

Hali continues:

'People who are not well-acquainted with Ghalib's temperament and his way of writing may think that Ghalib falsified his religion in order to safeguard his access to the King. But the truth is that all these rubais were written simply to amuse the King and raise a laugh among his courtiers; for there was not a man in the court who did not know that Ghalib was a Shia, or at least a tafzili [one who, though not a Shia, acknowledges the pre-eminence of Ali]. Ghalib frequently recited verses of this kind . . . for the King's amusement. On one occasion when the court was assembled the conversation turned on the close relations that had existed between [the medieval Muslim saint] . . . Nizam ud Din and [the Persian poet] Amir Khusrau. Ghalib at once composed and recited the following verse:

> Two holy guides; two suppliants. In this
> God's power we see.
> Nizam ud Din had Khusrau: Siraj ud Din has me.'

(Siraj ud Din was the King's real name. He took the name Bahadur Shah when he came to the throne.) The verse neatly combines a compliment to the King with a compliment to himself, suggesting that Bahadur Shah matches the great Nizam ud Din in holiness and spiritual power while Ghalib matches Amir Khusrau, who was universally honoured as one of the greatest of the old Persian poets.

Bahadur Shah may indeed have found these incidents as amusing as Hali says he did. Ghalib, for his part, gave him little opportunity to take him seriously. Whenever the King said anything which could suggest that he was chiding Ghalib for his religious shortcomings, Ghalib's rejoinder was generally flippant and irreverent. 'On one occasion,' writes Hali, 'after Ramzan was over the King asked him, "Mirza, how many days' fasts did you keep?" Ghalib replied, "My Lord and Guide, I failed to keep one",' and left it to the King to decide whether this meant he had failed to keep only one or failed to keep a single one. Colloquially, eating during the periods when one should fast (between daybreak and sunset) is called 'eating the fasts'. Ikram writes:

'It was perhaps on this same occasion that he read the following verse before the Royal Court:

> The man who has the wherewithal to break
> the fast when evening comes
> Must surely keep the fast; it is his
> bounden duty to.
> He who has nothing he can eat when it is
> time to break the fast
> Can only eat the fasts themselves; what
> else is he to do?'

At the same time he presented a rubai in which he wrote that to keep the fast was an article of faith with him—and he would keep it if only he had the means to do so in comfort. Ghalib wrote to Haqir on June 4, 1854 quoting both these short poems and adding: 'His Majesty was very amused, and laughed heartily'.

Ikram writes:

'In the ghazals of this period there are any number of flippant verses of this kind. . . . Towards the end of 1851 Bahadur Shah planned to make the Pilgrimage [to Mecca—an act of great religious merit]. Ghalib [who thought that if he could go he would enjoy the journey] included the following couplet in a ghazal which he wrote at this time:

> He goes to Mecca; if the King will take
> me in his company
> Gladly will I transfer to him the merit
> that accrues to me.'

One of his ghazals ends with the couplet:

> Ghalib, you write so well upon these
> mystic themes of Love Divine

> We would have counted you a saint, but
> that we knew your love of wine.

Hali says: 'I have been told that when Ghalib recited this ghazal, the King commented on the final couplet, "No, my friend; even so we should never have counted you a saint." Ghalib replied, "Your Majesty counts me one even now, and only speaks like this lest my sainthood should go to my head." '

Hali, after suggesting the reasons for Ghalib's changing from Persian to Urdu as the medium for his correspondence, continues:

'Ghalib probably at first thought it beneath him to adopt Urdu as the medium of his writing. But it sometimes happens that the very achievement which a man regards as trifling and of little weight becomes the basis of his fame and popularity. Wherever one looks, Ghalib's fame throughout India owes more to the publication of his Urdu prose [i.e. his letters] than it does to his Urdu verse or to his Persian verse or prose. True, people generally already regarded him as a very great Persian poet, and thought of his Urdu verse too as poetry of a high order beyond the comprehension of the ordinary reader, but these opinions were based on hearsay, and not on their own reading.'

He goes on to say that Ghalib was himself aware of this, and saddened by it.

One may share Ghalib's regret that his verse and his works of Persian prose were not generally appreciated, without belittling the achievement which his Urdu letters represent. In them one finds a vivid picture of the man and of the life he led, and one which, incidentally, assists substantially in the understanding of his avowedly literary work. Even among his Persian letters one occasionally finds one in the homely style and content more characteristic of his Urdu. For example, on December 1, 1848 he writes to Jawahir Singh, the son of his old friend Rae Chajmal Khatri:

'You will remember that I had a cap made of kid-skin. Well, it is moth-eaten now, and I am without a hat. I want a silk turban, the kind they make in Peshawar and Multan, and which distinguished men in those places wear. But it must not be of a bright colour or a youthful style; and it must not have a red border. At the same time it should be something distinctive and elegant, and finely finished. I don't want one with silver or gold thread in it. The silks in the material must include the colours black, green, blue, and yellow. You can probably get something like this quite easily in those parts. See if you can find one, get it for me, and send it me by post. And tell me how much it costs. I shan't accept it until you've told me what it costs. It's not a gift. A gift, a present, is something you send without being asked. You can't give a man something that he's asked for as a present. I don't mean that I wouldn't accept a present from you. Not at all. I only mean that I'm buying the turban, and I'll only accept as a gift something that I haven't asked for. Anyway, please send the turban without delay, and don't hesitate about telling me what it costs.'

In the Urdu letters it is this sort of informal, intimate writing on everyday personal matters that prevails. Most of those given in the last chapter relate either to Ghalib's employment at the Mughal Court or to poetry and criticism. But there are many more, and they cover a wide variety of themes.

Some of them express his love of children, a love which he perhaps felt all the more strongly because he had none of his own.

Little is known in detail about his family life, for in Indian Muslim society one did not (and does not) talk about one's wife and children. His marriage was, as far as we know, no more and no less successful than most in his society, but he seems always to have felt that a wife was an encumbrance he could very well have done without. Hali writes:

'Ghalib's wife, the daughter of Ilahi Bakhsh Khan Maruf, was an exceedingly pious and sober lady, meticulous in keeping the fasts and in saying her prayers. She was as strict in her religious observances as Ghalib was lax in these matters —so much so that she even kept her own eating and drinking utensils apart from her husband's. At the same time, she never failed one iota in her duty of serving him and looking to his welfare. Ghalib always spent his time in the men's apartments, but . . . at an appointed time every day without fail he would go into the zenana, and his treatment of his wife and her relations was always considerate in the extreme. . . .'

One wonders whether Ghalib really was so considerate to his wife as Hali makes out, but his description of the wife is entirely convincing. There were and are thousands like her. From a brief reference in one of Ghalib's letters, written many years later, we know that she bore him seven children, but none survived longer than fifteen months. There were times when, hard-pressed by financial worries, he counted this his good fortune, but at other times it grieved him, for he was genuinely fond of children. Having no son of his own, he gave a father's love to Zain ul Abidin Khan Arif, his wife's nephew; his verse includes a Persian poem in Arif's praise. 'He is the flame of the candle that lights my house,' he writes, 'and the pen in my fingers dances for joy as I write his name.' But Arif's health was poor, and in 1851 he fell seriously ill. In a letter to Haqir, written probably between April and July of that year, he describes his sickness:

'He has had a sudden attack of *ru 'āf*. In this disease there is usually a flow of blood from the nose, but he has been losing blood mainly from the mouth, and only a little from the nose. The blood flowed from his mouth like water from a water-carrier's goat-skin. In the course of a week—may God strike me if I tell a lie—he lost something like ten to fifteen pints of blood—black and foul-smelling. No one thought he would live, and all hope was given up. But in the end God saved him. You may imagine what he looks like now. Even before he was nothing but skin and bone, and now he has shrivelled up until he is as thin as a rake. He is still confined to bed. Not only can he not move about; he cannot even get out of bed. But his life is out of danger.'

Ghalib's concern was all the greater because Arif's wife was suffering from a prolonged illness at the same time. In the same letter he writes:

'For three months she has been suffering from fever and a persistent cough. God have mercy on her and on her children, and save her life. I cannot tell what will happen, but you may take it that if she lives it will be as though she had returned from the dead.'

Ghalib's fears proved only too well-founded. Arif's wife died in January 1852. Arif himself survived her for only three or four months. One of Ghalib's simplest and most moving ghazals was written on his death.

They left two small boys—Baqir Ali, aged five, and Husain Ali, aged two. If the letter to Tufta quoted above (p. 91-2) is correctly dated, he must have taken both of them into his care; but in that case it must have been a temporary arrangement, and the elder boy soon went to his grandmother, Arif's mother. The younger, Ghalib and his wife adopted as their own child. Hali says: 'Ghalib loved him more than if he had been his own child, and never let him out of his sight'. He often speaks of him in his letters.

He was also very fond of Haqir's children, and there are few letters to Haqir in which he does not ask after them and send them his blessing. The thought of them seemed to bring him some sort of consolation even in his keenest grief. The letter of January 9, 1850 already quoted, in which he wrote of the bitterness of his grief, his desire to leave Delhi and the insuperable obstacles that prevented him doing so, goes straight on:

'Today amid this same tumult of grief and sorrow, my thoughts turned to you and your children. It is a long time since I heard how you are faring, and how my dear little niece i.e. [Haqir's daughter] Zakiya is faring. Nor have I any news of [your sons] Munshi Abdul Latif and Nasīr ud Din. . . .'

Somewhere between August and October 1850 he wrote:

'How is my nephew and my dear little niece? You told me in an earlier letter that she takes her own pen and inkpot and sits down to write letters to me, and that when she quarrels with you she says, "I'll go off to stay with Mirza Sahib". Now you must tell her to stop calling me "Mirza Sahib" and call me "Uncle".'
D*

On January 8, 1853 he ends a letter with:

'My blessing to Munshi Abdul Latif and to Nasīr ud Din . . . and last of all I send my blessing to my dear niece Zakiya Begam: May Exalted God preserve her and grant that I may see her face; otherwise as the days pass by she will grow up and become a lady, a gentleman's daughter. And then I don't suppose she'll appear unveiled before me. She'll hide herself from me, because I'm not really her uncle; I've only laid claim to be her uncle on my own account.'

On March 27, 1854 he writes of her again. It seems that Haqir was anxious to give her a good education, but Ghalib urges what was in his time (and, indeed, continued to be long after his time) a more traditional view:

'Give my blessing to all the other children, especially Zakiya Begam. My friend, for women it's quite enough if you teach them the letters, so that they can read the Holy Quran at sight. Don't lay too much stress on her education.'

A few months later, on June 18, 1854, he expresses his satisfaction with her progress, but says:

'My friend, I can't make out whether you mean that Zakiya Begam has just read to the end of the *sipara*[1] amma yatasa alun or whether she has memorized it too. Praise be to God! If she's memorized it, that is a great achievement, and it will be a very great achievement indeed if she memorizes all thirty *siparas*. Anyway, tell me: you must have heard her read. She must have learned the letters, and learnt how to join the separate letters together. Or does she just read . . . parrot-fashion?'

He ends the same letter with a report on Husain Ali's progress: 'He can read the letters *alif, be, jim, he, khe.* God preserve my good name and grant that no fault remain in him, that people may not reproach me with having brought him up badly.' He speaks of Zakiya again in a letter of August 15, 1854: 'My blessing to Begam. [Then, addressing her directly:] Tell me, my dear. Even if I come to Aligarh now, shall I be able to see you? Or do nieces in your country observe parda from their uncles?' A month later, on September 15, 1854 he writes: 'From now on I shan't call Begam "Zakiya" or "Begam". From now on I shall call her 'Hāfiz Ji'. Give Hāfiz Ji my blessing. And my blessing and my greeting to Munshi Abdul Latif and his children.' Apparently Zakiya had by now memorized a part of the Quran. Hāfiz is the title given to one who knows the whole Quran by heart, and ji is a suffix of respectful address.

A little over a fortnight later he is writing that Husain Ali is seriously ill. On September 15, 1854 he had written:

[1] One of the thirty sections into which the Quran is divided. The one mentioned here is the last. It contains the shortest chapter of the Quran. It is this section which the Muslim child studies first.

'There has been an outbreak of fever here so widespread that I don't suppose there's a single house where half the occupants aren't down with it. It's a recurring fever. My steward Kallu, his mother, Madari's wife and his children are all ill. Your sister-in-law—that is, my wife—and the woman who looks after Husain Ali and runs the household are also ill. And the best of it is that both of them get the fever on the same day. Thank God that Husain Ali is well.'

But it must have been only a few days later that Husain Ali caught the fever too, for on October 3, 1854 Ghalib writes:

'Today it is thirteen days since he opened his eyes. He lies there day and night with the fever, unaware and unconscious. Yesterday, the twelfth day, he was purged, and he passed four motions. All he has to live on is medicine three or four times a day and barley-water two or three times. The outlook is not good. His grandmother [Ghalib's wife] is also ill. Every day at midday she gets a fit of shivering. It leaves her at evening. She has to miss the midday prayer, but manages to say the afternoon prayer at the right time. . . . My friend, I am not too concerned about my wife, but Husain Ali's illness drives me to desperation. I love him dearly. May God preserve him to survive me when I am gone. He has grown thin as a rake. I didn't write to you before, but sickness is spreading here on a huge scale . . . all kinds of fevers, most of them recurring ones. In other words if in a household of ten persons, six are sick and four well, three of the six will get well and the four well ones will fall ill. So far all ended well, but now people have begun to die. . . . In short it's a case of

> The seven heavens[1] are turning night and day.
> *Something* will happen: set your mind at rest.'

Three days later he had despaired of Husain Ali's recovery:

'I told you of Husain Ali's condition in my last letter. Today is the sixteenth day of the fever, and the ninth since he had so much as a grain of solid food. He has grown thin as a rake. Today he is being given an enema. I cannot bear to watch it, and am sitting in the sitting room writing this letter. . . . Let us see what the result is. I am in despair.'

But on October 15th he is able to write: 'Husain Ali is better now. That is, the fever has left him. His urine is cloudy and his stomach is hard. He is weak beyond all measure. God grant he may be spared and get completely well.' On November 5, 1854 he writes again:

'Husain Ali is better now, except for the hardness in his stomach and his stomach-orifice. And yes, there is still some swelling. Yesterday, for the first

---

[1] Whose movement determines men's destinies.

time in several days, he again had a fever. It left him as the night ended, and today he is well. Let me see how he is tomorrow. His real grandfather, that is, Zain ul Abidin Khan's [Arif's] father and my wife's sister's husband, Nawwab Ghulam Husain Khan, has died. His death is much to be regretted. He was a very humane and affectionate man.'

Less than a year later Arif's mother also died, and Ghalib took Arif's elder boy Baqir Ali into his care. His position caused him some anxiety. He wrote to Haqir on June 23, 1855:

'Let me inform you that Zain ul Abidin's [Arif's] mother, that is, Husain Ali Khan's grandmother, died on Wednesday, 28th Ramzan. Zain ul Abidin's elder boy, Baqir Ali Khan has come to live with me too. Do you see, my friend, the tricks that cruel fate plays on me? Load upon load it piles upon me. Wound upon wound it inflicts upon me. There is nothing I can do. My income is the same; my expenses have increased. But I must fear God. I cannot behave callously towards them. And there is no one to whom I can say, "Look after your own boys. I can't afford it." Anyway, I hold my peace and am at a loss what to do. May God safeguard my honour.'

The children are mentioned once or twice more in the letters to Haqir. The first, written during Ramzan, 1856 (June 4, 1856) says: 'Both your children, Bāqir Ali Khan and Husain Ali Khan, are well. They break the fast three or four times a day, and as the time for breaking the fast [sunset] draws near, stand sentry over the mouths of those that are keeping it.' The second comes just over a year later, on July 27, 1856: 'Both the boys are happy. They wander about the place demanding mangoes, but no one will give them any. Their grandmother [Ghalib's wife] has got it into her head that she mustn't let them eat their bellyful of food.'

He often wished that he could go to Aligarh to visit Haqir, and at one time planned to do this and then go on to Banda, further East, to visit other friends. But he found constantly that circumstances prevented him. Some time between August and October, 1850 he had written to Haqir: 'God willing, I shall find an occasion to come by the mail to Aligarh this winter to visit you, and stay with you for a few days'. On May 21, 1852 he concludes a letter:

'Today I felt like talking to you. And I *am* talking to you, not writing a letter. But, alas, there's not the same pleasure in this conversation as in actually talking together, because I'm doing all the chattering and you're not saying a word. And that's not the same as talking together, with you answering my questions and I answering yours. What can I do? It's a strange life I'm leading—everything goes absolutely against my own inclinations. What I want is to travel around, stopping a month here and two months there; and the position is that I, so to speak, lie here unable to move, with my arms pinioned behind me. And now, God help me, I've used up all the paper and I still have a lot more to say. I haven't even written my blessings to my children. *You* say them for me. And when you write, tell me how they are.'

More than a year later, on August 21, 1853, he writes:

'You ask me about the King. What am I to tell you? The diarrhoea has stopped, except for an occasional attack. The fever has left him, but he still gets a temperature from time to time. His hiccups are less violent than they were. He sometimes gets a burning in his chest and sort of belches now and then. They bring his open palanquin to the bedside, and move him from the bed on to it, and that is how he goes out. They carry him around within the precincts of the Fort and then bring him back to his apartments. You may take it—and this is what is being generally said—that the sickness has left him but he is still weak. Anyway, as long as he's safe, that's something; but I shall have to wait and see how long it is before what *I* want happens, and he takes his bath to mark his recovery[1] and receives his gifts in congratulation, so that I can take leave of him and go off by the mail to Banda. I shall have lost half the pleasure of the journey, for the mangoes and the rains are practically over. Oh well, let's see when I shall manage to meet my friend [Haqir] in Aligarh and see his children and meet my friends in Banda and see their children. . . . My friend, I tell you by God that my heart was—and is—set upon making this journey. It is just what I would like. But just see what has happened. If only things had not turned out this way, I would have been off to Banda by now, visiting you on the way. But what can I do? In the circumstances I cannot ask for leave; and I can't go off without taking leave. "God is recognized in the failure of man's plans." [i.e. Man proposes, God disposes.][2] I will write to you in more detail later. My blessings to the children.'

On September 3, 1853 he writes again:

'You can take it that my intention is absolutely unchanged—absolutely. The King has recovered. Once he has held his court after taking the bath and I have recited an ode or a poem of congratulation before him, I shall take leave of him, take my seat in the mail-coach, and come to Aligarh. I shall stay twenty-four hours there [with you] and then go on.

'One Shaikh Momin Ali Sahib, Sadr Amīn[3] at Aligarh, has been here. He came to see me one day, but I had gone out, so we were not able to meet. Two days later I went to visit him, and found him at home. We spoke of you too, and he spoke very highly of you. I was expecting him to visit me again, but three or four days ago I met Hakim Imam ud Din Khan in the Fort and asked

---

[1] Prescribed by Muslim usage.
[2] The saying is attributed to Ali, the cousin and son-in-law of the Prophet.
[3] A post in the judiciary.

him. "How is the Sadr Amīn from Aligarh whom you were treating?" He said, "He has gone back to Aligarh." The point is, if you meet him tell him, "An unworthy Asadullah [Ghalib] presents his respects and begs to state that he cannot presume to complain to you that you left without visiting him again. But he regrets that he was not informed of your departure; otherwise he would have waited upon you to bid you farewell.'

On October 2, 1853 he is still hoping, though not without misgivings:

'May God hold you and your children safe in His keeping, and bring me the happiness of meeting you and seeing them. My friend, the fate that I brought into the world has laid it down that nothing that I want comes to pass. . . . The enjoyment of the journey by the mail, the pleasure of coming to Aligarh, the joy of meeting you, my friend, the delight of seeing your children, the diversion of halting here and there on the way to buy mangoes—how can I tell you all the things I have missed? As you know, I got a windfall of money, and I intended to use it to pay the expenses of my journey. And then I was confronted with this state of affairs here. They say now that His Majesty will not celebrate his recovery until after Muharram [the month in which Muslims mourn the martyrdom of Husain]. My intention is unchanged. But where shall I find the money? Anyway, let a suitable opportunity present itself and I will take leave, borrow money, and be on my way—unless fate plays me some new trick in the meanwhile.'

Four days later, on October 6, 1853, he writes again:

'I am told that the King will celebrate his recovery after Muharram. He is well again—weak, it is true; but that is inevitable at his age. Anyway, after the 10th Muharram[1] I shall ask for leave—but only when a suitable occasion presents itself and when I have arranged for the expenses of the journey. Yesterday all day the sun was blazing and the wind as hot as it is in Jeth and Asarh [the months in the Hindu calendar corresponding to May-June and June-July] when the hot season is at its height. But as evening came on it got so cold that the rich had their big shawls taken out of their store-rooms and the poor untied their bundles and got out their quilts and blankets. The sky was completely overcast with black clouds throughout the night, but there was no rain. Now as morning dawned there was such a downpour that water lies in sheets every-where. I haven't been able to go to the Fort. It is still raining, and I am sitting here writing this letter. If it keeps on like this I shan't be able to send it off today. It's raining heavily. . . . My blessings to the children. God grant them long life and happiness and grant me the joy of seeing them. Here gram, wheat, and gram flour are selling for forty to forty-five pounds for a rupee.

[1] When the period of the most intense mourning for Husain ends.

Write and tell me the position there. Here the new moon was visible on Tuesday; so Wednesday was the 1st Muharram and today is the 2nd. . . .'

In the end it seems that his ambition of visiting Haqir was never realized. He
wrote on September 15, 1854: 'To go anywhere now is beyond my strength.
Even if I had not had these ties with the King, I should still have been stranded
here.'

Several letters throw a sidelight on the marital and other problems of a
common acquaintance of theirs. Somewhere between April and July, 1851 he
writes:

'My friend, for God's sake make Hasan Ali Beg see sense. Is this any way to
go on—to leave his wife for a boy? Even your mother takes no interest in what
has happened to her. The poor woman is stranded there with her aunt. Write
to your mother and tell her to write and persuade the girl to come to her so
that she can send her off to you. I mean, give Mirza [Hasan Ali Beg] this piece
of advice, and give him a good talking to.'

Sooner or later this advice seems to have had some effect, and Hasan Ali Beg
returned to his wife. But a letter of three years later shows that this did not
resolve all problems. On June 18, 1854 Ghalib writes:

'My heart bleeds for Hasan Ali Beg. His wife has, in cash and in kind, got rid
of five or six thousand rupees of his money. And it's not just the money. She's
as good as ruined him. What's he to do now, poor man? He's been to see me
two or three times, and one day when we were alone he told me the whole
story. I could see that the man was near to tears. How true it is:

> A good man married to an evil wife
> Tastes all the pains of hell here in this life.

Here in Delhi they have a term 'a new nawwab'. This term can be applied to
anyone, Hindu or Muslim. When a man dies—a wealthy man, that is—and his
property comes to his son, bad characters get together and begin addressing
him as "Lord of bounty" and "Your exalted lordship". They tell him, "Such
and such a courtesan is desperately in love with you", and "Such and such a
lord was praising you to his assembled friends. You must certainly send for this
courtesan and give a party for this lord. That is what worldly wealth is for.
You cannot take it with you. Did your father take anything with him? And
will you?" Anyway, to date your humble servant has seen three such new
nawwabs. One was Khatri Todar Mal. He had a hundred thousand rupees to
his name, and in six to seven years he lost it all, left Delhi, and disappeared
without a trace. The second was a Panjabi boy named Sa'ādat. He lost all he

had—some forty to fifty thousand rupees. The third was named Khan Muhammad—the son of Sadullah Khan. He too had twenty to twenty-five thousand
rupees and used to ride around in a buggy. Now he clip-clops around in down-
at-heel shoes. In short, I've heard of *men* becoming new nawwabs; but this
good woman is the only woman new nawwab I've come across. The root of
the matter is that there's a crafty, cunning whore, who has, only recently, got
round my brother-in-law, Zain ul Abidin Khan's [Arif's] uncle in his old age,
got herself installed in his house, and goes about fleecing the respectable young
wives of the household. It's this same woman who has got together with
[Hasan Ali Beg]'s wife and made a "new nawwab" of her, and got her to spend
all the money they had. You'll hear the whole story from him. He did his best
to persuade her to accompany him, but she absolutely refused to go.

> Seek not within my head for room where sound
>   advice may lodge—
> The music of the lute and viol has entered
>   every cell.

He'll be coming to you alone. You must hear all his tale of woe from his own
lips.'

Haqir perhaps suggested that Hasan Ali Beg's wife was probably behaving
like this to punish him for his own misdeeds. Ghalib rejects this idea in his
next (undated) letter:

'What you wrote about Hasan Ali Beg's household affairs is not so—that is,
his good woman hasn't done this out of spite.

> Another story lies behind this tale

A woman man-hunter, a bad character, a cheat, has got her claws into her. And
now she entertains guests every day, and is for ever ordering flowers and fruits
and all sorts of fancy things. She's doing all this out of mischief and a taste for
luxury, not out of anger and resentment.'

There are occasional comments on the British administration, which, in its
larger aspects, impresses him very favourably. Thus he remarks in passing in a
letter of October 2, 1853:

'The Lieutenant-Governor [of the North-Western Provinces] has died in
Bareilly. Let's see who is appointed in his place. Just see the way this nation
runs its affairs! [In former times] in India if so great a potentate had died,
what an upheaval there would have been! But now nobody turns a hair. People
hardly notice what has happened or who has died.'

There were still important British officials whom he knew and admired, and this attitude is implicit in a letter of November 7, 1853, in which he writes:

'Thomas Metcalfe Sahib, the Delhi Agent and Commissioner, has died. He was the only one left of those who knew us. The celebration of his funeral defies description. There was a crowd of a hundred thousand people stretching from the Kashmiri Gate to his residence. He was buried in the precincts of Sikandar Sahib's [Skinner's] church, beside Fraser Sahib.'

The British administration did not always impress him so favourably in its more detailed workings. On May 29, 1853 he wrote:

'You may well ask about the weather. I am in exactly the same plight as the animals that lap up water with their tongues. As Zuhuri puts it

> The dog's plight, and the cat's plight and the
> Jackal's plight.

You have to see me in this weather before you can understand how I pass my days.

'I have some news for you. An epidemic is raging in the city. That is, the [East India] Company's agent has examined the papers of past years to see who owes dues [i.e. income tax, says Mihr] to the government, and has presented a demand for them. In fact "demand" is too mild a word. He is fully determined to exact them. Among others, he found that I too owed dues—five hundred rupees and eight annas—and demanded this sum on pain of imprisonment. I'd be hard put to it to raise even the eight annas; where am I to find the five hundred rupees? In the end his honour decided that the money should be paid by instalments, and a monthly deduction of five rupees should be made from my British pension. I used to get sixty-two rupees eight annas a month. So that leaves me fifty-seven rupees eight annas. Five rupees a month comes to sixty rupees a year. So when can I look forward to getting my full pension again? In other words you may take it that my pension is now fifty-seven rupees a month.'

And he more than once comments unfavourably on a British invention of great importance to one who wrote so many letters—the post office. On June 4, 1854, he writes:

'What do you think of the state of the British postal services? I don't know what innovations they've introduced, but all organisation is at an end and you simply can't place any reliance on it. An Englishman had one or two of his letters in English go astray. He spoke to the post-office here about it and when nobody paid any attention to him, he addressed a complaint to the head post-master. He got a reply to say that they accepted no responsibility; he had handed in his letter and they had sent it off; it was not up to them whether or not it reached its destination. Complaints have come from Meerut too, and one hears the same thing in letters from Agra. So far no letter of mine has gone astray, but in a general epidemic who is safe? I've felt obliged to make a new rule. I've sent word to Major John Jacob at Agra and to you at Aligarh and to a cousin of mine—my mother's brother's son—at Banda, and one or two other friends in various districts, telling them that in future we should send our letters to each other unstamped. It works out quits, and it puts our minds at ease. In future if you send me a letter postage pre-paid I shall be cross with you. Send them unstamped; and get Munshi Hargopal Tufta to do the same; in fact show him what I have written. A lot of pre-paid letters go astray. Unstamped ones can be trusted to get there.'

A few months later he is even more dismayed. It seems that the British had for the first time introduced the letter-box. On October 3, 1854 he writes:

'The post office department has gone all to pieces. It may have been an idle foreboding, but I had thought it proper, as a precaution, to start sending my letters unstamped. The letter would go to the post-office and I would get a receipt—stamped with a red-ink stamp for a pre-paid letter and a black-ink stamp for an unstamped one. My mind was at rest, because I could look at my mail-book and remind myself on what date I had sent such-and-such a letter and how I had sent it. Now they've put a big box in the post-office. It has an open mouth and anyone who wants to post a letter can go and drop it in the box and come away. No receipt, no stamp, no evidence of posting. God knows whether the letter will be despatched or not. And even if it is, when it gets to the other end there's no prospect of a tip to tempt the postman to deliver it, and no incentive to the authorities to collect what is due on it. They may not even give it to the postman to deliver, and even if they do he may not deliver it. And if it doesn't arrive, the sender has nothing in writing to base a claim on— not, that is, unless he pays four annas extra and sends it registered; and we send off letters all over the place practically every other day. Where are we going to get eight annas and more a week to register them all? Suppose I calculate that a letter weighs three *masha* and stick a half-anna stamp on it. It turns out that it's two *ratti*[1] overweight, and the addressee has to pay double. So you're forced to keep a balance to weigh your letters. The tongue of every balance is different, and shows a slightly different weight. In short, sending off a letter is a headache; it's asking for trouble. I've written this letter on 10th Muharram. Tomorrow I'll send for the necessary stamps, stick them on the envelope and send it off. It's like shooting an arrow in a dark room. If it hits, it hits, and if it misses, it misses.'

---

[1] There are eight *ratti* to a *masha*.

In the remaining letters of this period all manner of subjects come up. Like the preceding ones, most of them are letters to Haqir, but there are letters to other correspondents too, notably to Ghalib's and Haqir's common friend Tufta. We give extracts below, generally speaking, in the order in which they were written.

May, 1848, to Tufta:

'What's wrong with our good friend Munshi Nabi Bakhsh Haqir, that you write that even goat's whey couldn't cure it? There is a recipe given in *Tibb i Muhammad Husain Khani* which has no harmful effects and does you good, though it takes a long time for its effect to show. This is it: Take six or seven quarts of water, and, in the proportion of half an ounce to each quart, put in it crushed China-root. Boil it until a quarter of the water has evaporated. Strain the remainder into a fresh, unglazed earthenware vessel. Leave it to stand some hours and then drink it. Follow your normal diet, but whenever you feel thirsty, either by day or at night, drink only this. Make a fresh supply every day. After a full year its beneficial effects will be evident. Give him this recipe with my regards. Whether he uses it or not is up to him.'

August–October 1850, to Haqir—it appears that Tufta had secured some nominal employment with the Raja of Jaipur:

'I received the news about Tufta. Well, I too entered the King's service. Tufta is my shagird: why shouldn't he enter the Raja's? What you say is quite right. He's not taken service because he's concerned with supporting himself, but because he's concerned to get his diwan printed. What can I do? I have no resources, and can do nothing. Otherwise would I not have given a hundred or two hundred rupees to help him? I am disgusted with myself and ashamed to face my friends. How can anyone tell how much I love my friends? Who respects a man whose pockets are empty? And who listens to what he says?'

On September 6, 1851, to Haqir:

'I read in the papers that epidemics are raging in Agra and in Patna. There was nothing about Aligarh, but now I've learned of the situation from your letter. May Exalted God keep all His servants safe and well. All is well here, except that, as usual with the changes that take place at the beginning of this season, there's a wave of fevers and agues and colds. But there's no epidemic. It's been very hot, but for the last two days there's been a cool breeze. The clouds are gathering, but there has been no rain. If Almighty God wills, there will be in a day or two. His Majesty is at the shrine of Qutub Sahib.[1] He'll be returning on the 20th of this month—i.e. of Zi Qad. I ought really to have gone for a few days to the shrine, but I got one or two boils on my foot, and these provided me with a lame excuse not to go.'

[1] The famous Muslim saint Qutub ud Din whose tomb is at Mihrauli, near the Qutub Minar.

On January 4, 1852, to Tufta, rebuking him for not writing: 'Brother, just for one day keep off the drink—or cut it down—and write me a few lines, for you are much in my thoughts.'

On March 9, 1852, to Haqir:

'There's no need to feel so concerned about the pain in my chest. Most of my ailments are recurring. A little while ago I had a bout of colic. Now I've started a bout of pain in the chest. The pain starts up, lasts for twelve hours, or eighteen hours, or six hours, and then goes away. Munshi ji's ghazals came. He wanted them back quickly, but that was the day my pain began. I wrote and told him that I should not be able to attend to them that day or the next. I returned them to him on the third day. He had no business to tell you about it and cause you concern. In short, I'm quite all right.

'I don't have Hakim Imam ud Din Khan Sahib to treat me any more. Hakim Ahsanullah Khan looks after me now. He told me that the season was changing and I should be purged. Accordingly I have had ten to twelve suppuratives and three purges. The third was today. I'm writing to you after taking my cool drink, and my servant has gone to [Ahsanullah] Khan Sahib with a note. Let me see whether he brings back the good tidings that I am finished with them now and can relax, or whether I'm to be purged once again the day after to-morrow. This was the reason for the delay in answering your letter. Now you please be kind enough to write me in similar detail about your own health,[1] and tell me how the children are. My blessing to Munshi Abdul Latif Sahib. And my blessing to Zakiya Begam. Zakiya Begam, I want to know how far you have got with your lessons, and what you are reading now. Write and tell me. My blessing to Nasīr ud Din and Abdus Salam. I've forgotten the name of the new arrival. Give him my blessing and write and tell me his name.'

On March 22, 1852, to Tufta:

'I have moved from Kale Sahib's house and rented a house in Muhalla Balli-maron. It was my affection for him that kept me there, not any consideration of the lower rent. I tell you this simply for your information, though letters to me don't need the house address: "Asadullah, Delhi" is sufficient. But don't write Lal Kuan any more; write Ballimaron.'

We shall see later how much Ghalib prided himself on being so well known that a letter addressed to him at 'Delhi' would reach him and how cross he got when people pestered him for a more detailed address.

On May 15, 1852, to Haqir:

'Today is Saturday, the 15th of May, and it's morning. I've written you two letters. One of them I have just sent off to the post and the other I am giving

[1] Haqir had had something wrong with his eye.

to Hakim Ilahi Bakhsh Sahib. He is a man of good family from Sikandra, and is the friend and pupil of him whom, without ever having seen him, I love—namely of Sahib i Alam of Marahra—may Exalted God preserve him! He brought me a letter from him. He spent several months here, studying *Mufarrih ul Qulub* ["The Rejoicer of Hearts"—presumably, from the context, a work on medicine] under Hakim Imam ud Din Khan Sahib. He is a very nice man, a cultured man, and a man of excellent disposition. Here it has proved quite impossible to get employment for him, and fortune has not favoured him. Now he is returning home, and when he reaches Aligarh, will call upon you. You must treat him with deference and think of him as an old friend. And bear in mind that in your district there are many contractors and landed gentry. If any of them needs a physician, see to it that he is given a favourable introduction to him. There is no hurry about this; but bear it in mind.'

On May 21, 1852 to Haqir:

'Strange things are going on here. It's the month of Jeth [the Hindi month corresponding to May–June, and associated with the worst of the heat that precedes the rains] and we are having rain every day and it's quite cold. People are wrapping themselves in quilts at night, and I am myself using a coverlet. Ever since Nauroz[1] I've witnessed the spectacle of rain day and night and piercing cold. For two days it was hot, and the third day we had rain. And the rain continued for three to four days. Write and tell me how it is where you are.'

On March 17, 1853, to Haqir:

'I had myself purged because I was feeling constant pain in my limbs, and my stomach was overloaded with accumulated waste. Well, by God's mercy I have attained my object and feel relieved and well again. I have as much faith as ever in Hakim Imam ud Din Khan, and he is as kind to me as ever. But I had drawn closer to Hakim Ahsanullah Khan Sahib, and we see each other frequently. And he too is second to none in learning and practical ability. That is why I followed his advice and had my bowels purged.

'You're drinking infusions of neem leaves, and you do well to do so; but it's a vulgar prescription you're acting on in following it with gram-flour cake dipped in clarified butter. The accepted thing is to make gram chapaties your staple diet in ailments of this kind. If you continue this for some time you feel considerable benefit from it.'

Letters both to Tufta and to Haqir in 1852 and 1853 show that Ghalib tried about this time to gain the patronage of the Raja of Jaipur. He never seems to have felt very confident of the outcome, for at quite an early stage[2] he writes to Tufta:

[1] New Year's Day in the Persian calendar—about March 21st.
[2] Though the date of the letter is disputed. Mihr places it at about May 1852.

'The Jaipur business was a chance affair. It came up without my really thinking about it or planning anything. My cupidity has turned my attention there. I have grown old and deaf. I stood high in favour with the British authorities, and was counted among those of noble descent, and used to receive a full robe of honour. Now I have a bad name, and a great stain upon my character. [Mihr suggests that this is a reference to his imprisonment in 1847] and cannot hope to gain the entry into any princely state—unless I can establish a link as an ustad, or a spiritual counsellor, or a panegyrist, and so gain some advantage, or perhaps get a foothold for some relation there. Let us see what turns up.'

Afaq Husain, the editor of the collection of Ghalib's letters to Haqir, summarises the history of this episode:

'Ghalib, through Jani Banke Rae, presented a copy of his Urdu diwan as a gift to the ruler of Jaipur, submitting a petition at the same time. Jani Banke Rae appointed . . . Hardev Singh to await the Raja's reply. . . . In the end it was decided that Ghalib should be given a grant of five hundred rupees. When Ghalib heard this he decided to give twenty-five rupees of it to Munshi Hardev Singh, and wrote to Jani ji to deduct twenty-five rupees and give them to Hardev Singh, and send a draft for the remaining sum. He later learned that Hardev Singh had spent twenty-nine rupees and some annas of his own money in this connection; so he again wrote to Jani ji to deduct [this sum also] from the draft. . . . But Jani ji paid Hardev Singh out of his own pocket, and sent Ghalib a draft for the full five hundred. [Two officials of the state] had promised their help to Ghalib, and he had felt confident of receiving a substantial sum from the Raja. But his hopes were dashed when the Raja died suddenly, and the two officials fell upon evil days. . . .'

But Ghalib had at any rate got the five hundred rupees, and was not too dissatisfied with such an outcome. He wrote to Haqir on June 22, 1853: 'Well, it's better than nothing. I couldn't assume that I would get just what I wanted.' A letter to Tufta written some days earlier, on June 9, 1853, elaborates the picture a little:

'If this your well-wisher attains to no high rank in other things, in want his rank is very high—that is, I am greatly in need, and a hundred or two hundred rupees will not quench my thirst. A hundred thousand praises to your generosity![1] If I could have got two thousand from Jaipur I could have cleared my debts, and, given that a few years more of life were granted me, could have borrowed as much again. This five hundred, my friend—I swear to you—will go (all but a hundred and fifty) on sundry items. What's left I shall need for my own expenses. The loans which I've borrowed on interest from money-lenders will still amount to fifteen-to-sixteen hundred rupees. The whole of

[1] Tufta had been instrumental in bringing about the approach, through Jani ji, to Jaipur.

the hundred which I asked Babu Sahib [Jani ji] to send me was due to the English merchants in payment for that thing which our religion forbids and yours permits [wine], and I have now paid it. . . .'

A fortnight later, on June 24, 1853, he writes:

'Three days after I last wrote to you I [received more money]. . . . All my miscellaneous debts are paid and I feel greatly relieved. I now have forty-seven rupees cash in my box, and four bottles of wine and three of rose-water in the store-room. Praise be to God for His kindness!'

On June 22, 1853—corresponding to Ramzan 14th—he writes to Haqir:

'You may well ask about the heat. Scorching winds and burning heat like this hasn't been seen for the past sixty years. On the 6th–7th of Ramzan there was heavy rain. No one had ever seen such rain in the month of Jeth [May–June]. Now the rain has stopped. The sky is overcast all the time. When there is a breeze it is not hot, and when the breeze drops the weather is unbearable. The sun is fierce. I'm keeping the fast—whiling it away, that is. Every now and then I take a drink of water or smoke the hookah, or eat a bite of bread. People here have warped minds and strange ways: here am I whiling away the fast and they inform me that I'm not keeping it. They can't understand that not to keep it is one thing, and to while it away is another.
    '. . . Two days ago someone mentioned to me that there had been a news-item in the Delhi *Urdu Akhbar* (Urdu News) that there had been a riot in Hatras and that the magistrate had been injured. Today I borrowed a sheet of the paper from a friend, and found that there really was such an item, reporting that there had been a riot over the demolition of houses and shops in connection with the widening of the roads, and that the people had pelted the magistrate with stones and injured him. If that was so, I can't understand why the magistrate left the place; and if he didn't leave it, how were *you* able to come away? I am consumed with desire to hear the full story from you. . . . Now I address myself to Begam. You are to know that I can't say anything for definite yet, but if I get the chance, I shall be seeing you round about Id or soon after, and shall hear how you read the Quran. But don't tell your daddy this. Keep it to yourself. Why? Because if he gets to hear of it he'll write and ask me all the details.'

On August 21, 1853, he comments to Tufta on the fact that he had pre-paid postage on a letter to him: 'Apart from Hatim and myself did any man ever show such generosity?' (Hatim was a hero of Arabic legend, and proverbial for his open-handedness.) Somewhere about the same time—Mihr places the letter between August and December 1853—he grumbles at him for not leaving room for him to enter corrections and answer questions on some pages of verse he has sent:

'You've left me no room for corrections, nor can I follow the convolutions of the lines you've written. Why didn't you write them out separately on a double page, and why didn't you space them out a bit? Now I've got to set out your questions. If there are any I haven't noticed and so haven't answered, don't blame me; blame the twists and turns of your writing.'

He then sets out the questions and his answers to them and concludes:

'I've hunted out your questions and answered them . . . I hope to God I've not missed any. And mind that you too when you read these enchanted pages, don't neglect any of my hints for correction. See to it that you never write like that again. It puts me off. . . .'

In another letter of the same period he writes:

'See what good fortune is mine! All these days I was thinking that any day now I should be getting a letter from Munshi Ji [Nabi Bakhsh Haqir] telling me that he is safe and sound; and now a letter has come and it tells me no such thing. He's not well, but has hurt his foot. But I tell you it's a good thing that the bone wasn't injured. And the only reason that it has swollen so much is that there was no one there to massage it and the injury became chronic. Anyway it will right itself after a while. Be sure to write and tell me as soon as it does. The thing will be on my mind. . . .

'I gather from the fact that your letter conveys the respects of Babu Hargobind Singh that he must have gone on holiday to Aligarh [where Tufta was]. He shouldn't have troubled himself. His house is at the most two hundred yards from mine, and he went off without coming to see me first. What do I want with his "respectful service" now?

'Oh, and another thing. What are you and Babu Sahib thinking of to address my letters to "Imli ka Muhalla"? I live in Ballimaron. Imli ka Muhalla is a good mile away from here, without any exaggeration. It's a good job the postman knows me: otherwise your letters would have been going the rounds undelivered. . . .'

On December 22, 1853, he writes to Haqir briefly and movingly of the death of a lady about whom we should have wished to know a great deal more—his father's sister. The opening sentence suggests that Haqir himself had recently suffered a similar loss.

'My friend I too have become a partner in your grief; because [two days ago] on Tuesday, 18th of Rabi ul Awwal, in the evening, the aunt whom from my childhood onward I looked upon as a mother, and who looked upon me as her son, died. I may tell you that the day before yesterday it was as though I had lost nine of my dear ones—three aunts, three uncles, my father, and his father and mother. Because so long as she was alive I felt that these nine lived too, and with her death I feel that now all these nine have died at once, "Verily we are for God, and verily to Him we shall return".'

The last words are a verse from the Quran; they are always quoted when someone dies.

On January 23, 1854, to Haqir:

'The late Mirza Najaf Ali Khan must have been a friend of yours. He has died here. His son . . . Mirza Yusuf Ali Khan, I look upon as my own son. He behaves as a son should, and for this, and for all his other good qualities, I love him. He has just gone to Aligarh. You must go and visit him . . . and hear his story from his own lips. He's a young gentleman who was brought up in the lap of luxury and knows nothing of the ups and downs of life. His father owned one or two houses there. God knows what he will do with them. You must act as a sort of well-wisher and guardian to him. But he'll be leaving on Thursday. Today's Monday, and I'm sending off this letter to you. I feel sure you'll get it tomorrow. As soon as you do, please go and see him. It would not be proper to send for him, because he is mourning his father; you should go to express your condolences. And read him this letter to you.'

On March 2, 1854, to Tufta:

'Your letter came that day—yesterday, Wednesday. For the last four days I have been afflicted by the ague, and the best of it is that this is . . . the fifth day and all this time I have had nothing to eat during the day, and no wine at night . . . and I don't feel at all hungry; I feel absolutely no interest in food. . . .'

On March 27, 1854, to Haqir:

'Sanaullah Khan Sana lives with his son in one of the cells of the Fatehpuri Mosque. I got him introduced to Ihtiram ud Daula Hakim Ahsanullah Khan. Five days ago the respected Hakim Sahib came to see me. Sanaullah Khan was there with an ode. He was asked to read it out. The next day he went to his house, and the Hakim Sahib gave him five rupees. Then he was sent with his ode to brother Nawwab Ziya ud Din. (He is the younger son of Nawwab Ahmad Bakhsh Khan.) He too gave him five rupees. So he's raised ten. Yesterday Sanaullah Khan didn't come to see me. He may come today. There's a courtesan named Chotam in the service of Maharaj Hindu Rao. He [Sanaullah] says that she is his shagird. Now he is planning to take leave of her. When she gives him something he'll set out to see you at Aligarh.'

On June 4, 1854, to Haqir:

'My friend, praise be to God everything else is all right, but the heat is so intense that we cry to God to protect us. I suffer from heating of the blood as it is, and there's this torture on top of it. I was taking only one meal a day, and now I've discontinued that too. All I have to eat is curd, and how long can I go on eating that? I don't know what to do. To keep the fast is well beyond my powers, but I'm in a worse state than those that do keep it—and it's hard to describe their state. I have four servants, and all of them are keeping the fast. By the end of the day they look like four corpses walking about. And amid all these troubles I've got nothing that would provide some relief from them—no cooled room, and no iced water.'

He then quotes the rubai translated, and the short poem summarized, on p. 101 above and continues:

'I recited this rubai and this poem yesterday to the King. He was very amused and laughed heartily.

'I'm dying of over-heating, but I'm on the alert to see when the mango crop is ready. I'm certain they must already have ripened in Bengal. I lived two years in Calcutta, and mangoes are on sale there in June. About three days ago a fruit-seller brought five mangoes, but they had no taste. The hot wind had ripened them.'

On June 18, 1854, to Haqir:

'My friend, I can't tell you how much your comment made me laugh—that I'd excused myself the fasting with a rubai or a qata, while you'd had to fast for full thirty days—as though you and I weren't each and severally bound to keep the fast; as though it were a task entrusted jointly to you and me, and I had done nothing, and left it to you to do both our shares! God guard you in his keeping!'

Later in the same month, to Tufta:

'My greetings to you. Your letter and the sheet of verses have reached me. For the present I shall leave them—and the ones you sent before—lying where they are. Although the hot season has passed and the rains have started, and a cool breeze has started to blow, I'm ill at ease and can't concentrate on anything. I'd already composed a complete ode to the King and another, all but the conclusion, to the heir apparent, and had put them aside. I managed to finish this with the greatest difficulty during Ramzan, and recited them at Id. . . .'

On September 15, 1854, to Haqir:

'I'll tell you what happened here at [Baqar] Id. But let me tell you first what they're saying here about what happened in Aligarh. God save us! Wherever people meet they were saying that there had been a great civil war in Aligarh. Hindus and Muslims had drawn their swords on each other and ten to twenty on both sides had been killed. I was intending to write to you about it when in the meanwhile your letter came and I learned the true situation. I expect the same sort of reports have been current there about Delhi—that swords were drawn, and so on. Well, my good sir, swords were not drawn and there was no fighting. For two days the Hindu shopkeepers kept their shops closed, whereupon the British magistrate and the Chief of Police toured the whole city. Persuading and cajoling and insisting and threatening, they got the shops opened, and both goats and cows were sacrificed.'

Baqar Id is the festival on which Muslims commemorate Abraham's preparing to sacrifice his son. Some of them kill a cow on this occasion—'baqar' in Arabic means 'cow'—and Hindus, to whom the cow is sacred, were protesting against this practice.

On November 5, 1854, to Haqir:

'Yusuf Ali Khan has told me about your hearing and your sense of smell. My friend, by God I swear to you that I've been in this position for ages. I can neither hear nor smell properly. Although I am here in Delhi and some of my friends are hakims, they can't prescribe anything for it. And you sit there and want some prescription or some medicine sent you from here which will cure you at once! It can't be done. It takes time. It takes effort. There are purgatives to be taken, electuaries to be taken, essences to be drunk. And then you wait and see whether they have done you any good or not. Hakim Ahsanullah Khan in his kindness wanted to treat me, but I couldn't contemplate the rigours involved. Anyway, that's another story. The point, as I have said, is that the treatment of these ailments involves a great deal of purging. And for that you need a physician present, and peace of mind.'

Some time in 1854—the letter is not more precisely dated—he writes to Qazi Abdul Jamil Junun, who had sent him verses to correct, making the same complaint as he had made to Tufta; but, since he was evidently on less intimate terms with him, he expresses himself more politely:

'In the margins and on the back of your first letter there are verses written, but the ink is so faint that I cannot easily read what is written. Though my eyesight is good, and I have no need of spectacles, it cost me some effort to read them. Moreover, there is no space left in which to enter corrections. Accordingly I am returning the letter to you lest you should think that I had torn it up and thrown it away. . . . You will see for yourself that there is no space for corrections. In future when you send a ghazal for correction would you please leave more space between each couplet and between each line? . . .'

It seems that some of his friends were equally short-sighted even where more important things were involved. He writes, perhaps in 1854 or 5, to Anwar ud Daula Shafaq, who had sent him an ode in praise of the King to present to His Majesty: 'Your ode . . . had no space at the top for the signature. I had to have it written out again on a double page. I then presented it to His Majesty, and your old ambition was realized, that is, he signed it with his own hand, signifying his pleasure. . . .' The letter is a long and rambling one. He goes on to speak scathingly of Indian 'scholars' of Persian, expresses his keen desire to meet Shafaq, explains at some length his relationship to the ruler of the small princely state of Banda, in Bundelkhand, and how he had planned to go there to see his relative and take the opportunity to visit Shafaq before returning to Delhi, and why this plan came to nothing. He concludes: 'Please forgive my crime in babbling on like this. I felt like talking to you and so wrote down whatever was in my mind.' He begins the next letter to Shafaq on the same note, ironically scolding himself for his informal style of writing, and for failing to observe the elaborate formalities generally considered essential in his time:

'How can I claim that I am not mad? The most I can say is that I am sane enough to recognize I am mad. I ask you! Where is the sanity in this, that I write a letter to you, revered sir, to whom the wise turn in veneration, and use no proper forms of address or of salutation, or assurances of respectful service and humble submission? Listen to me, Ghalib! I tell you plainly: don't presume to play the companion. "Ayaz, know your place!"[1] What if last night you did write a ghazal of nine couplets for the first time in several years? What if you do go into ecstasies over your own verse? Is *this* any way to write? First write the proper forms of address. Then, with joined hands, enquire after your correspondent's health, then express your thanks for the receipt of his kind missive. . . ."

And some months later he writes, 'I am not writing you a letter. I am talking to you; and that is why I do not use the formal style of address.'

In May 1855, to Haqir:

'I do not envy men their riches and wealth or rank and splendour, but how should I not envy Shaikh Wazir ud Din and Mirza Hasan Ali Beg, who have met my friend [Haqir] and talked with him before coming here. I write to tell you that both of these gentlemen have separately been to see me and I have learned from both of them that you are well. Shaikh Wazir ud Din was saying something about *Mihr i Nimroz*, but I am deaf, and I didn't understand a word he said. Perhaps he was asking me to send [you] a further copy when it is reprinted. . . . Well, my friend, it's past eight o'clock, and getting on for nine. You be off to the courts, and I'll visit the Fort.'

---

[1] A common saying. Ayaz was a favourite slave and catamite of Mahmud Ghaznavi who presumed too much upon his intimacy with his master.

On May 25—9th Ramzan—1855, to Haqir:

'You did well not to have Begam [Zakiya] keep the fast. God grant that the fever has left her now too. Write and let me know. You said in your letter that Abdur Rashīd's bismillah [a ceremony observed when a child begins to learn to read and write] would be in the month of Shaban. Who *is* Abdur Rashīd? It seems you meant Abdus Salam, but wrote Abdur Rashīd by mistake. Tell me about this too when you write. Munshi Abdul Latif too should take care and not keep the fast. Otherwise God knows what damage it may do his health. . . .

'Be sure to write and tell me how Begam is, and the position about Abdur Rashīd and Abdus Salam. And tell me the position about our young friend Abdul Latif's fasting.

'Husain Ali is well. He has got as far as the Sura [of the Quran] Lam yakun.'

On June 3, 1855, to Haqir:

'You, and I, and his father are all to be congratulated on Abdus Salam's starting his schooling. Your writing Abdur Rashīd by mistake was a good omen. It means that he will be *rashīd* (dutiful). I was glad to hear about Munshi Abdul Latif. It doesn't matter whether it's a hakim or a doctor who attends him. It's the results you're concerned with.

'Good wares we want, from any shop you please. My friend, you're involving the poor boy in the toils of [a second] marriage. [Abdul Latif's first wife had died.] But, God keep them, Abdus Salam and Kulsum are enough to preserve his name. For my part, my friend, I believe in Ibn i Yamīn's words:

> Wise is that man who in this world refrains
> from just two things:
> He who would pass his days in peace must
> steel himself to say,
> "I will not wed, though I might have the
> daughter of a king,
> I will not borrow, though I get till
> Doomsday to repay."

'I hope it's not the case that he doesn't want to marry and you are pushing him into this misfortune. Find out from men he confides in what is in his mind. If he is willing too, I've nothing more to say. But if he isn't, then in my opinion it would be an imposition.'

On July 5, 1855, to Haqir:

'My dear friend, congratulations upon Munshi Abdul Latif's marriage, first to him, then to his parents, and then to his sisters and brothers. I tell you again,

God grant that it has been done with his willing consent. Congratulations on Zakiya Begam's engagement.

'The air is very pleasant now, and it rains every day. . . . This time I had to wait a long while for a letter from you, and several days ago I felt like writing to complain. But the rain made it impossible for me to send my man out to the post, and after that your letter came two days ago. Yesterday it still rained, but today it's cleared up; that is, the rain has stopped. I've been to the Fort, and written this letter to you too.'

On July 26, 1855, to Haqir:

'It's rained until there's a river wherever you look, and the sun appears as briefly as the lightning flash—that is, it only shows its face very occasionally. Many houses in the city have collapsed. It's still raining as I write this. I'm writing the letter, but let's see when it can be taken to the post office. I'll tell my man to wrap a blanket round him and go.

'The mangoes this year have been ruined—so much so that if for the sake of argument a man climbs a tree and picks one from the bough and sits and eats it there, even then he finds that it's rotted and decayed. And, if all this were not enough, have you heard about Tufta? His beloved son Pitambar Singh has died. Alas, I can imagine what the poor man is feeling.

> What should His servant do that would not
> bow to God's command? . . .

You're not writing anything like so frequently these days. What's so difficult about writing once a week?'

On October 3, 1855, he writes to Haqir to explain a misunderstanding that had arisen between them. It seems that Ghalib had sent him a copy of the second edition of his diwan, which had recently come out, and that Haqir had given this to one of his friends and written to ask for another copy. Ghalib had not immediately responded, and Haqir, thinking that this was perhaps because Ghalib was cross with him for having given away the first copy, wrote and expressed regret at his attitude. Ghalib replies:

'Far be it from me to resent your displeasure. But, by God, it's not what you have assumed. I grant you I did think, "My friend doesn't care for my diwan, otherwise he would not have given a thing like that away." But your giving it away would not have made me refuse you another copy. The people at the press have sold as many as a hundred and two hundred copies at a time to the booksellers beforehand, and when I ordered a copy from the press I couldn't get one. Now I've spoken to various booksellers. As soon as I can get hold of a copy I'll send it. My position is that when I write anything I don't feel any peace until I've sent it to you. I regard you as a man who really understands poetry. Last night, after a lapse of several years, I wrote a [Persian] ghazal, and I'm sending it you first thing this morning. In God's name take note that this is what you *call* a ghazal. . . . Just listen to it, but concentrate your attention and listen attentively. You can copy it out and send it to anyone you like. [The full ghazal follows.]'

On November 20, 1855 he writes to Junun:

'Why are you worried in case your letters have not reached me? Several letters reach me every day from all over the place—occasionally even English ones. The postman knows my house. The post-master knows me. All my friends write to me giving only my name and "Delhi" as the address—there is no need even to add the name of the muhalla. Judge for yourself: you have gone on addressing me at Lal Kuan and your letters have always reached me at Balli-maron. . . . In short, none of your letters has gone astray. Every one you wrote has reached me. I am at fault in failing to reply sometimes, but there are two reasons for that. First, your honour writes from nine different addresses in the course of a month. How many can I keep track of? If there were only one address I could keep a note of it. Secondly, I can't keep on writing letters in reply, when you go on writing just for the pleasure of writing. What could I say? I have given up editing epistles, and only write now when I have something to say. What am I to write when there's nothing to necessitate my writing? In your last letter there were three points that demand a reply. First, the rubai which you sent to this disgrace to God's creation. The reply to that is my humble service, and obeisance, and respect. The second, your concern lest your letters were not reaching me. I have already replied to this. The third point, Maulvi Allah Yar Khan Sahib's calling on me when I was out. I really was extremely sorry to hear this. If you see him please give him my regards and tell him how sorry I was. Every morning I go to the Fort. It seems he must have come early in the day. But even when I go out, there are always one or two people in the house. Maulvi Sahib could have taken a seat and smoked the hookah. If I go to the Fort, I am always back in about three hours. What more need I write?'

An undated letter—perhaps of 1855 or 1856—to Shafaq expresses a more bitter mood:

'Lord and master, was it a sin if, to express my grievance against you, I addressed you as "umid-kah" instead of "umid-gah"? [The latter word means "centre of my hopes", the former "destroyer of my hopes". In the Urdu script the two key letters "k" and "g" very closely resemble each other.] You neither answered my letters nor acknowledged my ode. And

> In this distress seek not forgiveness from me:
> A servant in distress grows rude of speech.

And the answer you are pleased to give me is that this and this preoccupation prevented you writing the praises of my ode. Well, your humble servant knows his place, and does not ask for praise. I am surrounded by men who, except for Ihtiram ud Daula,[1] know nothing of poetry. When I send you my verse I am, so to speak, doing a favour to myself

> Lament that verse's fate that cannot reach
> A man who understands it.

I am sorry that you do not visualize the state in which I live and the vicissitudes which befall me. Otherwise you would know how much—even with this subdued, and broken and lifeless heart—I achieve. Nawwab Sahib, my heart no longer holds its former strength, nor my pen its former power. The one talent that remains to me is the gift of facile composition. I can write—without thought and without delay—whatever fancy comes into my head. The labour of poetic creation I cannot now sustain. As . . . Bedil says,

> Striving befits a man when he is strong:
> Weakness demands full freedom from all cares.

Your letter told me about the seal. First you must write and tell me what is to be engraved on it. 'Mahdi Husain Khan?' 'Mahdi Husain Khan Bahadur?' I am writing from memory, because the boys have taken your letter and lost it. I seem to remember that you said you would send the stone. But I want to confirm whether the stone is to be sent or whether it is to be bought here. And what is to be engraved on it? I need to know how many letters there will be in the engraving. When you write again I will send my reply. I have been almost informed of Hāfiz Sahib's arrival in that you send regards on his behalf. Accordingly I too send my humble service to be conveyed to him. . . .'

In 1856 he writes to Yusuf Ali Khan Aziz replying to various questions about gender:

'There is no generally agreed rule about gender. See! people in this [part of the] country regard "lafz" [meaning "word"] as masculine, while people further east [i.e. in Lucknow and what is now eastern U.P.] make it feminine. Anyway I write whatever comes to my tongue. In this matter nobody's poetical works can prove anything; one community agrees on one thing, another grouping settles on another. There is no definite rule.'

He goes on to give the genders of the letters of the alphabet and to answer queries about particular words. At one point he remarks in passing. 'English has been current in Bengal for the past hundred years, and in Delhi and Agra for the past sixty.'

[1] The title of Hakim Ahsanullah Khan.

Among the last letters we have before the momentous year of 1857 are two written to his friend Mir Ahmad Husain Maikash:

'Bravo! a thousand times bravo! I thoroughly enjoyed your chronogram. God alone knows how good the dates on which it was composed must taste. Look here, my friend!

A darwesh speaks only when he has seen.

I have seen the chronogram, and have praised it. When I've eaten the dates, I'll praise them too. Don't get the idea that this is a polite way of asking for some, and put poor Din Muhammad to further trouble. He has just brought your note; don't make him come again to bring me dates. God forbid! However, if by any impossible chance you do decide to do just that and send me some dates by Mr Din Muhammad, [then they'll be welcome].'

In the second he commiserates with him on his illness:

'It's a strange coincidence that I can't come to see you and you can't come to see me. . . . God preserve us! I haven't enjoyed these holidays at all. I get news of you from Yusuf Mirza and Mir Sarfaraz Husain, and grieve for you. May God take pity on your state and grant you recovery. I hope that you won't make your weakness an excuse not to write to me yourself.'

Before many more months had passed Maikash was taken and executed by the British for complicity in the 'Mutiny'.

Such are the varied themes of the letters of the years before 1857. Exactly what was going to happen in that year, Ghalib could not have foreseen. But he had seen for years the few remaining powers of the Mughal King being whittled away by the British, and by the early fifties had become fully aware of the threat that this involved to the stability of his own position. Close as he was not only to the Mughal Court but to influential British officials, he knew very well how to read the signs of the times, and already in 1852, when the King had been taken ill, he had expressed anxiety about his future in a Persian letter to a friend, Munshi Hira Singh: 'Since the evening of Id the King has been ill. What will happen now? And what will become of me, who sleep in the shade of his wall?' [i.e. who depend on him for my livelihood.] 1854, the year which brought him the most considerable accessions to his regular income he was ever to receive, also brought him fresh warning, for in that year the British decided that after Bahadur Shah's death the royal family was to vacate the Red Fort and live outside the city in the area of the Qutub Minar. He received a letter about this time from Junun in which he had apparently been asked about mushairas being held in Delhi. He replies:

E

'Mushairas are not held anywhere in the city. In the Fort the Timurid princes
gather to recite ghazals. . . . Sometimes I go, and sometimes I don't; and this
assembly [the Court] itself will not last many days more. . . . It can vanish at
any moment. . . .'

In 1856 he suffered two serious losses of income, with the death of the
Mughal heir apparent and the British annexation of Oudh. About the former
event he wrote to Haqir on July 27, 1856:

'You must bear in mind that the death of the heir apparent has been a great
blow to me. It means that my ties with the Empire [i.e. the Mughal Court] will
last now only as long as the King does. God knows who the new heir apparent
will be. He who appreciated my worth has died. Who will recognize me now?
I put my trust in my Creator, and resign myself to His will. And there is this
immediate loss: he used to give me ten rupees a month to buy fruit for Zain ul
Abidin Khan's [Arif's] two boys. Who will give me that now?'

He does not mention the stipend which he had received as the heir apparent's
ustad.

The whole future of the Mughal court now became even more uncertain,
for the British decided that Bahadur Shah's successor was to be styled 'Prince'
and not 'King', and that the allowance paid him by the British Government
was to be reduced. Not surprisingly, Ghalib thought it prudent to seek other
sources of support. First he decided to try his luck with the all-powerful
British themselves. He wrote a Persian ode in praise of Queen Victoria, and
sent it to the Governor-General, Lord Canning, for forwarding to London.
Along with it went a letter containing a none too subtle hint of his motives in
writing it. He later wrote of this letter:

'I indicated what my expectations were by saying that the emperors of Rum
and of Persia, and other conquering kings, had been accustomed to bestow all
manner of bounties on their poets and panegyrists. They would fill a poet's
mouth with pearls, or weigh him in gold, or grant him villages in fief or open
the door of their treasuries to shower wealth upon him. "And so your poet and
panegyrist seeks a title bestowed by the imperial tongue, and a robe of honour
conferred by the imperial command, and a crust of bread from the imperial
table." '

At the end of January 1857 he received a reply from London which greatly
encouraged him, saying that when enquiries had been made appropriate orders
in the matter of the title and robe would be issued. About the same time, early
in 1857, through his old friend Fazl i Haq, he established a link with the small
princely state of Rampur. On Fazl i Haq's suggestion, Ghalib addressed a
Persian letter to its ruler, Nawwab Yusuf Ali Khan, and followed this up by

presenting him a copy of his diwan. The Nawwab, who had once studied Persian under Ghalib in Delhi, now appointed him his ustad, and sent him occasional gifts of money.

Ghalib did not make these new contacts any too soon. A few months later, in May 1857, the Indian soldiers at Meerut rose in revolt against their British rulers. They entered Delhi on May 11th, and were to hold it for several months. But with the British victory in the struggle that followed, the Mughal power was finally swept away.

✿ Chapter 6 ✿

The Revolt of 1857

What Ghalib did during the 'Mutiny' we know, for the most part, from his own accounts. In a letter to Sarur written eighteen months later (November 18, 1858) he writes:

'On May 11, 1857 the disorders began here. On that same day I shut the doors and gave up going out. One cannot pass the days without something to do, and I began to write my experiences, appending also such news as I heard from time to time. But I made it a binding rule to write it in ancient Persian, the language of *Dasatir*, and except for the proper names, which, of course, cannot be altered, to use no Arabic words.'

It was the established tradition in Ghalib's day to choose the title of a work not to indicate its content but rather to assert in poetic metaphor its literary worth; he accordingly entitled this work *Dastambu* ('A Posy of Flowers'). It continued to occupy him on and off for fifteen months.

What else he did besides beginning *Dastambu* in the four months during which the rebels held Delhi we do not know in any detail. *Dastambu* itself treats this period very briefly, and his private letters too are noticeably reticent. But in a letter written much later—on January 14, 1858—to the Nawwab of Rampur he says,

'In those turbulent days I held myself aloof [from the Court]. But I feared that if I completely severed all connection with it my house might be destroyed and my very life perhaps endangered. Thus I continued inwardly estranged, but outwardly friendly.'

Several weeks earlier—on December 5, 1857, he had told Tufta, 'In this upheaval I have had no part in any matter of policy. I simply carried on with my verse-correcting. . . .'

No such statements are to be found in *Dastambu*, at any rate in the form in which it has come down to us. This qualification is necessary because, as we shall see later, Ghalib conceived the idea in 1858 of presenting the work to the British authorities as a means of winning their favour and patronage. With this in mind Ikram comments, 'To assume that Ghalib has recorded the whole course of events plainly and without inhibition would not be correct'. But if we may safely assume that he may on the one hand have omitted or toned down passages which could give serious offence to the British, and on the other may have added emphasis to his horror at the acts of the rebel sepoys, there is nevertheless no reason to believe that the book in any way misrepresents his essential attitudes, and it remains the clearest connected account we possess of his personal experiences during these months and his reactions to the momentous events taking place around him; for, as he writes: 'This book from start to finish records what has befallen me and what I have heard'. (He adds that where he records what he has heard, he does so in the conviction that it is true.) The book is also a work of remarkable literary power. For both these reasons we translate the greater part of it in this and the next chapter.

Because he conceived *Dastambu* primarily as a work of literature, he does not come immediately to its essential subject matter, but begins, as a true Muslim should:

'In the name of God, from Whom comes all success, and Who created sun and moon, and night and day.

'A Mighty Ruler is He, who raised the nine heavens aloft and endowed the seven planets with light, and great is His knowledge Who caused the soul to enter the body and taught reason and justice to mankind, and caused these seven and those nine, sustained by no foundation and no prop, to endure eternally....'

He goes on to argue that if the heavens influence human fortunes, they do so as the servants of His will: 'The stars are the servants of a Just Ruler, and the servants of His justice may not pass beyond the orbit of equity.' If then the stars bring misfortune upon man, all this is part of the working of God's purpose:

> The Minstrel's plectrum strikes against the strings
> But who does not know what his purpose is?
> Joy lies concealed in grief. 'Tis not in anger
> The washerman beats the clothes against the stone.

'In truth the annihilation of one thing serves only to bring another into being. Ease and toil, success and degradation, are all of God's gift, and whatever He sends tends to man's gain and betterment and happiness and delight.... Is this not gift enough to us, that He exists?... The heavens turn like a millstone, and neither heavens nor millstone move without a mover....

> God sets the skies in motion. Understand then
> Nothing that comes from them can be unjust.

'All praise to Him Who confers existence and sets a term to nothingness, Who nurtures equity and stamps out oppression, Whose justice saps the might of the mighty, and Whose kindness gives strength to the weak. What was it when the swallows dropped their pebbles and by their blows the proud, head-strong riders on elephants were levelled in dust and blood?[1] And when the sting of a gnat took Namrud's life away? Beyond doubt, these were the evident signs of the might and majesty of God, Who can make the mighty weak and the weak mighty. Tell me, were these two disasters, of two different ages, wrought by the conquering power of the fatal glance of some cruel, capricious star?

> Zuhak seized throne and kingdom from Jamshed
> And Alexander clave Darius' breast.
> A jinn can steal the ring from off the hand
> That holds both jinn and peri in its palm.[2]
> Reward and punishment are hidden from you:
> You harp upon the influence of the stars.

Yes, that God Who can transform nothingness into being, can in the same way annihilate all that is. If He who said "Be", and in a moment brought the whole universe into being, should in another moment say "Cease!" and annihilate all what man would dare to murmur against Him?'

In short, God is great, and God is good, and the wise man who knows this, accepts with equanimity and joy all that God sends.'

Ghalib then prepares to move towards his subject proper, and a passing reference to 'armies that throw off their allegiance to their commanders' foreshadows what is ultimately to come. Ultimately, but not yet. There follows a long comparison and contrast between the fall of Persia before the invading Arab Muslims and the revolt of the Indian sepoys against their British masters, each presaged, according to astrologers, by the same conjunction of Mars and Saturn in the same mansion.

'The wise man does not fall prey to such fancies. There, a foreign army fell upon a foreign land; here an army rises against its own leaders. . . . There, the issue was religion; the blessings of a new, exalted faith brought happiness to a ruined Iran, and freed it from the bonds of fire-worship. Here the issue is the order of the state. To what new order can the Indian look with joy? The people of Persia turned their face from the worship of fire and saw before them the road to the worship of God. The Indians have let go the skirt of their just masters' garment and fallen into a snare, so that they are become the comrades of raging beasts. . . . Judge truly: to hope for peace and ease from any order but the British is no better than blindness. To the wounds which the Arab

---

[1] A reference to chapter cv of the Quran, which alludes to a story of how a powerful force including a number of elephants moved against Mecca, but was miraculously destroyed by flocks of birds like swallows, who dropped pebbles which killed all whom they struck.

[2] A reference to Sulaiman (Solomon). His power over jinns and peris depended upon a ring on which the Great Name—the hundredth name—of God was engraved. On one occasion, in punishment for an omission, God permitted this ring to be stolen by a jinn for forty days.

scourges inflicted on the Iranians, the excellence of the blessed religion of Islam brought balm. . . . But now, if those who know the world can conceive of the rule of reason and of equity returning hereafter, then let them tell me, and by their kindness bring comfort to my grieving, terror-stricken heart. . . .

'I am not so blindly ignorant as to expect from the proximity of two inauspicious planets the same outcome as befell a thousand years ago. Grief-stricken, and sunk in irremediable sorrow, I conceive it better that we poor creatures who inhabit this earth, who have neither seen Cancer and Saturn and Mars nor heard aught of them but their names, should not talk of things unseen and unheard, but should think that Time, which preserves all the secrets of past and future in its breast, and whose age-old custom it is to bring destruction upon the works of good men, could not allow the wise men of Europe to be humbled by a foreign army, and so sent their own armies from every quarter to assail them.'

He then turns abruptly to his own position:

'Let the reader of this book understand that I, the motion of whose pen spills pearls upon the page, have from my childhood eaten the salt of the English government. So to say, since I cut my first teeth my bread has come from the table of these conquerors of the world. Some seven or eight years have passed since the King of Delhi summoned me and desired that in return for six hundred rupees a year I should write the history of the Timurid Kings. I accepted, and set myself to my task. After some time, when the old ustad of the King passed away, the correction of his verses too fell to me. I was old and infirm, accustomed to ease and solitude. And more than all this, my deafness made me a burden to the hearts of others, as in every assembly I gazed intently at the lips of every speaker. Willy nilly, I would go once or twice a week to the Fort. If the King came out of his apartments I would stand for some time ready to serve him; if not, I would sit there for a little while writing, and then return home. Whatever I had written I would either take to the King myself or send it to him by another's hand. Such was my occupation when the far-ranging thought of the swift-moving sky planned a fresh revolution, to destroy my insignificant and harmless ease.

> I swear by His name, Whose unheeding sword
> Strikes down impartially both friend and foe.'

He then describes how

' . . . this year, at midday on Monday 16th Ramzan, 1273 A H, which corresponds to May 11th, 1857 . . . the gates and walls of the Fort and the battlements of Delhi were suddenly shaken. It was not an earthquake: on that inauspicious day a handful of ill-starred soldiers from Meerut, frenzied with malice, invaded the city—every man of them shameless and turbulent, and with murderous hate for his masters, thirsting for British blood.'

He relates how they were admitted by the city guards and quickly overran the city, killing every Englishman they found and not resting until they had burnt their houses to ashes.

'There were humble, quiet men, who passed their days drawing some modest sum from British bounty and eating their crust of bread, living scattered in different areas of the city. No man among them knew an arrow from an axe. . . . In truth, such men are made to people the lanes and by-lanes, not to gird up their loins and go out to battle. These men, when they saw that a dam of dust and straw cannot stem the fast-flowing flood, took to their only remedy, and every man of them went to his home and resigned himself to grief. I too am one of these grief-stricken men. I was in my home. When I heard the noise and uproar, I would have made enquiry, but in the twinkling of an eye . . . every street and every lane was full of galloping horsemen, and the sound of marching men, coming wave upon wave, rose in the air. Then there was not so much as a handful of dust which was not red with the blood of men whose bodies were like the rose; and it seemed that every corner of every garden was stripped of its leaves and fruits, the graveyard of a hundred springtimes. Alas for those wise and just rulers, of good nature and good name! And woe for those fair ladies of delicate form, with faces radiant as the moon and bodies gleaming like new-mined silver! And alas for those children who had barely yet seen the world, whose smiling faces put the flowers to shame and whose dainty steps reproached the partridge's gait! For all of these were dragged down to drown in the vortex of blood. If Death itself, that rains burning coals and issues flames of fire, Death at whose hands men are compelled to lacerate their faces and blacken their clothes, should stand sobbing and lamenting at these victims' graves, and don black raiment in mourning for them, it would be no more than just. And if the heavens should turn to dust and settle on the earth, and the earth in panic move like a whirlwind from its station, it would be no more than fitting.

> Spring, wallow in your own blood, like a stricken bird;
> Age, plunge in blackness, like a night without a moon;
> Sun, beat your head until your face is bruised and black;
> Moon, make yourself the scar upon the age's heart.

'At last, when evening fell on that black day, and blacker darkness over-spread the earth, then these black-hearted men in their headstrong pride pitched their camps throughout the city and in the Fort, where they made the royal orchards a stable for their horses and the royal abode their sleeping quarters. Little by little, from distant towns the news came in, that in every cantonment sepoys had shed their officers' blood, and as the minstrel draws the melody from his strings, so had these faithless ones, with beating of drums raised the tumult of rebellion. Band upon band of soldiers and peasants had become as one, and far and near, one and all, without even speaking or confer-ring together, girded their loins to their single aim, and girded them so strongly that the buffetings of a torrent of blood could alone ungird them. It seemed that legions without number and warriors without count were bound in unity as a single thread binds the twigs that make the broom. . . . And now you will see a thousand armies, marshalled without marshals, and unnumbered bands, led by no commander and yet ready for war. Their guns and shells, their shot and powder are all taken from English arsenals, and are bent to war against the masters of those arsenals. All the ways of war they learned from the English, and now their faces are inflamed with hate and malice against their teachers. My heart is not stone or iron: how should it not burn in sorrow? My eyes are not sightless windows: how should they not shed tears? Yes, a man must both feel anguish at the death of its English rulers, and shed tears for the destruction of Hindustan. City after city lies open, without protectors, filled with men who have none to watch over them, like gardens bereft of their gardeners, studded with trees stripped bare of leaves and fruit. Robbers go freed from the fetters of the law, and merchants released from the burden of levy. House after house lies desolate, and the abodes of grieving men invite despoliation. Nameless men, who lay lost in the oblivion of their obscure homes, have decked themselves out and sallied forth to display their shamelessness. Row upon row, they go with daggers drawn like a line of eyelashes, while peace-loving men of good will venture out to the markets bowed down at every step under oppression's weight. The thieves and the light-fingered, in broad daylight, boldly loot and plunder men's silver and gold, and go home at nights to wrap themselves for sleep in silks and brocades; while illustrious families lack even the lamp-oil to illumine their homes. In the dark nights when raging thirst assails them they await the flash of the lightning, that they may see where the pitchers and the goblets lie. See and admire His serene indifference! Men of no rank, who once toiled all day digging earth to sell, have found bricks of gold in that earth; and men of high rank who once in the assemblies of music and wine lit the bright lamps of pleasure and delight with the rose's fire, lie now in dark cells and burn in the flames of misery and degradation. The jewels of the city's fair-faced women . . . fill the sacks of vile, dishonoured thieves and pilferers. All their remaining wealth was their airs and graces, and these the new-rich, beggar's sons, have stolen from them to swell the stock of their cheap ostentations. Lovers who were to bear the perverse fancies of fair-faced mistresses, must suffer now the whims of these scoundrels. Every worthless fellow, puffed up with pride, perpetrates what he will, like the eddying whirlwind, and every vain, trifling man, who, drunk with vanity, performs the cheap antics of self-display, is like the straw borne swiftly hither and thither on running water. One, once of high resolve and high renown, has seen his honour dragged in the dust of his own lane; and another, who once had nor name nor pedigree nor gold nor jewels, is suddenly become master of rank and status beyond reckoning and wealth and property beyond compute. He whose father tramped the streets and by-lanes as though blown by the idle wind, has made the wind his slave; and he whose mother begged fire from her neighbour, has the fire at his com-

E*

mand. Shallow men aspire to make fire and wind their servants, and we are of those ruined ones who long for one sigh of contentment and one cry proclaiming justice:

> My grievous tale to you is but a story:
> The stars weep tears of blood to hear it told.'

After a little more in this vein, in which Ghalib laments particularly the complete breakdown of the postal services, so that he no longer has news of his friends, he passes on to speak of the further development of the revolt.

'Fate mustered a sepoy from every street corner, a force from every lane and alley, and an army from every point of the compass, and set them marching on Delhi. The King was powerless to repulse them; their forces gathered around him, and he fell under their duress, engulfed by them as the moon is engulfed by eclipse, though eclipse befalls only the full moon [i.e. the moon at the height of its power] and the King was not like that [i.e. his powers were, already before the revolt, extremely limited].'

The prisons had been opened, and freed criminals contributed their part to the general anarchy and to the pressures on the King. He goes on to speak of the military situation, and the daily clashes between the rebels, now 'near enough fifty thousand strong' and the force of 'the . . . British rulers, who in all this wide area held only a hill to the west of the city'.

Meanwhile in the Fort a conflict developed between the King's advisers. On one side was Ghalib's old friend and benefactor, Hakim Ahsanullah Khan, and against him

'. . . a man who, engulfed in inordinate pride . . . made himself the secret rival of his patron and benefactor. Fearing that unless . . . [Hakim Ahsanullah Khan] were wiped out, his own malpractices, by which he had amassed his wealth and property, could not be for ever concealed, he fomented constant opposition to him and cherished malice against him, making it known that Hakim Ahsanullah Khan was a supporter and well-wisher of the English and fanning the flames of dissension between him and the rebel leaders. One day this man of evil intent, intent on the murder of this wise man, launched an attack upon his mansion. [He] . . . was at that time in the Fort, in attendance upon the King; some madmen from this band therefore entered the Fort and hemmed him in. The Lord and Protector of his servant [i.e. the King], whose grace and bounty have no flaw, covered him with his own body, and only thus in this fatal moment was his life preserved. But though his life was saved, these turbulent, unruly men could not rest until the ruin of his household was accomplished. They looted his palace, adorned in beauty like a Chinese painting, and set fire to the roof. Every beam and every joist, joined in that roof as firmly as the stone set in the ring, fell and was burnt to ashes. The walls were blackened with smoke, as though the palace itself had put on black to mourn its own destruction.

> Trust not to heaven's kindness: know that this cruel witch
> Can plunge him in disaster whom she held in her embrace.

'I say that the most damned and dishonoured of slaves could never, never practice such malevolence against his master but that his seed had entered his mother's womb in the time of menstruation. This unclean traitor, false to his salt, to whose pock-marked countenance were added great bulging eyes and an ugly broad mouth, but who counted himself a third in beauty with Venus and Diana, goes everywhere about, swinging his hips and gesturing, and thinks that his gait outdoes the pheasant and the quail in beauty. I will not write his name, for this son of a beggar has neither name nor honour. I call down curses upon him, for this is an act of merit, and bring back the steed of my pen on to its former course.'

He goes on to write how the knowledge that the King had given his name to the rebel cause spread far and wide, and brought a great accession of strength to the revolt. Rulers of Indian states, from Delhi to Lucknow, hastened to offer proof of their allegiance. They included the ruler of Farrukhabad and the Nawwab of Rampur.

'The famous Lord of Farrukhabad, Tafazzul Husain Khan, who had never owned himself the King's humble vassal, now . . . wrote of himself that he had long been the King's slave. . . . That radiant sun that warms the world, the noble ruler of Rampur (may no evil come near him) who rules his domain with regal pomp and majesty . . . and whose loyal solidarity with the English rulers is so strongly founded that though the hand of time assail it for a thousand years with a thousand tests of strength, it cannot break it, had no recourse but to send a simple message and so silence the tongues of his enemies.'

But the tide of fortune was beginning to turn. In Lucknow the rebels had enthroned a ten-year-old son of the deposed King, Wajid Ali Shah, and an embassy had been despatched to Delhi, bearing gifts for Bahadur Shah. Ghalib describes these gifts and then continues:

'It seemed that all these splendid presents would bring further lustre to the King's house. But Time was waiting to make them an eyesore to him. . . .

'His fate had been roused suddenly from its deep slumber[1] by the sepoys' tumult; but now its drooping eyelids again closed in sleep. But no! Rather did the star of the King's fate rise to such heights that the sight of us men of mortal

---

[1] In Persian and Urdu idiom 'the awakening of fate' means the sudden turn of one's fortunes for the better.

clay could no more discern it. . . . On the heels of the day when that inauspicious embassy fulfilled its duty and the King extended his generous kindness to them, came the next day—Monday, 24th of the lunar month and 14th of September—when they who lay in the shade of the hill made an assault on Kashmiri gate with such majestic force that the black forces had no choice but to flee before them. . . . And if May drove justice out of Delhi, September drove out oppression and brought justice back.

> When four months had passed, and another four days
> The bright sun again warmed the world with its rays.

Although from May 11th to September 14th is four months and four days, yet one may say that since the city was lost on a Monday and recovered on a Monday, it was lost and recovered on the same day.'

In point of fact, the recovery of the city took more than one day. The attack of September 14th penetrated to the Jama Masjid, the beautiful mosque built in the reign of the emperor Shahjahan (1627–1658) but it was then thrown back. However, it was renewed, and although fighting in the streets continued until the 20th, the city was by then firmly in British hands. It is characteristic of Ghalib's moral courage that in a work intended for presentation to the British authorities he makes no attempt to conceal what the city suffered in the British assault.

'Smiting the enemy and driving him before them, the victors overran the city in all directions. All whom they found in the streets they cut down. Those distinguished in the city by rank and wisdom one and all took to their houses and shut the doors, that their honour might be safe. Of the army of scoundrels still in the city many determined upon flight, while a few raged to resist the attackers. These few now grappled with the brave conquerors of the city to spill, as they thought, the blood of the alien enemy, but as I deem, the honour of the capital. For two to three days every road in the city, from the Kashmiri Gate to Chandni Chauk, was a battlefield. Three gates—the Ajmeri, the Turcoman and the Delhi—were still held by the rebels. My house . . . is situated, between the Kashmiri and the Delhi Gate, in the centre of the city, so that both are equidistant from my lane. When the raging lion-hearts set foot in the city, they held it lawful to slaughter the helpless and burn the houses, and indeed, in every territory taken by force of arms these are the sufferings that people must endure. At the naked spectacle of this vengeful wrath and malevolent hatred the colour fled from men's faces, and a vast concourse of men and women, past all computing, owning much or owning nothing, took to precipitate flight through these three gates. Seeking the little villages and shrines outside the city, they there drew breath to wait until such time as might favour their return. Or if even there they could not feel at ease, they journeyed on day and night to some other place. As for the writer of these words, his heart did not quake, nor did his step falter. I stayed where I was, saying "I have committed no crime and need pay no penalty. The English do not slay the innocent, nor is the air of this city uncongenial to me. Why should I fall a prey to groundless fancies and wander stumbling from place to place? Let me sit in some deserted corner blending my voice with my lamenting pen, while the tears fall from my eyelashes to mingle with the words of blood I write."

'The command which went forth on the first day of eternity is immutable. On that day the fate of all created things was written and the leaven of the bread of all that would befall was set to work; our ease and pain conform to that eternal command, and it is to our gain that we eschew sorrow and despair and, as children rejoice at every spectacle they see, so we too should in our old age sit and watch the wonders which ever-varying Time displays, and be content.'

He passes on to

'. . . Friday, the twenty-eighth day of the month of Muharram and the eighteenth day of September. . . . In these five days the black rebels who had strayed from the right path fled like pigs from within and without the city, and the conquerors gained full control of the city and the Fort. The tumult of arrests and killings reached this lane, and the heart of every man was rent with fear. You must know that there is only one means of egress from this lane, and the lane holds no more than ten to twelve houses. . . . Most of those who lived there, the women with children in their arms and the men with bundles of their possessions on their shoulders, left it and fled away. The few that remained . . . closed the gate to the lane from the inside, and piled stones all about it. . . .

'From September 15th every house and every room had been shut up, and neither shopkeepers nor shoppers were anywhere to be seen—no grain-dealer to supply our grain, no washerman to wash our clothes, no barber to cut our hair, no sweeper to clear away the refuse. For five days people had gone out, returning always with water, and sometimes, when they could find them, with salt and flour too. But in the end the doors were barricaded with stones and the mirrors of our hearts were rusted over. . . . With light or heavy hearts, we ate what we could get, and drank water so sparingly that a man might think it came from a well we had dug with our fingernails. And then the water in the jugs and pitchers, and the fortitude in the hearts of men and women, ran out, and there was no more. The stage passed where we could delude ourselves that we could sustain the burden of the day with patience or that food and drink would come, and for two nights and days we went hungry and thirsty. . . . But on the third day . . . release from our troubles came. It came about in this way. The ruler of Patiala, Maharaja Narendar Singh Bahadur . . . was with the victors in this war, and his army had from the outset been ranged at the British army's side. Some of his favoured servants were distinguished noblemen of Delhi, holding high rank at his court, and among them were Hakim Mahmud Khan, Hakim Murtaza Khan, and Hakim Ghulamullah Khan, all sons of that Hakim Sharif Khan who dwells in Paradise: and they lived in our lane. Their houses stretch in a long line, threshold to threshold, roof to roof, on both sides of the lane, and the writer of these words had been for ten years the neighbour of one of these beneficent men. The first of the three, with his wife and children, lived in the capital, in accordance with the tradition of the family, while the other two lived in Patiala, privileged to be companions to the Maharaja. Foreseeing the re-taking of the city, the Maharaja in his gracious kindness to his servants, had secured from the mighty warrior-lords [the British] a promise that when the flowing tide of time should bring them victory, protectors should take their stand at the gate of this lane so that the British soldiers . . . should do it no harm. . . .

'On the third day, then, the Maharaja's soldiers came, a guard was posted, and the dwellers in the lane were freed from the fear of looting and attack. They came out of their houses, saying to themselves "Now come what may," and asked the soldiers' permission to leave the lane. Since the guard was one of friends and not of enemies, their request was granted to this extent: they were told "You may go as far as Chandni Chauk: to go beyond is to go to the slaughter". In hardship, misery and fear and trembling they opened the gate. Water-skins and water carriers there were none, and a man from each house, and two of my servants, ventured out. Sweet water was far away, and far they must not go. Of necessity they filled their pots and pitchers with brackish water and brought them back home; and at last that fire whose other name is thirst was quenched. They who had gone out and fetched the water said that in the lane beyond which they were not permitted to go, soldiers had broken down the doors of several houses, but the sacks in them were empty of flour and the vessels empty of oil. I said, "God's true servant is he who speaks not of vessel or sack, of oil or flour. Our livelihood is in the hands of Him Who forgets us not. To fail in thanksgiving to God for His bounties is Satan's work".

'In these days we thought of ourselves as prisoners, and in truth the life we led was a prisoner's life: none could come to us that we might listen, nor could we go out to see what could be seen; thus our ears were deaf and our eyes were blind. And in this trouble and perplexity, a dearth of bread and water! One day out of the blue, clouds gathered and rain fell. We hung out a sheet and put a pitcher beneath it, and got water. They say the clouds draw water from the oceans and rain it down on earth: this cloud of great price and auspicious shadow brought water from the fountain of life, and that which Sikandar, for all his kingship, vainly sought, I, for all my wretchedness, found. . . .'

At this point he breaks off to tell of his present difficulties. The use of the present tense and 'this year' in the sense of 1857, shows the original character of *Dastambu* as a narrative of events written as they happened from day to day:

'This year [1857] I enter my sixty-second year, stirring the dust of this ancient world of dust. And for fifty years I have used up my strength in the pursuit of poetry. . . . [He then gives the history of his pension.] Until the end of April of this year—I write these words in 1857—I drew my pension from the treasury of the Collector of Delhi. But the doors of that treasury have been closed since May, and I am face to face with misfortune, and wild and fearful fancies throng my heart. Formerly I had none to support but my one wife, with neither son nor daughter. But some five years ago, I took to my bosom two orphaned boys from the family of my wife, prime source of all my troubles. They had just learned to talk, and love for these sweetly-speaking children has melted me and made me one with them. Even now in my ruined state they are with me, adorning my life as pearls and flowers adorn my coat. My brother, who is two years younger than I, at thirty years of age gave sense and reason to the winds and trod the ways of madness and unreason. For thirty years he has passed his life unaware, troubling no man and making no commotion. His house is apart from mine, at a distance of about two thousand paces. His wife and daughter, with the younger children and the maidservants, saw that their best course lay in flight, and went away, leaving the mad master of the house with the house and all it contained, with an aged doorkeeper and an old maidservant, to fend for himself. Had I had an enchanter's power I could not in those days have sent anyone to bring the three of them and their goods to me. This is another heavy sorrow, another calamity that has descended on me like an avalanche. Two tender children, tenderly reared and cherished, ask for milk and sweets and fruit, and I cannot give them. Alas! at such a stage the tongue falls silent. We live in anxious thought for bread and water, and die in anxious thought for shroud and grave. Constant care for my brother consumes me. How did he sleep at night? What did he eat by day? And no news comes, so that I cannot even tell if he be still alive or if the weight of constant hardship has broken and killed him.

> More than the cry which echoes the heart's strife would leave my lips
> God and my soul! the very breath of life would leave my lips!

The things that I have written sap my life; and things I have not written afflict my soul. I look to men who know of these things to give ear to my complaint and judge me justly. The end of life draws near, and I am like the flickering lamp of early dawn or the sun that sinks to rest behind the roof-tops. . . .'

He again breaks off to relate how he had two years earlier composed an ode in Queen Victoria's honour, and what had been the response to this, and how the revolt had prevented matters coming to a conclusion. Then he resumes:

'On Wednesday, September 30th, seventeen days after the taking of the city and the sealing of our lane, news was brought to me that robbers had attacked my brother's house and looted it, and the whole lane had been plundered. But they spared . . . [his] life and those of the old doorkeeper and old maidservant. These two old people, helped and accompanied by two Hindus who in the panic and uproar had fled there and found refuge with them, had spared no effort to find water and food. Be it known that in the uproar of tumult and reprisal that shook the city, just as the modes of violence and oppression varied from lane to lane, in the same way the ways of the soldiers in killing and plundering varied, and ruthlessness or mercy was shown according to each soldier's mood and temperament. I surmise that in this assault the orders were to spare the life of him who bows the head of submission and take only his goods, while he who resists must yield his life and wealth and property all three. . . . And this is the general belief. . . . And to cut down old people and women and children is not held lawful. . . . Ye men who worship God, exalting equity and justice and condemning violence and oppression . . . remember first the Indians and see their character who in enmity without cause and malice without foundation, in full knowledge that the murder of one's masters is a sin, drew the sword against their rulers and murdered helpless women and sent to their long sleep in the dust and blood children whom their mothers would have lulled to sleep in their cradles; and then behold the English, who when they rose to battle against this enemy, and marshalled their forces to take revenge upon the guilty, might in their just suspicion of Delhi's citizens have left not a dog or cat in the city alive. On fire with an anger whose flames could burn the heart to ashes, they yet restrained it, and harmed not a hair on the head of any woman or child. . . .'

Yet a few lines later he continues:

'Many of the wretched people of the city have been driven out, and the rest lie here, prisoners of hopes and fears . . . and there is perhaps no balm to soothe the pain of either those within or those without the city. If only those within and those without could have news of each other's lives and deaths! . . . All one can tell with certainty is that every man, wherever he is, is in want. Those . . . within the city who sigh deeply for their fate and those without, who rejected by fate, are condemned to rove aimlessly, their hearts alike carry a full burden of sorrow and their faces alike are pale with the fear of death.'

He then relates an incident which took place

'. . . suddenly at midday, on Monday, October 5th, when a small band of British soldiers came along the wall which runs from the gate to the lane, climbed onto a roof, and thence jumped down into the lane. The Maharaja's soldiers attempted without success to stop them, and disregarding the smaller houses, they came straight to the house of him who writes these words. In the goodness of their hearts they did not touch any of the household effects, but took me, and the two fair-faced boys, and two or three servants and a few good-hearted neighbours with them, using, however, no violence or harshness, and brought us to a point rather more than two furlongs from our lane, to the house of the merchant Qutub ud Din, on the other side of Chandni Chauk, where the wise and capable Colonel Brown[1] had his headquarters. He spoke to me courteously and humanely, asked me my name and the others their occupation, and there and then dismissed me with every kindness. I offered thanks to God, sang in my heart the praises of that gracious man, and returned to my house.'

Here he turns again to the wider scene. He is puzzled on October 7th to hear a salute of twenty-one guns, 'for the Lieutenant-Governor's approach is saluted by seventeen, and the Governor-General's by nineteen'; but he ultimately concludes that this must salute some further victory over the rebels, 'for be it known that in many places—Bareilly, Farrukhabad, Lucknow—band upon rebel band is still bent upon stirring up evil . . . their hearts—may God crush them to blood—are set upon war, and their hands—may God strike them useless—are set to their task.' Other disturbances have arisen too,

'. . . as though Hindustan has become the arena of the mighty whirlwind and the blazing fire. And if in these grievous days whose beginning none can remember and whose end none can tell, mine eyes have seen aught but weeping, may their windows be blocked with dust. Save the darkness of my fortunes, there is nothing I can claim my eyes have seen. . . . To leave the house, to set foot on the threshold, to walk the lanes and streets, and see Chandni Chauk in the distance—these, except for that one day when the English soldiers took me— have not fallen to my lot. It is as though the sage of Ganja [the Persian poet Nizami] spoke for me when he said

> I do not know what passes in the world
> Or what of good or bad befalls men there.

Afflicted by these ills without remedy, these wounds without balm, I must think that I have died, have been called to life to give an account of my deeds, and in punishment of my sins have been suspended head-down in the pit of Hell, thus to live for ever in misery and degradation. Woe upon me if all my todays and tomorrows are to be like this! . . .

'On October 19th, a Monday once again—that day whose name should be struck from the list of the week's days— . . . in the first watch of the day, my brother's doorkeeper with downcast face and dishevelled hair, brought me the joyous news of my brother's death. I learned that he had taken the road to oblivion and walked with hurrying steps: for five days he had burned in high

---

[1] It appears that, in fact, the Colonel's name was Burn.

fever, and then half an hour after midnight, had urged the steed of life to leap from this narrow pass. Think not of water and cloths, seek not for corpse-washers and grave-diggers, ask not for stone or brick, talk not of lime and mortar; but say how can I go to him? Where can I take him? In what grave-yard can I consign him to the earth? Cloth, from the dearest and finest to the cheapest and coarsest, is not to be had. Hindus may take their dead to the river and there at the water's edge consign them to the fire. But what of the Muslims? How could a Muslim join with two or three of his fellows and, joining shoulder to shoulder, pass through the streets carrying their dead to burial? My neigh-bours took pity on my loneliness and at length girded their loins to the task. One of the Patiala soldiers went in front, and two of my servants followed. They washed the corpse, wrapped it in two or three white sheets they had brought with them, and in a mosque at the side of his house dug a hole in the ground. In this they laid him, filled up the pit with earth once more, and came away. Alas for him who in his life of sixty years passed thirty happily and thirty in sadness . . . God grant him His mercy—for in his life he knew no comfort—and send some angel for his delight and grant his soul to dwell in Paradise for ever. Alas for this good man of ill fortune . . . who in the years of sanity never showed anger and in the years of madness troubled no man . . . but lived his life a stranger to himself . . . and on the 29th night of the month of Safar, died.

> Bow down your head and ask for God's forgiveness;
> Where'er you do so, there His threshold is.'

He turns to speak of what happened to his kinsmen of Loharu.

'In the same week in which the British army conquered the city, Amīn ud Din Ahmad Khan Bahadur and Muhammad Ziya ud Din Khan Bahadur, men renowned for their wisdom and justice, bethought them that their honour might best be safeguarded and their hopes for the future made stronger if they left the city. They set out with their wives and children, with three elephants and about forty fine horses, and took the road to the domain of Loharu, which had always been their estate. They first halted at Mihrauli, where in the radiance of that blessed burying ground[1] they partook of the provisions for their journey and rested for two or three days. While they were there, robber soldiers surrounded them, and robbed them of everything except the clothes they wore. Only the three elephants, whom their loyal and faithful companions had led away the moment the tumult began, survived to remind them of their former state, like three burnt granaries [on a plundered estate]. You may well imagine the plight of these victims of robbery and ruin, as they set out, without provisions and without equipment, for Dujana. They were welcomed by Hasan Ali Khan Bahadur, of noble name and fairest fame, who gave proof of his humanity and courage, telling them "My home is yours"

---

[1] Mihrauli is burial place of the great saint Qutub ud Din Bakhtyar.

and escorting them to Dujana. I will not speak at length: this laudable leader of men acted towards his peers with all the gracious generosity that Iran's emperor . . . showed to Humayun.[1] When the Commissioner[2] Sahib Bahadur heard the news, he sent for them to come to Delhi. Accordingly they returned to the city and presented themselves before him. For some time he spoke to them with unkind taunts, but they returned soft answers to him, and he fell silent. He directed them to a palace in the Fort, next to the hall of the King's Steward in Chief, and commanded them to take up residence there. Regard for the even flow of his writing did not permit the writer of these words to tell the full tale of loss and ruin that befell this family. Know then that while their owners fell a prey to pillage in Mihrauli, their empty houses in Delhi were plundered and laid waste. Of all they had taken with them, they brought only their fainting lives to Dujana, while the rest in its entirety fell to the robbers. While here, of their mansions and palaces nothing remained but bricks and stones and pebbles. They were stripped bare; not a trace of their silver and gold remained, and not a thread of their carpets and their clothing. God grant His mercy to these guiltless men, and an auspicious end to this inauspicious beginning, bringing them comfort out of distress. It was Saturday, the 17th October when these two men, unrivalled in wisdom, returned to the city, and, as I have said, took up their residence in the Fort.

'Two or three days later a force was ordered out, and returned bringing in the lord of Jhajjar, Abdur Rahman Khan, as criminals are brought in. He was lodged in a corner of that hall in the Fort which is called the Hall of Public Audience. The whole of his former estate passed into the power of the English government. On Friday 30th October the ruler of Farrukhnagar, Ahmad Ali Khan, was arrested and brought in in the same way, and given room in another corner of the Fort. The town of Farrukhnagar became the target of attack for skilled and practised robbers, and its citizens lost all they had. On Monday, November 2nd, the ruler of Bahadurgarh and Dadri, Bahadur Jang Khan was arrested and confined in the Fort. On Saturday 7th November, to these nobles, held in the fort in isolation from one another, the coming of the Lord of Ballabgarh, Raja Nahar Singh Bahadur, added another. Let him who seeks the truth understand that the number of those estates which are subject to the Delhi Agency is no more and no less than the number of the days of the week. Jhajjar, Bahadurgarh, Ballabgarh, Loharu, Farrukhnagar, Dujana and Pataudi—there are these seven. The rulers of five of these were now in Delhi Fort, as I have said, and the remaining two, Pataudi and Dujana, are the target of the shafts of fear. What has Fate yet to show? And what will be the outcome for these men?'

He goes on to speak of two other nobles, Muzaffar ud Daula Saif ud Din Haidar

---

[1] Humayun, second of the Mughal dynasty, reigned from 1530 to 1556. Early in his reign he was forced to flee for some years to Iran.
[2] Of Delhi.

Khan and Zulfaqar ud Din Haidar Khan, generally known as Husain Mirza. (Although Ghalib does not say so here, both were known to him personally.[1]) They too

'. . . had left the city . . . leaving behind them houses full of furnishings and treasures beyond price. These two men of noble lineage had several houses and halls and palaces, all adjoining one another, and it is certain that if one measured the land on which they stood it would equal the area of a village, if not a town. These great palaces, left without a soul to attend them, were utterly looted and laid waste, though some of the less valuable, heavier things, such as the drapings of the large halls, and pavilions and canopies and . . . carpets, had been left as they were. Suddenly one night—the night of the morning when Raja Nahar Singh had been arrested—these things caught fire. The flames rose high, and stone and timber, doors and walls, were all consumed by fire. These buildings lie to the west of my house, and are so near that from my roof at midnight I could see everything in the light of the leaping flames, and feel the heat on my face and the smoke in my eyes, and the ash falling on my body, for a westerly wind was blowing at the time. Songs sung in a neighbour's house are, as it were, gifts which it sends; how then should not fire in a neighbour's house send gifts of ashes? . . .

'About the princes no more than this can be said, that some fell victims to the rifle bullet and were sent into the jaws of the dragon of death, and the souls of some froze in the noose of the hangman's rope, and some lie in prisons, and some are wanderers on the face of the earth. The old and infirm King, confined in the Fort, is under trial. The lords of Jhajjar and Ballabgarh and he who adorned the throne of Farrukhnagar, have been taken separately, on separate days, and hung on the gallows tree, that none might say that their blood has been shed.'[2]

On this blunt note Ghalib ends his account of 1857, and though there is more in *Dastambu*, it is convenient to break off at this point and see what further light on his experiences is shed by other sources.

We have seen that in *Dastambu* he discreetly ends his account of his connection with the Mughal court at the point when the entry of the sepoys into Delhi 'destroyed his insignificant and harmless ease'; whereas in his letters to Tufta and to the Nawwab of Rampur already quoted he says that he continued during the rebel occupation to perform his duties as the King's ustad, and in general to maintain outwardly friendly relations with the court. There are similar differences in the period from September 14th, when the British launched the assaults that re-captured the city. The British soldiers did not behave with

[1] Cf. pp. 206–8 below.
[2] Much later, on June 13, 1858, he records that Bahadur Jang Khan had now been released, granted an allowance of Rs. 1000 a month, and ordered to take up permanent residence in Lahore.

quite the restraint which, while not concealing their ruthlessness, he praises in *Dastambu*; and Ghalib knew it. During the fighting many excesses were committed; and, much worse, they continued long after Indian resistance had ceased. All able-bodied men were assumed to be rebels and all who could be found were sought out and killed indiscriminately. Ghalib's feelings are expressed in a poem evidently written at the time, and appended without comment to a short letter on quite another topic written in 1858.

> Now every English soldier that bears arms
> Is sovereign, and free to work his will.
>
> Men dare not venture out into the street
> And terror chills their hearts within them still.
>
> Their homes enclose them as in prison walls
> And in the Chauk[1] the victors hang and kill.
>
> The city is athirst for Muslim blood
> And every grain of dust must drink its fill. . . .

Another thing missing from *Dastambu* is Ghalib's characteristic humour, which he no doubt felt to be inappropriate to such a work. That it did not desert him even in the worst days is evident from two incidents that occurred when he was carried off by the British soldiers to be interrogated by Colonel Burn. The first is related by Hali, and the second by Ghalib himself. Hali writes:

'I have heard that when Ghalib came before Colonel Brown [Burn] he was wearing a tall Turkish-style head-dress. The Colonel looked at this strange fashion and asked in broken Urdu, "Well? You Muslim?" "Half," said Ghalib. "What does that mean?" asked the Colonel. "I drink wine, but I don't eat pork," said Ghalib. The Colonel laughed, and Ghalib then showed him the letter which he had received from the Minister for India [*sic*] in acknowledgement of the ode to Her Majesty the Queen which Ghalib had sent.[2] The Colonel said, "After the victory of the Government forces why did you not present yourself at the Ridge?"[3] Ghalib replied, "My rank required that I should have four palanquin-bearers, but all four of them ran away and left me, so I could not come." The Colonel then dismissed him and all his companions with every courtesy.'

Hali evidently did not know that Ghalib himself had written an account of

---

[1] Mihr notes that after the mutiny the British hanged offenders in Chandni Chauk, in front of the police headquarters.

[2] Cf. p. 130 above.

[3] High ground outside the city, where the English forces were encamped.

this incident, and that his own version of his reply to the Colonel's final question is a little more elaborate. He says he told him:

'The rebel soldiers were posted outside the gates to prevent people leaving. How could I come? If I had made up some story to deceive the rebel sentry I might have got out of the city, but as soon as I came within range of the English sentry on the Ridge he would have fired at me. And let us suppose that I did get past the rebel guard, and the English sentry did not shoot me—just look at me and consider my condition. I am old and crippled and deaf, and as unfit to confer with as I am to fight. I do pray for your success, and have done all along; but I could do that from here.'

Ghalib's remark that he was 'half a Muslim' was not entirely flippant. 'At this point in his book *Dastambu*,' says Hali, 'Ghalib writes, "A free man does not hide the truth; I *am* 'half a Muslim', free from the bonds of convention and every religion; and in the same way, I have freed myself from grief at the sting of men's tongues".'[1]

In *Dastambu*, Ghalib puts a bold face on it and says of his decision not to flee before the British assault that 'his heart did not quake, nor his step falter', nor did he 'fall a prey to groundless fancies'. It is not to deny his courage to say that his letters tell a rather less confident story. A letter to Tufta written towards the end of the year, on December 5, 1857, looks back on what has passed since the re-taking of the city, and its whole tone is very markedly—and very understandably—apprehensive. He explains how the lane in which he lived received the protection of troops from Patiala, and continues:

'But for that I should not have been in Delhi now. Do not think I am exaggerating: everyone, rich and poor alike, has left the city, and those who did not leave of their own accord have been expelled. Nobles, grant-holders, wealthy men, artisans—none are left. I am afraid to write you a detailed account. Those who were in the service of the Fort are being drastically dealt with, and are harrassed with interrogations and arrests—but that is only those who entered the service of the Court during these months and took part in the revolt. I am a poor poet, attached to the Court for the past ten to twelve years for writing chronograms and correcting verses—call it Court service if you like, or call it wage-labour. In this upheaval I have had no part in any matter of policy. I simply carried on with my verse-correcting, and considering that I was innocent of any offence, I have not left the city. The authorities know that I am here, but they have found nothing against me either in the royal papers or in the statements of informers, and accordingly I have not been summoned to appear before them. Otherwise, when high-ranking nobles have been summoned or brought in under arrest, of what account am I? In

---

[1] The words which Hali quotes do not in fact appear at this point in *Dastambu*, but in another context. See p. 156 below.

short I stay in the house and cannot as much as step outside the door, much less get into the palanquin and go visiting. As for anyone coming to see me, who is there left in the city? House after house lies deserted, and the punishment of offenders goes on. Martial law was introduced from May 11th, and today, Saturday 5th December 1857, is still in force. No one knows how life goes on in the city. In fact, the authorities have not even turned their attention to such things. Let us see what will come of it all. No one can enter or leave the city without a permit. On no account should you think of coming here. We must still wait and see whether the Muslims are permitted to return to their homes in the city or not. Anyway, give my regards to Munshi Sahib[1] and show him this letter. Your letter has just come, and I have sat down and replied to it right away and given it to the postman.'

Well might Ghalib, even so late in the year, feel 'afraid to write', and well might he feel the need to assure Tufta that he was 'not exaggerating'. For the British reign of terror continued for weeks after the re-taking of the city, and the measures taken against the people of Delhi were so drastic as to seem almost incredible. As soon as the city was re-taken, the British expelled the whole population, and Ghalib, in the same letter to Tufta, vividly describes the uncanny sense of desolation that this produced:

'Do you understand what has happened, and what is going on? There was a former birth in which you and I were friends, and all the many things that happen between close friends happened between us. We composed our verses and compiled our diwans. In that age there was a gentleman who was our sincere friend—my friend and yours. Munshi Nabi Bakhsh was his name, and Haqir his takhallus. Suddenly that age came to an end, and all the friendly dealings and sincerity and love and joy ended with it. After a while we received another birth. But although to all appearances this birth is exactly like the first— I write a letter to Munshi Nabi Bakhsh Sahib and receive his reply, and today I get a letter from you, and your name is still Munshi Hargopal and your takhallus Tufta, and the city I live in is still called Delhi and this muhalla is still named Ballimaron muhalla—yet not one of the friends of that former birth is to be found. By God, you may search for a Muslim in this city and not find one—rich, poor, and artisans alike are gone. Such as are here are not Delhi people.'

The expulsion of the population had taken place in mid-September. By mid-October its sufferings were extreme. Mrs Saunders, wife of the Commissioner of Delhi, wrote in a letter on October 25th, 'The inhabitants of this huge place seven miles round are dying daily of starvation and want of shelter,' and accounts by contemporary English observers support Ghalib's statement that in December, when the cold at nights is severe in the Delhi region, the position was still unchanged.

[1] Munshi Nabi Bakhsh Haqir.

The anxious, defensive tone in which he describes the nature of his connection with the Fort is fully understandable. No reference to his name had been found in the Royal papers, but some reference might yet be found, and however harmless its nature, it could in the mood then prevailing have had the direst consequences for him. Similarly, informers were everywhere active, and men were paying off old scores against their enemies by denouncing them to the British as supporters of the rebel cause. Reports like these were being acted upon without any attempt at independent verification, and Ghalib knew from abundant evidence all around him that anyone who felt a strong enough grudge against him could put his life in immediate danger. For weeks together, therefore, fear and uncertainty continued to oppress him, so that even in his private letters he is afraid to speak of what is going on. On December 26, 1857 he writes to Hakim Ghulam Najaf Khan:

'I got your letter. . . . You say that I've never written to you. Be fair! What am I to write? What can I write? What news is there that can be put into writing? What did your letter amount to? And what does this letter of mine amount to? Nothing more than this, that both of us are still alive. And more than this neither you nor I can write.'

We shall see in the next chapter that weeks later he is still writing in the same vein.

Not until long after this does he feel that he can safely express his feelings about the heavy toll which the revolt and its aftermath took of his friends. It is in an undated letter to Tufta, written perhaps as late as June or July 1858, that he reveals all that he felt. We give it here in full. Though it speaks of other things besides his grief, the quotation from his own verse with which, without any preamble, he begins his letter, sets the tone of the whole, and the intensity of his emotion rises to its highest pitch as he approaches the end.

'If Ghalib sings in bitter strain, forgive him;
Today pain stabs more keenly at his heart.

My kind friend, first I have to ask you to convey my greetings to my old friend Mir Mukarram Husain Sahib. Tell him that I am still alive and that more than that even I do not know. Give my regards to Mirza Hatim Ali Mihr Sahib and recite this verse of mine on my behalf:

Keep strong your faith in the unseen—else you are no believer.
You who are hidden from my sight, love for you is my faith.[1]

I had already sent off an answer to your first letter. Your second letter came two or three days later. Listen, my friend, when a man has the means to devote

---

[1] In the original the verse is all the more apt because the word translated 'love' is 'mihr', which is also the takhallus of the man to whom it is here addressed.

all his days free of care to the pursuit of the things he loves, *that* is what luxury means. The abundant time and energy you give to poetry is proof of your noble qualities and your sound disposition; and brother, the fame of your poetic achievement adds lustre to my name too. As for me, I have forgotten how to write poetry, and forgotten all the verses I ever wrote too—or rather, all except a couplet-and-a-half of my Urdu verse—that is, one final couplet of a ghazal, and one line. This is the couplet. Whenever my heart sinks within me it comes to my lips and I recite it—five times, ten times—over and over again:

> Ghalib, when *this* is how my life has passed
> How can I call to mind I had a God?

And when I feel at the end of my tether I recite this line to myself:

> O sudden death, why do you still delay?

and relapse into silence. Do not think that it is grief for my own misery or my own ruin that is choking me. I have a deeper sorrow, so deep that I cannot attempt to tell you, and can only hint at it. Among the English whom those infamous black scoundrels slaughtered, some were the focus of my hopes, some my well-wishers, some my friends, some my bosom companions, and some my pupils in poetry. Amongst the Indians some were my kinsmen, some my friends, some my pupils and some men whom I loved. And all of them are laid low in the dust. How grievous it is to mourn *one* loved one. What must his life be like who has to mourn so many? Alas! so many of my friends are dead that now if I should die there will be none to weep for me. "Verily we are for God, and verily to Him we shall return." [1]

These letters and the narrative in *Dastambu* afford adequate materials for an assessment of Ghalib's attitude to the revolt, even though the conditions in which he wrote them prevented him from expressing all that he felt. The picture is substantially what one would have expected. When the revolt broke out he was fifty-nine years old, and his attitudes had long been formed. A Mughal aristocrat, steeped in the traditional culture of Mughal India, he was at the same time a highly intelligent, clear-sighted and unsentimental man who had seen Calcutta, the British capital, and had lived for more than forty years in Delhi, where, outside the precincts of the Mughal court, the British were in full control. He knew the material strength and vitality of the civilization to which, in the last resort, the British owed their success in the struggle for supremacy in India, and he had been deeply impressed by it. Equally well he knew how effete were the political representatives of the old Mughal order, and how

---

[1] Cf. p. 121 above.

powerless to resist the new force which confronted them. We have seen how some years before the revolt, he had written that the Mughal court would not survive many days more, and there is reason to believe that in letters written early in 1857 to the Nawwab of Rampur, he had convinced him too of the hollowness of the Mughal power. This is the view of Arshi, the editor of the volume of Ghalib's correspondence with Rampur, who writes:

'Only a few months after the renewal of Ghalib's relationship [with the Nawwab] as his ustad, signs of the coming Mutiny . . . began to appear. Ghalib wrote a number of letters to his shagird and benefactor which, on the latter's instructions, were destroyed. The only reason for these instructions which suggests itself is that their subject-matter was political.'

He goes on to say that the policy which the Nawwab pursued during the revolt [of *de facto* support for the British without overt hostility to the rebels] could not have been worked out had he not been 'provided beforehand with a correct appraisal of the situation and of the real causes that had given rise to it'.

At the same time Ghalib resented the encroachments of the British. In a letter of February 23, 1857 written to a friend in Oudh he speaks of his feelings about the British annexation of 1856: 'Although I am a stranger to Oudh and its affairs, the destruction of the state depressed me all the more, and I maintain that no Indian who was not devoid of all sense of justice could have felt otherwise.'

It is not likely that a man of such divided sympathies could have given wholehearted allegiance to either side when the great clash came, and the position was further complicated by the fact that there was a strong plebeian element in the revolt to which Ghalib's aristocratic temperament reacted with contempt and hatred. In Delhi in particular the plebeian element constituted the real driving force of the revolt, and *Dastambu* shows clearly that Ghalib was fully aware of this.

Thus Ghalib's letter to Sarur quoted at the beginning of the chapter probably does represent accurately enough his real attitude in the early days of the revolt. An absence of deep sympathy with either side impels him to shut himself up within his own four walls, while at the same time a sense of the momentousness of the events taking place impels him to record them. His decision to do so in ancient Persian is, no doubt, mainly due to his wish to set himself a task difficult enough to engross all his attention and keep him fully occupied, though his ever-present enthusiasm for Persian also inclines him to the exaggerated purism he describes. As events move to their climax and culminate in the savage British actions of September and after, he is deeply shocked and expresses his feelings in the bitter poem already quoted and even, in a more restrained way, in *Dastambu* itself. But what moves him most deeply and makes the most lasting impression upon him is the personal tragedy of individual men personally known to him, caught up and destroyed in the play of forces far beyond their control. He had friends in all camps—among the English, among the Hindus, among Muslims who aided the British and Muslims who supported the revolt—and he mourned all of them deeply and sincerely, and felt their death as an irreparable loss. This sense of loss forced into the background all his partial political sympathies, and overshadowed even his sense of personal danger.

Chapter 7

1858: the Aftermath

The crushing of the revolt brought changes in the life of Delhi which could never be reversed. Yet with the new year elements of normality were beginning to return. On December 5, 1857 Ghalib had written that while the Muslims were still excluded from Delhi, 'some of the Hindus, it is true, have returned to their homes'. The British held that it was the Muslims who had been mainly responsible for the revolt, and though Hindus and Muslims were penalized indiscriminately in the period immediately following the re-taking of the city, the Hindus were later freed from the most drastic of the restrictions which had been imposed. Those to whom Ghalib refers must however have been exceptional, for it was not until January 1858 that a general return of the Hindus to the city was permitted. He himself writes of this in *Dastambu*:

'In the early days of January, 1858 the Hindus' freedom was proclaimed, and permission was granted them to return to their homes in the city. From all quarters they hastened back. But on the walls of the homeless Muslims' homes the grass grows green, and its tongues whisper every moment that the places of the Muslims are desolate.'

Ghalib had some cause to rejoice that he was a man who formed sincere friendships in all communities. His Hindu friends were now able to send him wine and to help him in other ways. He writes in *Dastambu*:

'To tell the truth—for to hide the truth is not the way of a man free in spirit—I am no more than half a Muslim, for I am free from the bonds of convention and religion, and have liberated my soul from the fear of men's tongues. It has always been my habit at night to drink nothing but French [wine], and if I did not get it I could not sleep. But these days in Delhi foreign wine is very dear and my pockets are empty. What would I have done had not my stalwart God-fearing . . . friend, the generous and bounteous Mahesh Das sent me wine made from sugar cane,[1] matching French in colour and excelling it in fragrance? Had he not with this water quenched the fire in my heart, life would have left me, and the raging thirst of my soul would have laid me low.

> Long had I wandered on from door to door
> Seeking a flask of wine or two—no more.

[1] Presumably rum.

Mahesh Das brought me that immortal draught
Sikandar spent his days in seeking for.

Justice is not to be denied, and what I have seen, I cannot fail to speak. This
virtuous man has spared no effort that the Muslims might be allowed to return
to their homes. But heaven's decree was against him. . . . The Hindus' freedom
to return, all know to have come from the kindness of kind rulers, though in this
too the works of this man, who loves good and does good and wishes the good
well, have played their part. In short he is a good man, who does good to his
fellow men and leads a good life amid music and wine. Our acquaintance is not
of long standing; yet we talk whenever we chance to meet, and from time to
time he sends me a gift; and for both these things I am indebted to him; indeed
he does all that kindness could demand. Amongst my other friends and shagirds
is Hira Singh, a young man of good heart and of good name; he is very kind to
me. He comes to see me and beguiles my sorrow. Among others in this half-
desolate, half-peopled city, is that wise young man of illustrious birth, Shiv Ji
Ram Brahman. He is like a son to me. He knows my stricken heart, and seldom
leaves me all alone, but serves me with all the resources at his command and
prospers all my works. His son too, Balmukand, is at one with his father, ever
ready in service and unequalled in sympathy. Among the friends who are far
from me is that full moon in the sky of love and kindness, that sweetly-speaking
poet Hargopal Tufta, my old friend, a man of one spirit and one voice with
me. Since he calls me his master in poetry, his verse and all its God-given
excellence is a source of pride to me. In short, he is a man free in spirit, love
embodied, and kindness incarnate. Poetry is the source of his fame and he the
source of poetry's flourishing. In my abundant love for him I have taken him
into my heart and soul and dubbed him "Mirza Tufta".[1] He has sent me money
from Meerut, and is always sending me letters and ghazals.

'I had no need to record these things, but I have been at pains to do so, for
I wished to render thanks to God for my friends' love and human kindness. . . .'

The other source of comfort to him during the first six months of the year was
the steady successes of the British in crushing the revolt in its remaining centres.
He records his satisfaction at every fresh victory—on February 20th, when a
salute of twenty-one guns 'roaring like the giants of the land and the monsters
of the deep', celebrated the success of a major attack on the rebels at Lucknow;
on Wednesday, February 24th, when the Chief Commissioner, ' . . . upright
cypress of the garden of justice, bright moon of the skies of splendour . . .
commander of forces bright and innumerable as the stars, rode into Delhi . . .
while the voice of thirteen guns brought to men's grieving hearts the news of
coming balm of mercy and kindness, and the universal rejoicing made one think
that the days of Shahjahan had returned;' on Thursday, March 18th, when 'the

[1] Mirza is strictly speaking the form of address appropriate to men of Mughal (Turkish) stock,
such as Ghalib himself. It was also conferred as a title by the Mughal emperors.

azure vault of the sky rang with the voice of the guns, bringing the glad news of the expected recovery of Lucknow'; in early May, when Muradabad was taken and handed over to Nawwab Yusuf Ali Khan [of Rampur]; and with special satisfaction on June 22nd, when Gwalior was taken from the rebels.

'On June 22nd, a Tuesday, which is the day of Mars, the hours of that planet's influence had not yet passed and the lord of day . . . had not yet risen a lance's height from the eastern horizon, when the furious voices of the guns that roar to heaven—guns equal in number to the days of June already passed—caused the hearts of their friends to leap in their breasts from excess of joy, and rained on the heads and faces of their enemies ashes more hot than blazing fire. [They announced] the taking of the city of Gwalior, that fort of stones . . . carved from the mountain's heart.'

Ghalib seems to have seen this as sealing the fate of the revolt.

'It seems that all signs now proclaim the evident end of these lost men, who had fled from all directions to gather in Gwalior, and have now suffered such patent defeat. For some days more, broken and desperate, they will range the land, raiding and robbing on the roads, to meet in the end at every point, degradation and destruction. You will see their horses coursing the grassless deserts until they stumble and their breasts scrape the ground as they breathe their last. You will find their equipment weltering in the mud of flowing watercourses. Then Hindustan will be swept clear of thorns and straw, and every corner of the waste will bloom with luxuriant verdure, and every by-lane shine with the radiance of prosperity.'

But the over-all tone of *Dastambu*, and of most of his letters of this period, is not one of rejoicing. The passage of *Dastambu* quoted above, in which he says that he has written about the kindness of his Hindu friends because 'I wished to render thanks to God for my friends' love and human kindness' continues without a break,

'. . . and because I desired that when this tale reached my friends they should know that the city is empty of Muslims. No light burns in their homes at night, and no smoke rises from them by day. Ghalib, who knows this city, who had a thousand friends, who had a friend in every home and an acquaintance in every house, now dwells in loneliness with none but the voice of his pen to speak with him and none but his shadow to bear him company.

> My face is pale; only the tears of blood
> Bring colour to the cheeks whence colour fled.

My soul and heart are grief and fear entire
And briars and thorns the texture of my bed.

Had not these four men [i.e. the Hindu friends mentioned earlier] been in the city there would have been none even to witness my helplessness.'

His letters express his feelings more fully—his grief for the loss of his dead friends, the loneliness which oppresses him in his enforced isolation from those who still survive, and (what receives little or no emphasis in *Dastambu*) his continuing fears for his own position. On January 19, 1858 he tells Hakim Ghulam Najaf Khan:

'So far we are still alive—I and my wife and the children—but no one knows what may happen from one hour to the next. When I take up my pen there is a lot I should like to write. But I cannot write it. If we are fated to meet again I will tell you about it all. And if not, then "Verily we are for God and verily to Him we shall return." I heard about [the death of] the little girl. May Almighty God keep her mother safe, and give her patience to bear her loss. I look upon it as the little girl's good fortune. . . .'

A letter to Tufta dated January 30, 1858 speaks of his position *vis-à-vis* the British authorities. It is still the same, he says: the authorities know that he is in Delhi, but he has not been sent for. He goes on:

'. . . and I on my side have made no move either. I have not been to see any of the authorities, or written to them and made any application to them. I haven't received my pension since May. Judge for yourself how I have passed the last ten months. I cannot tell how it will all end. I am alive, but life is a burden to me. Hargobind Singh has come here, and has visited me once.'

But now Tufta was able to send him money from time to time. In a letter written only four days later he acknowledges a gift of a hundred rupees:

'Late in the afternoon of Wednesday, February 3rd the postman brought me a registered letter. I opened it and found your draft or bill, or whatever you call it, for Rs. 100 inside. I sent off the servant with the receipt with my seal on it, and in little more than the time it takes to get there and back, he was back with a hundred rupees in coin. I had borrowed twenty four . . . so I repaid that, gave fifty to my wife, and put the remaining twenty-six in my box; and as I had to open the box to do so, I wrote this letter at the same time. Kalian [Ghalib's servant] has gone to the shops. If he is back soon I will send him to post this letter today. Otherwise it will be tomorrow. May God reward you and keep you. These are evil days, my friend, and I cannot see them ending well. In short, everything is finished.'

Only two days later he had fresh cause to feel alarmed and depressed. *Dastambu* tells us:

'It seems to have occurred to the ruler of the capital [the Commissioner], perhaps at the prompting of black-hearted informers, that the houses of the physicians of Raja Narendar Singh had become a rallying centre and place of refuge for the Muslims. (And indeed it may well have been that this concourse harboured one or two fugitive rebels.) Accordingly on Tuesday, February 2nd, he came with a band of soldiers, and without doing them violence, took away the owners of the houses along with . . . some others. For several nights and days they were held in custody, but without dishonour to honourable men. On Friday, February 5th, orders were issued that Hakim Mahmud Khan and Hakim Murtaza Khan, with their cousin Abdul Hakim Khan, known as Hakim Kale, should be permitted to return home. On the Friday following, February 12th, a few more, and then on Saturday 13th three more, also returned. But more than half of those who had been taken were still detained.[1] My wounded heart could not be proof against my neighbours' troubles . . . and though in these arrests I was not questioned, I have not slept soundly by night or lived carefree by day from that day to this; and my care is not without cause.'

His anxiety is reflected in the letters which he wrote during these days. On February 7th he writes to Majruh:

'Today is Sunday, February 7th—i.e., I think, the 22nd of Jamadi us Sani 1270 AH. About midday Shaikh Musharraf Ali, who lives In Ustad Hāmid's Lane, came to bring me your letter dated 15th Jamadi us Sani. The letter you sent through the post never reached me; and yet I have not been out of the city, and am still living just where I was. God knows why your letter was returned to you. I ask you, is it possible that I should get a letter from you and send it back? You say yourself that "Addressee not here" was written on it. If it had reached me would I have written on it that I was not here? I regularly receive letters from Agra and Alwar and Aligarh.

'I was very distressed to hear of your mother's death. God grant you patience to bear it, and forgive her her sins. My brother too, Mirza Yusuf Khan, died insane.

'My pension? What prospect have I of getting that? I shall be lucky to survive—

A raging sea of blood lies in my path—
would that were all!
Time may show perils more than this
rise to confront me still.[2]

---

[1] The remainder were ultimately released, but not until April.
[2] Ghalib here quotes a couplet from one of his own ghazals.

If I live, and the day comes when we can again sit together, you shall hear my story. You write that you want to come here. If you do, don't come without a permit. You write that Mir Ahmad Ali Sahib is here. I don't know where. He would have done well to come and see me. I am not in hiding or living here secretly. The authorities know I am here; but I have neither been interrogated nor arrested; nor have I made any attempt to see them. All the same I am not out of danger yet. We must wait and see how it will all end. . . .

'Maikash[1] is enjoying himself, using his plausible tongue as he wanders around. He was in Sultan Ji; now he is in the city, and has been to see me two or three times. But he hasn't been for the last five days or so. He told me he had sent his wife and boy to Mir Wazir Ali in Bahrampur. He himself goes around buying up looted books. I was glad to hear that Miran Sahib is safe and sound; but you didn't say whether his family is with him or whether he is on his own there. If he is on his own, where is his family? Your younger brother, I know, is here and is well. Why didn't you write any news of your elder brother? I have not had much to do with him, but I regard you and him alike as my own sons. Don't hesitate to write to me, or have any qualms about sending your letters by post.'

On February 8, 1858, he wrote to Saqib:

'I got the letter you sent by Hakim Mahmud Khan's servant, and was glad to learn that you are safe and well. Be reasonable! Where would I find any books? The loot has been sold off in holes and corners, and even if it had been sold in the street, where would I have had the chance to see it? Be patient and say no more about it. . . .

'People are entering and leaving the city now. God grant that you get news from time to time of what is happening here. If we survive it and are fated to meet again I will tell you everything. Otherwise, to put it briefly, everything is finished. I am afraid to write anything, and what is there, anyway, that one would feel any pleasure in writing about? . . .'

In a letter to his old friend Hatim Ali Beg Mihr, undated, but written perhaps about this time, he suddenly breaks off and exclaims,

'Alas for Major John Jacob! What a fine man met his death. . . . He too is one of those whom I mourn. Thousands of my friends are dead—I cannot bear to think how many—and none is left to hear my lamentation. If I live, there is none to share my sorrow, and if I die there will be none to mourn me.'

February 27th brought a faint gleam of hope in that on that day, it seems, the authorities announced their readiness to receive petitions. But hope is hardly the keynote of Ghalib's entry in *Dastambu*:

[1] Cf. p. 129 above.

F

'The order to "Stand back" was withdrawn; sorrowing men who sought justice . . . were permitted to draw near. Know that in Delhi now the cells within the city and the jails without are so swollen with men that it seems that they meet and merge. None but the Angel of Death can tell the number of those from both jails that have . . . gone to the gallows. You will not find more than a thousand Muslims in the city, and of that thousand the writer of these words is one. Of those who took to flight some have fled so far that one would think that they had never inhabited this earth. Many men of high rank encircle the city four to five miles off, and lie waiting in mounds and pits and huts and houses of mud, half-sleeping like their fortunes.[1] Of these dwellers in the wilderness some are those who wish to enter the city, some the kinsmen of those in custody, some who like pensioners live on scraps. In all their petitions they beg for nothing more than the alms of release from jail, or return to their homes, or re-issue of their pensions. Already there are two to three thousand petitions before the courts. The petitioners' eyes are on the road and their ears alert to see and hear what may befall.'

Ghalib was one of them. In February, when the news came that the Chief Commissioner, Sir John Lawrence, would shortly visit Delhi, he had written:

'It has always been my custom to present an ode in his praise to every ruler who comes to govern this country, and especially to this city. I therefore wrote in the praise of this man of high splendour a ghazal on the theme of spring, congratulating him on his victories and singing of the freshness of the breezes of the unfolding season, and sent it off by post on Friday, February 19th.'

Hence he now writes:

'And my heart too is not pure of the desire for reply to the humble petition which I despatched by post. Sundry misgivings have so far prevented me from presenting myself at the Commissioner's house and seeking a meeting with him. In short, sorrows beset me like piercing thorns. . . .'

He at length received a reply to his letter of humble submission. First, on March 8th, it was returned to him, with instructions to re-submit it through the Commissioner of Delhi. He complied, adding a note asking that his pension be restored to him. 'On Wednesday, March 17th, from the Commissioner's headquarters came his command—that there was no call whatever for a letter comprising nothing but praise and congratulation.' One cannot help thinking that it was with his tongue in his cheek that he wrote the words which immediately follow: 'And I too reflected, "In these turbulent days what room indeed is there for kindness and humanity and praise and congratulation?" I am a slave to my belly; I need to eat. Let us see what response my second petition is thought to merit.'

[1] Cf. note to p. 139 above.

A little later he writes,

'Since March 22nd a sadness haunts my distraught soul: the world once held a month of Farwardin[1] and a day of Nauroz,[2] and that radiant day used to dawn among the todays and tomorrows of this time of year. But this year this city is perhaps a city of the silent,[3] for I do not hear the cries of welcome to greet the coming of spring. . . . But the sun has not forgotten to sojourn in the mansion of the Ram, that the grass may not grow and the flowers may not bloom. No, the order of nature does not change and the heavens may not revolve in any path but that ordained for them. My tears are for myself, not for the garden; my lamentations for my fate, not for the spring.

> The rose's scent, the tulip's colour,
> fill the world
> While I lie pinned beneath the heavy
> rock of care.
> The spring has come, but what have
> I to greet it with?
> Helpless, I close my door, that none may
> enter there.

I weep and think to myself how heedless is my fate, that I must sit sorrowing in a corner, with my face turned to the wall and may not see the greenery and the flowers, nor let the fragrance of the rose pervade the senses of my soul. Yet the radiant spring is not less radiant for that, and I may not claim recompense from the breeze.'

All the same, not all the letters, even in this period, reflect anxiety and dejection. While some were clearly written under emotional strain, others show that there were times when Ghalib's troubles weighed less heavily upon him. The letters themselves show his varying moods, and little or no comment is called for. On March 5, 1858 he writes to Mihr:

> 'Complaint itself bears witness that the
> pain has passed.
> The heart's pain comes out through the
> tongue, and finds release.

My friend, your humble servant does not take your complaint ill. But complaint is an art which no one knows but I. The excellence of a complaint consists in this: not to turn one's face from the truth, and not to leave the other person any scope for a rejoinder. Can I not make rejoinder to you that I had

---

[1] The first month of the Persian calendar. The 1st of Farwardin falls on the 20th, 21st, or 22nd of March.
[2] The Persian New Year's Day.　　　[3] The regular metaphor for a graveyard.

been told that you were going to Farrukhabad and so did not write? Can I not say that I wrote you several letters during this period, and all of them were returned to me? What you write is no complaint against me; you are simply laying your own sins at my door. When you left you sent me no word of where you were going, and when you got there you sent no word of where you were staying. Yesterday your kind letter arrived, and today I am sending you one in reply. Do I not then live up to my claims? It is not well to harrass the afflicted too much. You are displeased with Mirza Tufta simply because he has not written to you. I do not even know where he is these days, but I have today put my trust in God and written to him at Sikandarabad. Let us see what we shall see.'

Somewhere about the same time he writes to Hakim Ghulam Najaf Khan:

'Wake up, brother? When did I ever enclose a letter? And when did I ever write that I was forwarding a letter from Sher Zaman? It was just a joke. Sher Zaman in his letter to me had asked me to pay his respects and I said I was enclosing them in my letter. That was all. You have received his respects, wrapped up, so to speak, in my letter to you. So put your mind at rest.'

Tufta had evidently written to enquire whether he might send his verses for Ghalib to correct. Ghalib replies on April 12, 1858:

'Why do you ask whether you should send me your verses? Send them and think nothing of it, no matter whether there are four folios[1] or twenty. I am no longer a writing poet—only a poet-critic. Like an old wrestler who is only fit to teach others the holds. Don't think I am posing. I have altogether lost the ability to write, and when I see what I wrote in former days I am at a loss to understand how I could do it. But anyway, send me the folios soon.'

Tufta must have done so, for Ghalib writes again on April 25th:

'The postman brought the packet you sent me. . . . I am on my own, and have nothing to do all day long. I read it all attentively and thoroughly enjoyed myself. I tell you truly, your verses have delighted me. Long may you live! . . .'

On April 20, 1858 he writes to Majruh:

'The post brought me two letters from you. Yesterday shortly after midday a stranger—a dark-complexioned man, with a trimmed beard and big eyes— came with a letter from you. In due course I asked him his name. He told me, "Ashraf Ali". I asked his community, and was told he was a Sayyid.[2] His

---

[1] The Urdu word usually means a section of a book, consisting of eight leaves.
[2] A descendant of the Prophet through his daughter Fatima.

profession? He was a hakim. In short, Hakim Ashraf Ali. I was very pleased
to make his acquaintance. A nice man, and a resourceful man too. What a
mean fellow you are! *"Mustalihat ush Shuara"*, *"Mustalihat ush Shuara"*!
Yes, brother, the book is yours. I haven't misappropriated it; I've borrowed it;
when I've finished with it I'll return it. Why do you keep pestering me for it?
...'

In April 1858 he writes to Hakim Ghulam Najaf Khan:

'Hakim Sahib[1] was kind enough to call upon me one day. I cannot express the
heartfelt pleasure it gave me. May God grant him long life! Practically none of
my friends and acquaintances survived this upheaval; and for that reason those
that are still left are very dear to me. And now I pray to God that none of
them may die before me. For if I die there should be someone left in the world
to remember me and weep for me.'

About the same time, he writes to his young friends Shihab ud Din Khan and
Ghulam Najaf Khan; it seems they had been planning to bring out a fresh
edition of his diwan, and had sent specimen verses for him to see. It produced
an explosion:

'Brother Shihab ud Din Khan, what in God's name have you and Hakim
Ghulam Najaf Khan done to my diwan? God knows what child of adultery has
inserted the verses you have sent me. After all, the diwan is printed. If these
verses are in the text they are mine, and if they are entered in the margin they
are not mine. And if they do occur in the text the explanation is that some pimp
has scratched out the original verses and written in this trash. In short, curses
upon the scoundrel who wrote these verses, and on his father, and on his
grandfather and on all his bastard ancestors back to the seventieth generation.
What more than that can I say? What with you, and the boy Miyan Ghulam
Najaf, misfortune has come upon me in my old age that my verse has fallen into
your hands.

'After I had written these lines your letter came. I had already heard of this
second misfortune. It is all the doing of fate, and leaves no room for complaint.
Let us hope that permission will soon be granted you to return to your estates
so that you may all be re-united and live in peace. Tell your calligrapher not
to include that trash in his text, and if he has already written these two pages,
make him take them out and substitute new pages, written out afresh. You had
better send someone to me with the diwan that your calligrapher has written,
so that I can look through it and send it back. Well, that's all. I am sorry, but
today I haven't got either a stamp or the money to buy one. ...'

Having vented his wrath, he did not harbour any malice. In his next letter,

[1] Hakim Ahsanullah Khan.

dated April 12th he writes, 'I got your letter. There was nothing in it that called for a reply, but then I thought you might be upset if I didn't write, so today I am writing to you. . . .'

The same month he writes to Hakim Ghulam Najaf Khan:

'I expect you have heard about Mustafa Khan [Shefta]. God grant he may be released when the sentence comes up for review; for how can one who has lived in luxury stand a seven-year prison-sentence? Have you heard the news about Ahmad Husain Maikash? He has been hanged—as though there was no one else of that name in Delhi.'

The implication of the last sentence is, perhaps, that someone named Ahmad Husain (which is a common name) had been wanted for a capital offence, and that because this was Maikash's name, the authorities had assumed it was he. Ghalib continues in the same despondent tone:

'I have applied for my pension to be renewed. But even if it is, how far will it go? True, there are two points about it—first, it will mean I am cleared of suspicion, and secondly, as the people say, "I shan't starve". . . . I get some pleasure from Bedil's lines:

> Our evenings bring no tidings of a coming morn;
> Our mornings show no glimmer of the dawn's white grace;
> When all our strivings end in nothing but despair
> Take the earth's dust and fling it into heaven's face.

I felt like talking to you, and I have told you what I was feeling. I have nothing more to write now.'

In April 1858 he fell ill. On May 24th he writes to Tufta:

'After I had sent you my last letter I fell ill, so ill in fact that I thought I should die. It was the colic, and so bad an attack that it had me writhing in pain the whole day long. In the end I took gamboge and castor oil. For the moment I am better, but this is not the end of the story. I will put it briefly. You know the sort of meal I eat when I am in good health? Well, in ten days, on two occasions only, I ate half that amount—in other words, I regaled myself on one full meal in ten days. Mainly I lived on rosewater and essence of tamarind and juice of Persian plums. Yesterday I no longer felt that I should die, and it began to look as though I might survive. This morning I have taken my medicine and written you this letter, and I am sure that today I shall be able to eat my fill. . . .

'Well, are brother Munshi Nabi Bakhsh Sahib and Maulvi Qamar ud Din

Khan Sahib still absorbed in their fasting, or have they recovered consciousness now? Today is the 10th of Shawwal,[1] 1274 AH. Even the day to break the Shasha fast[2] has gone by. For God's sake write and tell me how they are. And submit this epistle to our brother's radiant gaze. Perhaps he'll write to me.'

To Majruh he writes in May:

'Well, my friend, what do you say? Am I a man to reckon with or am I not? When I read your letter I recited this verse two hundred times:

> The time when we shall meet draws near;
> Affection's flame burns brighter.

I sent Kallu [Ghalib's servant] to Maulvi Mazhar Ali Sahib with a message not to go out anywhere, as I was coming to see him. That was a smart move, wasn't it? After all he's not my father's servant, to come when I send for him. But he sent back word that I must not trouble myself, and that he would come to me. And so he did, within an hour or so. . . .

'Listen, I've discovered the knack of living without eating, so put your mind at ease on that score. During Ramzan I ate every day; and for the future, God will provide. If I can't get anything else I'll feed on sorrow. Well then, so long as there is something to feed on, even if it is only grief, why should I grieve?

'Give Mir Sarfaraz Husain a hug and a kiss for me. Give my blessing to Mir Nasīr ud Din and my greetings to Mir Ahmad Ali Sahib. To Miran Sahib I send neither greeting nor blessing; give him this letter to read and then send him on his way here. I've just had a good idea. There is no need for him to stay outside the city and wait for me to send for him. He can come in a carriage, a coach, a conveyance—that is, by the mail, and get off right by my house in Ballimaron muhalla. Maulvi Mazhar Ali lives in Mirza Qurban Ali Beg's house, and there is only Mir Khairati's mansion between his house and mine. Nobody dares to hold up the mail. If he acts on this plan and sets out as soon as this letter arrives he can still be here in time for Id.'

However, he seems to have had second thoughts about this last suggestion, for in a letter to Sarur—undated, but almost certainly written shortly after this —he says:

'I learned of how you had proposed to come here, and how at your uncle's advice you had postponed your intended visit because of the great heat. Your uncle's dissuasion was something of a miracle. If you had travelled by the mail you would have reached my house, but it would have been dangerous to stay

---

[1] The month which follows Ramzan.
[2] A period of six days in Shawwal when some Muslims fast.

in the city without first obtaining permission from the authorities. Had the matter not come to their knowledge, then of course all would have been well; but if they should come to know of such a thing, there would be trouble. On no account should you make the mistake of thinking that things are run here as they are in Meerut and Agra and the eastern areas. This comes under the Panjab, and there is neither law nor constitution. Anyone in authority may do exactly as he thinks fit. But anyway:

> I grieve because I cannot see my friends
> And for no other thing.

God willing, there will be peace and order here too in another two or three months. . . .'

We may note in passing that he speaks later in the same letter of the care he takes with verse sent to him for correction: 'I have, as usual, noted by each correction the reason I have made it.'

On June 19, 1858 he writes to Tufta:

'Well, what is it, Sahib? Why are you angry with me? It must be a month since I heard from you—or it will be in a day or two. Work it out for yourself. You know how many friends I had, and how I was never without two or three of them around me. And now there are only two—Shiv Ji Ram Brahman and his son Balmukand, who visit me from time to time. Then I would always be getting letters—from Lucknow, and Kalpi, and Farrukhabad and I don't know where else. And now I don't even know what has happened to all the friends who used to write them; I neither know where they are nor how they are faring. The old stream of letters has dried up. There are only you three[1] that I can expect to write, and two of you only occasionally. You, it is true, usually favour me once or twice a month. Listen Sahib, make it a binding rule to write to me once a month. If you have occasion to, write twice or three times. Otherwise just post off a line to tell me how you are. . . . If you are not cross with me answer this letter the day after it reaches you. Let me know how you are, and how Munshi Sahib [Nabi Bakhsh Haqir] is, and how Maulvi Sahib [Qamar ud Din Khan] is. Also be sure to tell me, in words suited to the needs of the times, whatever you know about the disturbances at Gwalior . . . and what the situation is in Agra. Are the people there afraid at all, or not?'

At the end of June—immediately after an entry for June 22nd—comes an entry in *Dastambu* recording his feelings as he enters his sixty-fourth year reckoned by the Muslim calendar:

[1] Ghalib means Tufta, Nabi Bakhsh Haqir, and Maulvi Qamar ud Din Khan.

'Sixty-three years of my life have passed, and the infinite woes which cease-lessly beset me proclaim the impertinence of looking to fate to grant me many more years of life; and involuntarily I hear the pleasing voice of the poet of Shiraz [Sadi], on whose shining spirit be all my blessings, singing the lines of his enchanting verse; and as one mourner draws consolation from another, his melody brings me, not happiness to be sure, but a moment's release from the bonds of grief:

> Alas for all those springs and all those flowers
> The world will look upon when we are gone!
> Springs, summers, winters—all will come and go
> When we are mingled in the dust and stone.'

On June 26, 1858, he writes to Tufta, who was busy at this time, it appears, with getting his diwan printed:

'God give you long life and happiness! . . .

God give you joy, because you gave me joy!

What gives me most joy is that you have made writing perform the function of speech. I already knew of all your busy activities in getting your diwan printed and so on. All your money in the bank will go on paper and calligraphy.
    'Well, God preserve you! People like you are precious these days. I am very fond of the verse which Rajab Ali Beg Sarur puts at the head of his story *Fasana i Ajaib* (The Tale of Wonders):

> Men such as we bring glory to an age.
> Remember us, the story of an age!

. . . I'd already heard of the birth of a son to Munshi Abdul Latif [Nabi Bakhsh Haqir's son] and sent a letter of congratulations . . . . Things with me are just as usual:

> The same old heart, the same old bed,
>   the same old pain.'

On July 18, 1858 he again writes to Tufta:

'Why haven't you written all this time? . . . I liked our friend Qasim Ali Khan's verse very much. By a lucky coincidence the letter came at an auspicious time. A few days earlier I had given a man a Persian cloak and a two-and-a-half-yard shawl to sell, and he brought me the money just as the letter arrived. I took the money and read the letter and had a good laugh to think at what a happy time it had come.'

F*

To Hakim Ghulam Najaf Khan, probably in July 1858, he writes:

'Have you made any plans to come to Delhi? . . . My dear boy, you know my
position. It's not as though I were here without the government's permission;
and I cannot leave Delhi without a permit. So what can I do? How can *I* visit
you?'

On August 8, 1858 he writes to Majruh:

'Mir Ashraf Ali gave me your letter. You write that the letter I wrote you was
delivered to someone else of the same name. That's *your* fault. Why do you
live in a city where there's another Mir Mahdi?[1] Look at me. In all the time I've
lived in Delhi, I've never allowed anyone else of the same name, or nickname,
or takhallus to live here. That's all there is to it.'

We have seen that as soon as circumstances permitted, Ghalib had raised the
question of his pension with the British authorities. A letter to Tufta on March
12th adds a little to the account already quoted from *Dastambu*:

'Let me tell you what has been happening. My petition came before the Chief
Commissioner, Sir Henry Lawrence. He wrote on it that it should be returned,
with the documents attached, to the petitioner, who should be instructed to
submit it through the Commissioner of Delhi. Now the proper course would
have been for the office superintendent to write me a formal letter. This was
not done, but the petition, with the Chief Commissioner's instruction written
on it, was returned to me. I wrote a letter to Mr Charles Saunders, the Commissioner of Delhi, and enclosed the petition with it. The Commissioner sent
it to the Collector, with orders to send him particulars of my pension. The case
is now before the Collector, but so far he has not carried out his instructions.
The matter came before him two days ago. We must wait and see whether he
makes any enquiry of me or just sends his own personal opinion. There can
hardly be any past papers there for him to consult. At all events, thanks be to
God that nothing has been found in the royal papers which implicates me in
the disorders, and that I have a clean enough record with the authorities to
warrant their asking for the particulars of my pension. . . .'

But the months passed by, and nothing more happened to encourage his hopes.
His last entry in *Dastambu*, made at the end of July, shows to what straits he
was reduced. Not only had every regular source of income ceased, but his wife's
jewellery—traditionally the very last reserve of an Indian family—was gone.
He writes:

'I marvel at the varied wonders of Fate. In the days of killing and looting, when

---

[1] Majruh's name. (Majruh is a takhallus.)

it seemed that every house in the city was emptied even of its dust, my house escaped the looters' grasping hands. Yet I swear even so that nothing but clothes to wear and bedding to sleep upon was left to me. The answer to this riddle and the key to this false-seeming truth is this: that at the time when the black rebels seized the city, my wife, without telling me, gathered her jewels and valuables and sent them secretly to the house of Kale Sahib.[1] There they were stored in the cellar, and the door of the cellar blocked up with clay and smoothed over. When the British soldiers took the city and were given leave to loot and kill, my wife revealed this secret to me. Now there was nothing to be done; to go there and bring them back was impossible. I said nothing and comforted myself with the thought that we were destined to lose these things and that it was well that they had not been taken from our own home. And now it is July—the fifteenth month—and I see no sign that I shall again receive the pension which the British government formerly granted me. And so I sell the clothes and bedding to keep body and soul together, and a man might say that where others eat bread, I eat cloth. I go in fear that when all the cloth is eaten I shall die naked and hungry. Of the servants who had long been with me there are some few who even in this tumult did not desert me. These too I must feed, for in truth, man may not turn his back on man, and I too need them to serve my needs. Besides these are those suppliants who in former days laid claim to a share in the gleanings of my harvest. Even in these bad times they cry to me, and their cry, more unwelcome than the cock's untimely crow, pierces my heart and adds to my distress. And now that these raging sicknesses and sorrows which oppress my body and soul have sapped all my strength and spirit, the thought comes suddenly to my mind, "How long can I occupy myself adorning this toy I call a book?" For this distress must end either in death or in beggary. In the first case, this tale must needs for evermore lack an ending . . . and so sadden its readers' hearts. And in the second case, the one clear outcome is that I must raise the beggar's cry from door to door, here gathering a crumb, there driven with abuse from the lane and humiliated in the open street. And for how long should I tell such a tale, myself spreading the fame of my disgrace? Now even if my pension is restored it cannot wipe clean the mirror of my heart, and if it is not, that mirror will itself be shattered, as by a stone. And . . . whichever may befall, the air of this city will be noxious to such ruined ones as I, and I must go and live in some strange land. From May of last year to July of this I have written what has befallen, and from the 1st August I stay my pen.'

He then expresses the hopes which even now he entertains, of a title, a robe of honour, and a pension granted by Queen Victoria's grace, and adds thirty-four lines of verse in her praise. The final paragraph reads:

'After completing this book I named it *Dastambu* (A Posy of Flowers), and

[1] Cf. p. 71 above.

sent it from hand to hand and from place to place to sustain the souls of the learned and steal the hearts of the eloquent. And it is my hope that this handful of the flowers of learning may be a posy of colour and fragrance in the hands of the God-fearing, and a globe of flame in the sight of them that are of Satanic nature. . . .'

However, on August 7th something happened which raised his hopes once more. He tells Majruh in a letter of August 8, 1858:

'The position about my pension is that the chief of police had been asked to furnish particulars. He reported favourably. Yesterday, Saturday August 7th, Mr Edgerton sent for me and put a few simple questions to me. It looks as though I may get the pension. The only question is, shall I get the fifteen months' arrears as well, or shall I only get it from now on?

'There has been some progress in the case of Ghulam Fakhr ud Din Khan, and the outlook seems favourable. God willing, he will be released. Sahib, I have got tired of that Persian work [*Dastambu*] and have brought it to a close. I have written that it contains an account of the fifteen months to August 1st, 1858, and is now concluded.'

The mention of the pension and of *Dastambu* in the same letter is significant. We have seen that whatever Ghalib's original intention may have been when he started writing it, he had at some stage conceived the idea of using it as a means of inclining the British authorities favourably towards him. It was after all a work of great virtuosity, such as a poet aspiring to win the patronage of the great could present with justified pride, and most of Ghalib's letters in which he refers to it regard it in this light.

Now having completed the book, he became increasingly keen to put his plan into effect. From August to early November his letters are full of it, and it is clear that the more he thought about it, the more important he thought it to be as a means to the recovery of his pension. By September 3, 1858 he is writing to Tufta, whose help he had sought in this connection, that the task with which he has entrusted him is 'one in which my whole being is involved, so many are the aims which I hope to achieve through it. In God's name I beg you not to regard it indifferently; put your whole heart into it.' During these months he is quick to note every sign that his standing with the British is improving. In a letter of September 29, 1858 he writes to Mihr:

'I do not know Mr Edmonstone by sight, as I have never seen him; but I have made his acquaintance by letter, because whenever a new Governor-General comes I send an ode to be presented to him. . . . When Lord Canning was made Governor-General, I posted off the customary ode, and when the Chief Secretary Mr Edmonstone replied, I found that despite the fact that we had never met, he had addressed me with greater honour than before. Up to then

I had been styled "Khan Sahib, our most kind well-wisher"; but Mr Edmonstone, true judge of worth that he is, had written "Khan Sahib, our most kind and affectionate friend". Shall I not then count him my patron and benefactor? I would be an infidel not to recognize where gratitude is due.'

Unfortunately for Ghalib, and perhaps still more unfortunately for his friends, conditions in Delhi in August 1858 were still so far from normal that there could be no question of his having *Dastambu* printed there under his own supervision. He therefore entrusted the task to his friends in Agra, and in the first place to Tufta, writing them repeated letters full of the most detailed instructions, and experiencing every kind of apprehension whenever they neglected to inform him at once how his instructions were being carried out. Extracts from these letters tell their own story.

On August 17, 1858 he writes to Tufta in terms which show that he had not previously told him that he had been writing a book, for he begins by telling him what the book is, and what sort of language it is written in. He goes on:

'I have written in it in the same hand as I am writing this letter—not too closely-written, but not with over-much spacing either, and it is on unlined paper, so that the number of lines to the page varies between nineteen and twenty-two. There are forty pages—i.e. twenty leaves. Closely written, at nineteen lines to a page, you might get it into a book of two sections.[1] There is no press here—or rather, I am told that there is one, but that its calligrapher doesn't write a good hand.[2] If arrangements can be made to print it in Agra, let me know. Short of money as I am, I could pay for twenty-five copies; but no press is going to print as few as that, and anyway we ought to print at least five hundred, if not a thousand. I feel sure that a print of five- to seven-hundred would work out at three or four annas a copy. Only one manuscript will be needed. As for paper, it won't need much. I've already explained about the writing of the text; true, the meanings of words will have to be written in the margins. Anyway, if possible get an estimate and work out the costs and write to me. . . . Be sure to let me have your answer on these points *without fail*. To impress this on you, I am sending this letter unstamped.'

Tufta apparently approached their mutual friend Hatim Ali Beg Mihr about this. Ghalib writes in his next letter:

'Why did you speak to Mirza Hatim Ali Sahib about it? All I had expected was a letter from you telling me that you had shown the work to Mirza Sahib and that he had liked it. As it is, give him my regards, and tell him I express my thanks to him for expressing his thanks to me. I understand what you say about the printing. When you read this letter you will understand. I want it

---

[1] The standard number of pages to a section of an Urdu or Persian book was sixteen.
[2] Urdu books were, and for the most part still are, produced by lithography from a text prepared by a professional calligrapher.

printed carefully and quickly, because I intend to present a copy to the Nawwab Governor-General Bahadur, and, through him, to send another to Her Majesty the Queen of England. . . .'

On August 28, 1858 he sends him good news:

'This letter will be sent to you by my great benefactor Rae Umid Singh Bahadur. As soon as you have read it, go and call on him, and as long as he is there continue to attend upon him, and to carry out all his commands with regard to *Dastambu*. Get him to read it and come to an understanding with him about the price per copy. He will pay the cost of fifty copies. Get that from him, and when the book is printed, send ten copies to him at Indore and forty to me, in accordance with his instructions. Be sure to tell me how matters stand with regard to the five *de luxe* copies I wrote to you about.'

In the same letter he gives him detailed instructions about inserting a rubai which he had inadvertently omitted from the manuscript.

The arrangements which Tufta and his friends were making on his behalf brought him into contact with Munshi Shiv Narayan Aram, an enterprising young man in his twenties who published a newspaper from Agra and owned a press. It appears that Aram's first letter to Ghalib was a request to see what he could do to get subscribers to his paper in Delhi; he also asks Ghalib to write an ode which he wants to present to an English official, and says that, hearing that Ghalib makes his own envelopes, he is sending off a packet to him to save him the trouble. Ghalib replies:

'I received your letter, and the newspaper, and the news of the envelopes you are sending me. You should not have troubled. Making envelopes keeps me amused. What else has an idle man to do? But, anyway, when they arrive you shall receive my grateful acknowledgements. For:

Whatever comes to us from friends, is good.

Where would I find anyone here to subscribe to your paper? The money-lenders and merchants who inhabit this city go around finding out where they can buy grain most cheaply. If they're exceptionally generous men, they'll weigh you out full measure. What do they want with a paper at a rupee a month?

'Your letter reached me yesterday. All last night I sweated blood to compose your ode, and managed one of twenty-one lines in fulfilment of your order. My friends—Mirza Tufta especially—know that I can't compose chronograms. But in this ode I have found a way of expressing "1858". I hope you will like it. You yourself appreciate poetry, and you have three friends [Tufta, Haqir, and Mihr] who are masters of the art. So my efforts will receive their due meed of praise.'

In his next letter he gets down to business. Aram's letter has just arrived, and he is replying at once. He proceeds to give the most detailed instructions:

'The point is I don't want the book to be of two or four sections only. There should be at least six. There should be ten or eleven lines to the page, with wide margins on three sides and a rather narrower one towards the binding. I have already written all this to Mirza Tufta, but, heedless fellow that he is, he's probably told you nothing. Also the text should be correct; there must be no need for a list of errata; you please attend to this yourself.'

Then follow instructions on what kind of paper is to be used and much more. Then:

'Someone who will buy fifty copies has come to Agra. For God's sake tell Mirza Tufta to go and see him—Raja Umid Singh Bahadur of Indore. He lives in Chali Int, at the back of the police station. It's surprising that your letter has come but that Mirza Tufta hasn't acknowledged receipt of the parcel. . . . Please tell him to go and see Raja Umid Singh; and oh yes! impress upon him to be sure without fail to insert the rubai I sent him—[here he repeats the detailed instructions which he had given Tufta only three days earlier]. You remind him, and see that he writes to me without fail.

'I was astonished to read in your letter that the Sahib[1] had liked it when you read it to him. ["It" presumably means *Dastambu*.] I can't think what part of it you must have read to him, because I can't imagine that he would understand this kind of writing. Write to me about it in detail.'

The tone of anxious impatience becomes stronger in succeeding letters, and, along with it, an anxiety not to offend the friends on whom he is depending and an occasional panic fear that he *has* offended them and that all is lost. On September 1, 1858 he writes to Tufta:

'Sahib, this is a strange state of affairs! I wrote to Munshi Shiv Narayan Sahib at your instance, and yesterday received a letter from him acknowledging the receipt of *Dastambu*. He can't have received it through the post. *You* must have sent it to him. So how is it that *you* didn't acknowledge receiving it and didn't answer my letter? Even if I assume that you were waiting until after you'd called on Raja Umid Singh, you must have done that too by now. It looks to me as though you've withdrawn from it all; you've handed over the book to the press and aren't concerned any more to see that it is printed correctly and nicely produced. If that is so, I give this edition up for lost, and all I hoped to attain by it will vanish. But why should you behave like that? I can only think

---

[1] Presumably some English official—perhaps the one for whom Ghalib had written the ode.

you must be cross with me. For God's sake write and tell me why. I am sending off this letter this morning, Wednesday, September 1st. If I get a letter from you by this evening, well and good. Otherwise I shall feel convinced of your displeasure, and because I shan't know the cause of it, I shall be in misery. I on my side can't think of any reason for it. For God's sake write quickly, and if you are cross, tell me why.

'I *know* you won't even have called on Rae Umid Singh. God forfend! I am put to shame. I had told him that oh, yes, Mirza Tufta would give him all the help he needed in reading *Dastambu*.

'Since I suspect you are cross and want to be rid of the whole affair, I ought not to ask you to do anything else for me. But what can I do when I have no choice? I *have* to tell you. The proprietor of the press addressed his letter to me "Mirza Nosha Sahib, Ghalib". For God's sake! What an incongruous phrase! I'm only afraid that he'll put the same thing on the title page of the book. Hasn't my Persian diwan or the Urdu one, or *Panj Ahang* or *Mihr i Nimroz* or any other of my printed books ever reached your city? He could have seen my name on them. And you too haven't told him. It's not just because I hate this nickname that I am wailing about it. The point is that the Delhi authorities know it, but from Calcutta to Britain—that is in Ministry departments and in the Queen's entourage—nobody is acquainted with this confounded nickname. So if the proprietor of the press puts "Mirza Nosha Sahib Ghalib" I am lost, finished, and all my efforts will have gone for nothing. They will think the book is by someone else. I write this and think to myself, "Let's see whether he'll pass on the message to the press or not." '

His much-harassed friend must have replied at once, for two days later, on September 3rd, Ghalib writes: 'Thank God you wrote to me and put my mind at rest'—after which he at once goes on to complain! 'You don't read my letters properly. I certainly never said that it should be a book of thirty-two pages. What I said was that it would *go* into thirty-two pages, but that I wanted it to be bigger.' Small wonder that, judging by a later passage in this same letter, Tufta seems to have asked him whether it was *really* impossible for the book to be produced in Delhi under Ghalib's own supervision.

On two other occasions the question of the name and style to be entered on the title page was discussed. On September 3, 1858 Ghalib writes to Tufta:

'Make it clear to Munshi Shiv Narayan that he is not on any account to use my nickname. The name and takhallus are enough. To write my titles [i.e. those conferred on him by the Mughal King] would be not only inappropriate but harmful. But he can put in the word "Bahadur" after my name, and my takhallus after that—"Asadullah Khan Bahadur, Ghalib".' Tufta then asked him whether he should not use his full name—Muhammad Asadullah Khan—and whether the name should be preceded by 'Mirza', 'Maulana' or 'Nawwab'. Ghalib replies on September 17, 1858:

'Listen, sahib; for every letter of that blessed word—*mim, ha, mim, dal*[1]—I would sacrifice my life. But since none of the authorities from here to Britain uses it in addressing me, I too have dropped it. As for "Mirza", "Maulana" and "Nawwab", you and our brother [Hatim Ali Mihr] can use your discretion and write what you like.'

These and other details continue to keep them fully occupied. Ghalib wants two more lines inserted at one point in his manuscript; he discovers that he has inadvertently used an Arabic word; this must be erased and a pure Persian one substituted; and so on and so forth. As one reads his letters one feels that he too deserves sympathy. He gives his instructions in the utmost detail, often taking the precaution of repeating them to two, or even to all three— Tufta, Mihr, and Aram, and regularly closing his letters with a point-by-point recapitulation of what he wants done. And despite all this he cannot get them to tell him whether they have received and understood his directions and acted upon them; while sometimes it is quite clear that they have overlooked or ignored them. Still, their joint efforts have succeeded by mid-October in the book being produced to Ghalib's entire satisfaction. Among the Indians to whom he must have sent it shortly afterwards was the Nawwab of Rampur. From a letter dated November 7, 1858 we gather that he sent him a copy of his Urdu diwan about the same time. Of this he speaks with characteristic in- difference; it is *Dastambu* that he urges the Nawwab to read:

'I learned from your letter that my Urdu diwan, and the book, had reached you. It is for you to decide whether you wish to read the diwan or not; but please be sure to read the book. . . . It is in ancient Persian, and has both beauty of meaning and skill in artistry. And along with these, I have used the utmost care and circumspection in everything I have written.'

The last sentence is significant.

Ghalib was particularly gratified by the care which Mihr had taken with the *de luxe* editions. On October 16, 1858 he had written about them to Tufta: 'Tell Mirza Sahib that my ears have heard of their beauty, but my heart will believe it more readily when my eyes have seen it.' Then, on November 20, 1858:

'Yesterday, Friday 19th November, I received a parcel of seven books from Maulana Mihr. My tongue cannot find words to praise them, they are so regally embellished. . . . It worries me to think that he may have spent his own money on it. You find out about it, there's a good fellow, and let me know.'

He wrote to Mihr himself on the same day:

[1] In the Urdu script short vowels and the doubling of consonants are represented by diacritical marks, not by letters. Hence the letters of the word 'Muhammad' are simply those which Ghalib names—equivalent to 'm h m d'.

'My dear brother, yesterday—blessed and auspicious day—was a Friday, and one which brought me all the joys of Id.[1] An hour and a half before sunset your letter of good tidings came, and an hour and a half later, at sunset:

'A parcel came, containing seven books. . . .

A man can hardly ever hope to attain all that his heart desires, but I have attained it beyond anything I could conceive of. I could never have imagined such a beautiful get-up. . . . As long as the world lasts, may you live on in it! . . . Now I am at a loss to know whether you have invoked the twelve Imams and they have imparted miraculous increase to the twelve rupees I sent, or whether you have spent money of your own. Postage on two parcels, two registration fees, three books with the titles in gold lettering—how could Rs. 12 run to all these things? And how can I find out? Whom am I to ask? God grant me that you will not stand on ceremony and will not hesitate to tell me the position. . . . When men love each other truly, with a religious and spiritual love, there is no room for ceremony. I am most grateful. Your kindness puts me to shame. What more can I write?

Silence alone can praise a thing that is
        beyond all praise.'

Even the harassed weeks and months which had preceded this satisfactory result had yielded their moments of pleasure. Ghalib enjoyed even the sheer volume of the correspondence involved. He writes to Nabi Bakhsh Haqir on September 22, 1858:

'Amidst all these troubles, how I laugh to think that you and I and Mirza Tufta have turned correspondence into conversation.[2] We talk together everyday. By God above! these will be days to remember. What letters upon letters we have written! I spend half my time making envelopes. I am either doing that or writing a letter. It's a good thing that postage is only half an anna. Otherwise we'd have seen what this conversation cost us!'

But there were deeper satisfactions than this. In 1857 Hatim Ali Mihr, with his uncle's help, had saved the lives of seven of the English by giving them shelter in his house. He was now rewarded by the British authorities with an estate of two villages and with other honours. It was probably in this period that Ghalib heard the news and wrote to express his sincere pleasure:

'You showed real courage, and staked your life on it. It is your manly and resolute conduct which has brought you this reward. What more can the world give than wealth with good repute? . . . How well I remember the time when

---

[1] The great day of rejoicing celebrating the end of the month-long fast of Ramzan.
[2] The idea and the turn of phrase clearly appealed to him. He repeats it in a letter of about this time to Mihr.

Mughal[1] spoke to me about you, and how she showed me the verses in praise of her beauty which you had written with your own hand. Now a time has come when letters pass between us. But if God Almighty wills it, the day will come when we shall sit and talk together and lay our pens aside.'

In October he discovered that there had been a long-standing connection between his family and Shiv Narayan Aram's. On October 19, 1858 he writes to him:

'Munshi Shiv Narayan, my son, I had no idea who you were. When I discovered that you were the grandson of Nāzir Bansi Dhar I felt I had discovered a beloved son. From now on if I address you formally I'll count it a sin. You won't know about the relations between my family and yours. Let me tell you.

'Your [paternal] grandfather's father and my [maternal] grandfather Khwaja Ghulam Husain Khan were companions in the days of Najaf Khan[2]. . . . When my grandfather retired from active service and returned home your great-grandfather also retired. This was further back than I can remember. But I can remember when I was a young man seeing my grandfather and yours, Munshi Bansi Dhar, together, and when my grandfather laid his claim for his estate . . . before the government, Munshi Bansi Dhar acted as his agent and managed the whole thing on his behalf. He and I were about the same age—there may have been a year or two's difference one way or the other. Anyway I was about nineteen or twenty and he was about the same. We were close friends and used to play chess together; we would often sit together until late into the night. His house was quite near mine and he used to come and see me whenever he liked. There was only Machia the courtesan's house and the two by-lanes between us. Our big mansion is the one that now belongs to Lakhmi Chand Seth. I used to spend most of my time in the stone summer-house near the main entrance. I used to fly my kite from the roof of a house in one of the lanes nearby and match it against Raja Balwan Singh's. There was a big house called Ghatia Wali, and beyond that another near Salīm Shah's takiya[3] and then another adjoining Kale Mahal and beyond that a lane which used to be called Gadariyon Wala and then another lane called Kashmiran Wala—that was the lane where the house was. Your grandfather had a man named Wāsil Khan who used to collect the rents for him.

'And listen! Your grandfather had made a lot of money. He had bought land and acquired a big estate which paid something like ten or twelve thousand rupees in land revenue to the government. Have you inherited all that? Write to me soon and tell me all about it.'

Of the three most directly concerned with seeing *Dastambu* through the press, it was poor Tufta who came off worst. Ghalib's friendship with him was

---

[1] A courtesan whom Ghalib and Mihr had both known, cf. p. 203 below.
[2] The last imperial minister of any distinction. He died in 1782.   [3] The abode of a faqir.

already of long standing and could bear the greatest strain; and moreover he was Ghalib's pupil in the art of poetry and, as a dutiful pupil, must carry out his master's commands. When Ghalib scolds him he does so bluntly—despite an occasional fear that he may have gone too far. When he addresses Mihr, on the other hand, he is more tactful about it, and adopts a humorous tone. He had asked Mihr to arrange for the regular dispatch of an Agra news-paper to Hakim Ahsanullah Khan, but Mihr had apparently neglected to carry out his instructions. Ghalib writes on September 20, 1858:

'Was it such a difficult matter, that you should not have done as I asked? And if it was, was it difficult to inform me that it was? At present I am not complain-ing; I only ask you whether you don't agree that these things warrant a com-plaint? I have written all about it in a letter to Mirza Tufta. Didn't he show you the letter either? I have racked my brains for some explanation of the delay, but I can't think of one, and now, leaving aside whether my request is carried out or not, I think to myself "Let's see whether I get a letter from Mirza Sahib [Mihr] in the next six months, or the next year, and, if so, what he has to say on the matter. I too am a poet, like him, and if a suitable theme had suggested itself I too would have thought of it." *I* can't think of any excuse worth listening to: let me see what *you* will think up when you write.'

On this occasion he must on the next day have felt profoundly thankful that he had been so tactful. On September 21, 1858 he writes:

'Forgive me that in my simplicity
I sin against you and still ask your praise!

Yesterday morning, Monday 20th September, I wrote a letter reproaching you, and posted it off unstamped. At midday the postman came and brought a letter from you and one from Mirza Tufta. I learned that the letter to which I was demanding a reply had never reached you. I felt ashamed of myself for complain-ing, and, equally at a loss to understand why my letter had not reached you. In the afternoon I opened my box to get a stamp for a letter I had written to Mirza Tufta, and saw a letter addressed to you lying there. I saw what had happened; I had written you the letter, but forgotten to post it. I cursed my forgetfulness and realized that there was nothing I could say. I hope you will forgive me.'

The publication of *Dastambu* seems to have suggested to Shiv Narayan Aram and Tufta the idea of collecting and publishing Ghalib's Urdu letters too. It is interesting to note his reaction. He writes to Aram on November 18, 1858:

'As for your wish to publish the Urdu letters, that too is unnecessary. Hardly any of them were written with proper thought and care, and apart from these few the rest are just what came on the spur of the moment. Their publication would diminish my stature as a writer. And leaving that aside, why should we let others read what only concerns us? In short, I do not want them to be published.'

Tufta must have tried to persuade him, for two days later, on November 20, 1858, he writes again both to him and to Aram. He tells Tufta: 'I don't want the letters to be published. Don't keep on about it like a child. And if nothing else will satisfy you, why ask me? Do as you like. *I* am against it.' And to Aram, a little more politely: 'I have already forbidden you to publish the letters, and you and Mirza Tufta must respect my wishes in the matter.' It is interesting that the reason which Ghalib puts first is that his letters are not good formal prose—which still meant, in his day, the elaborately contrived, rhythmical and rhyming prose based on Persian literary models. This, as we have seen, he could write extremely well; but it never seems to have occurred to him to have attempted anything similar in Urdu, and now he thinks about it, he wonders whether Urdu is capable of producing really good prose at all. In another letter to Aram on December 11, 1858 he refers to a request made to him by Mr Henry Stuart Read to write a book in Urdu prose for use in the schools. (Read was Director of Education in what was later to become United Provinces.)

'But, friend, you can imagine for yourself—if I write in Urdu how can my pen wield its full power, and how can I express the niceties of meaning? I am still wondering what to write. . . . If you have any ideas, write and tell me.'

Later on he was to be persuaded of the literary value of his Urdu letters, and helped to collect copies of them for the collections published in 1868 (the year before his death) and 1869. And there is no doubt that these collections helped to win the battle to make the colloquial Urdu of educated speakers the standard literary language also.

Ghalib's attitude to his Persian prose was different. Here too one can gather from his letters that Aram was trying to collect his past writings, perhaps with a view to publication. In the same letter of December 11, 1858, Ghalib writes to him:

'You must have been wondering why I did not answer your letter. The thing is that I cut my hand badly near the thumb when I was cutting a pen, and it swelled up so badly that for four days I had difficulty even in eating. Anyway, I am all right now. You did well to buy *Panj Ahang*. It was printed twice, once at the royal press and once at Munshi Nur ud Din's press. The first is defective, and the second full of mistakes. How can I tell you? Ziya ud Din Khan of Loharu is related to me and is my pupil in poetry. Whatever I wrote in prose and verse he used to take and keep. He had spent about a hundred and fifty

to two hundred rupees and had separate volumes made of my collected Persian
verse, in about nine hundred pages, *Panj Ahang, Mihr i Nimroz*, and the Urdu
diwan—some fifteen hundred to two thousand pages in all—with English
bindings, and embellished with gold and silver. And my mind was at rest,
knowing that all my writings had been collected and were available. Then one
of the princes had a copy made of all this collected verse and prose. So there
were two separate collections of my works. Then suddenly this turmoil descended on us, the city was looted, and both of these two libraries with the rest.
I have had people search everywhere, but they could not find any of these books.
They are all manuscript copies. The reason I tell you all this is that I want you
if you come across any of these books being offered for sale—the manuscript
Collected Persian Verse, the manuscript Collected Urdu Verse, the manuscript
Panj Ahang or the manuscript *Mihr i Nimroz*—to buy it for me and let me
know. I will send you the money.'

But he did not want *Mihr i Nimroz*, at least, republished. Aram had heard of
some such work and asked him about it in a previous letter. 'It is not *Mihr i
Nimmah*,' he had replied on November 18, 1858, 'its title is *Mihr i Nimroz* and
it gives the histories of the Timurid kings. The whole thing is over and done
with now and the book is not worth printing.' Ghalib does not say so, but he
knew it would hardly be tactful to publish a court history of the Mughal kings
at a time when he was trying to win the favour of those who had just forcibly
put and end to the dynasty.

It was the loss of his Urdu verse, which he had once belittled as not really
worthy of him, which seems to have grieved him most. A month or two earlier
he had written to Mihr:

'I have never kept any of my verse by me. Nawwab Ziya ud Din Khan and
Nawwab Husain Mirza used to write down everything I composed and keep it.
Both of their houses were looted, and libraries worth thousands of rupees
destroyed. And now I long for my own verse. A few days ago a faqir who has
a good voice and sings well discovered a ghazal of mine somewhere and got it
written down. When he showed me it, I tell you truly, the tears came to my
eyes. I am sending the ghazal to you, and ask in reward a reply to this letter.'

Ghalib's bald statements about the libraries in these two letters conceal a
shocking story of the senseless vandalism of the British troops. These libraries
and that of the Royal Fort which they destroyed really were of inestimable
value. Some indication of this may be obtained from Ikram's remark about
Ziya ud Din Ahmad Khan's library alone:

'The eight bulky . . . volumes of translated selections from histories of Muslim
India which Sir Henry Elliott and his collaborators produced comprise, without
any exaggeration, the essence of hundreds of books. Sir Henry Elliott's manu-

script papers in the British Museum testify to the fact that in this work it was Nawwab Ziya ud Din's library which was of the greatest assistance to him.'

In general, from the time *Dastambu* was printed to the end of 1858, Ghalib was in buoyant mood. But a letter to the Nawwab of Rampur sharply reminds us of his continuing financial distress. Still without any source of regular income, Ghalib had sought to develop the relationship with Rampur which he had initiated early in 1857, but which had been cut short by the revolt. The Nawwab seems to have shown no great alacrity in providing the regular support which a noble was expected to extend to a man of letters, and for which it should not have been necessary to ask in so many words. But desperation forced Ghalib to write in a tone which he must have felt it painful and humiliating to adopt, and on November 17th he tells the Nawwab bluntly: 'Whatever you send unasked, I do not refuse. Nor do I feel shame in asking when I am in need. The heavy burden of grief has crushed me. Once I had little in hand, and now I have nothing. Please hasten to help me. . . .' This blunt appeal brought him a gift of two hundred and fifty rupees.

Perhaps fortified by this he writes to Tufta on November 28, 1858:

'I have already sent the book *Dastambu* to the Chief Commissioner of the Panjab, and today, God willing, the parcels will go off to the Governor-General, to the Queen, and to the Secretaries. . . . Let's see what the Chief Commissioner writes and what the Governor-General will say.

> That friendship's tree may one day bring
> forth fruit
> Today we plant the seed and water it.'

Two letters to Mihr well illustrate his prevailing mood. Early in December 1858 he writes:

'First I want to ask you a question. For several letters past I have noticed you lamenting your grief and sorrow. Why? If you have fallen in love with some fair cruel one, what room for complaint have you there? Rather should you wish your friends the same good fortune and seek increase of this pain. In the words of Ghalib (God's mercy be upon him!)[1]

> You gave your heart away; why then lament
> your loss in plaintive song?
> You have a breast without a heart; why not
> a mouth without a tongue?

And what a fine second couplet!—

> Is one misfortune not enough to drive
> a man to beggary?

[1] Words always used of a saint after his death!

When you become his friend why should
the sky[1] become his enemy?

And if—which God forbid—it is more mundane griefs that beset you, then my
friend, you and I have the same sorrows to bear. I bear this burden like a man,
and if you are a man, so must you. As the late Ghalib says:

My heart, this grief and sorrow too is
precious; for the day will come
You will not heave the midnight sigh, nor
shed your tears at early morn.'

He goes on to speak of verses about which Mihr must have written to him,
recalls and quotes three couplets of a ghazal of his own with the same rhyme
as one of them, but in a different metre, and by the metre of another is reminded
of a short poem in the same metre which he had composed extempore during
his stay in Calcutta years ago.

'The occasion of it was this: I had a friend, Maulvi Karam Husain. We were
sitting with some of our friends when he put on the palm of his hand a polished
betel-nut and said to me, "Can you write a poem describing this in various
similes?" I sat down there and then and wrote a poem of nine or ten couplets,
which I handed to him; and I received the betel-nut as my reward. I am trying to
remember the couplets and am writing them down as they come back to me.'

He succeeds in recalling seven couplets—the full poem has twelve—and ends:
'Well, there you are, Sahib, I've answered your letter. . . .'
    In a second letter, dated December 20, 1858, he tells Mihr that he has sent
off copies of *Dastambu* in various directions, but has so far had no response.
Then he quotes his own verse:

The seven heavens[2] are turning night and day:
Something will happen—set your mind at rest.

This sets him thinking of the other verses of the same ghazal and he writes out
as many as he can remember, and for good measure follows it up with another.
He ends his letter: 'It's Monday morning, December 20th. I have a brazier
burning and am sitting by it warming myself and writing this letter. These
verses came to mind, so I wrote them out and am sending them to you.'
    With Aram he is by this time on sufficiently informal terms to tell him
something which in his first letter to him a few months earlier he had politely
kept to himself:

'Your letter with the package of envelopes has just come. Friend, I can't help

---

[1] i.e. fate.   [2] Whose movement determines men's destinies. Cf. p. 107.

it, but I don't like these envelopes with "From . . ." and "To . . ." and "Date
. . ." and "Month . . ." printed on them. The lot you sent me before I also gave
away to friends. I'm sending back this package of envelopes so that you can
send me plain ones instead—without "To . . ." and "From . . ." printed on
them—(like the ones you send your own letters in)—and take these in exchange.
And if you haven't got plain envelopes, it doesn't matter. I don't really need
them.'

Ghalib had promised to get a seal engraved for him, and Aram must have
asked if it could be done on an emerald. Ghalib's letter continues:

'As for the seal, where in this desolate city can you get an emerald?—and that
too the size of chick-pea, and eight-sided. The seal will be of cornelian, and of
a good colour—black or red, as you wrote in your earlier letter, and eight-
sided. *I* shall be sending you this seal—what concern of yours is it whether it
cost four annas a letter or six annas? If you want to get a seal engraved yourself, do—on an emerald or a diamond or what you like. *I'm* giving you one on
cornelian. . . .
    'Read Sahib is playing the sahib with me. How can I produce my best if I
am to write in Urdu? . . . At the most, my Urdu will be more elegant than other
people's. Still, I will do something. . . . Vomiting and diarrhoea? It sounds as
though you've been drinking some inferior kind of wine, and too much of it.
Take some sort of cooling medicine, and don't drink so much. . . . When I
wrote to Tufta that he was cross with me I did it in the same spirit as I once
wrote the same thing to you. Good heavens, he is like a son to me: I know very
well he wouldn't be cross with me. I have had two or three letters from him
since then, and am posting one to him by the same post as I send this letter to
you.'

    Tufta was indeed 'like a son' to him, and he had the satisfaction of knowing
that Ghalib relied on him more than any other to help him feel that life was
worth living. On December 27, 1858 he writes:

'Well, Sahib, are you still angry? And are you going to keep it up? Or will you
cool down? And if you won't cool down, then at least tell me what has upset
you. In this solitude it is letters that keep me alive. Someone writes to me and
I feel he has come to see me. By God's favour not a day passes but three or
four letters come from this side and that; in fact there are days when I get
letters by both posts—one or two in the morning and one or two in the afternoon. I spend the day reading them and answering them, and it keeps me
happy. Why is it that for ten and twelve days together you haven't written—
i.e. haven't been to see me? Write to me, sahib. Write why you haven't written.
Don't grudge the half-anna postage. And if you're *so* hard up, send the letter
unstamped.'

The light-hearted tone half hides Ghalib's pitiable position. What he had written to Tufta six months earlier was still true. A man whose house had never been empty was forced to spend his days in loneliness, and depend on a handful of correspondents to help him feel that his links with his friends were still there. He was still without any regular income; Delhi was still closed to its former Muslim inhabitants, and no-one knew when they would be allowed to return. Some were waiting in nearby villages. Others had dispersed further afield. Majruh, for example, was in Panipat. Ghalib sometimes felt that he and his friends would never be able to meet again. On September 7, 1858 he writes to Majruh:

'In short I fear that parted friends will never be reunited, unless it be on Judgement Day. And what chances are there even then? The Sunnis will assemble in one place, the Shias in another, the good on this side and the bad on that.'

In his financial straits he felt his wife and adopted children more and more a millstone round his neck. Already in April he had written to Ghulam Najaf Khan:

'Family cares are the death of me; they are a bondage in which I have never been happy. God had kept me childless, and I returned Him thanks. But my thanks were not pleasing and acceptable to Him . . . out of the same iron from which my collar of servitude was made He forged two fetters for my hands. Oh, well, it's no good crying over it. This imprisonment is for life. . . .'

Later in the same letter, speaking of the possibility of getting his pension back, he writes:

'If I had been on my own, how well and how carefree I could have lived, even on this small income! But it is madness to talk like this. *If* I were single, and *if* my pension were renewed, I *might* live in comfort. . . .'

In July he is even more depressed: 'Delhi is no longer a city, it is an inferno,' he writes to an unknown correspondent. By August he had actually decided to try and get his wife and the children taken off his hands. His relatives were now confirmed in the possession of their Loharu estates, and Ghalib writes to Alai, the son of Nawwab Amīn ud Din Ahmad Khan (on August 23, 1858):

'I have already explained fully to your father and to your grandmother and your uncle what I want of them. In brief, it is that my wife and children are their kinsmen and they should take them off my hands, for I can no longer shoulder the burden of supporting them. . . .'

This makes it virtually certain that an undated letter to Nawwab Amīn ud Din Ahmad Khan belongs to this time. In it Ghalib writes:

'My brother, for sixty years your forebears and mine were in close relationship to one another, and as for our own personal relations with each other, for fifty years I have given you my love, regardless of whether or not you also gave me yours. For forty years our love has been mutual; I continued in my love for you, and you in your love for me. And does not the general closeness of our families and our special closeness to each other demand that we begin to love each other as true brothers? Is that closeness and this regard any less than the bond of blood-relationship? How could I hear of your distress and not be myself perturbed and want to come to visit you? But what can I do? Do not think I exaggerate: I am a body from which the spirit has departed . . . and I grow worse with every day that passes. My cooling drink at morning, my meal at midday, my wine in the evening—the day that any one of these is not ready on time, I am prostrate. By God, I cannot come. I swear by God, I cannot. What beats in my breast may not be a heart, but it is not a stone; I may not be your friend, but I am not likely to be your enemy. I may not love you, but I am not likely to hate you. Today you two brothers occupy the place of [your ancestors] Sharf ud Daula and Fakhr ud Daula. I am a childless man, "neither begotten nor begetting".[1] My wife is your sister, and my children your children, and so are my niece and her children. Not for your own sake but for these defenceless ones I pray for you and for your long life. It is my heart's desire— and if God Almighty wills, it shall be so—that you may live, and I may die before you both, so that this tribe may receive its bread at your hands. And if you cannot give it bread, you will at any rate give it parched gram. And if you don't give even that, and take no thought for them, well, it will mean nothing to me. As I conceive it, grief for these wretched ones will not trouble me as I die.'

In the letter of August 23, 1858 to Alai, Ghalib continues:

'And they [Nawwab Amīn ud Din, his brother, and their mother] have agreed to my request, provided that they [the wife and children] go to Loharu. I intend to travel, and if my pension is restored I shall use it for my own needs. When I find a place I like I shall stay a while, and when I tire of it I shall move on.'

But nothing seems to have come of these plans. At the end of the year (December 19, 1858) in a letter full of rather grim humour, he writes to Tufta:

'Your letter has come and told me all I wanted to know. I feel sorry for Umrao Singh, and envy him too! Wonderful are God's ways! There is he, who has twice had the fetters struck from his feet,[2] and here am I hanging for the last fifty-one years with my neck in the hangman's noose—and the rope doesn't

---

[1] A quotation from the Quran of a verse which, in the Quran, describes God.
[2] i.e. he had twice been married, and both wives had died.

break, and I don't die. Tell him, "I'll look after your children; why do you let your troubles get the better of you?"[1] The line you quoted is one of Hakim Sanai's and the story is in his *Hadiqa*: "A son came weeping to his father and said, 'Please arrange my marriage' The father replied, 'My dear son, live in sin with some woman, but do not talk of marriage. Learn sense, not just from me, but from all the world. If you are caught in fornication you will still be released in the end. But if you marry you are bound for life, and if you leave your wife you are disgraced.' " [The original is in Persian verse.]

'So you've stayed in Sikandarabad. Why not? Where else would you go? You've spent all you had in the bank, and what will you live on now? My friend, nothing that I suggest and nothing that you think of will make any difference. The heavens keep turning and what is to be, will be. We have no power, so what can we do? We have no say in it, so what can we say? Mirza Abdul Qādir Bedil is right:

> Why should you covet power and wealth?
> And why forsake the world?
>
> Do this or that—it makes no odds,
> For all will pass away.

Look at me—neither bond nor free, neither well nor ill, neither glad nor sad, neither dead nor alive. I go on living. I go on talking. I eat my daily bread and drink my occasional cup of wine. When death comes I will die and that will be an end of it. I neither give thanks nor make complaint, and all my words are no more than a tale. But, after all, wherever you are and however you fare, write me a letter once a week.'

Not all of his troubles were so serious. On November 18, 1858 he writes to Sarur:

'My kind friend, your kind letter of November 15th reached me today, Thursday, 18th November. If a letter from Marahra [Sarur's town] reaches Delhi in four days, how is it that a letter from Delhi to Marahra takes longer? See, to please you I am sending this letter unstamped. ['From this,' notes Mihr, 'it seems that Sarur had himself asked Ghalib to send his letters unstamped.'] But let me know what day it reaches you.'

He then goes on to explain the circumstances in which he wrote *Dastambu*, and continues:

'So I am sending you a copy. As a matter of fact I am presenting it to my most revered and respected master, Sahib i Alam. Since he is your elder I could not

---

[1] Hali, in a note on this letter, says that Umrao Singh had argued that for the sake of his children he should marry a third time.

have the temerity to present it to you, telling you to give it to him to read too.

'Alas, what havoc these scribes play with the works of the masters! Well, you can expect anything of them. But I could not have thought that you and my master [Sahib i Alam] would have failed to recognize a scribe's mistake.'

He then quotes, in the scribe's incorrect version, a verse of the Persian poet Urfi and after some detailed comment continues:

'God save us! Even if Urfi had drunk a great mugful of Indian hemp or a full bottle of wine, he could never have written that. His line goes like this, poor fellow. [He then quotes it and explains its construction.]

'What I write next is addressed to my master, Sahib i Alam. Though we are of the same age, I am his disciple; though we practise the same art, he is my master; and I trust he will forgive my shortcoming. I am sixty-three years old; I have gone deaf; but there is no defect in my sight, nor do I wish to resort to spectacles. But if my sight is keen, my understanding is dim, and I cannot read your handwriting. In my two previous replies I had gone by guess work; I had not been able to read your letters properly. After all, Chaudhri Sahib [Sarur] is your devoted admirer, and as close to you as any of your kin. Let *him* write down faithfully whatever you command him. I will reply to everything as soon as I hear from you that you have received the book and when I receive your letter, re-written in Chaudhri Sahib's hand.'

This was not the first time that he had had to complain of Sahib i Alam's hand, and it was not to be the last. In an earlier letter (undated) he had written to Sarur, 'I am forced, in my complete perplexity, to return the enclosed letter to you. For God's sake copy out the revered words of my spiritual lord and master on another sheet and send it back to me, so that a miserable wretch can see what he wrote.' From another letter to Sarur dated December 1, 1858, it seems that Sahib i Alam had ignored the request he had so politely expressed in his letter of November 18th:

'I had requested [Sahib i Alam] to get you to write whatever he had to communicate. He has ignored this and has again written me something in his own special hand. I swear to God that neither I nor anyone else could read it. Don't say a word to him, but copy it out in your own hand and have it sent to me. Be sure to do this, and do it quickly.'

Burdened as he was by personal troubles, he was still alert to note what was going on in the wider world around him. On September 21, 1858 he writes to ask Mihr whether it is true what people are saying, viz. that 'in Agra proclamation has been made, and it has been announced at the beat of the drum, that the [East India] Company's contract has been ended and India brought under the British Crown.' If so, he says, it is good news. About a month later he writes to Aram:

'Let me tell you the news from this city. An order has been issued that on the night of Monday 1st November all well-wishers of the English are to illuminate their houses, and there are also to be illuminations in the bazaars and on the Deputy Commissioner Sahib's bungalow. Your humble servant, even in this state of penury, not having received his appointed pension for the last eighteen months, will illuminate his house, and has sent a poem of fifteen couplets to the Commissioner of the city.'

The purpose of this, which, it seems, was not revealed until the night in question, was to proclaim the end of the Company's rule and the bringing of India directly under the Crown.

On November 20, 1858 he tells Tufta of 'the general amnesty now proclaimed'. And finally, in a letter of December 22nd to Majruh, he surveys the Delhi scene, and calmly and humorously, if without much hope, speculates on what the new year will bring:

'Bravo, Sayyid Sahib! What distinguished prose you've started writing; and what a distinguished pose you've started striking! For several days I've been intending to answer your letter, but the cold has put me out of action, and today, now that it's cloudy and the cold less intense, and I've decided to write to you, I'm at a loss to match the enchantment of your style. You've lived so long by the watercourse in Urdu Bazaar that you've yourself become a river of eloquence—Urdu's Mirza Qatīl,[1] in fact! But never mind all that. I'm only laughing at you. Come, let me tell you what's happening in your beloved Delhi.

'The well near the pool in front of the Begam Bagh gate in [Chandni] Chauk has been filled up with stones and bricks and rubbish. Several shops near the entrance to Ballimaron have been demolished, and the road widened. There is still no order permitting anyone, rich or poor, to return to his home in the city, and as for pension-holders, the authorities are not concerned with them. Taj Mahal, Mirza Qaisar, the wife of Mirza Jawan Bakht's brother-in-law Mirza Wilayat Ali Beg Jaipuri—all of these have been released in Allahabad. The King, Mirza Jawan Bakht, Mirza Abbas Shah and Zinat Mahal have all reached Calcutta and will be embarked aboard ship. Let us see whether they will be kept at the Cape or sent to London. People here have hazarded a guess— you know what Delhi's inventors of news are like—and spread a rumour which has now spread throughout the city that in January 1859 there will be general permission for people to return to their homes in the city, and bags and bags of money will be given to pension-holders. Well, today is Wednesday, December 22nd. Saturday will be Christmas Day and the Saturday following January 1st. If we live we shall see what happens. Let me have a reply to this letter, and soon. . . .'

[1] A very left-handed compliment! Qatīl, to Ghalib, typified all that was objectionable in Indian 'authorities' on Persian.

❈ Chapter 8 ❈

1859

The experiences that were to befall him during 1859 were to justify his scepticism. The one substantial gain he could register when it ended was the establishment of a regular contact with the Nawwab of Rampur which eased to some extent his financial distress. His correspondence with Rampur shows that he was already receiving occasional gifts before July 1859, and that as from that month the Nawwab granted him a regular monthly allowance of Rs. 100. But this was not enough for his needs, and he continued to seek for other means of supplementing it—without success. Until June, he had rising hopes of the restoration of his pension from the British, but these were dashed—at any rate temporarily —by an adverse report about him made by the Commissioner of Delhi, and the reception of *Dastambu* similarly failed to justify the hopes he had placed in it. He hoped also to receive something from Wajid Ali Shah, the ex-king of Oudh, whom the British had removed to Calcutta when they annexed his kingdom in 1856, but whose resources still permitted of the exercise of a measure of patronage. But here too his hopes were disappointed, and by the end of the year he had ceased to expect anything from that quarter.

Meanwhile, in Delhi, conditions continued far from normal, with British policies alternating unpredictably between leniency and severity. Not until August was the regulation withdrawn whereby entry into and exit from the city required a permit; and even then a residence permit was still needed for a stay of even one night in the city. It was November before Muslims were finally allowed to enter and take up permanent residence, more than two years after their original expulsion. The very face of Delhi was changing, and large scale demolition of historic buildings was making way for open expanses and new roads.

News from outside was also often bad enough. Ghalib's old friend Fazl i Haq was sentenced to transportation for life, and his appeal was rejected. His friends Husain Mirza and his family, for whom Ghalib held a sort of watching brief in Delhi, tried in vain to make some progress in their negotiations with the Delhi authorities over their extensive properties there, and by the end of the year were at a loss where to go and to whom to turn for help in securing their future.

In these circumstances it is hardly surprising that the letters for 1859 are often anxious, despondent, and occasionally written in great distress and bitterness, though even in the deepest dejection Ghalib's humour will unexpectedly assert itself in a sudden flash. But with this short introduction the letters may be left to speak for themselves.

On January 3, 1859 he writes to Tufta:

'See here, sir. I don't like your ways. I write to you in 1858 and you reply in 1859; and if I speak to you about it you will reply that you answered my letter on the very next day. And the best of it is that both of us are right!'

The same day he writes to Bekhabar:

'Today is Monday, 3rd January 1859. It must be about nine in the morning. The sky is overcast, and a fine drizzle is falling. A cold wind is blowing. I have nothing to drink, so I have had to eat instead.

> The clouds of spring are spread across the sky
> But in my cup of clay there is no wine.

'I was sitting here feeling depressed and despondent when the postman came with your letter. I saw that it was addressed in your own hand, and felt very pleased. I read it, and found that it did not bring me the news I wanted; and again felt sad:

> Oppression's force has driven us from home.
> How should good tidings come from lands like ours?

And in this sadness I felt like talking to you. So although your letter did not call for a reply I began to write you one.

'So first let me tell you that your letter has been delivered to your friend; but he has twice written to me to say that he has already posted off a reply to the address given on the envelope, and now awaits a reply to his reply.

'You know that when despair reaches its lowest depths there is nothing left but to resign oneself to God's will. Well, what lower depths can there be than this that it is the hope of death that keeps me alive? And my resignation gains strength from day to day because I have only another two to two-and-a-half years to live; and somehow the time will pass. I know you will laugh and think to yourself I am talking nonsense. But call it divine revelation or call it superstition, I have had this verse kept by for the past twenty years:

> Who am I to expect eternal life,
> When Naziri has gone, and Talib died?
> If they ask you the year of Ghalib's death
> Simply tell them in answer, 'Ghalib died'.

[In the original 'Ghalib died' is 'Ghalib murd', and is a chronogram.] It is now 1275, and "Ghalib murd" gives 1277. Let me experience whatever happiness may come to me in this short space; and then I shall be gone.'

The next day he again laments to Aram that he is called upon to write a work of Urdu prose.

'My friend, how can I write in Urdu? Is my standing so low that this should be expected of me? Still, it *is* expected of me. But where am I to turn, hunting for tales and stories? I haven't a book to my name. Let my pension be restored and I'll get the peace of mind to think of something.

> Give me food and drink
> Then see how I can think!'

(It is interesting that this jingle which he quotes is in Panjabi.)

On January 26, 1859, he writes to Tufta: 'I got your letter . . . I am late in replying because I had gone by the mail to Meerut to see Mustafa Khan [Shefta]. I stayed three days, and came back yesterday.'

A letter of February 2, 1859 to Majruh gives more details:

'Now let me tell you what I have been doing. Nawwab Mustafa Khan Shefta had been sentenced to seven years' imprisonment. Now he has been pardoned and released. So far that is all. No orders have yet been issued regarding his Jahangirabad estate or his properties in Delhi or his pension. So he is obliged to stay where he is in Meerut as the guest of a friend. As soon as I heard the news I took the mail and went to Meerut to see him. I stayed four days and then returned home, also by the mail. I can't remember the dates, but I went on a Saturday and returned on a Tuesday. Today is Wednesday, 2nd February, and I have been back nine days. I was waiting for a letter from you so that I could answer it when I wrote. Your letter came this morning, and I am writing this reply at midday.'

He goes on to describe conditions in Delhi:

> 'The city gets fresh orders every day—
> But what is going on, no one can say.

When I got back from Meerut I saw how strict they are here. Not content with the guard of British soldiers, the police officer at Lahori Gate sits on a chair overlooking the street, seizes anyone who has slipped past the British sentries and sends him to the cells, where he receives five strokes of the cane by the Commissioner's orders or pays a fine of two rupees. After that he is kept in prison for eight days. Also, orders have been issued to all police stations to find out who in the city has a permit and who is living here without one. Lists are being drawn up at the police stations. An inspector from our district came to see me too about this. I told him, "My friend, don't enter my name on your list. Write a separate statement about my position, to the effect that the pensioner Asadullah Khan has been living since 1850 in the residence of the brother

G

of the Patiala hakim. He did not move during the days when the blacks held
the city, nor did he leave it (nor was compelled to leave) when the whites came.
His residence there was authorized by the verbal order of Colonel Brown
Sahib Bahadur, and no one in authority has hitherto modified that order. Now
it is for the authorities to decide." The day before yesterday the inspector
forwarded this statement, with his list for the muhalla, to the office of the
Chief of Police. Yesterday an order was issued stating that people were building
themselves houses outside the city without authority. All such houses are to be
demolished, and proclamation made that for the future such building is prohibited. It is also rumoured that five thousand permits have been printed; any
Muslim who wishes to take up residence in the city will have to make a contribution according to his means—of which the Commissioner will be the
judge—and will then receive a permit. In other words, "Pull your houses down
and settle in the town."

'My blessings on the light of my eyes, Mir Sarfaraz Husain and my son Mir
Nasir ud Din; and to his honour Miran Sahib, both my greeting and my
blessing. He may choose whichever he likes.'

On January 30, 1859 he writes despondently to Bekhabar. The first part of
the letter is in rhyming prose, but very simple and straightforward language:

'Respected sir, does it never occur to you that you have a friend named Ghalib?
Do you never wonder whether he has the wherewithal to eat and drink, and
how he maintains life? Twenty-one months have passed since his pension was
stopped, and still in his simplicity he hopes for fresh largesse. The matter of
the pension is in the hands of the Panjab authorities, but it seems to be their
way neither to send money nor to answer letters, neither to bestow kindness
nor to visit their wrath upon me. Well, leave that aside, and consider this:
Since 1856 I have entertained the hope of a royal gift, for the Minister's letter
gave me grounds to hope.[1] Were I guilty of any crime I would feel ashamed to
press my request. But had I been guilty I would have been shot or hanged. . . .
Whenever I have sent any communication to the Government in Calcutta
I have always had a reply from the Chief Secretary. This time I sent two books[2]
—one for the Government and one for presentation to the Queen; but I have
heard neither of the acceptance of the one nor of the despatch of the other.
Neither has his excellency William Muir Sahib Bahadur showed his kindness,
for he too has not written to me.'

He goes on to ask for accurate information regarding recent transfers and
appointments of high British officials and concludes:

'I have given up all hope and resigned myself to lamenting my evil fate, but I
want full and accurate information of the true situation to comfort my soul

------

[1] Cf. p. 130 above.   [2] I.e. copies of *Dastambu*.

and set my mind at ease. And if you will put yourself to the trouble of answering my questions—not in general, but in detail; not later, but now—you will, so to speak, make me your slave. . . .'

Tufta had apparently sent a letter containing a message for Raja Umid Singh asking him to send him his full address. Ghalib replies on February 19, 1859:

'My friend, you are a man of intuition, and your knowledge of the unseen is accurate. I was expecting a letter from you so that I could reply when I next wrote, and yesterday evening I got one. I am replying this morning.

'The point is that a letter addressed to anyone who is well-known doesn't require to be addressed to any muhalla. I am only a poor man, yet letters addressed in Persian and in English reach me safely. Some of the Persian letters do not give the name of the muhalla, and the English letters carry no address at all other than "Delhi". I have had three or four letters from England. Do you think anyone there knows or cares what "Ballimaron Muhalla "is? And he [Raja Umid Singh] is a much more important man than I am. He gets hundreds of letters in English every day. But, in short, I again sent a man to him to show him your letter to me. He told my servant, "Give the Nawwab Sahib [Ghalib] my respects and ask him if he would himself kindly send the necessary information". Well, I've told you the position about this, but in accordance with your wish I now inform you that his house is in Dason ka kucha, muhalla Balli-maron.

'The position about *Dastambu* is that on one occasion I sent him [Aram] a draft for seven rupees, ordering twelve copies and an almanac. Then I sent a stamp for eighteen annas asking him to despatch two copies direct to Lucknow. And then I again sent an eighteen-anna stamp and asked him to despatch two more copies direct to Sardhana. I write all this because I want you to know that after the first fifty copies I have had a further sixteen from him, but I paid cash. I have never ordered them on credit. Once I paid by draft, and twice in stamps. Now, by my life, you are to write to him and ask him by the way how many copies Ghalib has ordered, and did he pay cash or take them on credit? Write and tell me what he says in reply.'

Ghalib obviously felt strongly about this matter, for his next (undated) letter to Tufta is again mainly devoted to it:

'I was pleased to get your letter. It seemed from what you had written that you had got it into your head that I had ordered the books from Agra without sending the money for them. This is presumably what you meant when you wrote about "the author's rights". My friend, do you think I'd lie to you? And even if Shiv Narayan [Aram] didn't say anything about my sending the money, neither did he say that I'd ordered the books without sending the money. Now by my head and by my life I adjure you, just ask Shiv Narayan how many copies Ghalib has ordered after the first fifty and whether he sent the money with his order or whether he still has to collect it. See, I have bound you by oath; you are to do exactly as I say.

'Raja Umid Singh Sahib is still here. I haven't met him during these last few days, so the question of his mentioning your letter doesn't arise. But I am certain it must have reached him. You say that if it didn't reach Dason ka kucha it would be delivered to me. Well, it hasn't been. My friend, what are you worrying about? He is a noble and a celebrity. *Of course* letters addressed to him reach him.'

His next letter, dated February 27, 1859, is short and to the point:

'What is this, Mirza Tufta? Our friend Munshi Nabi Bakhsh Sahib is asking anxiously after you. Why have you stopped writing to him? He writes to me that if I have any news of you I am to be sure to write to him.'

In the same month—the letter does not bear the precise date—he had written to Majruh:

'Why are you surprised that Yusuf Mirza has not written to you? He is all right where he is. He calls upon the authorities and is looking for employment. Husain Mirza is there too, and is in contact with the authorities there. He is making application for a pension. I get one or two letters a week from both of them, to which I reply.[1] My friend, Lucknow enjoys a peace and security such as never existed either under Indian administration or under British administration before these disorders. The nobility and gentry meet the authorities and are received with the honours and deference appropriate to their rank. The issue of pensions is general, and there is no order preventing people returning to their homes. On the contrary, they are being re-settled with every kindness and consideration. And listen to this: The Commissioner there observed that his staff consisted entirely of Hindus and that there were no Muslims. So he posted them off to other districts and appointed Muslims in their place. It is Delhi alone that has suffered this catastrophe. Not only in Lucknow, but in all the other cities too the administration is again what it was before the mutiny. Now they have printed permits here. I've seen them myself. The wording is in Persian, and runs, "Permit to reside in the city of Delhi, on condition of the payment of a fine." The amount of the fine is in the discretion of the Commissioner. To date, five thousand permits have been printed. Tomorrow, being Sunday, is a holiday. On Monday we shall see how they are issued.

'But this is the position in the city in general. Now let me tell you my position in particular. The day before yesterday, after twenty-two months, the Chief of Police called for a written statement of the position of the pensioner Asa-

[1] Cf. p. 206–8 below.

dullah Khan, stating whether he has means or is destitute. In accordance with regulation, he has required me to produce four witnesses. So tomorrow four witnesses will present themselves at his verandah and testify to my lack of means. Don't get the idea that once my poverty is proven I shall get the arrears of my pension, and henceforth receive it regularly. No sir, there's no question of that. After my poverty is established I shall be put down as entitled to receive a sum corresponding to six months', or perhaps a year's payments. . . .

'Give my blessing to Mir Sarfaraz Husain, and give him a hug and a kiss for me. And give my blessing to Mir Nasīr ud Din and my congratulations to Miran Sahib.'

The next letter continues the story:

'My dearest friend, may God grant you a hundred and twenty years of life! Old age is upon you; there are white hairs in your beard; but understanding has not yet come to you. You're all confused about the pension—and what confusion! You know that in Delhi no pensioner has received his pension since May 1857. This is February 1859—twenty-two months later. Out of the twenty-two months' arrears, a few people have been given twelve months' arrears as a grant in aid. No instructions have been issued regarding either the rest of the arrears or the regular monthly re-issue of the pension henceforth. And now recall your question and tell me whether or not it has anything to do with these facts? . . .'

He then quotes a number of actual cases which exemplify the general position he has described, beginning with that of his wife's brother, Ali Bakhsh Khan, and goes on to give news of his own position to date.

'No grant in aid was made to me. Successive letters at length brought an instruction from the Commissioner that the applicant was to be given Rs. 100 as a grant in aid. I did not claim it, and again wrote to the Commissioner that my pension had been Rs. 62 As. 8 a month, and that this worked out at Rs. 750 a year; in all other cases a full year's arrears had been granted; how was it that I was granted only Rs. 100? Like the others, I too should be granted a full year's arrears. So far I have had no reply to this.

'As for re-settlement, the position is that Mr Edgerton [the Delhi Magistrate], having had public proclamation made and permits printed, has gone off by the mail to Calcutta, leaving all the people who are hanging on outside the city gaping like idiots. Perhaps people will be allowed to re-settle after his return— or perhaps there will be some fresh development.'

His next letters are full of optimism. In an undated letter written early in March he writes:

'My dearest friend, listen to my story. The Sahib Commissioner Bahadur of

Delhi, i.e. . . . Mr Saunders . . . sent for me. On Thursday 24th February I went to see him, but he was mounted and ready to go out hunting, so I had to return without seeing him. I went again on Friday, 25th February, and this time I saw him. He gave me a seat, and after enquiring after my health, picked up a four-page letter in English, which he read. When he had finished reading it, he said, "This letter is from Macleod Sahib [Financial Commissioner of the Panjab]. He writes that I am to enquire into your circumstances and send him a written report. So first tell me about this request to Her Majesty for a robe of honour." I told him the position. I had brought with me a letter I had received from England, and this was read to him. Then he asked, "What is this book you have written?" I told him. He said, "Macleod Sahib has asked for a copy to look at; and let me have one too." I said, "I will bring them tomorrow". Then he asked me about my pension. I told him the facts and returned home feeling very pleased with myself. . . .

'Now see, Mir Mahdi, what does the Commissioner of the Panjab know about the proceedings in England? How does he know about the books? What is his object in asking about the pension? These enquiries are being made at the order of the Governor-General. And this is a favourable augury for a successful outcome of it all. Anyway, next day, being Saturday, was a holiday, and I stayed at home. On Monday, February 28th, I went again. I sat down in an outer room and sent word that I had come. I was asked to wait. After a very short time a letter arrived from the garrison commandant. The Commissioner ordered his carriage, and when it arrived, came out. I said, "I have brought the books". "Leave them with Munshi Jiwan Lal," he said, and got into his carriage. I too . . . went home. On Tuesday, 1st March I went again, and we talked for some time in a very friendly and informal atmosphere. I showed him some certificates from various Governors that I had brought with me. I had brought a letter for Macleod Sahib Bahadur, and I gave it him with the request that it should be sent to him along with the book. "Very well," he said, and took it. Then he said, "I have written to Edgerton Sahib Bahadur about your pension. Go to see him". "Very well," I said. As you know, Edgerton Sahib was away, but he came back yesterday, and today I have written to him. I shall act on whatever instructions he sends and go to see him when he sends for me. See how the Lion of God, the Prevailer[1]—peace be upon him!—has helped me, his slave, and preserved me. In twenty-two months he never let me go hungry and thirsty. And see from what an exalted quarter . . . he has favour bestowed on me, honour shown me by the authorities. My patience and steadfastness has received its reward. And that patience and steadfastness too was his gift. . . .'

Further letters follow in the same vein. One of March 7, 1859 begins with good-humoured, and perhaps slightly ironic, praise of Majruh's prose style.

---

[1] Ali—cf. p. 35, n. above. In Arabic his title reads 'Asadullah al Ghalib'—i.e. almost identically with Ghalib's own name and takhallus.

'You've developed real style in your Urdu writing, so much so that I've begun to feel jealous of you. Let me tell you, all Delhi's wealth and property and gold and jewels have been looted and carried off to the Panjab. This style of writing was my own personal wealth, and now a tyrant from Panipat, who lives in the Ansaris' muhalla, has carried it off. [Majruh had left Delhi at the time of the revolt and gone to Panipat, in the Panjab, where he was living in the Ansaris' muhalla.] But I have pardoned him. May God prosper him.

'I want you to understand the exact position about my pension and the emoluments I expect from England. "God bestows his blessings by stealth." The way in which things were initiated is something special. The Governor-General wrote to the Governor of the Panjab to the effect that he was to get a report from the Commissioner of Delhi on the possibilities of the arrears of such and such a man's pension being given him as a lump sum and then continued by regular monthly payments. He was to note his approval, and then forward the report to receive his sanction and be returned. Accordingly, by the proper procedures, this order will be put into effect. In about two months—more or less—I shall get the full sum. Oh yes, and the Commissioner also told me that if I needed money I could draw Rs. 100 from the treasury. I said, "Sahib, how is it that others have received a full year's arrears and you are authorizing only Rs. 100 for me?" He replied, "In a few days I shall be authorized to pay you in full and re-issue your pension. It will be years before the others get as much. . . ." So I said no more. Today is Monday, 1st Shaban, and 7th March. Come midday I shall send my man with a receipt and draw Rs. 100. But, my friend, I trust in God alone to bring me my reward from England. An order about this came along with the order calling for the report, but it simply called for a statement of opinion. Let's see what opinion the two Commissioners—of Delhi and of the Panjab—express. . . . Your letter, and one from Yusuf Mirza, have just come. I have enjoyed a talk with you, and have replied to both of you right away. Now I'm going to have my lunch. . . .'

On March 27, 1859 he writes of further good news. The Lieutenant-Governor has written from Allahabad in the same style as of old, addressing Ghalib by his old styles of address, to express his appreciation of *Dastambu*. He now hopes to receive a similar response from the Governor-General.

From a letter to Aram dated April 19, 1859 it appears that Aram was trying to collect Ghalib's Urdu ghazals. Ghalib writes:

'Where would I find Urdu ghazals to send you? The printed diwans are defective. There are many ghazals which they do not include. The manuscript diwans, which were comprehensive and complete, were looted. I have told everybody here to buy them if they see them offered for sale, and I wrote the same to you. And remember another thing: I have very few ghazals indeed of fifteen to sixteen couplets. Generally there are not more than twelve couplets and not less than nine. [Mihr here notes: "This generalization is not valid.

Ghalib has numerous ghazals of less than nine couplets."] The ghazal of which you have sent me five couplets has nine in all. I have a friend who has a more complete Urdu diwan than the printed one. He has got together various manuscripts from here and there. It was from him that I got the ghazal rhyming "pinhan hogain, wiran hogain". I have just now written to him, and now I am writing to you. I will keep this letter open, and when he sends a ghazal I will enclose it with this and post it off. It will go off either today or tomorrow.

'I have written an ode in praise of my old patron and benefactor Mr Frederick Edmondstone, Lieutenant-Governor of the North Western Provinces, and another in praise of Mr Montgomery, Lieutenant-Governor of the Panjab. If you wish I can send you these. But both are in Persian, and about forty to forty-five couplets in length.

'I was pleased to hear of the sales of *Dastambu*. I sincerely hope that before you sold them you corrected those two or three mistakes you know about. You didn't say whether it was Britishers or Indians who bought them. Be sure you write and let me know about this. And see! You were apprehensive, but the books have sold, and you are not left stranded with them. My friend, India has become a realm of darkness. Hundreds of thousands are dead, and hundreds of those who still live, languish in prison. Those who have life (freedom) have no means.

'My guess is that the books you have just sold went either to Englishmen or to the Panjab. You won't have had much demand from the east [the region extending from the neighbourhood of Lucknow to the borders of Bengal].

'My boy, I regard you as a son, no matter whether letters pass between us or not. You have your place in my heart. Now I am going to see what I can do about the ghazal you sent. I am writing it out; God grant that I remember all nine couplets.'

Here the full ghazal follows, and he continues:

'It is your good fortune that I've remembered all nine couplets. So what with this ghazal and the two that are on their way you will have three weeks' supplies in hand. ["He means," says Mihr, "that Aram can print one a week in his paper."] If you want them I will send the two odes as well.'

From the next letter, written only three days later, we learn that Aram's discoveries included a ghazal which was not Ghalib's at all:

'My friend, God forbid, and God forbid again that this ghazal should be mine! [He then quotes a line and goes on] I won't say anything against the poet who wrote it, poor fellow. But a thousand curses on me if *I* wrote it. On one previous occasion somebody quoted its closing couplet to me:

> Asad, so loyal to your cruel idol?
> Bravo, my lion-heart! God's mercy on you![1]

[1] There is a play on words in the original. 'Asad', which Ghalib too used as his takhallus in his earlier verse, literally means 'lion'.

And I said the same thing to him, "If this couplet is mine, then a curse upon me!" The thing is that there was another Asad, and this ghazal comes from his wonder-working works . . . True, I did use Asad as my takhallus for a year or two when I first started writing verse; but since then I have used only Ghalib. [Mihr notes that Ghalib is exaggerating here. "There is evidence that Asad remained his takhallus for ten to twelve years; in fact, even after he changed it to Ghalib he wrote Asad when occasion demanded. . . ."] You haven't paid attention to the thought and expression either. Could such rubbish be *my* work? Let's hear no more about it.

Before you print the ghazal I sent you, make a copy and give it to Mirza Hatim Ali Mihr. Do it the day you get this letter, and send it to him.'

He goes on to speak of the recent sale of *Dastambu* mentioned in his previous letter. (It *had* gone to the Panjab, as he had suspected.) Then he again gives full details of the two odes, concluding, one suspects with a good deal of secret regret,

'But then they are in Persian, and you will of course not want to print them along with Urdu ghazals. So let them be. As for my old ghazals, I will send them as they come to hand. My dear boy, I swear to you by my life, I never feel like writing Urdu verse now, nor could I even if I did feel like it. Apart from that ode of twenty-five couplets which I wrote and sent out of regard for you, I haven't written an Urdu verse for these last two years; God punish me if I have. In fact, by God, I haven't even written a Persian ghazal—only the two odes. I can't describe the state of my thoughts and feelings. . . .'

A few days later, in a letter to Junun dated April 29, 1859, he has improved upon his reply to the gentleman who congratulated him upon the couplet which was not his. The story is recalled to him by a similar enquiry from Junun about yet another ghazal which Junun has wrongly assumed to be his.

'Lord and Master, your servant has been ever ready and never failing in your service; and I fulfil your every command. But to bring the non-existent into being is beyond the scope of my powers. I have never written a ghazal in this metre and rhyme. . . . God knows . . . why Maulvi Darwesh Hasan Sahib thought the couplet was mine. Although I thought hard I could not recall any ghazal of mine in this metre and rhyme. But there are a few copies of the printed edition of my diwan about, so I did not simply trust to my memory but looked at that too. There was no such ghazal in it. Let me tell you that it quite often happens that people recite someone else's ghazal and attribute it to me.'

He then goes on to relate the story of Aram's enquiry, without however mentioning his name, and says that his rejoinder to the man who praised 'his' couplet was: 'Sir, as for the gentleman whose couplet this is, to use his own

G*

phrase, God's mercy on him! And if it is mine, then a curse upon me.' After which he goes on to explain in somewhat more detail than he had to Aram the many features of the verse which distinguish its whole style from his.

Some time in April he is writing again to Majruh:

'Friend your incessant demands for answers to your letters will be the death of me!

'A curse upon the heavens, that move so perversely! What harm had I done to them? I had no wealth or goods or rank or majesty—only a few possessions and a corner where a handful of poor beggars would gather together to laugh and talk. But

> That too you could not bear to look upon,
> o cruel sky,
> Although to look upon each other was
> our only wealth.

Remember, this couplet is Khwaja Mir Dard's.[1] "Since yesterday I keep thinking of Maikash," [you write]. So? You tell me, what am I to write? When the memories of all the times we and our friends used to sit and talk come back to you, all you can think of doing is making me write you letter upon letter. But a man cannot quench his thirst with tears. And my writing is no substitute for their talking. Anyway, I'll write you something. Let's see what I can think of to write.

'I must tell you that I haven't heard any more about the report on my pension. "Slow but sure."

'My friend, I've got a bone to pick with you. You tell me that Miran Sahib is better, but you express no pleasure, nor do you congratulate me. In fact you write as though you didn't like him getting better. You write, "Miran Sahib is back to what he was before, jumping and leaping and roaming about the place." In other words, "Oh God! what a trial! Why did he have to get well?" Well, I don't like your attitude. You must have heard Mir's[2] couplet? I write it with a word or two changed. [He then quotes a verse which means "Be thankful that at least you have Miran—the only one left among Delhi men", and compares it with Mir's original verse, which means, "Be thankful that at least you have Mir—the only one left of men of former times."] Don't you think it's a fine adaptation?

'Oh, and there's more news. Have you heard? Yesterday I had a letter from Yusuf Mirza in Lucknow to say that Nasīr Khan's (Nawwab Jan's) father has been sentenced to life imprisonment. I'm astonished that such a thing could happen. But Yusuf Mirza wouldn't tell me anything that wasn't true, and I can only hope that the news he heard wasn't true.

---

[1] A famous Urdu poet of the eighteenth century.
[2] The great eighteenth-century Urdu ghazal poet.

'Well, my friend, *you* can sit here or not as you like, but *I'm* going off for my lunch. Everyone here, in the zenana and outside it, is keeping the fast—even the elder boy, Baqir Ali Khan. Only I and my son Husain Ali Khan are eating—the same Husain Ali Khan whose daily cry is, "Get me some toys" and "I want to go to the shops." Give my blessing to Mir Sarfaraz Husain and mind you read him this letter. And my blessing to my boy Mir Nasīr ud Din '

The letter illustrates a very lovable side of Ghalib's character. No one could have felt more deeply than he the loss of Maikash and all his other friends, but he is ready to respond to Majruh with a letter to cheer him up.

In March or April he writes to Hatim Ali Beg Mihr:

'Keep strong your faith in the unseen—
else you are no believer.
You who are hidden from my sight, love
for you is my faith.[1]

Your auspicious portrait has gladdened my sight. Do you know what Mirza Yusuf Ali Khan Aziz meant by what he said to you? I must have said some time in the company of friends, "I should like to see Mirza Hatim Ali. I hear he's a man of very striking appearance." And, my friend, I had often heard this from Mughal Jan.[2] In the days when she was in Nawwab Hāmid Ali Khan's service I used to know her extremely well, and I often used to spend hours together in her company. She also showed me the verse you wrote in praise of her beauty.

'Anyway, when I saw your portrait and saw how tall you were, I didn't feel jealous because I too am noticeably tall. And I didn't feel jealous of your wheaten complexion, because mine, in the days when I was in the land of the living, used to be even fairer, and people of discrimination used to praise it. Now when I remember what my complexion once was, the memory is simple torture to me. The thing that *did* make me jealous—and that in no small degree—was that you are clean-shaven. I remembered the pleasant days of my youth, and I cannot tell you what I felt. But as Shaikh Ali Hazin says:

I rent my clothes when I was young
and felt a lover's frenzy.
Now I may wear my woollen cloak and feel
no sense of shame.

When white hairs began to appear in my beard and moustaches, and on the third day they began to look as though ants had laid their white eggs in them—and, worse than that, I broke my two front teeth—there was nothing for it but to . . . let my beard grow long. But remember that in this uncouth city [Delhi] everybody wears a sort of uniform. Mullahs, junk-dealers, hookah-menders,

---

[1] The same verse as he had quoted in a letter to Mihr in 1857—(cf. p. 152 above).
[2] The style of name shows that she was a courtesan.

washermen, water-carriers, innkeepers, weavers, greengrocers—all of them
wear their hair long and grow a beard. The day your humble servant grew a
beard he had *his* hair shaved off—But God save us! what am I prattling about?

'Sahib, your humble servant sent a copy of *Dastambu* as a present to . . .
George Frederick Edmonstone Sahib, Lieutenant-Governor of the North-
Western Provinces. In reply I received by post a letter in Persian, written on
March 10th, praising the book and expressing his pleasure. I then sent a Persian
ode of congratulation on his Lieutenant-Governorship, and received a reply in
Persian, dated 14th, expressing appreciation of the poem and satisfaction at its
contents. Then I sent a Persian ode of eulogy and praise to . . . Robert Montgomery Sahib Bahadur, Lieutenant-Governor of the Panjab, sending it through
the Commissioner of Delhi. Yesterday a letter bearing his seal reached me
through the Commissioner of Delhi. About my pension, instructions have so
far not been received. But grounds for hope continue to grow. Slow but sure.
I never eat bread; just a pound of meat during the day and eight ounces of
wine at night.'

He then quotes the first couplet of one of his ghazals and says: 'If my insight
is true and the person who wanted this ghazal is a man of sound taste, then the
ghazal will have reached him before this letter. As for my greetings, I'll send
them now.'

His next letter—undated—begins with a reference to his own verse:

'The condition of Delhi is

> My home was wrecked; what further
> > ruin could your love inflict?
> The yearning to rebuild it filled my
> > heart and fills it still.

What is there left here for any one to loot? . . . The late Nasikh was your ustad
and my true and loving friend, but he was a poet with a single skill. He wrote
only ghazals and never touched the ode or the masnavi. Praise be to God!
You've written an ode that Insha[1] would have envied. And I cannot tell you
how much I enjoyed the couplets from your masnavi. . . . God grant you long
life. In days like these men like you are precious. . . .'

On June 12, 1859 he writes again to Aram. Mihr's note gives the necessary
background information to the letter:

'Aram had named his newspaper *Aftab i Alamtab* ['The Sun that Lights the
World'] and along with it had also begun to print *Halat i Darbar i Shahi*

---

[1] An Urdu poet of the late eighteenth and early nineteenth century.

['News of the Royal Court']. He had also brought out a literary journal named *Miyar ush Shuara* ['The Criterion of the Poets']. This was a fortnightly. He was proposing also to bring out another periodical publication giving an account of the Mutiny, for which Ghalib suggested titles. In the end the title chosen was *The Indian Revolt.*'

Ghalib writes:

'The position here is that among the Muslim nobles [who might have been expected to subscribe to your publications] there are three—Nawwab Hasan Ali Khan, Nawwab Hāmid Ali Khan, and Hakim Ahsanullah Khan; but their position is such that if they feed themselves they cannot clothe themselves. Moreover, it is uncertain whether they will stay here. God knows where they are to go and where to live. Hakim Ahsanullah Khan has subscribed to *Aftab i Alamtab,* but he is not likely to take *Halat i Darbar i Shahi* too. Apart from the moneylenders there are no rich men here, and *they're* not going to be interested in such things. You'd better forget any idea of getting subscribers here.'

It will be remembered that he had sent a similarly discouraging reply a year earlier. If he really means what he says about the Muslim nobles whom he names, their present straitened circumstances made a striking contrast with their former wealth. Mihr's notes on the two first-named are as follows:

'Nawwab Hasan Ali Khan: younger son of Nawwab Najabat Ali Khan, ruler of Jhajjar. He received a pension of Rs. 3,000 a month. Nawwab Hāmid Ali Khan: nephew and son-in-law of Itimad ud Daula Mir Fazl i Ali Khan, Minister to the King of Oudh. When Fazl i Ali Khan died, Hāmid Ali Khan came to Delhi, where he deposited his money in the treasury, drawing Rs. 4,500 a month in interest. He was kept in confinement for fourteen months after the Mutiny, but was released in February 1859.'

Ghalib continues his letter:

'As for the name of the publication [on the Mutiny], never mind about making it a chronogram. [He then suggests three possible titles.] And now tell me: does your paper *Miyar ush Shuara* go to the Nawwab of Rampur? I saw in the last number that you had written, "A poet named Amir[1] sends us his ghazals, but we cannot print them until we know his full name and other particulars." So let me inform you that he is a friend of mine. His name is Amir Ahmad and his takhallus Amir. He is a distinguished Lucknow gentleman, and was at one time a courtier and companion of the Oudh Kings. He is now with the Nawwab of Rampur. You can print his ghazals giving my name as a reference—something like, "These ghazals were sent to us by Ghalib, who also informed us of

---

[1] Amir Minai, at this time relatively unknown, later became a famous Urdu poet.

the poet's name and supplied the particulars which follow." Then print the information I have just given you. Put this in the forthcoming issue and send a two-page or four-page section to him at Rampur. Address it as follows: "Maulvi Amir Ahmad Sahib Amir, His Highness's Court, Rampur." And let me know whether your paper goes to Rampur or not.'

On June 17, 1859 he writes to Tufta:

'Four days ago, that is on Tuesday, at about ten in the morning I was un-expectedly honoured by a visit from Raja Umid Singh. I asked him about his travels and he told me that he had just returned from Agra. He has bought Joras Sahib's mansion in Basavan Lane, near Hakim's Lane; and he has also bought the adjoining land and is building on it. I spoke about you and told him that you ask after him whenever you write and also that you say you have sent him several letters, but had no reply. He said he had had one letter from you, and had replied to it, but had not had any more letters from you after that. Anyway, I've got boils, so I haven't returned his visit. I think he is going away today or tomorrow. (He's again going to Agra.) I'll send my man to him today. Yesterday I had a letter from Mirza Hatim Ali Mihr. He was asking after you—where you were, and how you are. Write to him, my friend.'

On June 29, 1859 he writes to him again:

'I had a letter from you the day before yesterday in which you said you were going to Meerut. This morning I had another in which you said you would be leaving on July 1st and would see me before you left. In both letters you speak of a parcel which you sent off on 20th June. Well, that's ten days ago, and during these ten days no parcel or pamphlet packet has reached me. The last pamphlet I had from you was the one with the two masnavis. (One of them was about that incident at Bulandshahr—about the boy that died, and how his lover stood by the funeral pyre, and how while the flames of the pyre consumed the boy's body, the flames of love consumed him too.) I made my corrections on both masnavis and posted them off to you; in fact I seem to remember your acknowledging them. But I have an idea that all this was before 20th June. Anyway, I've not had any parcel since that one. I don't keep things sent to me for correction more than two days, wherever they come from—least of all yours. But I can't do anything about things which don't reach me. In fact, *I* sent *you* a letter to which you owe me a reply. Perhaps that didn't reach you, or else you didn't think any reply was necessary. . . .'

In June comes the first of the Urdu letters to Husain Mirza which have survived, though Ghalib had told Majruh as long ago as February that he was in regular correspondence with him.

We are fortunate in knowing a good deal about Husain Mirza and his nephew[1] Yusuf Mirza from Mihr's account, which is based upon materials in the possession of Husain Mirza's family. The family was an old and distinguished one, and shared a common ancestor with the Kings of Oudh. For generations it lived in Lucknow, but Husain Mirza's father Hisam ud Din Haidar Khan had migrated to Delhi where, while continuing to draw a large income from Lucknow, he acquired considerable wealth and high rank. Husain Mirza was his third child, and second son, and was ultimately married to the daughter of a noble who was Steward to the Royal Household. On his father-in-law's death, Husain Mirza was appointed to succeed him in this office. He still held it when the Mutiny broke out. We know that he was one of the two nobles—the other being Ziya ud din Ahmad Khan—who preserved every thing that Ghalib wrote.[2] Once the rebel sepoys occupied the capital, Husain Mirza would have been in no position to relinquish his office at the Mughal Court even if he had wished to, and the British re-occupation of Delhi in September therefore put him in a position of great danger. The fate of his elder brother Muzaffar ud Daula was soon to underline the jeopardy of his situation. Mihr writes:

'When the English forces entered Delhi, Muzaffar ud Daula, with a number of others, went to Alwar, where the Raja was his friend. But he was taken prisoner there and brought to Gurgaon, where the British officers, without any trial or investigation or inquiry, shot him, along with a number of others. . . . Husain Mirza and his dependants first made their way to Safdar Jang's tomb [outside Delhi]. . . . From the Ajmeri Gate to the tomb must be about four to five miles, and in this short distance . . . robbers extorted ten thousand rupees from them. Then Nawwab Hāmid Ali Khan secretly got them all away to his village . . ., which is near Panipat. He had been Steward at the royal court, and could not be overlooked. A widespread search for him was made, and when the English discovered that he was in the village, a warrant was issued for his arrest. But before he could be taken he got to Panipat, where the Ansaris saved him at the risk of their own lives. He then made his way in disguise to Lucknow, where he lived in hiding. After the proclamation of general amnesty he returned to Delhi. [At the time when Ghalib writes he was out of danger, but still in Lucknow.] He had two sons, the elder named Sajjad Mirza and the younger Akbar Mirza. . . . Ghalib was on intimate terms with the whole family, and especially with Husain Mirza, whom he loved as a brother.'

Ghalib's own writings bear out this estimate. We have seen that Husain Mirza's father, Hisam ud Din Haidar Khan, was one of those to whom Ghalib offered his advice on the writing of poetry[3] and when his Urdu diwan was published, Ghalib wrote an introduction to it. The warmth of his feeling for the family is also evident in his account of the burning of their mansions after their flight from Delhi,[4] while in a letter he speaks of the death of Muzaffar ud Daula as

---

[1] Sister's son.   [2] Cf. p. 182.   [3] Cf. p. 93 above.   [4] Cf. pp. 147-8 above.

'ranking with the tragedy of Karbala'.[1] In the series of letters to Husain Mirza
and Yusuf Mirza which begins at this time there are two recurring themes—the
possibility of help from Wajid Ali Shah, the exiled King of Oudh, and the
position of the family's Delhi properties—but the first, dated June 18, 1859,
speaks also of a matter of great importance to Ghalib's own personal fortunes.
He writes to Husain Mirza:

'My dear Nawwab Sahib, it's easy to complain. Your honour got hold of some
green ink from somewhere without having to pay for it, and proceeded to
complain to me. And Yusuf Mirza Sahib has issued his command that I am to
send him something in verse and prose. Well, my friend, I have already written
a reply to you and sent it off. I don't propose yet to draft any petition [for you]
on my own to the Lord of the World,[2] and when I do, I shall send it through
my master[3]—may God preserve him! *You* should write out what you want to
say in the current, accepted Persian and then send it to me. This is what I have
said in my letter to you, and this is the answer to Yusuf Mirza too.

'Mirza Agha Jan Sahib came here the day before yesterday, bringing me the
news that Bhara Singh and Kashi Nath have come. I told him, "They can't do
anything either for you or for me. What can they do? It's out of the question.
What's going on is of the same order as the coming of the morning, or the
coming of evening, or the gathering of the clouds, or the falling of the rain.
Man's efforts, and plans, and desires don't enter into it." The talk about re-
settlement has died down again. Somewhat less than a hundred houses in the
area near Lahori Gate have been re-occupied. There are several thousand
houses in that area, and if God Almighty wills, it will be re-occupied within
the next three or four years. And when that area is re-occupied a start will be
made on the next. Don't worry about it. What's the hurry?'

After this sarcastic comment he goes on to give news of the comings and
goings of various people known to both of them, and then turns to his own
troubles.

'Well, so much for that. Now listen to my tale of woe. I didn't run away; I
wasn't arrested; nothing about me was found in the Fort records; no stain of
indifference or disloyalty [to the British] was found on my character. But some
newspaper proprietor, Gauri Shankar, or Gauri Dayal or something, used to
send his paper here during the days of the Mutiny, and some correspondent
sent in a news item, which he printed, that on such and such a date Asadullah
Khan Ghalib composed this inscription for the King's coinage and presented
it to him. [The inscription then follows.] When the Commissioner interviewed

---

[1] Cf. p. 210 below.
[2] Wajid Ali Shah, King of Oudh until the English annexed the kingdom in 1856, and removed him
to Calcutta.
[3] The *mujtahid ul asar* (leading Shia divine) at Wajid Ali Shah's court.

me he asked me, "What is this that he writes?" I said, "It is incorrect. The King was a poet, his sons were poets, his servants were poets—God knows who wrote it. The correspondent has ascribed it to me; but if I had written it, some paper in my writing would have been found in the Court records. You should ask Hakim Ahsanullah Khan about it." At the time he said nothing more. Now he has been transferred. Two weeks before he left he wrote a minute in Persian to the effect that this Asadullah Khan is famous for his unique knowledge of Persian, but we are not concerned with that. He was in the King's employ and composed an inscription for his coinage. In my opinion he does not merit a pension. Just see. I am here in Delhi; I have personal dealings with his staff; no one will tell me the date of this minute, or whether it has been forwarded to higher authority or not. I am at a loss to know what I should do. I shall go to see the new Commissioner, and if he consents, will get a copy of this minute from him. I also took the precaution of sending a reply before his predecessor's departure. But [no attention was paid to it and][1] only the statement of the charge against me is receiving attention. My friend, I put my trust in Ali—let me live, or let me die. If once I get a flat refusal I shall leave this city, and consign these two rupees a day[2] to the grave of the accursed tyrant who out of ten thousand rupees a year[3] saw fit to grant me just this. And may curses and torment be his lot.

'Give my blessings to Yusuf Mirza.

'Friend, Mir Ahmad Husain (Mir Raushan Ali Khan's father) has just told me that when Bahadur Shah came to the throne he was in Murshidabad, and he remembers hearing this inscription there. When he told me this I remembered that when Maulvi Muhammad Baqir printed [in his newspaper] the news of Akbar Shah's death and Bahadur Shah's accession, he also printed the news that Zauq had composed and presented this inscription. Bahadur Shah came to the throne in October 1837 or 1838.[4] Some people keep files of newspapers. If you can trace it there and send me the issue of the original newspaper just as it is, you will be helping me a great deal. I have written off to friends in Agra, Farrukhabad, Marahra and Meerut; and now I've written to you too. Now I only have to write off to Kalpi, and I'll do that within the next day or two. We have to examine twelve issues of the paper—covering the three months October, November and December of 1837 and 1838.'

In the same month he writes to Yusuf Mirza:

'My dearest friend, dear to me as the sight of my eyes,

> The child has left you and returned to dust.
> Grieve not; he came pure and departed pure.

---

[1] The words in square brackets are a surmise. Mihr gives a dotted line, with a note that it represents a passage in the original which is illegible.

[2] The pension was Rs. 62 As. 8 per month.   [3] Cf. p. 44-5 above.

[4] The former date is correct.

He was God's servant, and found favour in his Creator's sight. He came into
the world bearing a good soul and a good fortune. What would he have wanted
with staying here? You must not feel the least regret. And if the thought of
having children pleases you so much, well, you yourself are no more than a
child: God give you long life and children in abundance. Why do you write
about the death of your grandfather and grandmother? Their time had come.
The death of his elders is the common heritage of man. Did you want them to
go on living in times like these and see their honour destroyed? Yes, grief for
[your uncle] Muzaffar ud Daula [who was killed in the Mutiny] is another
matter. It ranks with the tragedy of Holy Karbala, and will live on as long as I
live. You should never feel any regret for what you have done to serve your
father. For anything in your power which you failed to do, you would have
been justly censured. When you are powerless to help, what are you to do?
The problem which faces us all these days is, where are we to live and what
are we to eat? You sent me news of Maulana [Fazl i Haq];[1] now let me send
you some. The court of appeal has upheld the sentence of life imprisonment; in
fact it has gone further and recommended that his transportation should be
expedited. You will get the news of this in due course. His son is going to
appeal to England, but what is the use? What had to happen, has happened.
"Verily we are for God, and verily to Him we shall return." Give . . . [Husain
Mirza] my regards and tell him that I have already written him a full account
of my position. If he can get that issue of the Delhi *Urdu Akhbar* it will be a
great help. But anyway I have nothing much to fear. The higher authorities
won't pay much regard to such things. I didn't compose the inscription, and
if I did, I did it under duress, to preserve my life and my honour. That's no sin,
and if it *is* a sin, is it so grave a sin that even Her Majesty's proclamation[2]
cannot wipe it out? Good God! Can the artilleryman who made ammunition
and sited the guns and looted the bank and the magazine be pardoned, and a
poet's couplet not be pardoned?

'Let me tell you a funny story of something that happened two days ago.
Hāfiz Mammu has been cleared of all guilt, and been released. He attends upon
the Commissioner asking for the return of his property. The fact that it *is*
his property has already been verified, and only the Commissioner's order is
required. Two days ago he presented himself, and his file was laid before the
Commissioner. "Who is Hāfiz Muhammad Bakhsh?" the Commissioner
asked. He replied, "*I* am." Then he asked, "And who is Hāfiz Mammu?" He
replied, "*I* am. My real name is Muhammad Bakhsh, but people call me Mammu.' He said, "That doesn't make sense. Hāfiz Muhammad Bakhsh is you;
Hāfiz Mammu is you; everyone in the world is you. Who am I to hand over
the house to?" The file was sent back to the office and our friend Mammu
went home . . .'

---

[1] One of Ghalib's oldest friends. Cf. p. 33 above.
[2] Of general amnesty.

An undated letter to Sahib i Alam clearly belongs to about this time, as internal evidence shows:

'I spend my days and nights thinking to myself, "This is what life was like; now let me see what death will be like."

> I lived my life waiting for death to come
> And dead, I still must see what else I face.

The couplet is my own, and it aptly describes my state of mind.'

He goes on to speak of the trouble over the inscription he was alleged to have written, repeating the information he had given in letters to others and adding:

'I searched the whole realm of Hindustan for the Delhi *Urdu Akhbar*, but I could not get it anywhere. The stain upon me remains; my pension is lost, the tokens of my noble rank, the robe and the durbar, are wiped out. Well, when all that happens, happens by the will of God, how can I complain?

> God sets the skies in motion. Understand then
> Nothing that comes from them can be unjust.[1]

... The story is told that Abul Hasan Khirqani (God's Mercy be upon him) was asked, "How are you faring?" He replied, "How will that man be faring of whom his God demands the fulfilment of his religious duty, and his Prophet the observance of his own standards, and his wife his wealth, and the angel of death his life?"

'In short, I live on in hope of death. . . .'

On July 15, 1859 he writes to Yusuf Mirza:

'I'm not going to correct your masnavi until I have the whole of it. You can put forward as many plausible arguments as you like, or appeal to my sense of shame, but until I get a complete ghazal or a complete masnavi, how am I to correct it? Give your uncle [Husain Mirza] my regards (because I love him) and my humble submission (because he is a Sayyid)[2] and my blessing (because he is my intimate friend and I am his ustad) and ask him what else he expects me to write. He asks me for a copy of the order; but where am I to get the original to take a copy from? It's true that everyone is saying that those who were formerly in [the King's] service are not being called to account; but my own observation tells me otherwise. Just see, only a few days ago Hāmid Khan was brought in under arrest, fettered hand and foot. He is in prison. Let's see what orders are finally issued. He contented himself with Navind Rae alone to represent him. What is to be, will be. People's cases are being decided on the

---

[1] Cf. p. 133.   [2] A descendant of the Prophet.

basis of whatever reports about them the authorities have. No law, no regulation matters. No precedent, no plea has any effect. A report has been forwarded
sanctioning a full pension of Rs. 200 to Irtiza Khan, son of Murtaza Khan, and
his two sisters, who received a monthly pension of Rs. 100 each, have been
officially told that their brother has been found guilty, and that their pensions
are therefore forfeit; but that on compassionate grounds they will each be
granted Rs. 10 per month. If that is compassion, what must indifference be like!
Here am I myself. I know the higher authorities, but I can't even pluck out a
pubic hair [i.e. there is absolutely no move I can make]. For fifty-three years
I've been drawing a pension, appointed by Lord Lake, and approved by the
Government; and yet I don't get it and am not likely to. Anyway, I can still
hope. You know that I am Ali's slave, and that I never take his name in vain.
Believe me then, at this moment Kallu[1] has one rupee and seven annas left;
and when that is spent, there is nowhere I can turn for a loan and nothing I
have left that I can pawn or sell. If money comes from Rampur, well and good.
Otherwise "Verily we are for God, and verily to Him we shall return."

'Some people have the idea that instructions about pensions will be issued
this month. Well, we shall see whether they are or not, and if they are, whether
I am among the chosen or the rejected. . . .'

As we have seen, money did come from Rampur; from this month onwards
Ghalib received from the Nawwab a regular income of Rs. 100 per month.

On July 23, 1859 he writes to Aram:

'Your letter reached me, and the issue of *The Indian Revolt* reached me a few
days before it. The firmness of your resolution pleases me. God be praised,
that now I shall look upon you, Bansi Dhar's grandson—my own grandson.
See that *The Indian Revolt* reaches me every month and *Miyar ush Shuara*
every fortnight. We'll talk about other things when we meet. I told my dear
friend Master Ramchandar the news that you were coming. He was very pleased.
I am sending his reply to my letter for you to read. If there are any copies of
Dastambu left, bring them with you."

On July 26, 1859 he writes to Yusuf Mirza:

'My friend how is it that you have got this skin irritation? And how did Husain
Mirza fall ill? O God, bestow peace of mind upon these wanderers in the
deserts of strange lands whenever it be Thy will, but preserve them in good
health, in Ali's name. Alas! Alas! Husain Mirza's beard has turned white. These
are the blessings which these extremes of grief and distress confer. As soon as
this letter arrives, write and tell me how you both are.

'You read my letter to you in a place [Lucknow] which exemplifies the poet's
lines:

---

[1] Ghalib's servant.

He said to me, "Our state is like the
                    lightning's—
Born in a flash, and vanished in a flash" . . .

He is my master and, God keep him safe, my revered elder. Agha Baqir's
Imambara,[1] besides being the house in which my master goes to mourn, is an
ancient foundation of exalted fame. Who would not grieve at its destruction?
Here two roads are forging rapidly ahead—the cool road and the iron road
[i.e. a road with water-courses, and the railway]—each in its own location.
More than that, barracks for the British soldiers are to be built in the city, and
in front of the Fort, where Lal Diggi is, there is to be a great area of open
ground. It will take in the whole area right up to the Khas Bazaar, from . . .
[here Ghalib lists a number of other localities]. Put it this way: from Ammu
Jan's Gate to the moat of the Fort, except for Lal Diggi and one or two wells,
no trace of any building will remain. Today they have begun demolishing the
houses of Jan Nisar Khan Chatta. I should rejoice in the desolation of Delhi.
When it's citizens have gone, then to hell with the city.

'Baqir Ali and Husain Ali have gone with their grandmother to Qutub
Sahib [the area around the Qutub Minar], to Ziya ud Din Khan's mother's.
Ayaz and Niyaz Ali are with them. So two "humble submissions" and one
"blessing" and two "respects" are deferred till later.' [These are the forms of
greeting which, respectively, the two boys, their grandmother, and the other
two named would have sent had they been there.]

Two days later, on July 28, 1859 he writes to Husain Mirza:

'O Husain, son of Ali, I pledge my soul to thee! . . .[2] My friend, what Muhammad Quli Khan wrote was false. Neither Hasan Ali Khan, nor Hāmid Ali Khan,
nor Hakim Ahsanullah Khan have been imprisoned. In the end no order was
issued against any of them. Hakim Ahsanullah Khan has obtained possession
of his houses. There is an Englishmen living in the zenana, at the back of the
baths. He pays a rent of thirty-five rupees a month. The other two are still
held up by the same difficulties. Ahsanullah Khan has moved into his house.
He has turned the main hall into the zenana, and made his own quarters where
the stable used to be. Debi Ram and Salig Ram have also got their houses back;
in fact I have heard that even their buried valuables were intact. Now they've
brought Hāmid Ali Khan from Qutub ud Din the merchant's mansion to their
own house . . .'

In an undated letter of about this time he writes to Majruh:

'My devoted son, did you see the poem? It's a faithful reflection of my state;

---

[1] Cf. p. 49 above.
[2] A play upon the name of his correspondent. Husain, son of Ali, was the grandson of the Prophet.

there's no poetry left in me. I had meant when I sent it off to write a letter too, but the children were pestering me, "Come on, grand-dad, dinner's ready. We're hungry." I had already got three letters written and I thought to myself, "Why should I write any more now?" So I just put the paper in the envelope, stamped it, addressed it, gave it to Kalian [Ghalib's servant] to post, and went to dinner. I did it to provoke you too. "This will annoy Mir Mahdi [Majruh]. Let's see what he says," I thought to myself. And that's just what happened. A real outburst of indignation! Well, here I am, sitting down to write to you. Tell me, what shall I write? Miran Sahib will have told you all about what's going on here. But don't believe what he's told you. The question of my pension is now before the Governor-General in Calcutta. The Commissioner here left a minute when he went, but what harm can that do me?

'I had written this much when two friends came to see me. It was not long before sunset. I shut up my box and went out to sit with them. It got dark, and and the lamp was lighted. I was lying on the bed, with Munshi Sayyid Ahmad Husain sitting at the head on a rush-chair, when all of a sudden that Eye and Lamp of the family of Faith and Learning, Sayyid Nasīr ud Din arrived, riding-whip in hand, and accompanied by a servant carrying on his head a basket covered over with green grass. I said to myself, "Aha! Good! Good! The King of Divines, Maulana Sarfaraz Husain of Delhi has sent me a fresh supply [of wine]." But it turned out not to be that, but something else—not special bounty, but general largesse; not wine, but mangoes. Well, no harm in such a gift either; in fact it's better than the other. I thought of each mango as a sealed glass, filled with the liquor of the grape, and filled with such superb skill that not so much as a single drop spilled from any of the sixty-five glasses. The man said there had been eighty, but fifteen went bad—rotten, in fact—and he threw them out in case they should affect the others. I said, "There are plenty left, my friend". I was not pleased, though, that you had put yourself to such trouble. You haven't enough money to go spending it on mangoes. God grant you prosperity and increase of wealth.

'There's a kind of English drink called "likur" [liqueur]—an exquisite liquor with a fine colour, and as sweet to the taste as a thin syrup of sugar. Let me tell you, you won't find its meaning in any dictionary, except perhaps in Sarwari.

'Give my blessing to the Authority of the Age [Mir Sarfaraz Husain], and to Hakim Mir Ashraf Ali, who is the key to his learning, and has gathered halfpenny pamphlets to the value of forty to fifty rupees.'

In July 1859 he again writes to Majruh:
'My friend, you talk like a child. There was indeed ground for anxiety . . . but your letter removed it. So what are you weeping and wailing for? The higher authority is favourable; and the subordinate, who was unfavourable, has gone. So what's all the fuss about? . . .

'The word "fahmaish" is a coining of old Budha, son of Jumma, and Lala Ganesh Das, son of Lala Bhairun Nath. Have you ever heard *me* use it?'

He then goes on to explain the rules governing the formation of certain types of Persian words, and concludes:

'Give Hakim Mir Ashraf Ali first, my blessing, and next my congratulations on the birth of his son. Last night, my boy, when I was slightly merry, I thought up a name which would be a chronogram of his birth—Mir Kazim Din. It works out at 1275, but, like "fahmaish", no literate person would use it.'

On August 18, 1859 he writes to Yusuf Mirza:

'May God Almighty grant you long life and wealth and happiness and honour. There was nothing in your letter of 2nd that called for a reply—only the news of Mirza Haidar Sahib's death. Yesterday morning, Wednesday, the 17th of both months [Muslim and Christian], Mirza Agha Jan Sahib came. He told me that Husain Mirza's wife had come from Lucknow . . .but had now gone on to her son at Pataudi. She had told him that Nāzir ji [Husain Mirza]—may his troubles befall his enemies—was very ill. . . . Yusuf Mirza, I tell you I felt desperate. What could I do? And how could I get news of him? I began to repeat to myself 'O, Ali! O, Ali! O, Ali!'' and I must have repeated his name ten times when Madari's son came running and brought me three letters. He was downstairs in the house when the postman came and handed him the letters; and Niyaz Ali brought them up to me. One was from Aziz, one from Hargopal Tufta, and one from Maulvi Zulfaqar Haidar.[1] My friend, I was near to tears with joy. At length I put his letter to my eyes[2] and then kissed it.

'Now just look at this: His letter of 13th Muharram reaches me on 17th. In it he writes that on Friday 19th he will be leaving by the mail for Calcutta. And then, the gentleman demands a reply! Yes, once he gets to Calcutta, and writes to me from there, and gives me the address where he is staying, then I'll write whatever I have to write. . . . Ziya ud Din has been here for the last two weeks. He is staying in the grounds of his old house. He has been to see me twice, and stayed about an hour on each occasion. It seems that he has chosen to show some regard for our former intimacy. God willing, I'll get him to send something to Sajjad Mirza, and once I hear from him from Calcutta, to Nāzir ji.

'Things are still just the same with me. I don't go hungry, but I am incapable of being of any service to anybody. If I speak to anyone I shan't be believed, and in any case it's not a matter for words, but for action; and I haven't the means to do anything. . . . Our friend Fazlu is staying in Arabsara. He's been here two days now. He runs around presenting petitions, but nobody takes any notice of them. He sends you his regards.

'Entry and exit permits have been discontinued. Beggars and people bearing arms are not allowed in, but anyone else—Hindu or Muslim, man or woman,

---

[1] Husain Mirza's name. Husain Mirza was the familiar name used by his family and close acquaintances.

[2] A sign of love and devotion to the writer.

mounted or on foot, can come and go as he pleases. But no one can stay over-night unless he has a residence permit. You remember all the talk about new roads being laid and a cantonment for the British troops being built? Well, nothing has happened. After all the fuss, all they've made is the new road in the area of Jan Nisar Khan's Chatta. People here in Delhi have been spreading all sorts of rumours about Lucknow. They say that thousands of houses have been demolished to make an open expanse. But I don't suppose that's so. I expect that nothing more has happened than what you wrote to me. Anyway, however that may be, write and tell me if Nāzir ji went off all right, and if Sajjad and Akbar and his mother and your father are all well.'

On September 8, 1859, he writes in great depression to Junun:

'The letter with the verses . . . enclosed reached me, and I replied to it, without writing anything about them. I can't contemplate writing Persian. I have no spirit left in me. My friends, my brothers, have all been killed or have disap-peared without trace. I have a thousand friends to mourn, grieving alone and comforting myself alone. More than ruined and destitute; my life is ending, and "my foot is in the stirrup". . . .'

He goes on to speak contemptuously of a Persian dictionary which, pre-sumably, Junun had quoted as an authority, corrects a line which Junun had misquoted from the chronogram which he had composed in anticipation that he would die in 1277 A H, denies indignantly that he could ever use the wording that Junun had given, and then gives the full verse (with a slight variation, however, in the first line), concluding: 'I learned this date not from the stars, but by revelation. "Verily we are for God, and verily to Him we shall return."'

He is still in the same mood when he writes on October 1, 1859 to the Nawwab of Rampur: 'I am your servant, and to praise and bless you is my task. Old age has laid me low, and in a little while I shall breathe no more.'

It was perhaps in the same period that he wrote an undated letter to Tufta:

'My friend, the way your mind works beats me! When did I say that your poetry was not good? When did I say that you will find none in the world to understand it and appreciate its worth? But it's true that you are intent on poetry, while all my faculties are intent on attaining oblivion. To me the learning of Avicenna and the poetry of Naziri are alike wasted, and pointless and illusory. To pass one's life one needs a little ease—and all the learning and power and poetry and magic are nothing. What of it if an avatar comes to the Hindus? And what of it if a prophet arises amongst the Muslims? What of it if a man wins fame in the world? And what of it if he lives out his life un-known? Let a man have something to live on, and physical health, and the rest is nothing, my dear friend. As a matter of fact these too are nothing, but I have not yet reached the stage where I realise it. Perhaps in due course this veil too will fall from my eyes, and I shall pass beyond the stage where getting a living, and enjoying health and pleasure mean anything to me, and pass into a world where sensation ceases.

'In the desolation in which I live I am lost to the whole world, indeed to both worlds. I go on giving my answers to suit the questions I am asked, and behave with every man as our relationship warrants; but it is all illusion in my sight—not a river, but a mirage; not reality, but fantasy. You and I are not bad poets. Suppose I grant we win the same fame as Sadi and Hāfiz. What did their fame bring them? And what would ours bring us? . . .'

But by October 15th he seems to have recovered. He writes to Majruh:

'My dear, you have nothing to do, and you fill in the time by writing letters. Your pen and ink is always ready. If a letter comes back you reply to it; if not, then you take up your pen to grumble and complain and get cross and call me names. Hakim Ashraf Ali came to see me. He had shaved his head. . . . By God, he's a sight to be seen. He told me that Mir Ahmad Ali had come, and that all was well with him again. I gave thanks to God. God grant us once in a while to hear such good news of our friends. Give him my regards and my congratulations. Mind you don't forget!

'My answer to your unwarranted complaints is this: The letter you sent from Panipat said that you were leaving for Karnal. I planned to write to you when I heard from you at Karnal. Well, today is Saturday, 15th October. It is morning. The food isn't even cooked yet. I have just had my cool morning drink. Your letter came; I read it; and I wrote this reply. Kalian is not well, so I'm sending Ayaz with it to the post office. Well, what have you to say? Was your complaint unwarranted, or wasn't it? If you want to complain to anyone, my friend, complain to yourself for waiting so long after you got to Karnal before you wrote to me. . . .

'As for my pension, don't talk about it. If I get it, I'll let you know. There was talk about re-settling the city, and houses could be had for rent. Four to five hundred houses were re-occupied, and then the order was cancelled. God knows what rule is in force now or what will happen next. . . .'

On October 29, 1859 he writes to Husain Mirza:

'I have already sent off replies to your and Yusuf Mirza's letter . . . Kashi Nath[1] is a careless sort of man. You should send off a letter of instructions to him too. He is always saying that when Husain Mirza writes, it is always to Mirza Nosha.[2] Don't let him know that I told you this; but write to him about your affairs.

'What can I do? I could say that my very life is yours to command, but that would be mere formal politeness. No one gives his life for another, or asks

---

[1] Who was acting on Husain Mirza's behalf in Delhi.
[2] Ghalib's nickname.

another to give his life for him. But the Lord my God knows the thought I take for you and what resources I possess. My resources you too know. . . .

'I write these few lines to tell you that your creditor Chunni Lal came a little while ago. He was asking me about you. I told him a mixture of truth and lies and got him to consider sending you another hundred to two hundred rupees. I talked to him like a *baniya*.[1] "Lala," I said, "when a man wants the fruit of a tree, he first waters it. Husain Mirza is your farm. Water it, and it will give you grain." My friend, that softened him a little. He got me to write down your address and took it away with him saying that he would discuss the matter with his son Ramji Das and would come and let me know what they decided. If he sends you money, what more do you want? And if he writes to you first, be sure to tell him in your reply that what Asadullah told him was quite true and that the matter will shortly be coming to fruition. . . .'

On November 2, 1859 he writes to Aram, asking him why he had not answered the questions which Ghalib had put to him, in some cases as long ago as August:

'If you're cross with me, say so. I am sending this letter unstamped to show you that I want a reply. And listen; there's something else I have to say to you. There are you, behaving as though you'd sworn an oath not to write to me, and here am I, anxious to get all the news about the Governor-General. Keep writing to me, and pass on all the news you hear, especially about what happened in Agra; I want to hear about that in detail. Did the Lieutenant-Governor accompany him there, or did they proceed there separately and meet after their arrival? What happened at the durbar? What awards were made to their well-wishers? Were any new administrative changes introduced, and if so, what are they? Keep me informed of all these things. Now mind, you're not to be idle about this. What have you heard just lately? How far have they come from Lucknow? Will they be coming to Agra via Kanpur and Farrukhabad? Where have they met the local nobility? And whom have they met? Write me whatever you've heard about the durbar at Lucknow. People here get the newspapers regularly, and I read them too, but I want *you* to write regularly and keep me informed, because you will write in greater detail and make matters clearer. I am sure my beloved nephew, your respected father, must have settled that Matter of Mirza Yusuf Ali Khan's successfully with Lala Joti Parshad. I need to know about this too. I expect a reply from you.'

On November 7, 1859 he writes to the Nawwab of Rampur telling him of the honours which the British had once shown him, and the uncertainty of his present position:

'My standing with the British government is that of a hereditary noble. My

---

[1] A caste of Hindus who deal in grain and in money-lending. 'Lala' is the title by which they are addressed.

income is small, but I am treated with an honour out of proportion to it. In the Government durbars I occupy the tenth place to the right, and the marks of honour prescribed for me comprise a ceremonial robe, seven gifts of cloth, a turban with an embroidered velvet band and jewelled gold ornament to wear in it, a string of pearls and a cloak. I used to receive these up to Lord Hardinge's time. Lord Dalhousie did not come here [to Delhi]. Now the present . . . [Governor-General, Lord Canning] has come. The complexion of the times has changed. I know no one in authority, and no secretary. My great patron and admirer was Mr Edmonstone; he too is no longer Chief Secretary; he has become Lieutenant-Governor [of the Panjab]. Had he still been Secretary I should have had nothing to worry about. To this day I do not know whether I am to regard myself as innocent or guilty, accepted or rejected. Granted that I performed no service to the British that I should merit new honours, still I committed no act of disloyalty, that my former honours should be abridged. Anyway, this is my predicament. My troubles are with me, and the road to remedy is closed. . . .'

The Nawwab wrote in reply that he often spoke of Ghalib in conversations with high British officials, and felt certain that the government would continue the honours formerly shown to him.

On November 8, 1859 he writes to Majruh:

'Friend, I have neither paper nor stamps, and only one unstamped envelope left. I've torn this paper out of a book to write to you, and I'll post it off in the unstamped envelope. Don't worry. Last night some booty came in, and today I'll send out for paper and stamps. It is the morning of Tuesday, 8th November —what the people call "high morning". I got your letter two days ago and today I felt like writing to you; so I'm writing these few lines. . . .

'How should *I* know what's going on in the city? There's a thing called "Pown Tuty" been introduced. ["Town Duty"—i.e. a tax levied on all commodities entering the city.] Except grain and cow-dung cakes[1] every single thing is liable for it. All round the Jama Masjid to a radius of twenty-five feet there's to be an open space. Shops and houses will be pulled down. The Dar ul Baqa[2] will vanish. [There is a play on words here: Dar ul Baqa means literally "House of Eternity".] Nothing but the name of God abides. From Khan Chand's lane to Shah Bula's banyan tree everything will be demolished. The picks and shovels are plying from both sides. Otherwise all is well. We hear that the Highest Ruler [the Governor-General] is coming this way. Let's see whether he visits Delhi, and, if he does, whether he holds a durbar, and if he does, whether this sinner will be invited, and if he is, whether he will get a robe of honour. I've heard nothing about the pension, and no one knows anything about it.'

[1] Used for fuel.
[2] The seminar for the teaching of literature, medicine and the religious sciences, established by Azurda. The students were maintained free of charge and provided with books.

He gives further news in a letter of November 9, 1859 to Husain Mirza:

'These days a lot of the officials from the Panjab are here. There was a conference about the Pown Tuty [Town Duty]. It was introduced on November 7th, two days ago, and the levying of it has been given to Salig Ram . . ., Chunna Mal and Mahesh Das. Every commodity is taxed except grain and cow-dung cakes. General re-settlement is now permitted,[1] and people are pouring in. Formerly only owner-occupiers were allowed in, and no one was allowed to rent a house; but since the day before yesterday this too has been permitted. But don't get the idea that you or I or anyone else can let any part of his house to a tenant. People who never owned a house and always lived in rented accommodation are taking up residence, but the rent they pay goes to the government.

'Judge for yourself. How can your sister's application be put forward? If she comes in person, and submits an application, and the application is approved, and she gets a house, then somewhere in this great desolate city she will have a mansion, and she will have to live there. How will she manage all alone in this wilderness? She'll be scared to death. And suppose she can steel herself to live here, how will she eat? . . .

'Hakim Ahsanullah Khan has got back his houses in the city, and has been forbidden to leave the city, or indeed to step outside his own door. He is to keep to his house. All Nawwab Hāmid Ali Khan's houses have been confiscated. He and his wife[2] are living in rented accommodation in Hauz Qazi. He too is not permitted to go out. Mirza Ilahi Bakhsh has been ordered to Karachi. He has stayed put, and is living in Sultan Ji. He is appealing against the order. Let's see whether *he* stays, or whether the order does.'

On November 13, 1859 he writes to Aram:
'I have had two letters from you, and today the newspaper arrived. My cousin Ziya ud Din Khan gets this "*Avadh Akhbar*" and sends it on to me. So I don't need it. Why waste my postage and your own on it? All I wanted was that since you are not far from Farrukhabad and news from there must be reaching you all the time, you should write and tell me whatever you hear. And when the . . . [Governor-General] comes to Agra you should write and tell me what you yourself observe. That's all. I'm putting the newspaper you sent me in a fresh envelope and sending it off today. . . .

'I am very concerned about your father. I pray for him. May God grant my prayer and send him a complete recovery. . . . I got your news of Mirza Yusuf Ali Khan Aziz. He is a man of distinguished family, brought up in every luxury. God will reward you for anything you can do to serve him. . .'

---

[1] More than two years after the population of the city had been expelled.
[2] In the original the word used is 'mamtua'. This indicates that Hāmid Ali Khan was a Shia. In the Shia sect a man may contract with a woman for a specified period of marriage. A 'mamtua' is a woman married under such a contract.

On November 28, 1859 he writes to Yusuf Mirza in an outburst of bitterness:

'Yusuf Mirza, none but my Lord and God knows my plight. Men go mad from excess of cares and sorrows; their reason deserts them. And if amid the griefs that beset me my reflective power is failing, that is no ground for surprise; indeed, not to believe it is monstrous. Grief and cares for what? you may ask. For death; for separation; for my livelihood; for my honour. Whose deaths? Leave aside the Inauspicious Fort,[1] and count up only the men of Delhi: Muzaffar ud Daula;[2] Mir Nāsir ud din; Mirza Ashur Beg; my nephew's[3] son Ahmad Mirza, a mere child of nineteen; Mustafa Khan, son of Azam ud Daula; his two sons Irtiza Khan and Murtaza Khan; Qazi Faizullah. Did I not love these as much as my own kin? Yes, and two more names that I forgot: Hakim Razi ud Din Khan and Mir Ahmad Husain Maikash. O God, O God! What can replace these men? Separation from whom? From Husain Mirza, and Mir Mahdi [Majruh] and Mir Sarfaraz Husain and Miran Sahib—may God preserve them! If only they could have been happy where they are! But their homes are sunk in darkness and they are condemned to wander. When I think of the state in which Sajjad and Akbar are living my heart breaks within me. These are words that any man can say, but I swear to you as Ali is my witness that, grieving for the dead and parted from the living, the world is plunged in darkness in my sight.

'I had one brother, and he died insane. His daughter, his four boys and their mother, my sister-in-law are stranded in Jaipur. In these three years I could not send them a penny. What will my niece be thinking? She must wonder whether she *has* an uncle. Here the wives and children of men who were once wealthy nobles are begging in the streets, and I watch them helplessly. To bear such affliction needs a stout heart.

'Now listen to my own tale of woe. I must support my family—a wife and two children; then there are the servants—Kallu, Kalian and Ayaz. Madari's wife and children are still here as usual; in short, it's as though Madari were still here. Miyan Ghamman had only left me a month when he came back. "I've nothing to eat." "Very well, my friend, you too can stay." Not a penny comes in, and there are twenty mouths to feed. The allowance I get from you know where [Rampur] is just enough to keep body and soul together. And I have so much to do that during the twenty-four hours I get practically no time to myself. There is always something to worry about. I am a man; not a giant, and not a ghost. How am I to sustain such a heavy load of care? I am old and feeble. If you could see me, you would know what a state I am in. I can sit for an hour or two, but I spend the rest of the time lying down—practically confined to my bed. I can neither go out visiting regularly, nor does anyone come to see me. That liquid which sustained me, I can no longer get. And more than

---

[1] The Red Fort had been called the Auspicious Fort in the days when it was the seat of the Mughal Court.

[2] Husain Mirza's elder brother and Yusuf Mirza's own uncle.   [3] Sister's son.

all this, is all the bustle because of the Governor-General's coming visit. I used to attend the durbar, and receive a robe of honour. I cannot see that happening now. I am neither one of the accepted nor one of the rejected, nor a culprit, nor an informer, nor a conspirator. Well, tell me yourself: if a durbar is held here and I am summoned, where am I to get an offering to present?[1]

'I have sweated blood day and night for the past two months to write an ode of sixty-four couplets. I have given it to Muhammad Afzal the painter, and he will let me have it on December 1st. . . . I set myself the task of recording the events of my life in it. I will send you a copy. . . . See how I can write, even though my heart lacks fire,—indeed, lacks life.

'I could not manage a new ode to the Refuge of the World [Wajid Ali Shah, the deposed King of Oudh]. This one [i.e. the one I have already sent] was never presented; so I have put Wajid Ali Shah in Amjad Ali Shah's[2] place. After all, God himself did the same. Anwari[3] repeatedly did this, altering an ode in one man's praise for presentation to another. So if I alter the father's ode to suit the son, that's nothing so terrible, especially amid all the afflictions which I have briefly related to you. And I wrote it not to show my prowess in poetry, but to beg.

'Anyway, tell me, did the ode arrive safely? I had a letter from your uncle two days ago, but he didn't say whether the ode had reached him. Put me out of my uncertainty and write plainly whether it arrived or not. And if it did, has it been presented to His Majesty? And if it has, by whom was it presented? And what orders were given? Write to me quickly about all this. . . .

'I'm waiting for a final decision about my pension; then I shall go to Rampur. Jamadi ul Awwal to Zil Hij[4] is eight months. Then, with Muharram, the year 1277 will begin. I have to live through perhaps two, perhaps four, perhaps at the most ten or eleven months of it—nineteen to twenty months in all. For that space I shall face whatever grief or joy, whatever humiliation or whatever honour is fated for me, and then, repeating Ali's name I shall depart for the land of oblivion—my body to the realm of Rampur, my soul to the realms of light. O Ali, O Ali, O Ali!

'Let me give you another piece of news, my friend. Brahma's son fell ill; he lay ill for two days, and on the third day died. Ah me, what a nice, inoffensive boy he was! His father Shivji Ram is distraught with grief. Thus I have lost two more companions, for one is dead and one is sick at heart. . . .

'Ziya ud Din Khan went off to Rohtak without attending to that matter [i.e. without sending money to Sajjad Mirza and Husain Mirza—cf. the letter to Yusuf Mirza dated August 18, 1859, given on p. 215 above]. Let's see what he says when he comes back. If he didn't get back last night, he'll be back by this evening. What am I to do? To whom can I open my heart? I promise you by

---

[1] It was considered obligatory for a man granted audience at court to bring a present suited to his status.

[2] Father and predecessor of Wajid Ali Shah on the throne of Oudh.

[3] The great Persian poet.   [4] Months of the Muslim calendar.

Ali, I had made up my mind beforehand that I would divide whatever the King of Oudh sends between us, like brothers—half for Husain Mirza and you and Sajjad, and half for me. The poor sustain life by such fancies, but it is by these fancies that the goodness of their hearts is known. Goodbye, and may all end well.'

This letter crossed with one from Yusuf Mirza, and Ghalib writes again on the very next day, November 29, 1859:

'Friend, I posted off a letter to you yesterday morning, and yesterday evening I had another letter from you. It's surprising that Hazrat Zubdat ul Ulama hasn't yet reached there [Calcutta, to ex-King Wajid Ali Shah]. God Almighty protect and preserve him, wherever he may be . . . All I want is that the ode should be presented and bring something in for you and me. But the few lines in Nāzir Ji's [Husain Mirza's] hand on the back of the envelope have dashed all my hopes. I can't see us getting anything."

He goes on to speak of the virtual impossibility of the family recovering its Delhi properties, and goes on to quote the verse of

'Maulana Ghalib—Peace be upon him:

> He who lives on because he hopes to die—
> *His* hopelessness is something to be seen.

I cannot describe the state in which the few lines in your uncle's hand put me. Alas! Alas! that Husain Mirza should have to write, "Where am I to go? And what am I to do?", and that I, wretch that I am, can give no answer. We had high hopes of him [Wajid Ali Shah], and, granted that he could not take him into his service or confer rank . . . upon him, what was so difficult about granting him a pension of a hundred rupees or so a month? Delhi men, and especially those who held rank under the King, are in such disgrace in every city that people even flee from their shadows. There was a princely court at Murshidabad, and Hyderabad is a really big court; but when you have no one there to provide a link, how can you go? Whom would you make contact with if you did? And what would you say to him? There's nothing for it but to stay where you are, and hope that somehow you can gain access to the King of Oudh. Where else can I advise you to go? . . .'

About this time he writes to Majruh of leaving Delhi, but says he cannot go until he knows how he stands in relation to the coming durbar and how the question of his pension will be settled.

'And even if my pension is restored there is nowhere I can go except Rampur;

and there I shall go, for certain. When I have been steadfast these three years why should I get agitated now? Say no more about it, and whatever happens, don't imagine that it grieves or worries me. . . .'

On December 2, 1859 he writes again. Majruh must have asked him what Delhi was like these days. He replies:

'My friend, what a question to ask! Five things kept Delhi alive—the Fort, the daily crowds at the Jama Masjid, the weekly walk to the Jumna bridge, and the yearly fair of the flower-men.[1] None of these survives, so how could Delhi survive? Yes, there was once a city of that name in the realm of India.

'The Governor-General will be here on December 15th. We shall have to see where he stays and what arrangements are made about the durbar. In former durbars the lords of seven principalities used to be in attendance, and each was received separately—Jhajjar, Bahadurgarh, Ballabgarh, Farrukhnagar, Dujana, Pataudi and Loharu. Four of these have gone. [The British abolished the four first-named after the Mutiny.] Two of the others—Dujana and Loharu—come under the Hansi-Hissar authorities. That leaves Pataudi. If the Hissar Commissioner brings his two here, that will make three nobles. Otherwise only one. In the general durbar all the Hindu notables and so on will be there. Only three [prominent] Muslims are left—Mustafa Khan [Shefta] in Meerut, Maulvi Sadr ud Din Khan in Sultan Ji, and that slave to the things of this world Asad [Ghalib] in Ballimaron. And all three are despised and rejected, destitute and distressed.

> We smashed the wine-cup and the flask;
> > what is it now to us
> If all the rain that falls from heaven
> > should turn to rose-red wine?

If you're coming, come along. Come and see the new road through Nisar Khan's Chatta, and the new road through Khan Chand's Lane. Come and hear how Bulaqi Begam's Lane is to be demolished and an open expanse cleared to a radius of seventy yards from the Jama Masjid. Come and see Ghalib in all his despondency. And then go back. . . .'

On December 13th, 1859 he writes again:

> 'I have no wine: the pen I hold will not
> > move on.
> The wind is cold. O smokeless fire,
> > where are you?

Mir Mahdi Sahib, it is morning, and freezing cold. The brazier is before me.

[1] Cf. p. 302 below.

I write a word or two, then warm my hands. True, there is warmth in the fire, but alas! where is that liquid fire, two sips of which run coursing through your body the moment you swallow them, bringing strength to the heart, and illumination to the mind and ecstasy to the power of speech? O cruel fate that the lips of one who serves the saki of Kausar,[1] should be parched!

'My friend, you keep on and on about the pension, but . . . it's the durbar and the robe of honour that worries me to death. . . . The Commissioner here has not included my name in the list. I have appealed against this to the Lieutenant-Governor. Let's see what he says in reply . . .'

Three days later, on December 16, 1859, when he writes to Husain Mirza, he has already given up hope:

'. . . On the 19th or 20th December the Governor-General will pitch camp in Meerut, and the durbar will be held there. As for Delhi, it is not certain whether he will come. . . . Your friend too [Ziya ud Din Ahmad Khan] will be going to Meerut tomorrow or the day after, on the orders of the Commissioner of Hansi-Hissar. . . . All *my* hopes of going there and receiving a robe have vanished. And I don't expect to get the pension either. . . .

'Give my blessing to Yusuf Mirza. Kallu fetched the shoes two days ago. We packed them in a parcel open at both ends, but the post office people sent them back saying that we should pack them in a closed parcel. We did that, and he took them back. "We will accept it at two o'clock," they told him. So he sat and waited, and at nine o'clock at night it was despatched in his presence. He got a receipt for it and came back home. God grant that the shoes reach you safely and that you like them.

'I've given up all hope in the matter of the ode,[2] but anyway write and tell me what happens just by way of keeping me informed. I was glad to hear that *An Adverse Wind*[3] had arrived. All the buildings in Fil-Khana, and Falak Paira and around Lal Diggi[4] have been pulled down. The fate of Bulaqi Begam's Lane is still undecided. The military is for pulling it down, but the civil authorities want to preserve it. Let's see what happens in the end.'

On December 23, 1859 he writes to Tufta. It seems that someone named Abdur Rahman, a distant kinsman of Ghalib's, had behaved badly towards Tufta, who had asked Ghalib to remonstrate with him. He writes in reply:

'My dearest friend, what are you thinking of? Can every created mortal be a Tufta or a Ghalib?

'Each man was made to fill his proper role. "Last thoughts are best"[5] Sugar is

---

[1] Ali, the son-in-law of the Prophet, whom Ghalib specially revered, will pour the wine of purity for the blessed in Paradise. Kausar is the name of a spring in Paradise.
[2] To the ex-king of Oudh.   [3] Cf. p. 48 above.   [4] Names of localities in Delhi.
[5] i.e. one must think a thing out to the end before deciding how to act.

H

sweet, salt savoury; and nothing can change a thing's inherent taste. If I write and remonstrate with this man, can't you see what he will think? He will think to himself, "How would Ghalib know who Abdur Rahman is? And what have I got to do with him?" And he's sure to realize that you must have written to me. I shall make myself cheap in his eyes and he'll be even more cross with you. As for what you write about my numbering him among my kinsmen, my gracious friend, I hold all mankind to be my kin and look upon all men—Muslim, Hindu, Christian—as my brothers, no matter what others may think. And as for that kinship which the world calls affinity, in that, community and caste and religion and way of life all have their place, and there are grades and degrees of affinity. Viewed by these standards, you will find that this man isn't related to me in the smallest degree. If I was polite enough to write of him as kinsman, or speak of him of kinsman, what of that? Zain ul Abidin Arif was the son of my wife's sister, and this man is the son of *his* wife's sister. Make what you can of that! In short, when *he* can't behave with ordinary decency, to write to him is pointless, useless, and even harmful.

'I had already heard of your journey to Meerut and your meeting Mustafa Khan [Shefta] there. Now your letter tells me of your arrival at Sikandarabad via Muradabad. May Almighty God in His glory keep you well and happy.'

On December 29, 1859 he writes to Husain Mirza:

'The Lord Sahib's [i.e. the Governor-General's] party arrived about nine in the morning. His tent is pitched opposite Bhula Shah's tomb near the city wall by the Kabuli Gate. The accompanying force occupies the area up to Tis Hazari Bagh.'

He continues after two days:

'Now listen to the tale of Ghalib's troubles. . . . Two days ago I went to [the Governor-General's] camp and saw the Chief Clerk, in whose tent I waited while word was sent to the Secretary. Kallu went along with the orderly. He brought the reply, "Present my compliments and say that I am not free." Well, I returned home. Yesterday I went again, and sent in word that I had come. A message came in reply, "In the days of the Mutiny you took care to keep in the good books of the rebels. Why do you ask to see us now?" The world became dark in my sight. This reply announces an end for ever to all my hopes. . . .

'Yesterday morning Muhammad Quli Khan came with a petition[1] written in English in his hand. He said that Talib Ali . . . had returned it, saying that this was not the occasion to present it. I was just going out at the time. I left, feeling your disappointment and the wound of the unfulfilled desires of my own which I have told you about.

[1] Husain Mirza's.

'Ibrahim Ali Khan has died of dropsy in Alwar. God forgive him his sins and grant me the same fate. . . . I hear that it is proposed to establish in Lahore a department to award compensation, to ten per cent of its value, to citizens whose property was looted by the blacks [the rebel sepoys]. That is, a man who asks a thousand rupees will be given a hundred. As for the plundering which the whites did, that's all pardoned; there will be no compensation for that. . . .

'Why do you speak of "Hāmid Ali Khan's houses"? They were confiscated long ago, and became government property. The grounds look quite different now. There were British soldiers occupying the zenana and the big house. Now the main gate and a whole row of shops have been pulled down, the brick and stone sold by auction, and the proceeds sent to the treasury. Don't get the idea that the rubble sold was Hāmid Ali Khan's. It was its own seized property that the Government demolished. Well, when the King of Oudh's properties are treated as they are, who is going to care about the properties of ordinary citizens? You haven't yet got it into your head what the authorities intend, and you never will. Your Navind Rae, and copies of orders, and appeals mean nothing. The orders issued here in Delhi are the decrees of fate and destiny, against which there is no appeal. Say to yourself, "We never were nobles; rank and wealth were never ours; we had no property, and never drew a pension."

'Rampur shall be my dwelling-place in life and my resting-place when I am dead. It makes me laugh when you write pressing me to go there. I am certain that I shall see the new moon of the month of Rajab . . . in Rampur . . .

'Give my blessings to Yusuf Mirza Khan. I understand the position about the ode and the *mukhammas*.[1] My revered master treats me as a father treats his son. . . . It is his wish that my prayer and praise should each receive its separate reward and recompense. . . . But, my dearest friend, you may judge for yourself that I cannot live on such rewards. And it is futile even to think of it. How much life is left to me? Seven months of this year and twelve of next year. Then in this very month I shall go to my Master, where hunger and thirst and piercing cold and raging heat will be no more. No ruler to be dreaded, no informer to be feared, no rent to be paid, no clothes to be bought, no meat to be sent for, no bread to be baked. A world of light, a state of pure delight.

> O Lord, how dear to me is this my wish:
> Grant Thou that to this wish I may attain!
>
> The slave of Ali, son of Abi Talib,
> Who longs for death's release,
>   Your servant,
>   Ghalib.'

On this despondent note the letters for 1859 end.

[1] A poem written in stanzas of five lines.

✺ Chapter 9 ✺

1860

He begins 1860 on a more cheerful note, writing to Majruh, on January 1, 1860:

'Where are you, my boy? Where are you roving? Come here and listen to the news. [He then tells him of the Governor-General's durbar and subsequent visit to Delhi and his own lack of success. But he continues:] As for the pension, although there is still no decision one way or the other, I am planning something and we shall see what comes of it. . . .

'Orders have been issued for the general return of the Muslims' properties. Those who had been paying rent for them have now been exempted from paying it. . . . If you think fit, come and take possession of your property. Then stay on here or return [to Panipat] just as you like. . . . Give my blessing to Hakim Mir Ashraf Ali and tell him to write out the prescription for those pills he gave me and send it to me quickly. . . .'

What he was planning in relation to his pension does not become clear until March, when in a letter to Bekhabar (dated only 'March, 1860') he explains what he did after being told that the Chief Secretary would not receive him because he had been a well-wisher of the rebels.

'The next day I wrote a letter[1] in English to the effect that it was sheer conjecture to think that I had been a well-wisher of the rebels, and requesting an investigation so that my name could be cleared and my innocence established.'

Then, either because he decided after all that his hopes were futile, or because he saw no need to stay on in Delhi waiting for the British to reply, he decided to carry out his intention to go to Rampur.

The Nawwab had long been pressing him to come—ever since early 1858, in fact—and letters from him in November 1858 and April 1859 had repeated the invitation. Ghalib had replied that he wished to wait until the British restored his pension, as he was generally confident that they ultimately would. Thus he had written to the Nawwab on April 18, 1859: 'The day after I receive the [pension] money I shall ask you for money to pay for conveyance and porterage; and the day after I receive it I shall start out for Rampur.'

---

[1] i.e., presumably, had a letter written.

But, as we have seen, 1859 passed by, and the restoration of his pension was not yet in sight. On December 8, 1859 he had had to ask the Nawwab bluntly for extra money:

'Your draft of Rs. 100 for . . . November 1859 reached me. I drew the money and spent it, and was again hungry and naked. Whom should I tell if not you? If you will send me Rs. 200 over and above my regular allowance, I shall be able to breathe again—provided that it is not reckoned against my allowance, and that you send it very soon.'

The Nawwab sent him the money, and at the same time repeated his invitation to him to come to Rampur. Ghalib had in any case intended to accept the invitation in due course, and in the circumstances probably felt that he could not reasonably delay much longer.

On the way to Rampur, on January 21, 1860 he wrote to Tufta:

'My friend, I have left Delhi for Rampur. I reached Muradnagar on Thursday 19th and Meerut on Friday 20th. Today, Saturday 21st, I am staying on at the insistence of our friend Mustafa Khan [Shefta], and I'm posting off this letter to you from here. Tomorrow I shall stay at Shahjahanpur and the day after at Garhmukteshar, and then go on to Rampur via Muradabad. So send your next letter to me to Rampur. All the address you need write is my name, and Rampur. This is enough for now. I will write to you again from Rampur.'

He also wrote from Meerut on the same day to Hakim Ghulam Najaf Khan giving him the same information and adding:

'It's nine o'clock [a.m.], and I'm sitting here writing to you. I am getting my food free, and shall stuff myself to my heart's content. . . . I've got the two boys to write to their grandmother [Ghalib's wife] and am sending their letters off. Go to my house with this letter and read it out to your teacher [Ghalib's wife] and tell her that I am safe and sound. . . .

'I've thought it best to tell you the stages of my proposed journey, but now if anyone asks you, tell him plainly that I'm in Rampur. Don't make a secret of it. I want every one to know the position plainly.'

Tufta, as usual, was not content to address his letters in the (in his view) inadequate style Ghalib had suggested. Ghalib's next letter (undated) rebukes him:

'You say that your son doesn't know the world, but you're no better yourself. Tell me first, who in Rampur doesn't know me? Do you think they know Maulvi Wajīh uz Zaman Sahib better? [Tufta had presumably addressed Ghalib in his care.] His house is a long way from mine. And I'm not at the

Nawwab's court. He entertained me in his own mansion for four days, and then I asked for separate accommodation. . . . It so happens that the post-office is near where I am living, and the post-office clerk has got to know me. Letters reach me from Delhi all the time addressed with my name and "Rampur", and that's all. . . . In fact if you address me c/o the Maulvi Sahib and the Court your letters may go astray. . . .'

He was very well satisfied with the treatment he received at Rampur. He writes to Hakim Ghulam Najaf Khan on February 3, 1860:

'Write and tell me in detail any fresh news of what is going on in Delhi. And now let me tell you my news: I am treated with great honour. I have met the Nawwab three times, and have been given a house which is three or four houses in one. There is no stone here . . . and only a handful of the houses are brick-built. Mud walls and tiled roofs—the whole population lives in this kind of house, and my houses too are of the same kind. So far we have not discussed anything together. I shall not make the first move, and he too will not speak to me directly, but through his officials. Let me see what he has to say and what allowance he will make me. I had thought that once I arrived here, things would be settled very quickly, but so far—and today is Friday, my eighth day here—nothing has been said. The Nawwab has both meals sent to me every day, and there is enough food for all of us. It's not unacceptable to my taste either. As for the water, I cannot find words to express my thanks to God for it. There'a a river here called the Kosi. God be praised! Its water is so sweet that you would think it was diluted sherbet—clear, light, refreshing and quickly assimilated. For these eight days I have been safe from attacks of constipation. I develop a really good appetite in the mornings. The boys are thriving and my servant [unnamed] well and strong. True, Inayat [another servant, says Mihr] has been out of sorts for the last two days, but he'll soon be well. . . .'

On February 14, 1860 he writes again to Hakim Ghulam Najaf Khan: 'My friend, you ought to have opened the letter. . . . It wasn't from the Lieutenant-Governor, but from the Chief Secretary to the Governor-General.' [He then translates it into Urdu. It is dated January 27, 1860, and is to the effect that the Governor-General has received Ghalib's petition and will reply after due enquiry has been made.]

'The position here is that the Lieutenant-Governor is coming to Muradabad from Agra. Muradabad is twelve *kos*[1] from here. The Nawwab is away on a tour of his dominions, but he will be back in three or four days, and if he goes to Muradabad to meet the Lieutenant-Governor, I shall go with him. True, the Lieutenant-Governor of the North Western Provinces has nothing to do

[1] About 18 miles.

with Delhi, but let me see what comes of the interview. I will write and let you know what happens.

'What is this that you write, telling me to write home[1] more often? The letters I write to you are in effect written to her too. Is it too much to ask of you to go and read them to her? Now she will be wondering what was in the English letter. Take this letter of mine with you and go and read it to her word for word.

'The boys are both well. Sometimes they amuse me, and sometimes they plague me. Their goats, and pigeons, and quails, and their kites—small and big—are all in good order. I gave them their two rupees apiece for February, and they spent it all in the first ten days. Then two days ago the younger gentleman came to me and said, "Grand-dad, give me something on indefinite loan." So I gave him something. Today is the 14th, and the end of the month is a long way off. Let's see how many times he comes back to borrow more. . . .

'Ask at home whether Kidar Nath has paid all the servants. I have sent the pay for all of them—even the sweeper. . . .'

On March 1, 1860 he writes to Tufta:

'Nothing is fixed yet. At present it seems that the Lieutenant-Governor will be coming to Muradabad, and thence to Rampur. After he leaves I shall be in a position to know whether I am going to stay here or not. If I do, I intend to send for you at once, so that we can spend together whatever days of life are left to me.'

However, he did not stay on in Rampur. In a letter to Aram dated March 14, 1860 he says, 'I am leaving for Delhi on Saturday, March 17th'—without, however, giving any explanation of his departure. There is a hint in a letter to Yusuf Mirza written on April 2, 1860, which tells us that he arrived back in Delhi on March 25th, the first day of Ramzan, the Muslim month of fasting, and adds: 'The children made my life a misery: otherwise I would have stayed a few days more.'

But a letter of April 6, 1860, to Majruh is more explicit. Majruh had apparently been surprised to learn of Ghalib's return to Delhi. Ghalib rebukes him with mock solemnity:

'Mir Mahdi, have you forgotten my accustomed ways? Have I ever once missed listening to the recitation of the Quran at the Jama Masjid during the blessed month of Ramzan? How could I stay in Rampur during this month? The Nawwab tried to detain me, and tried very hard, in fact, tempting me all the time with the prospect of the mangoes I would get there during the rains. But, my friend, I would have none of it, and moved to such purpose that I reached here on the night of the new moon [from which Ramzan begins]. The holy

[1] i.e. to his wife.

month began on the Sunday. And from that day to this I have been present
every morning at Hāmid Ali Khan's mosque to hear the reverend Maulvi Jafar
Ali Sahib's reading of the Quran. Every night I go to the Jama Masjid to say
the *tarawih* prayer.[1] Sometimes, when I feel so inclined, I go into the Mahtab
Garden at sunset and break my fast there and take a draught of cold water.
And, oh, how happily the days pass by!

'And now let me tell you the real facts. I took the boys with me to Rampur
and they made my life there a misery. I didn't like to send them back on their
own. If anything should happen to them on the way, I thought, I should never
live it down. So I came away sooner than I had intended; otherwise I should
have passed the hot season and the rains there. Now, if I live, and if I can go
there alone, I shall return after the rains,[2] and not come back here for a long,
long time. The position is that ever since July 1859—that is, for the last ten
months—the Nawwab has been sending me a hundred rupees a month. When
I got to Rampur he paid me an additional hundred rupees a month, calling it
"hospitality allowance". This meant that as long as I stayed in Rampur I
should get two hundred a month, whereas in Delhi I should get only a hundred.
Well, my friend, the point is not whether I get two hundred or a hundred. The
point is that the Nawwab treats me as his friend and his ustad, and gives me
my allowance in that spirit, and not as though I were his employee. It was as a
friend too that he always met me, with the deference and warmth which friends
observe in their intercourse with one another. I had the boys offer presents when
we were received, and that was all. Anyway, I'm fortunate; I must be thankful
that my daily bread is well provided for. Why should I complain that it is not
enough?'

He goes on to speak of the unjust (as he believed) reduction of his pension all
those years ago to a mere 750 rupees a year, but recalls with satisfaction the
honour formerly shown him both by the British and by the Mughal King. He
goes on:

'And so, my dear friend, things are back to where they were. I sit in my little
room with the *khas* screen in place.[3] A breeze is blowing; a full pitcher of water
is beside me, and I am smoking the hookah and writing you this letter. I felt
like talking to you, so I did. . . .'

Ghalib's return to Delhi gave rise to a good deal of speculation, some of
which he reports in a letter to Tufta dated March 30, 1860:

'You know that I went to Rampur at the end of January and returned at the

---

[1] A special prayer of twenty genuflexions performed at night-time during Ramzan.
[2] '—that is, late in October or early in November,'—letter of April 29, 1860, to Yusuf Mirza.
[3] In the hot season screens of a particular fragrant grass called *khas*, drenched in water, are placed
at the doors so that the air is cooled as it passes into the rooms.

end of March. Do you know what people here are saying about me? One lot says, "This man was the ustad of the Nawwab of Rampur and has been to visit him there. If nothing else, the Nawwab must have given him at least five thousand rupees." Another group says, "He went there to look for a job, but he couldn't get one." Another says, "The Nawwab gave him a job, and fixed his salary at two hundred rupees a month. But the Lieutenant-Governor came to Rampur from Allahabad, and when he found out that Ghalib was employed there he told the Nawwab that if he wanted to continue in his favour he must dimiss him; and so the Nawwab gave him the sack". And now you've heard all that, let me tell you the facts. Nawwab Yusuf Ali Khan has been my friend for thirty-one years and my shagird for five or six years. He used to send me money from time to time and now regularly sends me a hundred rupees a month—since July 1859. He had often invited me to Rampur, and now I have been there. I stayed two months, and then came back. If I live, I shall go again after the rains. But by God's grace I shall get my hundred rupees a month whether I am here or there.'

He had suffered one disappointment before he left Rampur. The letter of March 1860 to Bekhabar, already quoted above, tells us that in February he received an official letter rejecting his request for an investigation into his conduct during the Mutiny. Not for the first time, he concluded that he could no longer hope for anything from the British.

It is with some astonishment, therefore, that he writes to Tufta on April 16, 1860:

'I have something remarkable to tell you—something which will occasion you the greatest astonishment and the greatest pleasure. I had given up all hope that the British authorities would renew my pension. The list of pensioners had at last been made out here and sent to higher authority, and the Commissioner here had written of me that I did not merit a pension. The government has acted in despite of his opinion and issued orders for the renewal of my pension. The order has reached here, and has become generally known; and I too have heard of it. Now it is said that payments will begin next month, that is from May 1st. Let us see what instructions have been given about the arrears.'

At the end of the same month of April he is able to report to Sarur:

'My position, in general terms, is this, that my relations . . . with the authorities . . . have been restored. I had sent by post to the Lieutenant-Governor of the North Western Provinces a copy of *Dastambu*. I have received . . . a reply from him in Persian, praising its style and accepting the sincerity of my devotion and love. Then I had sent an ode celebrating the spring and telling his praises. I have had an acknowledgement of this, in which I am addressed in my former style of "Khan Sahib, our most kind well-wisher and friend", written on paper

H*

sprinkled with gold dust. Then I had sent a panegyric in praise of Mr Robert Montgomery, Lieutenant-Governor of the Panjab, through the . . . Commissioner of Delhi. In reply to this too came a letter, through the Commissioner, expressing his pleasure.'

Subsequent letters show that Ghalib's information proved to be reliable, and that furthermore the arrears due to him for the whole period since May 1857 were granted him. They also show how little was left of them once he had settled, for the time being, with his creditors. There are several letters which give the details, but the fullest is that to Tufta dated May 6, 1860:

'I've just had your letter, and am writing this reply immediately after reading it. How do you make out that three years' arrears amounts to some thousands of rupees? My pension is seven hundred and fifty rupees a year. Three years at this rate comes to two thousand, two hundred and fifty. I had been given a grant in aid of a hundred. This was deducted, and another hundred and fifty was accounted for by miscellaneous items. That left two thousand. My agent in these matters is a baniya, to whom I owe a debt of long standing. He kept the two thousand, and asked me to settle accounts with him. The principal and interest worked out at Rs. 1493. We calculated other miscellaneous debts at the same rate and they came to a few rupees over eleven hundred. So the 1500 and the 1100 made 2600—six hundred more than the two thousand. He wants me to pay him his 1500, and keep the 507. I want him to share the 2000 half and half, arguing that the miscellaneous debts come to 1100, leaving 900. He came with the money two days ago—on the 4th—and up to yesterday we hadn't reached a settlement. I'm not hurrying matters. One or two other moneylenders are involved. The thing will take a week to settle. . . .'

What exactly was settled we do not know, but we find him writing two months later, on July 8, 1860, to Ala ud Din Ahmad Khan Alai: 'After paying off all my debts I was left with four hundred rupees still to pay, and only eighty-seven rupees, eleven annas in hand.'

Not only was the lump sum swallowed up in this way; a change was introduced in the method of payment which involved him in further debt. He writes to Tufta on July 20, 1860:

'At the end of June orders were received from the Panjab authorities directing that established pensioners should in future be paid not monthly but twice-yearly. I was obliged to go to the moneylender and borrow money on interest, so that I should have something to supplement my income from Rampur. I shall be paying interest on the loan over the next six months, and that means a substantial loss.

> We know the rite in hour of the dead
> Called the 'six-monthly'—all observe it here.
> But see *my* case: men, while I still live on,
> Celebrate *my* six-monthly twice a year.'

In actual fact the changed method of payment was not introduced right away, as a letter of September 1860 to Sarur shows:

'I am getting my money month by month; but this will last only three months more—September, October and November. As from December 1860 it will be paid twice-yearly. Moroever there is going to be a cut of 4 per cent. At this rate I shall lose two and a half rupees a month.'

There has been much speculation about what led the British authorities to restore Ghalib's pension. Ghalib himself had hoped that the Nawwab of Rampur could influence them in this direction, and his efforts may indeed have played a part, for Ghalib's statement in one of his letters that the restoration of the pension was not the Nawwab's doing, but God's, does not necessarily contradict this. Ikram argues that the efforts of Sir Sayyid Ahmad Khan probably played a decisive part. He writes:

'Maulana Abul Kalam Azad says that Sir Sayyid exerted every effort to get Ghalib's pension restored . . . and there are signs which support this statement. . . . On his return journey [from Rampur] he stopped at Muradabad, and Sir Sayyid, who was at that time Sadr us Sudur[1] there, went to the inn where he was staying and brought him to his own house. It is reasonable to assume that during his stay he told all his troubles to Sir Sayyid, and that Sir Sayyid used the influence which he had acquired after the Mutiny to remedy them. Possibly because Sir Sayyid was a government employee, or perhaps from some other consideration, it was not considered advisable to speak of these efforts. Maulana Abul Kalam Azad's statement also seems plausible because it was in March 1860 that Ghalib stayed with Sir Sayyid and the restoration of the pension was made only a month or two later, in May, 1860.'

However that may be, Hali's account (in his life of Sir Sayyid) of Ghalib's stay at Muradabad on this occasion is interesting. It shows amongst other things that any sense of estrangement that may have arisen over the *Ain i Akbari* incident some years earlier was now ended. He writes:

'Sir Sayyid used to say that when he was in Muradabad, Ghalib had gone to visit . . . Nawwab Yusuf Ali Khan at Rampur. "I did not know he had gone there, but during his return journey to Delhi I heard that he had stopped at Muradabad and was staying at an inn. I at once went there and brought him

---

[1] A judicial post of some importance.

and his luggage and all his companions to my house." It would seem that when Sir Sayyid had refused to print Ghalib's introduction [to *Ain i Akbari*], the two men had kept at a distance and felt a certain reserve towards each other, and that this was why Ghalib had not informed him of his coming to Murada-bad. Anyway, when Ghalib arrived at Sir Sayyid's house from the inn and got out of the palanquin, he had a bottle [of wine] in his hand. He took it into the house and put it down in a place where anyone who passed could see it. Sir Sayyid later picked it up and put it in a store-room. When Ghalib found the bottle missing he got very upset. Sir Sayyid said, "Don't worry, I've put it in a safe place." Ghalib replied, "Show me where, my friend." Sir Sayyid then took him to the store-room and produced the bottle. Ghalib took the bottle from him and held it up to look at it, and then said with a smile, "There's some missing, my friend. Tell me truly, who's had it? Perhaps that's why you took it away to the store-room. Hāfiz was right:

> These preachers show their majesty in mosque
> and pulpit
> But once at home it is far other things they do.'

Sir Sayyid laughed and made no reply, and in this way the sense of strain be-tween them that had lasted for several years was removed. Ghalib stayed on for a day or two and then returned to Delhi.'

When the arrears of his pension were swallowed up in paying off his accumulated debts, Sarur suggested that he should write an ode in praise of the Nizam of Hyderabad and allow him to have it presented on Ghalib's behalf by an intermediary at the Nizam's court. The proposal depressed him, and he replied in an undated letter showing how fate had always frowned on him in these matters:

'First let me write of some matters which you will at first sight think irrelevant. I was five years old when my father died, and nine when my uncle died. In place of the income from his estate, I and my blood relations were to be granted ten thousand rupees a year from the estate of Nawwab Ahmad Bakhsh. He refused to give more than three thousand a year, of which my own personal share amounted to seven hundred and fifty. I pointed out this misappropriation to the British government. Colebrooke Sahib Bahadur (the Resident of Delhi) and Stirling Sahib Bahadur, Secretary to the government at Calcutta, were in agreement with me that my rights must be restored. But the Resident was dismissed and the Secretary met an untimely death.

'After a lapse of many years the King of Delhi appointed me to a pension of fifty rupees a month, and the heir apparent to one of four hundred rupees a year. Two years later, the heir apparent died.

'Wajid Ali Shah, King of Oudh's court appointed a sum of five hundred rupees a year to be paid me in reward for my odes of praise. He too did not survive more than two years, by which I mean that though he still survives, his kingdom was destroyed, and destroyed within those two years. The kingdom of Delhi was a little more tenacious of life. I drew my daily bread from it for seven years before it was destroyed. There are no stars so baneful as those that kill my patrons and destroy my benefactors. Now if I turn to the ruler of the Deccan [the Nizam's dominions, Hyderabad], mark my words, my intermediary will die, or fall from office, or if neither of these things happens, then his efforts on my behalf will be fruitless and the ruler will give me nothing. And if by any chance he does, then his state will be levelled in the dust and put under the asses' plough.

'And suppose I put all that aside and make up my mind to write a panegyric. Well, I can make up my mind to it, but not carry it through. Fifty to fifty-five years of practice have given me a certain talent, but I have no strength left in me. I sometimes look at the prose and verse which I wrote in former days; I know that it is mine, but I am lost in wonderment that I could write such prose and compose such verse. Abdul Qādir Bedil spoke as though with my tongue when he wrote:

My story echoes round the world—and I am
nothing.

My life is ending, and my heart and mind are spent. My hundred rupees from Rampur and my sixty rupees' pension suffice amply for my maintenance. Fluctuations of prices are always with us. For better or for worse, the work of this world goes on. Caravan upon caravan is ready to depart. See, Munshi Nabi Bakhsh [Haqir] was younger than I, but he died last month. Where shall I find the strength to write a panegyric? And if I make up my mind to it, how shall I find the leisure? And if I write it, and send it to you, and you send it to the Deccan, when will our intermediary find an opportunity of presenting it? And if he does, what will be the response? Do you think I shall live to see all these stages passed? "Verily we are for God, and Verily to Him we shall return. There is no god but God, and none who may be worshipped but He, and nothing exists but God, and God was when no other thing was, and God is now just as He was." '

All the same, the restoration of his pension and of his standing with the British must have been a source of much satisfaction to him. Another welcome event of the same time was a move to re-issue his Urdu diwan. Here he inadvertently landed himself in difficulties. He explains in a letter to Aram dated April, 1860:

'Let me tell you the facts about my diwan being printed at Meerut. Then you can have your say. I was still in Rampur when I received a letter headed "Petition of Azīm ud Din Ahmad, of Meerut". May God strike me if I know who this Azīm ud Din is or what profession he follows. Anyway, I read the letter and learned that he wanted to print my Urdu diwan as a business venture, and expected to make a profit out of it. Well, I made no reply. When I got to Meerut from Rampur, I stopped off at friend Mustafa Khan's [Shefta's]. There my old friend Munshi Mumtaz Ali came to see me. He said, "Send me your Urdu diwan. A bookseller named Azīm ud Din wants to print it." Now listen to this: where was I to find a fully complete copy of the diwan? True, before the Mutiny I had had a copy made and sent to Nawwab Yusuf Ali Khan Bahadur at Rampur. When I was about to leave Delhi for Rampur, brother Ziya ud Din urged me strongly to get the diwan from the Nawwab, get it copied by a scribe, and send it to him. Accordingly, during my stay there I got it copied by a scribe and posted it to Ziya ud Din at Delhi. Now let me return to what I was saying. When Munshi Mumtaz Ali said that to me, all I could say was, "Very well, I'll get the diwan from Ziya ud Din and send it you. But who will be responsible for correcting the proofs?" Nawwab Mustafa Khan [Shefta] said, "*I* will." Now, tell me, what could I do? When I got to Delhi I got the diwan from Ziya ud Din and sent a man with it to Nawwab Mustafa Khan. If I had been in a position to make what arrangements I pleased for printing it, do you think I'd have ignored our own press [i.e. Aram's] and sent it to someone else's? I am writing this letter to you and at the same time writing off to our friend Nawwab Mustafa Khan to tell him that if printing has not already started, he is not to give it for printing, but is to send it back to me as soon as possible. If it comes, I'll send it on immediately to you; if the scribe there has already started it, then there's nothing I can do. I am not at fault; and if, now you've heard what happened, you think I am to blame, well, my friend, then please forgive me. People will be involved with Ramzan and Id; I feel sure that the copying won't have begun; my diwan will be sent back to me, and shall then be sent on to you. . . .'

Some good-humoured sarcasm in a letter to Yusuf Mirza on May 9, 1860 shows that the situation was unchanged up to then:

'As for our friend Fazlu, Mir Kazim Ali, how could he know what "book" means and what weapon is called "Agra" and what tree bears the fruit called "Sikandar"? My Urdu diwan went to Meerut; Sikandar Shah took it for me and delivered it to Nawwab Mustafa Khan. . . .'

It transpired that Azīm ud Din, having once got his hands on the diwan, was not prepared to give it up. Ghalib writes to Sayyah on June 11, 1860:

'What can I say about the printing of my diwan? That unknown stranger known as Azīm ud Din, who got me to send him the diwan, is not a man but an apparition, a horror, a ghoul—in short, a very uncouth sort of person—and I don't want to put the printing of my diwan into his hands. I am asking him to return it, but he won't. God grant that I get it back. You too must pray for it.'

But in the end all turned out well. He was able to write to Aram on June 25, 1860:

'Friend, I have sinned against you, and kept your book [i.e. the diwan] to myself. It cost me a lot of effort and labour to stop it being printed there and to get it back. Today, Monday, 25th June, I have sent it off by parcel post. So now forgive me my sin and restore me to your pleasure and write and tell me you have done so. The book—my Urdu diwan—I give over to you entirely. Now it belongs to you. I don't say, "Print it" and I don't say "Don't print it." Do whatever it pleases you to do. If you print it, put me down for twenty copies. And, yes, my son, do please take great care to see that it is printed correctly.'

He writes again on July 3, 1860:

'My son, you make me laugh. The diwan I sent you is comprehensive and complete. What are these "two or three ghazals in Mirza Yusuf Ali Khan Aziz's possession, which are not in the diwan"? On this score you can set your mind completely at rest. I have not written a single line which is not in this diwan. However, I'll speak to him too and get him to send these ghazals for me to look at. What do you want with a picture of me? And how can Aziz, poor fellow, get my portrait done? If it's all that important, write to me about it. I'll get a portrait done and send it to you. You don't need to present anything, not even your respects. I love you like a son, and I give thanks to God that you are a dutiful son. God grant you long life and give you all that you desire.'

Ghulam Rasul Mihr thinks that an undated letter to Nawwab Ziya ud Din Ahmad Khan relates to this same period—or at any rate to the same year. 'Diwan,' he writes, 'here means the collected Persian verse. . . . The letter would seem to be one of 1860, when he contemplated getting his collected Persian verse printed at Munshi Newal Kishor's press.' The letter reads:

'Reverend sir, why are you so reluctant to give me the diwan? It's not as though you studied it every day. Nor is it so dear to you that you can't digest your dinner until you see it. So why won't you let me have it? There'll be a thousand copies instead of just one. My verse will win fame. My heart will rejoice. The whole world will see my ode in your praise. Everyone will be able to read the prose encomium on your brother. Are not these advantages enough? As for fear that the book may be lost, that is just a baseless feeling. Why should it? And if by any chance it is lost, if the mail is robbed between Delhi and Lucknow, then I'll travel at once by the mail to Rampur, and bring you the copy transcribed by the late Nawwab Fakhr ud Din Khan.

Perhaps you'll tell me, "Go to Rampur and send it off from there." But don't you think they would ask me why I don't send the Delhi copy? And if I write and tell them that Nawwab Ziya ud Din Sahib won't give it to me, don't you think I'll be told, "When your own relation and neighbour won't give it to you, why should I, who am so far away, give you my copy?" And if you tell me to borrow Tafazzul's copy and send that, what am I to do if he refuses to part with it? And if he does part with it, what use is it to me? In the first place it's incomplete, and then it's defective in other ways. There are some panegyrics in it in which I've altered the names for presentation elsewhere, and which in his edition still bear the earlier names. Shihab ud Din's copy too, which Yusuf Mirza has taken, has both these defects, and moreover is full of mistakes. Not a couplet, not a line is free of them. This thing can't be done without your help; and you lose nothing by it. You may *think* you do, but that's just a baseless fear, a bogy. And if you do, I'll guarantee to make good your loss, as I have already said. So make up your mind to grant my request and write to me accordingly so that I can inform the man who has asked me for it, and when he asks again, can send it to him.'

For the rest of 1860 there is no further mention of either the Urdu or the Persian verse. We find him in the middle of the year pre-occupied with the weather, with the Delhi scene, and with the problems of moving house—and on occasion with other themes, some more weighty, and some less so.

In May 1860 Yusuf Mirza had written telling him the news that his father had died. He replies on May 19th:

'Yusuf Mirza, how can I bring myself to write the words, "Your father is dead"? And if I do, what am I to write next? What am I to tell you to do now? To bear it patiently? That is the well-worn custom of the world—formal condolence and formal repetition of the phrase, "Bear it patiently". Alas that when a man's heart is cut out people can tell him to be still! How *can* he be still? This is not the occasion to offer advice, nor one where prayers and remedies have any place. First your son died, and now your father. If anyone were to ask me what it means to have nowhere to turn I would say, "To be in Yusuf Mirza's place."

'Your grandmother [the dead man's mother] writes that the order for his release had been passed. Is that true? If it is, then our stalwart broke both his bonds at a single effort—the bonds of existence and the bonds of English captivity. And she writes also that his pension-money had come, and that it would help to pay the expenses of his funeral. I don't understand this. When a man is found guilty and sentenced to fourteen years' imprisonment, how can it be that his pension is paid him? At whose request? Who would sign the receipt? Mustafa Khan's [Shefta's] release was ordered, but his pension was forfeited. There's no point in asking about it now, but it's a very strange thing; write and tell me any explanation that occurs to you. . . . Anyway, I've sent on your grandmother's letter, which your brother had sent me, to your uncle [mother's brother]. Orders have been issued for the restoration of his property. ... Let us see what happens. ...'

He was conscious that the year in which he had predicted he would die— 1277 AH, due to begin on July 20, 1860—was now approaching. On June 6, 1860 he writes to Majruh:

'Dear friend, I have just been so ill that I myself felt sorry for myself. For four days I couldn't eat. Now I am fit and well again. To the end of Zil Hij [the last month of the Muslim year], 1276, I have nothing to fear. From the 1st Muharram [the first month of the Muslim year] God knows.'

On June 11, 1860 he writes to Sayyah:

'It grieves me to hear of the desolation of Lucknow, but remember that there this destruction will give way to creation—that is, the roads will be widened and the bazaars improved, so that everyone who sees it will approve what has been done. In Delhi destruction is not followed by creation, and the work of destruction goes on all the time. The whole appearance of the city, except for the street of shops that runs from the Lahore Gate of the Fort to the Lahore Gate of the city ["i.e.," says Mihr, "Chandni Chauk and Khari Baoli"] has been spoiled, and will go on being spoiled. ...' But he laments the fall of Lucknow all the same. On June 30, 1860 he writes again to Sayyah: 'What praise was too high for Lucknow? It was the Baghdad of India, and its court— may God be praised!—a mint of rich men. A man could come there penniless and become wealthy. Alas that autumn should come to such a garden!'

On July 8, 1860 he writes to Ala ud Din Khan Alai:

'For the last ten to twelve years I have lived in Hakim Muhammad Hasan Khan's mansion. Now Ghulamullah Khan has bought the house, and at the end of June he asked me to move out. I've been trying to find two adjacent houses somewhere, so that I can make one the zenana and have the other for my own use. I couldn't find any, so I had to content myself with looking for a house in Ballimaron to which I could move. But I couldn't get one. Your aunt came to my rescue, and gave me Karorawali mansion to live in. It wasn't what I wanted, in that it wasn't near the zenana, but anyway, it's not all that far away. I shall move in tomorrow or the next day; so I have one foot on the ground and one in the stirrup. ...

'Yesterday . . . at about nine in the morning your letter came. About an hour or so later I had news that [your father] Amīn ud Din Khan Sahib had come to dignify his mansion with his presence. In the evening he was kind enough to pay me an unexpected visit. I found him thin and dejected, and that upset me. Ali Husain Khan [Alai's younger brother] also came, so I met him too. I asked why *you* hadn't come. Your father said, "Someone has to stay there while I am away: besides, he is very fond of his son." I said, "As fond as you used to be of him?" He laughed. In short, I found that he seemed to be a better man than you. But what is in your hearts only God knows.'

To Tufta he describes his house-moving difficulties in more detail, writing on July 20, 1860:

'I had been living in these narrow confines for the last ten to twelve years. For seven years I had paid four rupees every month. Now I paid three years' rent—something over a hundred rupees—in a lump. The owner sold the house, and the new owner told me—insisted, rather—that I must move out. That's all right if you can find another house. But he had no consideration and began to pester me by starting on the repairs. He put up scaffolding by the balcony (about two yards deep and ten yards long) overlooking the courtyard. That's where I slept at nights. What with the oppressiveness of the heat and the closeness of the scaffolding I felt as though it was the scaffold nearby, and, come morning, I should be hanged. I passed three nights in this state, and then on Monday, July 9th at midday, I got a house. I moved in, and felt as though my life had been saved. This house is a paradise as compared to the other, and the best of it is that it's in the same muhalla, Ballimaron. . . .'

Letters of the same period to Shafaq review the whole Delhi scene. He writes in a letter dated only '1860', but evidently belonging to early July:

'Lord and Master, it was twelve o'clock, and I was lying on my bed practically naked smoking the hookah when the servant brought your letter to me. As luck would have it, I was wearing neither shirt nor coat, otherwise I'd have rent my clothes in frenzy. (Not that your lordship would have lost anything by that—*I* would have been the one to suffer by it.) Let's begin at the beginning. I corrected your ode and sent it off. I received an acknowledgement. Some of the cancelled verses were sent back to me with a request to be told what was wrong with them. I explained what was wrong with them, wrote in words that were acceptable in place of those to which I had objected, and said that you might now include these verses too in the ode. To this day I have had no reply to this letter. I handed over to Shah Asrar ul Haq the paper addressed to him and wrote to you the verbal message he gave in reply. This letter too your Lordship has not answered.

> My heart is vibrant with complaint as
>   is the harp with music.
> Give it the slightest touch and hear the
>   strains it will pour forth.

I think to myself, "I sent both letters unstamped. I cannot conceive that they should have been lost." Anyway, it was a long time ago. No point in complaining now. You don't re-heat stale food, and "service means servitude".

'Five invading armies have fallen upon this city one after another: the first was that of the rebel soldiers, which robbed the city of its good name. The second was that of the British, when life and property and honour and dwellings and those who dwelt in them and heaven and earth and all the visible signs of existence were stripped from it. The third was that of famine, when thousands of people died of hunger. The fourth was that of cholera, in which many whose bellies were full lost their lives. The fifth was the fever, which took general plunder of men's strength and powers of resistance. There were not many deaths, but a man who has had fever feels that all the strength has been drained from his limbs. And this invading army has not yet left the city. Two members of my own household are down with fever, the elder boy and my steward. May God restore both of them speedily to health.

'The rains have been plentiful here too, but not as plentiful as in Kalpi and Banaras. The farmers are happy, and the fields ready for harvest. Anxiety about the autumn harvest is at an end. For the spring harvest they need rain in the month of Pus [December-January].

'. . . Mughal Ali Khan died of dropsy not long before the Mutiny. Alas! how difficult it is to write of these things! Hakim Razi ud Din Khan was shot by a British soldier during the general massacre, and his younger brother Ahmad Husain Khan was killed on the same day. Both of Tale Yar Khan's sons had come here on leave. Then the Mutiny prevented them leaving, and they stayed on here. After Delhi was re-taken both of them were hanged, though they had committed no crime. Tale Yar Khan is in Tonk. He is alive, but I am certain that he would be better off dead. Mir Chotam too was hanged. As for Miyan Nizam ud Din's[1] son, he fled from Delhi when all the other prominent men did. For some time he was in Baroda, for some time in Aurangabad, for some time in Hyderabad. Last year, during the winter, he came here. The government has made its peace with him but only to the extent that his life is pardoned. Raushan ud Daula's seminary (behind the police headquarters) and Khwaja Qasim's mansion (where the late Mughal Ali Khan used to live) and Khwaja Sahib's mansion—all these were designated as the personal properties of Kale Sahib, and after him, of Miyan Nizam ud Din; they were confiscated and sold by auction, and the proceeds went to government funds. True, Qasim Jan's mansion, the deeds of which were in the name of Nizam ud Din's mother, was given to her. At the moment Nizam ud Din has gone to Pakpattan. Perhaps he'll be going to Bahawalpur too.

There is more about the weather in a letter of July 19, 1860:

'What is the weather like? The hot season, the cold season and the rains have all

[1] Son of 'Kale Sahib'—cf. p. 71 above.

come together, not to speak of the hailstorms. . . . I always find this season hard to bear. In the hot weather I feel the heat as badly as an animal that pants for water, especially now when I have to bear not only the heat but the innumerable griefs and anxieties that beset me.

> The flames of Hell cannot give out such heat—
> For hidden griefs burn with a different fire.'

And in the next letter too: 'It rained last night and the wind was cold enough to be dangerous. Now it's morning, and a cool, harmless breeze is blowing. The sky is covered with light cloud. The sun is up, but you can't see it. . . .'

In July 1860 he writes:

'I have a story which will amuse you. The postman who delivers letters to Ballimaron these days is some baniya—somebody Nath or something Das— and he can just about read and write. I live on the upper storey. He came into the house, handed a letter to my steward and said, "Say that the postman presents his respects and his congratulations. The King of Delhi made him a Nawwab, and now there's a letter from Kalpi giving him the title of Captain." I wondered what on earth he was talking about. When I looked carefully at the address I found that my name was preceded by the words "makhdum i niyaz keshan" ['Master of his humble servants'—an honorific term of address]. The poor pimp had ignored the other words and read "keshan" as "kaptan"!' [In the Urdu script the two words resemble one another more closely.]

On August 24, 1860 he writes:

'The dearness of grain is a calamity from heaven, and disorders of the blood make life a misery. Swellings everywhere, and huge boils—and no remedy avails, and no effort counts for anything. Was it the rebel army from Meerut that descended on Delhi that morning of May 11th, or was it the onset of repeated visitations of divine wrath? From end to end of the realm of India the doors of disorder and disaster are opened wide—and Delhi, distinguished before, is just as distinguished now in this too. "Verily we are for God, and verily to Him we shall return." '

In September 1860 he writes to Sarur:

'Here it seems as though the whole city is being demolished. Some of the biggest and most famous bazars—Khas Bazar, Urdu Bazar, and Khanam ka Bazar, each of which was practically a small town, have gone without a trace. You cannot even tell where they were. Householders and shopkeepers cannot point out to you where their houses and shops used to stand. It is the rainy season, but there has been practically no rain, and it is under the rain of picks and shovels that houses are collapsing. Food is dear, and death is cheap, and grain sells so dear that you would think that each grain was a fruit. *Mash*-lentils sell at sixteen pounds to the rupee, millet at thirty-two pounds, and wheat at twenty-four pounds; gram at thirty-two, *ghi*[1] at three. Vegetables too are expensive. And to crown it all, the month of Kunwar [September-October], which they call the threshold of the cold season, is as hot as Jeth and Asarh— the water is warm and the sun fierce, and the hot wind is blowing. . . .'

He goes on to address Sahib i Alam:

'. . . How is it that you are expecting a visit from me? In what letter . . . did I express any such intention? Who conveyed any verbal message from me . . .? It is true, I long more than I can say to kiss your feet and to set eyes once more on Anwar ud Daula—and I think I shall carry this longing with me to the grave. . . . Lala Gobind Parshad has not arrived yet. I am not a worldly man, but a humble faqir, and hospitality is part of my nature . . . God willing, he will be happy and content with me.'

Then to Muhammad Amir:

'It grieves me that you thought I had been anxious [in 1857] and had fled from my home. Who could have told you anything so contrary to the facts? I have always stayed here in Delhi with my wife and children—swimming in this sea of blood.'

In another, undated letter he had in fact hinted at a visit to Sarur in the cold season:

'You invite me to Marahra and remind me that I had planned to come. In the days when my spirits were high and my strength intact, I once said to the late Shaikh Muhsin ud Din how I wished I could go to Marahra during the rains and eat mangoes to my heart's content and my belly's capacity. But where shall I find that spirit today, and from where recover the strength I once had? I neither have the same appetite for mangoes nor the same capacity to hold so many. I never ate them first thing in the morning, nor immediately after the midday meal; and I cannot say that I ate them between lunch and dinner because I never took an evening meal. I would sit down to eat them towards evening, when my food was fully digested, and I tell you bluntly, I would eat them until my belly was bloated and I could hardly breathe. Even now I eat them at the same time of day, but not more than ten to twelve, or, if they are of the large . . . kind, only six or seven.

> Alas! how the days of our youth have departed!
> Nay, rather the days of our life have departed!

[1] Clarified butter.

Now I would make the journey only to see you; and I can stand the troubles of travelling only in the winter, not in the rains. . . .'

When it came to the point he seems to have felt unable to face the physical strain which travel involved. Thus he had written to Ala ud Din Khan Alai on July 2, 1860: 'I should very much like to see you, but that can happen only if you come here. I wish you could have come with your father and visited me. . . .

> Meet with my rival if you like:
> I leave that to your whim.
> But what is wrong with asking after me
> as well as him?'

It was certainly not lack of interest which held him back. On December 31, 1860, he replies to a letter which his friend Sayyah had written him from Banaras:

'My friend, I like Banaras: it is a fine city. I have written a poem in praise of it called "The Lamp of the Temple". It is in my volume of Persian verse. Have a look at it. . . . You have written an account of your journey from Lucknow to Banaras, and I'm expecting you to go on with it. I am very fond of travelling and sight-seeing. . . . Oh well, if I cannot travel, never mind. I will content myself with the thought that "To hear of pleasure is to experience half of it", and will think of Sayyah's account as itself a journey.'

Among his other preoccupations during the latter half of the year was the correcting of the verses which his friends sent him. He writes to Ala ud Din Alai on July 2, 1860 that this is the most that his remaining poetic powers enable him to do:

'You ask me for recent verses. Where from? Verses on themes of love are as far from my taste as faith is from unbelief. I was the government's hired bard. I wrote my panegyrics and got my robes in reward. But the robes stopped coming, and I stopped writing. No ghazals, no odes. Lampoon and satire is not in my line. So, tell me, what am I to write? I am like an old wrestler, who can only explain the holds. Verses keep coming in from all directions, and I correct them. Believe me, I am telling the literal truth.'

On more than one occasion he has to protest, not for the first time, his inability to write chronograms. He writes to Sayyah on July 31, 1860:

'My friend, I swear to you by your life and by my faith that I am a complete stranger to the art of the chronogram and the riddle. You won't have heard of any chronogram by me in Urdu. I have composed a few in Persian, but the position there is that while the verses are mine the words giving the date were supplied by others. Do you understand me? Calculation is a headache to me, and I can't even add up. Whenever I work out a chronogram I always find that I've calculated it wrongly. There were one or two of my friends who, if the need arose, could work out for me the words which gave the required date, and I would fit them into a verse.'

He goes on to say that whenever he has attempted a chronogram himself he has had to make provision for additions and subtractions to such an extent that the whole thing becomes laughable. 'In Calcutta a mosque was built at the tomb of the late . . . Siraj ud Din Ali Khan. His nephew . . . asked me for a chronogram, and I wrote one which you will find in my volume of Persian verse.' He then quotes it, and shows by what tortuous methods he gets the right date, by selecting a key word which gives far too large a total and then finding ways of indicating that from this must be deducted numbers yielded by two other words. He concludes, 'I ask you, can you call this a chronogram?' This leads him on to quote two other examples which he likes better, because they incorporate a method which he had himself invented. He goes on:

'You write that "Sayyid Ghulam Baba" doesn't fit into any metre. How do you make that out? [He then writes two four-line verses, each in a different metre, and each incorporating this name, and goes on:] Produce some indicating word which fits into this metre and you'll have your chronogram. The friends who used to produce the key words for me have all departed for Paradise. And I, as I wrote above, am helpless in the matter.'

Perhaps the best chronogram which Ghalib composed himself was that on the Mutiny—*rustkhez i beja*—which he worked out and included in *Dastambu*; and since it well illustrates some of the points which his letters of this time discuss, it is convenient to analyse it here. The phrase is indeed an apt one, for it both fixes the date of the Mutiny and expresses Ghalib's view of it. It is not easy to translate. 'Unseasonable tumult' is an approximate equivalent, but 'unseasonable' does not convey the sense of outrage which 'beja' here carries. The other word, rustkhez, means 'Judgement Day', but is also used to describe any great tumult or upheaval, including emotional tumult such as the stunning impact of a woman's beauty, or the sudden news of a friend's death, might cause. If one adds up the numerical values of the letters of the word *rustkhez* as written in the Urdu script, they give a total of 1277. From these must be deducted the combined values of the two letters 'ja'—for 'beja' may be read as a single word (and, indeed, must be so read to give the meaning required), or alternatively as two words 'be ja' ,meaning 'without (or, minus) ja'. The total of 'ja' is 4, and 1277 minus 4 comes to 1273, which gives the date of the Mutiny in the Muslim era.

All this is relevant to the understanding of the letter which follows. Despite his dislike of the chronogram, Ghalib did not like to disappoint his friends if he could help it. A letter to Tufta of November 19, 1860, expresses his attitude:

'I consider the art of chronogram-writing beneath the dignity of poetry, nor do I believe, like you, that you pay any debt of love by writing a chronogram on a man's death. But anyway I wrote and sent off a verse which gave the date of death of the late Munshi Nabi Bakhsh Haqir. Munshi Qamar ud Din Khan Sahib didn't like it. Here it is: [He then quotes it.[1]] There is another way of doing it simply by producing some word which adds up to the required total, and not even bothering about it meaning anything. . . . Take a look at the odes of Anwari [the great classical Persian poet]. You will find three or four passages at the beginning of his odes which yield the right total and give the year he wants, but have no meaning. [By contrast] see in what good taste is the word *rustkhez* [which I used]—how meaningful and, moreover, how suited to the occasion. Of course, if I had used the word in a chronogram of a birth or marriage it would certainly have been objectionable. Anyway, to cut it short, if composing a chronogram pays a debt of love, then I have fulfilled the demands of friendship. What more is there to write?'

We may not unreasonably assume that his previous use of *rustkhez* in his chronogram on the Mutiny made him quick to realize that it gave him the date he now needed, this time without any modification being required. And, as he quite justly says, the word is indeed appropriate to the occasion it commemorates.

Some time during 1860—the letters are undated—he wrote to Mihr the last two letters to him which we possess. They are of exceptional interest. Mihr had written to tell him of the death of his mistress, a courtesan named Chunna Jan. Ghalib replies:

'Mirza Sahib, I received your letter with its grievous news. When I had read it I gave it to Yusuf Ali Khan Aziz to read, and he told me of your relationship with her—how devoted to you she was and how much you loved her. I felt extremely sorry, and deeply grieved. Listen, my friend: in poetry Firdausi, in ascetic devotion Hasan of Basra, and in love Majnun—these three are the preeminent leaders in these three arts. The height of a poet's attainment is to become a second Firdausi, the limit of an ascetic's achievement to rival Hasan of Basra, and the ideal of a lover is to match Majnun. His Laila died before him, and your mistress died before you; in fact you excel him, for Laila died in her own home, while your beloved died in yours. Friend, we "Mughal lads" are terrors; we are the death of those for whom we ourselves would die. Once in my life I was the death of a fair, cruel dancing girl. God grant both of them His forgiveness, and both of us, who bear the wounds of our beloveds' death, His

---

[1] The key word is *rustkhez*.

mercy. It is forty years or more since it happened, and although I long ago abandoned such things and left the field once and for all, there are times even now when the memory of her charming ways comes back to me, and I shall not forget her death as long as I live. I know what you must be feeling. Be patient, and turn your back on the turmoil of earthly love. . . . God is all-sufficient: the rest is vanity.'

We have no means of knowing how long an interval elapsed between this letter and the next, but it seems that Mihr could not overcome the grief he felt at his mistress's death, and Ghalib adopts quite another tone in an effort to rally him:

'Mirza Sahib, I don't like the way you're going on. I have lived sixty-five years, and for fifty of them have seen all that this transient world of colour and fragrance has to show. In the days of my lusty youth a man of perfect wisdom counselled me, "Abstinence I do not approve: dissoluteness I do not forbid. Eat, drink and be merry. But remember that the wise fly settles on the sugar, and not on the honey." Well, I have always acted on his counsel. You cannot mourn another's death unless you live yourself. And why all these tears and lamentations? Give thanks to God for your freedom, and do not grieve. And if you love your chains so much, then a Munna Jan is as good as a Chunna Jan. When I think of paradise and consider how if my sins are forgiven me and I am installed in a palace with a houri, to live for ever in the worthy woman's company, I am filled with dismay and fear brings my heart into my mouth. How wearisome to find her always there!—a greater burden than a man could bear. The same old palace, all of emerald made: the same fruit-laden tree to cast its shade. And—God preserve her from all harm—the same old houri on my arm! Come to your senses, brother, and get yourself another.

> Take a new woman each returning spring,
> For last year's almanac's a useless thing.'

After which he drops the subject completely and goes on to talk of other things.

Although Mihr lived for another nineteen years, no letters written to him after this survive.

As the year draws to a close he again feels despondent. On December 18, 1860 he writes to Majruh:

'You tell me that I'm not to invite Miran Sahib to Delhi until you say so—as though *you* are the only one that really loves him, and I don't. My friend, come to your senses and just think. I haven't got the means to invite him here and fix him up with a separate house to stay in and, if nothing more, give him thirty rupees a month, and say, "Here you are, take this and tour the ruins of Dariba and Chawri Bazar and Ajmeri Gate Bazar and Bulaqi Begam's lane and Khan Dauran Khan's mansion". Mir Mahdi, I think to myself how you lie abandoned and helpless in Panipat, and how Miran Sahib lies there wishing all the time that he could visit Delhi, and how Mir Sarfaraz Husain wanders around looking for employment. Do you think that such heart-rending sorrows are easy for me to bear? Had I had the means, I would have shown you what I would have done. "Alas, how many yearnings have turned to dust!" O, God! O, God!'

As the Christian year ended, nearly half of A H. 1277 had already elapsed and Ghalib still believed in his own prediction, he had at the most another six to seven months to live. He perhaps has this in mind when he writes to Sayyah on December 31, 1860:

'My weakness is at its height, and old age has made me useless. I am weak, slothful, lethargic, depressed, and weary of life. My foot is in the stirrup and my hand on the bridle. I have a long, long journey to travel, and no provision for the road, for I go empty-handed. If I am forgiven without being questioned, well and good. If I am called to account then I shall dwell in hell and damnation will be my station. Alone to face eternal torment. How well some poet[1] has said:

> Tired of all this, we look to death
> for our release
> But what if even after death we find
> no peace?'

[1] Zauq—cf. p. 85 above.

Chapter 10

1861

Ghalib's first letter of 1861 is addressed to Majruh. He writes on January 9th about conditions in Delhi:

'Kashmiri Katra is in ruins. Alas for those tall gateways and spacious rooms on either side of the road! You cannot even see now where they were. The coming of the railway and the clearing of a path for it are still postponed. For the last four days an easterly wind has been blowing. Clouds gather, but we have had only a few spots of rain. It hasn't really rained. Wheat, gram and millet are all selling at the same price—eighteen or nineteen pounds to the rupee. . . .I can't really make out whether Mir Sarfaraz Husain and Miran Sahib are here or in Jind. Mir Nasīr ud Din came to see me twice, but I don't know where he is now.'

In the next letter, written only two days later, on January 11, 1861, he takes up this last point:

'Just look at this! Here am I asking you where Mir Sarfaraz Husain and Miran Sahib are; and Mir Nasīr ud Din is in Delhi and doesn't come to see me, while Mir Sarfaraz Husain came here and didn't stay with me. In fact—God save us!—he not only didn't stay with me: he didn't even come to see me. Alas that those whom I look upon as my own kin regard me as a stranger. You will ask me, "How did you find out that Nasīr ud Din was in Delhi and . . . [Mir Sarfaraz Husain] had been there?" Well, my friend, today is Friday, the 28th of Jamadi us Sani, and the 11th of January, and it's morning. At first light I awoke, and I was lying there wrapped in my quilt when all of a sudden Mir Nasīr ud Din honoured me with a visit and announced, "I am leaving now, and so is Mir Hasan Sahib." I thought he meant Sarfaraz Husain. But as he went on I discovered that Mir Hasan had come from Jaipur and had stayed somewhere or other and was off somewhere or other. Alas, alas! He must have counted me a stranger or thought that I was dead, that he never came to my house to see me. He stayed with his in-laws and kept away from his own parents. By God, I would have loved to see him. Now I'm up. Let the cold go and the sun come out and I'll send a man to Agha Jan's house. Curse it, I don't even know where Agha Jan lives. But I'll send my man to Mir Ahmad Ali's wife, by Habsh Khan's Gate. When I find out Agha Jan's address and the man has been there to see the house, and found out whether Mir Hasan Sahib is there, then if he is, I'll . . . go to see him. Be quick and answer this letter and tell me why your uncle has come to Delhi and how he is getting on. . . .'

In further letters to Majruh he returns again to conditions in Delhi. In one dated only '1861' but perhaps written in April or May, a verse which Majruh had sent him for correction starts him off. He quotes the verse,

> 'My friend, this is the language
> Delhi people speak.'

and comments:

'Oh, Mir Mahdi, aren't you ashamed of yourself? My good sir, "Delhi people" now means Hindus, or artisans, or soldiers, or Panjabis or Englishmen. Which of these speak the language which you are praising? [It's not like Lucknow.] The population of Lucknow hasn't changed. The state has gone [the British annexed Oudh, of which Lucknow was the capital, in 1856], but the city still has its masters of every art.

'The grass screens and the breeze from the east? Not in *this* house. These were the advantages of the old house. Now I am in Mir Khairati's mansion, the house faces in another direction. Anyway, I get along all right. The great trouble now is that Qari's well has been closed, and in all the wells in Lal Diggi the water has suddenly turned brackish. Well, we might have drunk it even so, but it comes up warm. I went out . . . two days ago to find out about the wells—past the Jama Masjid towards the Rajghat Gate. I tell you without exaggeration that from the Jama Masjid to the Rajghat Gate is a barren wilderness, and if the bricks piled here and there were taken away it would be absolutely bare. You must remember that on the far side of Mirza Gauhar's garden was a hollow twenty to thirty feet deep. Now the place is level with the wall of the garden courtyard. Even Rajghat Gate itself has been blocked up. The parapet of the battlements has been left clear, but the rest is all buried. You saw Kashmiri Gate for yourself when you were here. Now they've cleared a path for the railway from the Calcutta Gate to the Kabuli Gate. Panjabi Katra, Dhobi Wara, Ramji Ganj, Saadat Khan's Katra, Jarnail ki Bibi ki Haveli . . . [and other localities]—you won't find a trace of any of them. In short, the city has become a desert, and now that the wells are gone and water is something rare and precious, it will be a desert like that of Karbala[1]. My God! Delhi people still pride themselves on Delhi language! What pathetic faith! My dear man, when Urdu Bazar is no more, where is Urdu? By God, Delhi is no more a city, but a camp, a cantonment. No Fort, no city, no bazaars, no watercourses. . . .'

His next letter, dated May 23, 1861, again takes up the theme. Majruh had

[1] The place where Husain and his companions were martyred, after their access to water had been cut off.

evidently protested that Ghalib had painted too black a picture. He replies, speaking this time of the once-famous poets of Delhi who are now no more, or are silent:

'Oh, my friend . . . Delhi's devoted lover, dweller in the now-demolished Urdu Bazaar, jealous maligner of Lucknow, fierce of heart, and stranger to shame, where is Nizam ud Din Mamnun? And where is Zauq? And where is Momin Khan? Two poets survive: one, Azurda—and he is silent: the other Ghalib—and he is lost to himself, in a stupor. None to write poetry, and none to judge its worth. . . .'

Other things depressed him too. He had written to Tufta on January 20, 1861, evidently replying to a letter in which Tufta had told him that he was having his collection of Persian verse printed; he had entitled it *Sumbulistan* (The Hyacinth Garden). Ghalib replies gloomily:

'I got your letter from Meerut . . . God prosper you in publishing *Sumbulistan*. He alone guards your honour. Most of my life has passed, and only a little more remains; and I have no complaints either about the past or the future. I ask myself, "What good did the fame of Urfi's odes do Urfi, that the renown of mine should profit me? What fruit did Sadi reap from his *Bostan* that you should reap from your *Sumbulistan*? Apart from God, all that exists is unreal, a fantasy—no poetry, no poets, no odes, no desire to write. Nothing exists but God.

'If you meet our friend Mustafa Khan [Shefta] give him my regards. The news of the renewal of his sister's pension gave me great pleasure—and even greater surprise. What wonder if something even more pleasing and even more surprising should happen and he himself should get his pension restored? God's is the power.'

He wrote again on April 19, 1861, when *Sumbulistan* had appeared and Tufta had sent him two copies:

'Mirza Tufta, my dear sir, you've thrown your money away, and shamed both your own poetic power and my corrections. Alas! What a wretched production the book is! Had you been here you would have seen the true parallel to your verse and its printed form; you would have seen the ladies of the Fort moving about the city, their faces fair as the moon and their clothes dirty, their trouser-legs torn, and their shoes falling to pieces. This is no exaggeration. Your *Sumbulistan* is like a lovely woman meanly clad. Anyway, I've given the two copies to the two boys and told their teacher to set their lessons from it. And they've started on it today.'

On February 22, 1861 he had complained to Junun of his deteriorating physical and mental powers:

'My memory is as good as gone, my sense of smell diminished, and my hearing defective. There is nothing wrong with my sight, though it is not so sharp as it was:

Old age, a hundred ailments, as they say.'

But, in general he is not in bad humour during these months, and even where he has something distasteful to say he handles it with a light touch. A letter of April 4, 1861 to Ala ud Din Ahmad Khan Alai, is typical:

'The lion feeds its cubs on the prey it has hunted, and teaches them to hunt their prey. When they grow up they hunt for themselves. You have become a competent poet, and you have a natural talent. Why should *you* not compose a chronogram on the birth of your child? Why should *you* not work out a name that yields the date? Why trouble me, an old man grieved at heart? Ala ud Din Khan, I swear by your life: I worked out a chronogram-name for your first son and put it into a verse; and the child did not live. The fancy haunts me that this was the effect of my inauspicious stars. No one whom I praise survives it. One ode apiece was enough to dispatch Nasīr ud Din Haidar and Amjad Ali Shah [Kings of Oudh]. Wajid Ali Shah [the last king] stood up to three, and then collapsed. A man to whom I addressed ten to twenty odes would end up on the far side of oblivion. No, my friend, may God protect me, I will neither write a chronogram on his birth nor work out a chronogram-name. May Exalted God preserve you and your children and confer long life and wealth and prosperity on you all.

'Listen to me, my friend. It's a rule with men who worship beauty that when they fall in love with a youngster they deceive themselves that he's three or four years younger than he really is. They know he's grown up, but they think of him as a child. Your tribe is no better. On my faith I swear: here is a man whose honour and fame are known and established among men; and you too know it, my friend. But you can't feel happy until you shut your eyes to all that and think of the poor fool as a nobody, whom no one has ever heard of. I have lived fifty years in Delhi. Thousands of letters come in from every quarter. Some who write don't even give the name of the muhalla. Some address me at the muhalla where I formerly lived. Letters from the authorities, in Persian and in English—even letters from England—come addressed simply with my name and "Delhi". You know all these things. You have seen such letters. And then you ask me for my address! If you don't class me as a noble, well and good. But at any rate I'm not an artisan, that the postman can't find me unless you write the muhalla and the police station. Address me by name at "Delhi". I'll stand guarantee that your letters reach me.'

He concludes an undated letter (probably of May or June 1861) to Majruh:

'These days Maulana Ghalib (God's mercy be upon him) is in clover. A volume of the *Tale of Amir Hamza* has come—about 600 pages of it—and a volume of the same size of *Bostan i Khayal* (The Garden of Fancy).[1] And there are seventeen bottles of good wine in the pantry. So I read all day and drink all night.

> The man who wins such bliss can only wonder
> What more had Jamshed? What more Alexander?'

In June 1861 he writes to Nawwab Amin ud Din Ahmad Khan's son Ala ud Din Khan Alai that he loves him as any man would love the son of one who has been a friend to him:

'You are the fresh fruit of that tree which came to maturity before my eyes, and in whose cool shade I have rested, blessing his name. How could you be otherwise than dear to me? As for our seeing each other, there are only two possibilities: you should come to Delhi, or I to Loharu. But you cannot come, and I must be excused. Do not listen to my excuse—I tell you this myself— until you have heard from me who I am and what my story is:

'Listen: there are two worlds, the world of spirits, and this world of earth and water. The Ruler of both these worlds is One Who has Himself proclaimed the question: "Whose shall be the kingdom this day [Judgement Day]?" and has Himself given the answer: "That of the one God, the All-Powerful". Though it is the general rule that those who sin in this world of earth and water receive their punishment in the world of the spirits, it has sometimes happened that those who have sinned in the world of the spirits are sent to undergo punishment in this world. Thus I, on the 8th Rajab 1212 AH[2] was sent here to stand trial. I was kept waiting in the cells for thirteen years, and then on the 7th Rajab, 1225 AH[3] I was sentenced to life-imprisonment. A chain[4] was fastened on my feet, and the city of Delhi having been designated my prison, I was committed there, and condemned to the hard labour of composing prose and verse. After some years I escaped from prison and ran away to the east [Calcutta] where I roamed at liberty for three years. In the end I was appre- hended in Calcutta and brought back and thrown into the same jail. Seeing that I would try to escape again, they fettered my hands as well.[5] The fetters chafed my ankles, and the handcuffs wounded my wrists. My prescribed hard labour became a greater burden to me, and my strength departed from me entirely. But I am a man without shame. Last year I got my feet free, and, still

---

[1] Enormously long medieval-style romances. The *Tale of Amir Hamza* runs into eighteen bulky volumes.
[2] The date of Ghalib's birth.   [3] The date of Ghalib's marriage.   [4] Ghalib's wife.
[5] The two boys whom Ghalib adopted as 'grandsons'.

handcuffed, ran off, leaving my fetters in a corner of my cell. By way of Meerut and Muradabad, I made my way to Rampur. A few days short of two months had passed when I was apprehended and brought back again. Now I have promised not to run away again. And how can I? I no longer have the strength. I await now the order for my release. When will it come? There is just a faint possibility that I may get out this very month—Zil Hij, 1277.[1] But, be that as it may, a man released from jail makes straight for home, and I too, when my deliverance comes, will go straight to the world of spirits.

> Happy that day when I shall leave this prison
> house of earth,
> Forsake this barren vale, and reach the city
> of my birth.'

His words make it clear that he now felt it unlikely that his prophecy that he would die in 1277 was going to be fulfilled.

A letter of this same month of June 1861 to Junun suggests that he has deliberately changed his mind about it:

'Why have you written like that about the mangoes? Gifts do not have to be repeated for evermore, especially when the gift is itself something that does not last. My dear sir, this year mangoes are scarce everywhere, and what few there are, are dry and tasteless. And it is not to be wondered at. There was no rain in the winter months and none in the rainy season. You can ford the rivers on foot, and the wells are dried up. How can one expect the fruit to be juicy? Please do not think anything of it. I shall prove my own revelation false, and live on till next year's rains to eat your . . . mangoes.'

And 1277 did indeed elapse with Ghalib still surviving. In due course, as we shall see, he thought up an ingenious explanation, but for the moment he had other things to occupy his mind. His patron the Nawwab of Rampur, had just celebrated with great pomp the marriage of his second son. Arshi describes the occasion:

'Preparations had been started months beforehand. Robes of honour had been distributed to the courtiers, and food sent to every citizen of the capital; and throughout the city gatherings were held where dancing girls and musicians entertained the people. Dependants of the court outside the state were sent invitations to come to the wedding. Ghalib too received one, but he was not well enough to come. . . .'

The Nawwab then sent him a gift of Rs. 125 in lieu of the tray of choice food and the robe of honour traditionally conferred on such occasions. Ghalib was

---

[1] Because Zil Hij is the last month of the Muslim year, and Ghalib had prophesied that he would die in 1277.

either exceptionally short of money at the time or else he felt that where the Nawwab had spent so much, he might be persuaded to spend a little more. Accordingly he writes on July 11, 1861:

'I am not writing to you but conversing with you, and, seeking your pardon for my impertinence and your permission to speak my mind, what I have to say (and I say it by way of a joke) is this: You have presented me with Rs. 125 to provide myself with a feast and a robe of honour. I am starving. If I spend it all on feeding myself, and don't use any of it for getting the robe made, will your highness still owe me money for a robe or will you not?

> May you live on another thousand years
> And every year have fifty thousand days.'

At the same time he composed and sent the Nawwab some poems in honour of the occasion, of which the Nawwab expressed his appreciation. However, an incident now occurred which aroused his displeasure. Ghalib's friends, Miran Sahib and Mir Sarfaraz Husain, had, with Ghalib's approval, gone to try their fortunes at Rampur, and Ghalib had given them a letter of introduction to the Nawwab's Chief Steward. This perfectly reasonable action seems to have upset the Nawwab, who presumably thought that Ghalib ought to have approached him direct, and Miran Sahib and Mir Sarfaraz Husain had to come away empty-handed. Ghalib's distress is evident from the letter he wrote the Nawwab on July 22, 1861:

'It is seven or eight years since I entered your service and began to share in your bounty. I have made it a binding rule never to make an improper request of you or recommend anyone to your favour. . . . I did not send Mir Sarfaraz Husain or Miran Sahib—I swear by God I did not. They went looking for employment. That is Mir Sarfaraz Husain's profession; and Miran Sahib recites elegies [on the martyrdom of Husain], and is outstanding amongst his fellows here in this art. When I wrote to your Chief Steward that they had such-and-such qualifications, what I had in mind was that during Muharram when half a dozen or more reciters are retained for the occasion, Miran Sahib might make one of them; and since, after all, there are numerous officials needed to take charge of your police stations and of the administrative sub-districts, Mir Sarfaraz Husain, who is an intelligent and able man, might be appointed to some such post in some district. Had both or either of these things been done, well and good. They have not been done; well and good. What I wrote was indeed not a recommendation; my aim was simply to introduce them. Had I wished to recommend them, could I not have written to you? Where I am concerned, you may set your mind at rest.

> For years and years no breath has passed my lips
> But such as tended to your happiness.'

I

To Majruh he wrote, understandably, in different terms. In a letter dated simply 'July, 1861' he writes:

'Your letter came yesterday in the middle of the afternoon. I feel sure that Mir Sarfaraz Husain must have reached you at much the same time, or at any rate that same evening. You will hear from his own mouth how he fared on his journey. I don't know what *I* can write. Whatever I have heard, I too have heard from him. His coming back empty-handed was not what I had wished and not what I had intended; but it accords with what I had believed and expected. I knew that he would get nothing there. He has spent a hundred rupees for nothing, and since he spent it trusting in my suggestion, I feel ashamed. In my sixty-six years I have often been shamed and disgraced in this way, and when a man bears a thousand such scars, well, he can bear one more. But my heart feels keenly the pain of his loss.

'Why bother to ask about the epidemic?[1] This was the one arrow left in the quiver of Fate, the unerring marksman. Where killing has been so general, and looting so merciless, and famine on so great a scale, why not an epidemic too? "The Voice of the Unseen"[2] had proclaimed ten years ago:

> Ghalib, all other woes have come to pass
> And only unexpected death remains.

'My friend, I was not mistaken about 1277, but I thought it beneath me to die in a general epidemic. Really, it would have been an action most unworthy of me. Once this trouble is over we shall see about it.

'The printing of my collected Urdu verse is finished. Most probably you'll be receiving a copy through the post this week—or at the latest by the end of the month.

'There are plans for printing the collected Persian verse too. If everything works out, that too will be printed. . . .

'The epidemic has died down somewhat. For six or seven days it raged everywhere. Two days ago Khwaja Mirza (son of Khwaja Aman) came to Delhi with his wife and children. Yesterday night his nine-year-old boy contracted cholera and died. "Verily we are for God and verily to Him we shall return."

'The epidemic affects Alwar too. Alexander Heatherly, known as Alec Sahib, has died. I tell you truly and sincerely, he was very dear to me, a man who wished to advance my interests and served as a link between me and the Raj. And it was for this crime that death has taken him. Well, this is the world of causes and effects. What are its workings to us?'

Mihr notes of Alexander Heatherly:

---

[1] There was a severe epidemic of cholera in Delhi at the time.
[2] A title by which the Persian poet Hāfiz is often known. Here Ghalib applies it to himself.

'His father was French,[1] and he had married an Indian woman. He was a very good Urdu poet, one of the disciples of Zain ul Abidin Arif [the "nephew" of Ghalib who died young and whose two children Ghalib adopted as his "grandsons"]. His usual pen-name was Azad, but he sometimes used Alec, the shortened form of Alexander. He died at the age of thirty. His younger brother Thomas had his collection of Urdu verse printed at Agra in 1863.'

In his next letter, dated August 8, 1861, he returns to the Rampur fiasco: 'My friend, you are right when you say

Nothing befalls the sons of man but passes by.

But what pains me is that they went there on the strength of my letter, and suffered by it. . . .' But after a few lines he returns to other themes.

'The volume of my Urdu verse is printed. Alas! When the Lucknow press prints a man's diwan it raises him to heaven. The calligraphy is so good that every word shines radiant! May Delhi and its water and its press be accursed! They call for the poet of the diwan as a man calls for his dog. I looked at every proof as it was brought to me. But the copyist was not the man who brought the pages to me, but someone else. Now that the copies are printed and I have received my author's copy I find that not a word has been corrected. The copyist has left them just as they were. All I could do was make a list of errata, and this has been printed. Anyway, no matter whether I like it or not, I'll buy several copies, and, God willing, a copy each will reach the trinity of you this very week. But I got no pleasure from it, and you won't either.

'And what's this you write—"There are customers here: write and tell me the price"? I'm not an agent, nor a merchant, nor the manager of the press. The Ahmadi Press is owned by Muhammad Husain Khan, and managed by Mirza Amu Jan. The press is in Shahdara—Muhammad Husain Khan, near Painters' Mansion, Rae Man Lane, Delhi. Price of the book: six annas [about sixpence]. Postage to be paid by the customer. Give this information to anyone who wants the book. Anyone who wants to order copies—two, or four, or ten, or five—should write to Muhammad Husain Khan, Painters' Mansion, Rae Man Lane, Delhi, and ask him to send them off by post. The books will come by post, and payment can be sent off in cash or in stamps, as you like. What's it got to do with me and you? You know what to tell anyone who asks.

'I can't tell you whether an epidemic's mounting or subsiding unless there *is* an epidemic. There is a man of sixty-six here [Ghalib] and a woman of sixty-four [his wife]. If either of them had died we would have known that there *was* an epidemic. A fig for such an epidemic! It's Thursday, August 5th, but there's no sign of the lunar month. Last night we put one stool on top of another, and several people kept climbing on them to look. But the new moon

[1] This is incorrect. His father was English, and his mother an Indian Muslim lady.

was not to be seen.' (The Muslim month begins when the new moon is actually seen.)

This letter makes it unmistakably clear that the Urdu diwan had not been printed in Agra after all. Not until January 10, 1862 do we find any indication why. But on that date he writes to Aram:

'It seems to me that Maulvi Mir Niyaz Ali Sahib has not presented my case to you properly. What I wanted him to make clear to you was that the printing of the Urdu diwan in Delhi had already begun before Hakim Ahsanullah Khan could bring me the proof-sheet you had sent him, and that I had authorized the press here to print the diwan because I thought you no longer proposed to do so. Just consider: remember how Muhammad Azīm, the owner of the press at Meerut, implored me to let him have the diwan, and how in order not to incur your displeasure I compelled him to return it to me. How could I then give anyone else permission to print it? You had left off writing to me, and I thought you must be cross with me. I told Maulvi Niyaz Ali Sahib, "You must please persuade my son Shiv Narayan to forgive me!" My friend, I swear to God, I regard you as a dear son. Why speak of the diwan and the picture? It was for you alone that I got the diwan copied out and brought it from Rampur. It took me a lot of searching to find the portrait in Delhi, but I found it, and bought it, and sent both things to you. They are yours. You may do as you like with them—keep them, give them away, or tear them up and throw them out. You had a fine edition of *Dastambu* prepared and made me a present of it: I sent you my portrait and my Urdu diwan. You are the living memorial of my cherished friend Nāzir Bansi Dhar:

> O fragrant flower, your fragrance pleases me
> Because it holds another's fragrance too.'

On September 22, 1861 he writes again to Majruh. He had corrected some verse of Mir Sarfaraz Husain and returned it, apparently with only a brief covering note. Majruh seems to have objected, for Ghalib now writes:

'Yes sir? What do you want of me? I corrected the manuscript . . . and returned it. What more did you want me to write? . . . You prefer the ways of Muhammad Shah's reign [he was Emperor from 1719 to 1748]: "Here all is well, and I desire to know of your welfare also. I had received no letter from you for many days. I was pleased to hear from you. The manuscript, duly corrected, is returned herewith. Please give it to my dear son Mir Sarfaraz Husain, and give him my blessing also. And further, give my blessing to Hakim Mir Ashraf Ali and to Mir Afzal Ali. It behoves you as a dutiful son always to continue writing to me in this way."

'What do you say? Isn't it a fact that this is the way they used to write letters in those days? Good heavens, what an attitude—that unless it's written like that, a letter's not a letter but a well without water, a cloud without rain, a tree without fruit, a house without light, a lamp without radiance! I know that you are alive: you know that I am alive. I wrote what was necessary, leaving it to another time to write the superfluities. And if I can't please you without writing like this, well, my friend, I've written you a line or two in that style now—and when a man makes up for a prayer he has missed, his atonement is accepted.[1] . . . So forgive me, and don't be cross.

'Mir Nasīr ud Din came once, but he hasn't been since. I haven't written any more Persian verse, so how can I send it to your uncle or to you? Nawwab Faiz Muhammad Khan's [Lord of Jhajjar's] brother, Hasan Ali Khan has died. Hāmid Ali Khan has been awarded a hundred and thirty thousand and some hundred rupees from the former King's treasury. Kallu, my steward, was ill, but today he's quite recovered. Baqir Ali Khan has had fever for the past month, and Husain Ali Khan has two swollen glands on his neck. The city is silent. No sound of shovels plying, no houses being blown up, no work on the railway going on, no mounds being raised. Delhi city is a city of the dead. I've used up all my paper, otherwise I'd have written more, just to please you.'

Two days later, on September 24, 1861, he sends a letter of recommendation to Shihab ud Din Khan:

"Light of my eyes Shihab ud Din Khan, my blessing upon you! This is to tell you that the man who has come with my note is named Hasan Ali, and is a Sayyid. His skill in making medicines is unmatched, and in making pickles and preserves, unparalleled. His father Jan Muhammad was employed at the King's court, and his uncle [father's brother] Mir Fatah Ali now holds a post at Alwar at a salary of Rs. 15 a month. Anyway, I have told him that he will get Rs. 5 a month and will have to go to Loharu. He refused, saying that on an income of five rupees he could neither keep himself nor send anything to his wife and children here. I replied, "It's a big establishment. If your work pleases them, they will raise your salary." He said, "Very well, on the strength of that I'll accept the small salary; but I must be provided with two meals a day. Otherwise I can't possibly manage."

'Listen, my son. The poor fellow is quite right. Unless he gets his keep he can't manage. I'm sure that when you report the facts, you can get this authorized. So much for that. Now he says, "Let me have two months' salary in advance so that I can get some clothes made and leave them something at home to be going on with. And let me have money to cover the expenses of food and conveyance for the journey. Here too I think he's in the right, but I'm not in a position to say anything on this point. Anyway, you can send on this note I've written you to our lord and master [Ala ud Din Khan] Alai.'

---

[1] A Muslim unable to say one of the five prayers at the prescribed time is permitted to make good the omission later.

He writes to Alai himself the next day. Alai must have asked him how it was that he could go to Rampur (as he had done the previous year), but could not come to Loharu. He replies on September 25, 1861:

'Lord and master Alai, I've just received your letter, and sat down to answer it the moment I finished reading it. Here's a fine thing! I am to be your ox, and my ties with Rampur your goad—or I your horse and taunts about Rampur your whip. Why should my ties and commitments to Rampur hinder and prevent my coming to Loharu? I'm not the Nawwab's representative, posted to a certain area. Just as nobles provide for the upkeep of faqirs, so does the court of Rampur provide for mine. The only difference is that a faqir is expected to call down God's blessings on his patron while I am expected to correct his verse. If I like, I can stay in Delhi, or in Agra, or in Lahore, or in Loharu—just as I like. I have only to hire a conveyance for my clothing, pack a dozen bottles of wine in my trunk, contract for the services of eight palanquin-bearers, leave two of my four servants here, take two along with me, and set off. Any letter from Rampur can be sent on by the boys' tutor. I can arrange for the conveyance; I can get the wine; I can find the palanquin-bearers. But where shall I get the strength? When I go for my meals from my own quarters to the zenana (which is quite near) it takes me almost half an hour to get my breath back, and the same when I get back to my drawing room. And after all, the Nawwab of Rampur too invited me to his son's wedding and I told him the same thing, "I hardly exist any more. Your auspicious influence sustains me to correct your verse, but expect no service from me beyond that."

'I would love to see both my brother [your father] and you. But what can I do? I can hope to come when the sun is in Scorpio or Sagittarius, that is, in November or December, but I wish it were only Gurgaon or Badshahpur I had to get to instead of Loharu. You'll say, "Is Rampur any nearer, then?" But it's two years since I went there, and my strength fails and declines with every day that passes. You can't come here, and I have not the strength to go there. So if in November or December my final assault succeeds, well and good. Otherwise

> I grieve because I cannot see my friends
> And for no other thing. . . .'

He writes again on October 15, 1861:

'My dear child, what are you saying? What more do you want? The breeze is cool again, the water cold again; the harvest has been good, and grain is plentiful. I have conferred the honour of succession upon you. [He means that he has declared him his literary successor, but he goes on to use the terms appropriate to a saint handing on his powers to a disciple.] I have bestowed my cloak upon you, and I would not grudge you rosary and prayer-mat too, were there any sign of them here. More than that, my brother [your father] has recovered his health. Master Mir Jan has arrived [at Loharu], and at the end of October or the beginning of November you will be welcoming [your uncle, Nawwab Ziya ud Din Ahmad] Nayyar i Rakhshan. Then why think anything of the sun of Scorpio and Sagittarius?[1]

> Springs, summers, winters—all will come and go
> When we are mingled in the dust and stone.[2]

'To Master Mir Jan, since my father's sister was his father's brother's wife, and since he is younger than I am, my blessing: and, since he is my friend, and friendship takes no regard of whether a man is older or younger, my regards: and, since he is called "Master", my humble service; and, since he is a Sayyid, my reverence: and, since, as the verse tells us,

> Apart from God, is nothing: all that is, is God—

my worship . . .
    'You may eat all the fried gelded goat's meat you like, and all the meat and onion, curries, and pulaos and kababs. I swear to God I don't give it a thought. But I only pray that sugar-crystal from Bikaner is denied you. Whenever I imagine Mir Jan Sahib munching lumps of it, I eat my heart out with envy.'

Alai evidently responded by sending him a present of Bikaner sugar-crystal, for he writes again on November 12, 1861:

'Today at the time I usually go to the zenana for lunch Shihab ud Din Khan arrived with your letter and a bag of sugar-crystal. I had it taken along with me and had the crystal weighed in my presence. It came to about four ounces over the four pounds. God prosper your dwelling-place! That is enough and more than enough, and I don't need any more. When I came out again after having my lunch, your cousin's [Shihab ud Din Khan's] servant was waiting to ask me for an answer to your letter, saying that the camel-man was about to leave. I usually lie down after lunch, so I've written this acknowledgement lying here. I'll answer the other things in your letter tomorrow.'

Only a few letters speak of things that saddened or distressed him. In a letter to Sayyah dated October 4, 1861, he writes:

'Munshi Mir Amir Ali Sahib and I have never met, but I hear him spoken of as a good man of exceptional qualities. Maulvi Izhar Husain Sahib I have met

---

[1] Cf. the previous letter. Ghalib had said he would hope to visit Loharu 'when the sun is in Scorpio or Sagittarius'. There is a play upon words here. 'Nayyar i Rakhshan' literally means 'the dazzling sun'.
[2] Cf. p. 169 above.

on two occasions, here in Delhi, but I did not find him the sort of man to feel friendship and consideration for a poor faqir. He is all right for the rich. Alas for Maulvi Muhammad Hasan and Maulvi Abdul Karim! If either of them had still been here in these times I would have had no occasion to lament my fate. Time passes, but one does not forget.

'And yes, Khan Sahib, now you have reached Calcutta and met everybody there, make full enquiries about Fazl i Haq, and write and tell me why he has not been released and under what conditions he lives there in the islands [the Andaman Islands, where criminals sentenced to transportation were sent] and how he is.'

A letter from Shafaq, in which he had apparently complained of ill-treatment by his relations, provokes an outburst of bitterness on Ghalib's part against his. He writes on October 22, 1861:

'Most reverend sir, . . . In matters of feeling, the union of two opposites is beyond the bounds of possibility. How can it be that at one particular time one particular matter can be at once the cause of joy and the grounds of grief? Yet in reading your letter I found just that, for I felt both pleasure and pain. Glory to God! I find that in so many things you and I have shared the same fate—ill-treatment from our relatives, grievance against our kin. Throughout the realm of India I have no fellow-countryman. One or two in Samarkand and a hundred or two among the nomads of the deserts of the Khifchaq [Central Asia] there may be. But relations by marriage I have; and I fell into their toils when I was only five, and for sixty-one years have borne their tyranny.

> Ghalib, were I to tell the tale of all my
> kin have done to me
> Then hope—that custom men observe—would
> leave the world for evermore.

You cannot come to my support, nor I to your aid. Oh God! I have swum the river, the further shore is near, and two more strokes will bring me to the land.

> I lived my life waiting for death to come
> And dead, I still must see what else I face.

. . . You are a prey to grief and sorrow, but . . . to be the target of the world's afflictions is proof of an inherent nobility—proof clear, and argument conclusive. . . .'

His depression must have been enhanced by the fact that he was ill at the time, as a later letter shows. On November 11, 1861 he writes to the Nawwab of Rampur:

'Your loyal well-wisher has been ill for a full month. It began with the same old bouts of colic. Then because I took the heating medicines which one has to for this ailment, I fell a prey to fever. I suffered several bouts, and now for the last two times a bout was due, I have felt nothing. But my strength is completely spent, and mental exhaustion has brought me to death's door. For the present I am taking apple juice.'

A letter of November 20, 1861, to Sayyah shows that he had still not made a full recovery:

'These days I suffer so much from giddiness and mental exhaustion that even a lot of the Nawwab of Rampur's verse is put to one side just as it is until I can attend to it. . . . The ghazals you sent me are all safe. You may rest assured. When I have corrected the Nawwab Sahib's ghazals, yours shall be corrected too.'

Otherwise, he had gone on consistently with the correction of his friend's verses—Sayyah's, Junun's and Tufta's, to name only three—throughout the year, praising and rebuking alike with the same forthrightness as ever. Thus he writes to Tufta on August 19, 1861: 'My friend Mirza Tufta, a thousand times bravo! What a fine ode you have written! All praise to you! . . . The construction is excellent, and the simplicity of the language admirable. . . .' On the other hand, on September 9, 1861, he scolds him for entertaining a doubt 'which only a schoolboy or a beginner ought to feel' and on October 4, 1861, for making a mistake 'astonishing in so practised a poet'.

In an undated letter to Rana which perhaps belongs to about this time he writes: 'My friend, Delhi and Lucknow are agreed that "*jafa*" is feminine. No one would ever make it masculine, except perhaps in Bengal, where they make even "cow-elephant" masculine.'

The same good humour pervades an undated letter to Sahib i Alam:

'Lord and Master, to what can I compare the couplets you write in my praise and how can I thank God sufficiently for them? It is God's goodness to His servants that makes His chosen favourites speak well of such a disgrace to creation as I am. It seems that this great good fortune was written in my fate that I should come through this general epidemic alive. O God, my God, praise to Thee that Thou hast saved one who deserved death by sword or fire, and then raised him to high estate! I sometimes feel that the throne of heaven is my lodging and Paradise my back garden. In God's name, compose no more verses in my praise, or I shall not shrink from claiming Godhead myself!'

From what follows, it is clear that Sahib i Alam's handwriting had not improved over the years.

1*

' "*Panj Ahang*, that book replete in instruction, that work so fair and fine . . ."—what follows that, your slave could not read. All I could make out were the three names, Chaudhri Sahib, and Hazrat Shah Amir Sahib and Maulvi Fazl i Ahmad Sahib. Even then I am doubtful about the second name, and wonder if my guess corresponds with the facts or not. About the other two—Chaudhri Sahib and Maulvi Fazl i Ahmad Sahib—I do not feel any doubt. Further, I could not make out what it is you want. If it is *Panj Ahang* you ask for, the answer is that I have a cousin by marriage, Nawwab Ziya ud Din Khan (God preserve him) who used to collect all my verse and prose. The collected prose and the Urdu poetical works were in his library. It is with fear and trembling I tell you that his library—it must have been worth twenty thousand rupees—was looted. Not a single page survived. True, the printed *Panj Ahang* is still on sale; but it is faulty in two respects. First, it does not include such prose as I wrote after it was printed; and secondly, the copyist made "corrections" in my prose of which only my heart can tell. Were I to tell you that no line is free of mistakes I should be pitching it too high. But I can say without exaggeration that no page is free of mistakes. Anyway, if you wish, I can send it. Please offer my due respects to your noble sons, first to the first, whose name I could not decipher, and then to Sayyid Maqbul Alam. My desire to see them grows day by day.'

Chapter 11

1862

Ghalib's first letter of 1862 was that to Aram already quoted in the previous chapter—the only one to Aram in this year. A second, dated January 19, 1862, to Maududi tells the welcome news of the release of Ghalib's old friend Azurda:

'Our revered Maulvi Sadr ud Din [Azurda] had been in detention for a long time, but he was brought before the court for trial, and at the end of the proceedings the court ordered that his life be spared. He lost his employment, and his property was confiscated. Willy nilly, in his penury he made his way to Lahore. There the Financial Commissioner and Lieutenant-Governor, as an act of clemency, returned half his property, and he now has possession of it. He lives in his own mansion and lives on the rent which he receives [from his other property]. He can manage on it, for he has thirty to forty rupees a month coming in, and there is only himself and his wife. But Imam Bakhsh's children are closely related to him, and there are about ten to twelve of them. So he doesn't live very comfortably. He is old, and very infirm, and getting on for ninety years old. May God preserve him. We must be grateful for such as he these days.'

Most of February and early March are taken up with letters to Alai, dealing with the real or imagined ailments of Alai's father, Amīn ud Din Khan, and, side by side with this, a delicate diplomatic matter in which Alai wants Ghalib's help. For some reason Alai is anxious that his father should take the two brothers Qurban Ali Beg Salik and Shamshad Ali Beg Rizwan into his entourage, and he wants Ghalib to put in a good word for them. Ghalib writes on February 1, 1862:

'On Friday morning I wrote you a letter, which I sent off right away. About nine in the morning I heard he [your father] had had another turn the previous night. I went to see how he was . . . and was told by Muhammad Ali Beg that this attack had been lighter than previous ones, and he had felt relief more quickly. Yesterday Mirza Shamshad Ali Beg told me that Ali Husain had told him, "The Nawwab Sahib is asking whether you will consent to come to Loharu and eat his bread". He had replied, "I want to eat your bread, provided I can eat my fill".' Ghalib draws the conclusion from this that the Nawwab is not favourably inclined to Salik [Qurban Ali Beg] and that 'his head is full only of Shamshad Ali Beg.

> The secrets of their states are known to kings alone:
> Sit in your corner, Hāfiz. Why bestir yourself?'

Alai must have expressed concern over his father's health, and even a fear that some enemy had cast a spell on him. Ghalib replies reassuringly on February 15, 1862:

'Your father is ill in the sense that he is not feeling entirely fit, and this depresses him; but there is absolutely nothing to fear. I had quite forgotten, but now that he tells me, I remember that twelve to thirteen years ago this feeling quite suddenly overcame him one day. He was young in those days, and not accustomed to use opium. He was treated at once with an emetic and a few days later with a purgative. Now he is getting on in years, and moreover he uses opium; and he has had several turns in quick succession. But my concern for him is based on my love for him; there are no medical grounds for concern.'

He goes on to list some of the famous Delhi hakims, remarking that some of them are no longer in Delhi, but that all the same there are still excellent hakims who will be in attendance upon him. And what more does he want?

'True there are one or two doctors, who have a reputation because they are of the same race as our rulers, and an obscure *baid* or two [a man who practises the ancient Hindu system of medicine] lurking in holes and corners.

'God save us! You think it necessary to commend Amīn ud Din Khan to my attention? Have I no heart in my breast? Or is the faith—otherwise called love—in my heart no more than an ant's head or a mosquito's wing? The hakims will take care of the treatment, and I will not fail in companionship or sympathy, or I shall stand convicted.'

He then goes on to describe the standard treatment which the hakims will be applying, and goes on:

'The names of God and the verses of the Holy Quran used in effecting recovery, breaking spells, and driving out spirits are all established, and may be expected to exercise their due effect. (True, the maulvis and reciters know nothing and introduce all sorts of complications to impress people.) And who would want to put a spell on your father? Poor man, he lives in such an out-of-the-way corner of his own that no one ever passes that way unless he specially decides to. You can dismiss that idea. Yes, and he can give alms to the poor and ask them to pray for him, and ask the saintly for their succour. Well, there are more poor in Delhi than a man can count, and one saint—Hāfiz Abdul Aziz. So that is that, and all will be well.'

A second letter written the following day, February 16, 1862, shows that his letter had crossed with one of Alai's. He begins in the same tone:

'I have already replied to your letter yesterday; it must have reached you by now. I went to see your father this morning. Ziya ud Din Khan and Shihab ud Din Khan[1] were there too, and Maulvi Sadr ud Din [Azurda] came while I was there. It has been settled that he is to be treated as Hakim Mahmud Khan prescribes—that is, he has written the prescription, the pills have been made up, and the materials for the medicines sent for so that they can be put in soak today ready for use tomorrow immediately after he has taken the pills. But it looks to me as though the noble patient and his well-wishers are in two minds about going through with the cure. They are weighing the prescription in the balance of scrutiny. Master Mir Jan was also there, and so was that half-fool Mirza Asad Beg. Everything is all right.'

Then a remark in Alai's letter evokes a more serious theme:

'At two separate points in your letter yesterday I see that you have written that Delhi is a big city and there must be plenty of people with all sorts of qualifications there. Alas, my dear boy, this is not the Delhi in which you were born not the Delhi in which you got your schooling, not the Delhi in which you used to come to your lessons with me to Shaban Beg's mansion, not the Delh, in which I have passed fifty-one years of my life. It is a camp. The only Muslims here are artisans or servants of the British authorities. All the rest are Hindus. The male descendants of the deposed King—such as survived the sword— draw allowances of five rupees a month. The female descendants, if old, are bawds, and if young, prostitutes. Count the number of Muslim nobles who are dead: Hasan Ali Khan, the son of a very great father, who had once drawn an allowance of a hundred rupees a day, died in despair, his pension reduced to a hundred rupees a month. Mir Nasīr ud Din,[2] descended on his father's side from a line of pirs and on his mother's from a line of nobles, was unjustly put to death. Agha Sultan, son of Paymaster Muhammad Ali Khan, who has himself held the rank of Paymaster, fell ill; without medicine, without food, at last he died. Your uncle provided for his shroud and his burial. Then let me tell you of my friends: Nāzir Husain Mirza, whose elder brother was numbered amongst the slain, is left penniless—not a farthing comes in. He has been granted a house to live in, but let us see whether he is left in possession or whether it will again be confiscated. Buddhe Sahib sold off all his property, lived on the proceeds while they lasted, and has now gone empty-handed to Bharatpur. Ziya ud Daula had properties returned to him that brought in a rent of five hundred rupees a month, but they have again been seized, and he has left for Lahore in a

---

[1] The brother and nephew of the sick man.   [2] Known as Kale Shah—cf. p. 71.

sorry plight. He is stranded there now. Let us see what becomes of him. To put it briefly, the Fort, and the estates of Jhajjar and Bahadurgarh and Ballabgarh and Farrukhnagar—with an income of something like three million rupees, have been wiped out. Where then would you find men of talent here? . . . Set your mind at rest about your respected father, and put any idea of enchantment or possession by spirits right out of your mind. God willing, once he has taken his purgative he will be quite all right. In fact, by God's grace, he's quite all right already.'

On March 1, 1862 he writes:

'Yesterday, Friday, the Nawwab was purged. I left him at eleven o'clock. His pills were made up of ingredients which are rather painful in their effects, and he was in a good deal of distress; he passed nine or ten motions, and by the end of the day was quite recovered. His system has been thoroughly cleansed, and by God's grace he is now quite well again; and it is certain that there will be no relapse.

'Leave it to your father to decide how long to stay on in Delhi. When he decides to leave I shall certainly say as much as I think appropriate on your behalf. But I shall not insist. I know his temperament better than you do. He is a self-willed man, and moreover he doesn't like having people recommended to him. The case of your two Mughal lads Qurban Ali Beg and Shamshad Ali Beg will have to be adjusted to what proves possible. I shall not intervene— unless of course I am asked, or the matter is discussed in my presence, in which case I shall speak, and to effect.

> Tear out the tongue that speaks
> what it should not.

Don't take offence: if he takes one or both of the brothers as his companion, the companionship *may* well be a happy one for life. But how many years, or months, or weeks can you guarantee them?'

Alai must have continued to pester him on both points, for he writes on March 7, 1862:

'Sir, my exalted brother your respected father is now cured. There are no rational grounds for fearing a relapse. As for irrational fears, even Luqman[1] had no remedy for them. To whatever you've written—and whatever you may write in future—about Mirza Qurban Ali Beg and Mirza Shamshad Ali Beg, my answer remains the same as I have already given you: My part is simply to observe; if your father mentions the matter to me, I will put in a good word for them.

[1] A wise man of legend, sometimes identified with Aesop.

'Your exalted uncle's pronouncements about Ghalib—that he sits there conjuring up all sorts of visions and fancies—shows that he judges me by himself, thinks that since *he* is a prey to illusory and superstitious fears, others too must be caught in . . . their toils. But it's a false comparison. . . . For I have drained the heavy goblet of the pure wine that teaches "Nothing exists but God", and I sit here above the radiance of religion and the fire of infidelity alike. . . .'

Letters in May—to Majruh and to Qadr Bilgrami—show that Ghalib's collected Persian verse, and a prose work, *Qāte i Burhan*, (of which we shall hear much more later) were now published. He had been asked to compose a chronogram of the date of printing of the collected verse, but refused. 'Why should I write a chronogram . . .?', he asks in a letter of May 24, 1862 to Qadr Bilgrami, 'The people at the press . . . can write it themselves. Printing began in '78 [AH] and finished in '79.'

On June 19, 1862 he again writes to Alai:

'Oh, my nephew! . . . May God protect me! I am not what Nayyar[1] imagines me (according to what you have written)—a prey to groundless fears and a victim of my own imaginings; nor am I what Mirza Ali Husain Khan Bahadur must think I am:

'O for just one man who would know me as I am!

To await me at Dujana and think that my coming depends upon the wedding is to fall prey to some of those mad fancies which make your uncle suspect that *I* am mad. I am not a lord, that a lord should invite me; nor a musician, to go along with my gear and tackle and earn a fee for playing at the wedding. Nor would I go to a wedding there in a season when the world is like a ball of fire and *not* go to see my brother at Loharu at the height of the cold season.

'Yesterday Master Mir Jan Sahib showed me your letter. . . . If Ghulam Husain Khan comes some time I will impress upon him the gist of what you wrote. And may Exalted God in His glory give one or both of these two the grace, or me the strength, or you the judgement, to persuade you that it is not any attachment to Delhi that prevents me coming. For I envy the men transported to the Islands, and still more the Lord of Farrukhabad, who was taken by ship and set down on the Arabian shore.[2] Oh for a place where

If I fall ill there would be none to visit me
And if I die there would be none to weep and wail.

'I cannot see the printing of the collected verse being finished during my life-time. The printing of *Qāte i Burhan* is finished, and I have received the

[1] Ziya ud Din Ahmad Khan, Alai's uncle.
[2] 'Tafazzul Husain Khan, Lord of Farrukhabad, who was charged with complicity in the Mutiny, and at his own request was sent to Arabia. He died in Mecca.'—Mihr.

one copy which is the author's right. I have sent that to your renowned uncle. Other volumes I have ordered as a customer, and the order is with the publishers. But they can't be sent until I've paid for them. I am trying to raise the money. If I manage it, I'll send it off. If the copy which has reached you is the printed edition, it's correct. Where you're in any doubt, look up the list of errata which is appended, and if you still need clarification write and ask me. If it's a manuscript copy, then it's not to be regarded as my work. In fact you . . . should tear it up. . . .'

In an undated letter that seems to follow this he writes:

'Your father refuses to believe me, and numbers me among the living. . . . Here am I concerned to provide camphor and a shroud for my corpse, and there is he, hard-hearted man, demanding verse from me. Had I been living, would I not have come to Loharu? Relieve me of this burden: write a few verses on this model and send them to me. I will correct them and send them back. . . .'

He ends his next letter, on July 17, 1862: 'Stopped drinking wine on 22nd June: started again on 10th July:

Thanks be to God! The tavern door is open
once again!'

He was asked to explain what this was all about, and in his next letter (of July 28, 1862) he does so. But he has something more remarkable to write of first:

'Listen, my dear boy: Thursday to Thursday makes eight days; Friday nine, Saturday ten, Sunday eleven. And not for a single moment has it stopped raining. At this very moment it is pouring down. I have had a charcoal brazier lit beside me, and after every two lines I write, I hold the paper to the fire to dry it out. What else can I do? Your letter demands an answer. So listen. . . .
  'Fifty years ago the late Ilahi Bakhsh Khan produced a new metre and rhyme scheme, and at his command I wrote a ghazal in it. [He then quotes what he regards as its best couplet, and its concluding couplet, and continues:] Now I find that someone has added an opening couplet and four more, included these two couplets of mine, and made a ghazal out of them which is being sung all over the place. The last couplet and one other are mine, and the other five some idiot's. . . .
  'Pay my respects to your father and tell him that the days are past when I could take one loan from Mathura Das, and touch Darbari Mal for another, and come away with loot from Khub Chand Chain Sukh's house. They all had my notes of hand, sealed with my seal and carefully preserved. Not that it did them any good, for they got neither principal nor interest. More than that, my

aunt paid my living expenses, and the Khan [?Ahmad Bakhsh Khan] would occasionally give me something besides, or would manage something from Alwar, or my mother would send me money from Agra. But these days all I have is the sixty-two rupees eight annas of my pension from the authorities and my hundred rupees from Rampur, and only the one agent from whom I can borrow and to whom I must pay interest and an instalment of the principal month by month. There is income tax to pay, the night-watchman to pay, interest to pay, principal to pay, the upkeep of my wife, the upkeep of the children, the upkeep of the servants—and just the Rs. 162 coming in. I was in difficulties, and could hardly make my way. I found I could not even meet my day to day needs. I thought to myself, "What shall I do? How can I solve the problem?" Well, a beggar's anger harms no one but himself. I cut out my morning cool drink, halved the meat for my midday meal, and stopped my wine and rosewater at nights. That saved me twenty rupees or so a month, and I could meet my day to day expenses. My friends would ask me, "How long can you go on without your morning and evening drinks?" I said, "Until He lets me drink again." "And how can you live without them?" they asked. "As He vouchsafes me to live," I replied. At length, before the month was out I was sent money from Rampur, over and above my stipend. I paid off the accumulated instalments on my regular debt. That left the miscellaneous ones—well, be it so. My morning drink and wine at night were restored, and I again began to eat my full quota of meat.

'Since your father asked why I had stopped drinking and then started again, read this part of my letter to him. . . .' He then turns upon one Hamza Khan, a maulvi who had once been tutor to Alai in his childhood and had now been ill-advised enough to have Alai write to Ghalib that it was time to act on the words of Hāfiz:

> Hāfiz, old age besets you: leave the tavern now.
> Debauchery and drinking go along with youth.

Without even breaking the sentence Ghalib goes straight on: 'and give my respects to Hamza Khan and tell him:

> You who have never known the taste of wine
> We drink unceasingly

'You see how He vouchsafes me drink? To make a name as a maulvi by teaching the baniyas and brats of Dariba, and to wallow in the problems[1] of menstruation and post-natal bleeding is one thing: and to study the works of the mystics and take into one's heart the essential truth of God's reality and His expression in all things, is another. Hell is for those who deny the oneness of God, who hold that His existence partakes of the order of the eternal and the possible, believe that Musailma shares with the Prophet the rank of the Seal of the

---

[1] In Islamic observances.

Prophets, and rank newly-converted Muslims with the Father of the Imams.
My belief in God's oneness is untainted, and my faith is perfect. My tongue
repeats, "There is no god but God", and my heart believes, "Nothing exists
but God, and God alone works manifest in all things." All prophets were to be
honoured, and submission to each in his own time was the duty of man. With
Muhammad (peace be upon him) prophethood came to an end. He is the Seal
of the Prophets and God's Blessing to the Worlds. . . . Then came the office
of Imam, conferred not by the consensus of men, but by God: and the Imam
ordained by God is Ali (peace be upon him), then Hasan, then Husain, and thus
onwards until the promised Mahdi (peace be upon him):

In this belief I live, in this I die.

'Yes, and there is this more to be said, that I hold free-thinking and atheism
to be abhorrent, and wine-drinking to be forbidden, and myself to be a sinner.
And if God casts me into Hell, it will not be to burn me, but that I may become
added fuel to the flames, making them flare more fiercely to burn those who
deny God's oneness and reject the prophethood of Muhammad and the Ima-
mate of Ali. Listen to me, maulvi sahib. Perhaps you will be stubborn and
think it no sin to hide the truth; but if not, you will remember, and confess
that you remember, how once in the days when you taught the *Gulistan* and
Bostan[1] to Ala ud Din Khan [Alai] you slapped the poor boy two or three
times. [His father] Nawwab Amīn ud Din Khan was in Loharu at the time, but
Ala ud Din's mother turned you out of the house. You came to me with tears
in your eyes, and I told you, "My friend, the sons of nobles and of gentlemen
may be scolded, but not struck. You were at fault. Never do such a thing again."
And you repented your folly. And now you graduate from school-mastering
and take up preaching to seventy-year-olds. By dint of repeated fasting you
memorize one verse of Hāfiz:

Hāfiz, old age besets you, etc.

and recite it—and that before one who has written twice and three times as
much verse as Hāfiz did, to say nothing of prose. And you do not observe
that as against this one verse, Hāfiz has thousands which contradict it:

Come, mystic, for the cup is clear as crystal
That you may see the ruby-red, pure wine.

Drink the pure wine and look upon the faces of
fair women
A fig for *their* religion! Gaze upon the beauties
here.'

---

[1] Works of the classical Persian writer Sadi, commonly used as elementary Persian texts.

He quotes two other couplets of Hāfiz in the same sense and then drops the
subject and turns again to address Alai:

'My son, I'm in great trouble. The walls of the zenana have collapsed [because
of the continuous rain]. The lavatory is in ruins. The roofs are leaking. Your
aunt [Ghalib's wife] keeps saying, "We'll be buried! We'll be killed!" My own
apartments are in an even worse state. I am not afraid of death, but I can't
stand discomfort. The roof is like a sieve. Where the sky rains for two hours,
the roof rains for four. The landlord can't do any repairs even if he wants to.
If only the rain would stop he could attend to everything, but even then how
can I sit here while the repairs are going on? If you can manage it, get your
father, for as long as the rains last, to let me have the mansion where Mir
Hasan used to live for your aunt [Ghalib's wife] and the upper apartment and
the downstairs sitting-room of the house where the late Ilahi Bakhsh Khan used
to live, for myself. Once the rains are over and the repairs are done, then the
sahib and memsahib and the babas will go back to their old house. Where your
father has so often made sacrifices to help me, let him show his kindness once
more and do me this favour in my closing days.'

The next day, July 29, 1862, he writes to Majruh:

'. . . Speaking of the rains, let me first give the over-all picture. First came the
mutiny of the blacks, then the wrath of the whites, then the disturbance of the
demolitions, then the disaster of the epidemics, then the calamity of the famine;
and now the rains have come like all these things rolled into one. This is the
twenty-first day. The sun appears as briefly as the lightning flash, and when
occasionally the stars appear at night people think they are fireflies. The dark
nights are a boon to the thieves, and not a day passes but what two or three
burglaries are reported. Do not think I am exaggerating: thousands of buildings
have collapsed, and hundreds of people have been buried beneath the ruins.
Every lane is like a river. The earlier famine was caused by lack of water. There
was no rain, and so no grain. This one is caused by excess of water. The rain
has fallen in such torrents that the sown seed has been washed away, and those
who have not yet sown their fields cannot do so. So that's how things are in
Delhi. Apart from that there's nothing new.'

Ghalib's appeal to Alai had the desired effect. On August 6, 1862 he writes.

'I do not fear death, nor do I lay claim to patience. And I believe not in freewill
but in predestination. You played the role of my go-between, and my brother
[your father] helped me like a brother. Long may you live, and long may God
preserve him! And may we lodge till Judgment Day in this same mansion!
    'To clarify the obscure and add detail to the general picture, the position was
that the rain fell in torrents. The younger boy was afraid and his grandmother

too [Ghalib's wife] was disturbed. I remembered the door of the private apartment that faces west, and, opposite it, a room with three doors. When you hurt your foot I used that door when I came to see you. With this in mind I planned to make that room the zenana, thinking that carriages and palanquins could come there and the various maidservants, and the tribes of women who come to sell vegetables, and oil, and betel, and what not . . . could use that door, while the children and I could come and go through the drawing room. God protect us if all of them were to come trooping through the drawing room, and we and the visitors were to have the spectacle of these witches forever before our eyes!

'Bi Wafadar[1]—you know her a little, and your father knows her well—has had the title of Wafadar Beg conferred upon her by your aunt [Ghalib's wife]. She goes out to do the shopping. At least, she doesn't do much shopping, but she's an affable soul, and sociable, and trots around talking to the people she meets in the street. Once she's out of the house it's unthinkable that she shouldn't take a walk along the canal and talk to the sentries at the gate and pick flowers and bring them back to show to her mistress, with "These flowers are from your nephew's garden."[2] Alas, alas, that so fine a drawing room should suffer such a fate and that a crazy, sensitive man like me should be so plagued! On top of that, I could not contemplate the idea that the small room would suffice for my servants and for the children to have their lessons in. For could the [children's] peacocks and pigeons and sheep and goat be kept outside with the horses? I muttered the verse "God is recognized in the failure of man's plans",[3] and said nothing more. But let your refined mind be at rest: all cause for uneasiness and fear has gone. The rain has stopped; the landlords have had repairs put in hand; the boy is no longer afraid; the mistress is no longer disturbed; I no longer suffer discomfort. I have the open roof, the moonlit night, the cool breeze. All night long Mars can be seen in the sky, and an hour before first light shining Venus comes into view. As the moon sinks in the west, Venus rises in the east: and I enjoy my morning draught of wine amid this radiance.'

Letters to Majruh and Tufta dominate the remainder of the year. Majruh had had fever, and it seems that on his recovery he had written about himself in what Ghalib felt to be quite unnecessary detail. Ghalib replies on September 16, 1862:

'Bravo, your lordship! What a letter! What's the point of writing all that nonsense? All it amounts to is that you're back in your own bed, back in your own bedclothes, and again have your own barber and your own lavatory, that

---

[1] 'Old Faithful'—nickname of an old maidservant.
[2] In the original, these words are quoted in the old woman's own peculiar speech.
[3] The equivalent of 'Man proposes, God disposes.'

you no longer disturb the night with, "Come quickly! Come quickly!" That
your life is saved and your servants too no longer plagued to death.

And now my nights are nights and days are days.

But you haven't said whether Miran Sahib got my letter or not. I suspect that
he didn't. Because if he had, you would certainly have seen it too, and he
would have asked you for the facts of the matter, and in that case you would
surely not have filled your letter with all that trash but would have told me
instead what passed between you. So if, as I suspect, the letter never reached
him, never mind. But if it did—well, you kept pestering me to answer Miran
Sahib's letter: why don't you keep on at him to answer mine? . . .

'You have seen for yourself what things are like here. The water is warm;
the breeze is warm; there is fever everywhere; and grain is dear. . . . Don't
ask me to describe the rains. God's wrath has descended on us. Qasim Jan's
Lane is like Saadat Khan's Canal. The gate of the house I'm living in which
opens on to Alam Beg Khan's Katra has collapsed. The stairs are on the point
of collapse. The walls of the small room where I sit in the morning are leaning.
The roofs are like sieves. If it rains for half an hour, they rain for an hour. My
books and writing materials have all been stored in the store-room. Here and
there on the floor are bowls and basins [to catch the water that leaks from the
roof]. Where can I sit to write a letter? Still, for the last four or five days things
have been better. The landlord is seeing about getting repairs done. Today I
had the chance of a few minutes' peace and decided to answer your letter.

'Alwar's displeasure, the hardships of your journey, the burning of the fever,
the ill effects of the heat, your dejected mood, your overwhelming troubles,
your present worries, your concern for the future, your grief at your fallen
fortunes . . . nothing you can say exaggerates them. These days everyone is in
the same boat. I hear that in November the Maharaja of Alwar's powers are to
be restored, but it will be the same sort of power as God has given to His
creatures—all power is in His mighty hand, and we mortals are disgraced.

'Tell me more of how you have got over your illness. God grant that your
fever has gone for good and that you are quite well again. Mir[1] says:

It is a thousand blessings to be well.

Mirza Qurban Ali Beg Salik has supplied another line to precede it. It's a good
one, and I like it very much:

Salik, if you are free from poverty
It is a thousand blessings to be well.'

On November 20, 1862, he writes again:

[1] The great eighteenth-century Urdu poet.

'Where would *I* have a copy of it . . . [the Nawwab of Rampur's] diwan? The Nawwab Sahib didn't present me with a single page of it. There are some copies that were sent here for sale. I bought one to send to Mustafa Khan [Shefta] at Jahangirabad. Now I'll speak to Muhammad Bakhsh and Pirji about it. If one of them can get me a copy I'll send it off . . . at once.

'I know very well exactly what your expectations of employment are. It's a case of "the King's salary". You buy a job—i.e. you present your offering of money [which convention demanded of a man presented at court] on the understanding that you will be given employment. Then you serve without pay for six months or a year until the pay due to you equals your offering.'

Mihr explains:

'In the last days of the Exalted Fort the court officials instituted a practice of taking sums of money by way of "offerings" and giving employment in return. The employee would have to serve without pay until his arrears equalled the sum of the offering. Moreover, men whose salary was several months in arrears would be given a part of the arrears in a lump sum on condition that they signed a receipt for the whole.'

Ghalib goes on to answer various questions on Urdu usage and then talks about various items of news.

'News of the King's death appeared in *Avadh Akhbar*, but I've not seen it confirmed anywhere. . . . They say that the Jama Masjid is to be given back. I shouldn't be surprised if it's true. It's also rumoured that the King of Oudh's property has been restored to him.

'Well, what more can I write? I'm writing this sitting in the sun by the parapet of the balcony overlooking the road . . .'

He writes again a month later, on December 16, 1862:

'You who seek news of Delhi and Alwar, accept my greetings. The Jama Masjid has been returned. On the steps on the Chitli Qabar side, the kabab-sellers have set up shop, and eggs and hens and pigeons are on sale. It has been put in charge of a committee of ten—Mirza Ilahi Bakhsh, Maulvi Sadr ud Din [Azurda] Tafazzul Husain Khan, and seven more.

'On Friday the 7th of November and the 14th of Jamadi ul Awwal of the present year (1279 AH and AD 1862) Abu Zafar Siraj ud Din Bahadur Shah was freed from the bonds of the foreigner and the bonds of the flesh. "Verily we are for God, and verily to Him we shall return."

'It's getting cold, and I have only enough wine left to last me for today: from tomorrow night only the brazier's heat will support me, and the glass and bottle will be put aside.

'The Raja of Patiala has died. His son retains the same title . . . and forms of address. At present Nihal Chand is Minister there. It seems that the future of the state will be made clear when the Governor-General comes. He will be coming here in February.

'Things are as usual in Alwar State. The Governor himself will confer powers—that is, things will be settled for Alwar and Patiala at the same time. . . .

'I'm sitting in the sun, and Yusuf Khan and Lala Hira Singh are with me. Food is ready, and when I've written this letter and sealed it I shall give it to my man to post and go to the house. There is a room there that gets the sun. I shall sit there. I shall wash my hands and face, soak a light chapati in the curry and eat it, wash my hands with gram-flour, and return here. After that God knows who will come to keep me company. . . .'

Letters to others are mainly on literary themes. On June 19, 1862 he writes to Shafaq:

'The target of the arrows of oppression, the old dotard—i.e. Ghalib—presents his respects. When I read your kind letter I realized that I had crossed out your line. . . . I had intended to write "*svad*" [the first letter of the word "sahih", meaning "correct"] against the verse. God knows how my pen came to cross it out. I am no longer in full possession of my senses. I have lost my memory. I often write words which I do not mean to write. I am in my seventieth year, and must expect such stupidities now. I have sinned against your verse and am put to shame before you. Please forgive me.'

In an undated letter of about the same time he writes to Tufta: 'Don't think that everything men wrote in former ages is correct. There were fools born in those days too. . . .' And on August 27, 1862 he writes at some length on his own qualifications as a Persian scholar and a poet:

'Persian as we know it is a compound of two languages—Persian and Arabic. In the colloquial, Turkish words are also used, but only to a small extent. I am no scholar of Arabic, but I am not completely ignorant of it either. All I mean is that I have not studied the language deeply. There are points on which I have to consult the scholars, and I have to ask them to quote authorities for various words. In Persian, from the Bounteous Source I received such proficiency that the laws and structure of the language are as deeply imbedded in me as the temper is in steel. Between me and the Persian masters there are two differences: first, that their birthplace was Iran and mine India; and second, that they were born a hundred, two, four, eight hundred, years before me. . . .

'It makes me laugh when I see how you think that I am like other poets, who set some master's ghazal or ode before them, or copy out its rhymes and then fit other words to them. God preserve me from such things! Even in my childhood when I began to write Urdu verse, may I be accursed if I ever set an Urdu poem or its rhyme-scheme before me. All I did was look at the metre, the rhyme and the end-rhyme, and then set to to write a ghazal or ode on the same pattern. You write that I must have had Naziri's diwan open before me when I wrote my ode . . . I swear to God that until I got your letter I never even knew that Naziri had written an ode in this scheme. . . . My friend, poetry is the creating of meaning, not the matching of rhymes. . . .

'Listen, my friend. My fellow-countrymen, Indians who claim to be masters of Persian, invent rules as they think fit. Thus that mongrel cock Abdul Wāse Hansoi says that "na-murad" is an incorrect form. And that son of an owl Qatīl declares . . . [other words] . . . to be incorrect. Do you think I am like them . . .? No, I hold the scales, the balance, of Persian in my hand. Praise be to God! Thanks be to God!'

On November 27, 1862, he writes:

'What you have written is unkind and suspicious! Could I be cross with you? May God forbid! I pride myself that I have one friend in India who truly loves me; his name is Hargopal, and his pen-name Tufta. What could you write which would upset me? And as for what someone else may whisper, let me tell you how matters stand there. I had but one brother, who died after thirty years of madness. Suppose he had lived and had been sane and had said anything against you: I would have rebuked him and been angry with him.

'My friend, there is no strength left in me now. The hardships of the rains are past, but I feel increasingly the full effects of old age. I lie about all day. I can't sit up, and generally write lying down. Besides, I feel now that you're a mature and practised poet, and I feel confident that I shall find nothing in your verse that calls for corrections. More important than that, all your odes are on themes of love, not written to serve any material purpose.[1] Anyway, I'll look at them some time. There's no hurry. There are three things involved: my sloth-fulness, the fact that your verse stands in no need of correction, and the fact that no particular gain is to be expected from any of your odes. And in view of these things I have left them on one side. A parcel from Lala Bal Mukand Besabr came ages ago, and I have not even opened it. And ten to fifteen of the Nawwab Sahib's [of Rampur] ghazals are also laid aside.

> Ghalib, old age has left you fit for nothing,
> Else you were once man to reckon with.

This ode of yours came yesterday. Today I've already gone through it, before the sun is really up, corrected it, and given it to my man to take to the post.'

---

[1] e.g. not to a patron, in expectation of reward.

❀ Chapter 12 ❀

1863

The physical weakness of which he complained to Tufta was to grow worse in 1863, so that in August he had to write to Sayyah: 'For the last year I have been a prey to ailments caused by disorders of the blood. . . .' But it is not until the end of March that he begins to show acute distress. Meanwhile his troubles are lighter ones, and there is even one great piece of good news.

On January 11, 1863 he writes to Ghulam Najaf Khan:

'. . . And now tell me, when are you coming? How many more years or months or days will you keep me waiting? Things here are the same as ever—you saw how it was when you were here:

> The earth is hard, the sky is far above.

It's really cold now; the mighty are stiff with pride, and the poor are stiff with cold. The new excise regulations have struck me a heavy blow, and so has the restriction on distilling. On the one hand the prohibitions of the excise authorities, and on the other the high price of foreign wine. "Verily we are for God, and verily to Him we shall return."

'. . . Well, Zahir ud Din [Ghulam Najaf Khan's son], don't you think I deserve a separate letter from you, or a separate note on your father's letter sending me your respects in your own hand? Hakim Ghulam Najaf Khan sat down to write to me, and while he was about it sent your respects to me too. And even your guardian angels knew nothing of it! What pleasure can such "respects" bring me?'

About the same time, in a letter to Majruh he writes:

'We've had several showers of winter rain. There'll be a good crop of wheat and gram, and the spring harvest looks hopeful.

> The clouds of spring are spread across
> the sky,
> But in my cup of clay there is no wine.

I have a wound on my right hand, a sore on my left arm, and a boil on my right thigh. That's how it is with me. Otherwise everything's all right.'

In March 1863 he received a quite unexpected piece of good news. The fullest account is in a letter to Bekhabar dated only 'March, 1863':

'In hopelessness hope still sends forth a ray—
The black night's end brings in the white
of day.

Reverend sir, today for your pleasure and happiness I write you the record of what has befallen me. Preamble: In 1860 the Lord Sahib [Governor-General] came . . . to Delhi. I went . . . and sent in my name to his Secretary. . . . The reply came, "During the Mutiny you spent your time flattering the rebel king; now the Government cannot agree to receive you". I am a persistent beggar, and was not to be put off by this prohibition. When the [Governor-General] returned to Calcutta I sent him an ode, in accordance with my old custom. It was returned to me with instructions that in future I was not to send these things. I gave up hope and stopped calling upon the Delhi authorities.

'Event: At the end of last month, February 1863, the Lieutenant-Governor of the Panjab [Sir Robert Montgomery] came to Delhi. People here ran to the Deputy Commissioner and the Commissioner to get their names on the list. I was outside all this, a man under a cloud in the eyes of the authorities. I stayed in my corner and called upon no one. The durbar was held, and all attained their wishes. On Saturday 8th February I went on my own account to visit Munshi Man Phul Singh in his tent. I sent in my card to the Secretary and was called in. Finding him well disposed towards me, I asked if I might meet the Lieutenant-Governor. This request too was granted, and these two distinguished officials showed me more kindness than I could ever have contemplated.

'Digression: I had had no previous dealings with the Lieutenant-Governor's chief clerk, on the strength of which I could hope to meet him. But he indicated, without saying it in so many words, that he would like to see me; so I went. When the two high officials had immediately acceded to my requests to see them, I can well imagine that it was on their prompting that he indicated his wish to see me. "God sends his blessings by stealth."

'Conclusion of the record: On Monday 2nd March the Governor encamped on the outskirts of the city. Towards evening I went to see my old friend Maulvi Izhar Husain Khan Bahadur. In the course of conversation he said, "Your attendance at durbars and robe of honour have been restored." I was astonished, and asked him, "How can that be, my good sir?" He replied, "The present Governor-General [Lord Elgin] on his arrival from England examined all the papers in your case, both in English and Persian, and gave orders in council that Asadullah Khan's [Ghalib's] attendance at durbars, and order of precedence, and robe of honour was to be restored in accordance with previous practice". I asked him, "Sir, what gave rise to this decision?" He said, "I do not know. All I know is that fourteen to fifteen days after the order was minuted, it was sent on here." I replied, "Glory to God".

> He who achieves our ends devises means to
> them
> While *our* devisings for our ends increase
> our pains.

'On Tuesday 3rd March at twelve o'clock the . . . Lieutenant-Governor sent
for me, presented me with a robe of honour and told me that my place and my
robe of honour at the Governor-General's court too had been restored, and
that if I went to Ambala I should be called to the durbar and receive the robe.
I replied: "I have looked upon your honour's feet and received my robe at
your hands. I have heard the Lord Sahib's [Governor-General's] order and
rejoice. What need to go to Ambala now? If I live, I will attend his durbar
another time and receive honour at his hands:

> No man has yet completed all life's tasks:
> Let all you undertake be of small compass." '

A letter to Tufta written earlier, on March 4, 1863, a day after his meeting with
the Lieutenant-Governor, shows that he had not in fact at once excused himself from attending the Governor-General's durbar at Ambala. After telling
him the good news he goes on: 'I was delighted, but at the same time at my
wit's end. Where am I to get the things I need to travel to Ambala? And the
enormous sum it will cost me? And on top of all this, my accustomed offering
at the durbar is an ode. So on the one hand I have to compose the ode, and on
the other think of some way to raise the money. I don't know where to turn.
I need all my wits and all my concentration to write the ode; and both are
exercised with the money problem. The Lord my God will solve this problem
for me too, but these days I can neither rest by day nor sleep at night. I'm
sending off these few lines to you and a few more to the same effect to the
Nawwab Sahib. If I live I will write to you after I get back from Ambala.'

The 'Nawwab Sahib' [of Rampur] responded by sending him on March 11th
the sum of Rs. 200, which Ghalib gratefully acknowledged in a letter of
March 16, 1863. But now some uncertainty arose. In the same letter he tells the
Nawwab:

'After the [Lieutenant-Governor's] departure the rumour went round the city
that Delhi people were prohibited from going to Ambala. I felt concerned at
this and went to the Commissioner, and personally delivered a letter to him.
Verbal enquiry brought a verbal reply, and then, in reply to my letter, came a
letter from him dated 7th March. So as not to make extra weight, I am not
sending the envelope, but I forward the letter to your honour just as it is.
'Since yesterday another rumour is abroad that . . . the Lord Sahib [i.e. the
Governor-General] is indisposed, and will not be holding a durbar at Ambala

but going off to Simla instead. Now . . . I am uncertain whether I should make
the journey or stay where I am. . . .'

The Nawwab replied on March 19th saying that in his view it would not be
advisable to go.

On March 27, 1863, he writes to Mir Sarfaraz Husain: 'I shall probably not
be able to write again for some days. . . . During the month of Rajab I got a
spot on my right hand, which developed into a boil, which burst and formed a
wound, which got worse and became a great cavity. Now the flesh has putrefied
over an area as big as the palm of my hand. That is why I couldn't go to Ambala.
For the last two weeks I've been under English treatment. A black[1] doctor
comes every day, and he's decided that today he'll cut away all the putrified
flesh. He'll be here any time now. So I've written this in a hurry and sent it off
before I get to work on my hand and send the pieces flying.'

A letter to Aram—the last to him which we possess—dated May 3, 1863,
shows how long his hand continued to trouble him:

'It is six months now since a spot on my right hand turned into a boil . . . Indian
surgeons treated me, but things got worse and worse. A black doctor has been
treating me for the last two months. He has been cauterizing the wound and
cutting the flesh away with a razor; and for the last twenty days it looks as
though it has begun to mend. . . .'

In this year we find for the first time evidence that Ghalib had now revised his
earlier opinion about his Urdu letters. In 1858 he had strongly opposed sug-
gestions from Tufta and Aram that they should be collected and published.
But now he writes to Alai in a letter dated only '1863' but placed by Mihr
between March and May:

'I write to tell you that some of my friends want to get together my Urdu
letters and publish them. They have asked me to send such letters to them, and
have collected others from various quarters. I don't keep copies of what I
write. I just write the letter and send it off to its destination. I am sure you must
have a lot of my letters. If you will parcel them up and send them by post or
by anyone who may be coming here during the next few days I shall be grateful
to you. And I think you too will be pleased to have them printed. . . .'

Alai, however, raised objections, and Ghalib's next letter reproaches him very
bluntly:

'What you wrote about sending my Urdu letters was something I could not
have expected from a man of your good nature. I am very upset about it, and

[1] I.e. an Indian practitioner of modern medicine.

if I were to write and tell you all the reasons why, it would probably cover a whole sheet of paper. So let me say just this, in the fewest possible words: Listen, my friend. If you want to keep the letters to yourself and the idea of their becoming generally known goes against the grain, then don't send them— not on any account. That will be an end of the matter. And if you are afraid they may be lost, then keep the originals by you, get some clerk to copy them, and either send the copies off by post or give them to someone to bring by hand. But for God's sake don't get angry and send the originals in the spirit of "I throw your gift back in your face". That's not at all what I want. I tell you, my friend, I'm afraid of what you might do.'

It seems that Alai did not respond immediately, but that in spite of this Ghalib did not raise the matter again. At this Alai seems to have felt concerned, thinking that Ghalib might be cross with him. Ghalib's next letter, of May 30, 1863, reassures him:

'Nothing exists but God, and in the name of that God Whom I think of in these terms and in Whom I believe, and besides Whom I hold all else to be non-existent, I swear that it was not because I was cross with you that I didn't press you again to send me the letters. I dropped the matter for the time being because I found that the man who wanted them had cooled off somewhat. His intermediary was a man of high rank, while he himself is only a dealer in books, concerned with estimating what he'll gain or lose, what he'll have to pay out and what he can save. I'd been under the impression that his intermediary was the man who was going to manage the whole affair, and thought it was he who was going to have them printed. I collected thirty letters from one source and sent them off to him. When he wrote to acknowledge them he as good as said that he had asked for them at the instance of a bookseller, and that the book-seller had now disappeared. Presumably he's gone off somewhere to sell his books or to get fresh supplies. The twenty-three envelopes and the thirty-four letters you sent me are still safe in my box. If the intermediary starts pressing me for them, I'll send copies of them to him and the originals back to you. And if not, then all the papers will go back to you.

'My friend, when you sent the letters you did the same to me as I did to you in Dujana. Well, I'm a doddering old man, and at my age absent-mindedness is to be expected. But what were you thinking of when you wrapped the letters in cloth and sealed the parcel with your seal? You could have wrapped them in a piece of paper and sent them off. If Munshi Bihari Lal had not been a friend of mine and Shihab ud Din's, you'd have set me back fifty rupees.

Calamity befell me, but all ended well.'

On June 11, 1863 he writes to Alai again:

> 'To lose one's life is bad, but just as bad
> Is to fall prey to your suspicious mind.

I have twice written to you that I never kept a copy of the ode. I have twice written that I can't remember which quatrains you want. And again you write, "Send the quatrains; send the ode". My friend, I swear by the Quran and by the Gospel and by the Pentateuch and by the Psalms and by the Hindus' Four Vedas and by the [holy books of the Zoroastrians], and by the Guru Granth [of the Sikhs] I haven't got the ode, and I can't remember the quatrains. As for my [Persian] collected verse, I have already told you

> So this is our position; here we stand,
> And here we shall continue in our stand.

'When I order fifteen to twenty copies I'll present one to your father and one to you. And if your father is in a hurry, he can order as many copies as he likes from Lucknow, from the *Avadh Akhbar* Press, proprietor, the famous Munshi Newal Kishor. Anyway, I will send two copies as soon as I get the opportunity.'

On June 19, 1863 he writes to Junun:

'Both your letters reached me. I am alive, but half dead. I lie here for twenty-four hours of the day, confined to my bed in the full sense of the words. For the last twenty days my foot has been swollen. It began with the sole and the instep, but the swelling has gone beyond that now and reached the calf. I can't get my foot into my shoe, and it's difficult for me to get up and go to the lavatory. But leave all that aside: the pain is torture to me. I was not allowed to die in 1277 [the year in which he had foretold he would die] so that I should be proved a liar; but for these last three years I have tasted death anew every day, and I am at a loss to know why I live on when I lack all the requisites of life.

'My soul dwells in my body these days as restless as a bird in a cage. I find no joy in any pursuit, nor in any man's company, nor in any gathering or assembly. Books I hate, poetry I hate, my body I hate, my soul I hate. There is no exaggeration in these words: I state a fact:

> Happy that day when I set out
> to leave this barren wilderness.

If in this distracted state I fail to answer your letters I must be forgiven.'

On June 21, 1863, he writes to Alai:

'My dear boy, Mirza Ali Husain Khan has been here, and came to see me. I gave him all the letters that you had sent me; now it's up to him whether he sends them to you or not. Of course I shall be waiting to hear that you've received them. I asked him what had brought him here and how long he would be staying. He said he'd taken forty days' leave; his wife was ill and he wanted to arrange treatment for her. If it were any good to him I'd give my life for Ali Husain Khan. Well, that's an exaggeration—hyperbole, in fact; no doubt about it. But I would not stop far short of that; anything within the bounds of possibility I would do. But what does sympathy and fellow-feeling demand of me? He doesn't go astray, that he should need my preaching. He has no case pending in any department, that he should require my counsel and advice. And as for his family affairs—his dealings with his wife and her elders and her brothers— that is a field where neither you nor I can intervene. . . .'

About the same time he writes to Tufta: 'Two days ago, in the morning, I put all your papers [presumably, corrected verses] in an envelope and sent them off to the post office. "Now I shall have some peace for a day or two", I thought; but the same evening I got another letter from you. Well, I'm sending that off too. I told you all about myself in my letter of two days ago. It's enough to say that now I do all my writing lying down. And it's diverting to see that you don't believe my own account of myself and *do* believe what somebody else tells you about me: "The swelling on Ghalib's leg has gone now; and he drinks wine in the day time too". And your lordship believes it! Twenty years ago the position was that during the rains I used to drink three glasses either before lunch or towards evening, and that without making any reduction in the amount I drank every night. In these last twenty years twenty rainy seasons have passed by, and torrents of rain have fallen; but let alone drinking [during the day], the very thought of it has never crossed my mind; and in fact I've reduced the quantity I drink at night. The swelling on my leg has increased beyond all measure. It turned out that it had not reached the stage where the matter can be drawn off, and inflammation set in. Two or three hakims are attending me, and on their advice a poultice of neem leaves will be applied from tomorrow. When that brings things to a head they will think about lancing it. So I have open wounds in the sole of my foot and in my calf too. If the hard-hearted eunuch who gave you that news [that I was better] is a liar, then curses upon him; and if *I* am lying then a hundred thousand curses upon me.'

On July 3, 1863 he tells Alai the history of the trouble:

'More than a month ago my left foot began to swell, and the swelling spread from the sole to the instep and from there to the calf. If I stand up it feels as though the veins in the calf are going to burst. Anyway I would get up; but instead of going to the zenana for my food I had it sent here. I *had* to get up to make water, but I had a chamber-pot kept here. I can't manage without squatting down. I pass a motion only every second or third day, but, anyway, the time comes when I do have to go. Imagine all these different occasions and think for yourself what I must be going through. And over and above all this it looks as though a hernia is developing:

> Old age, a hundred ailments, as they say.

I repeat my own line to myself again and again:

> O sudden death, why do you still delay?

And it's not "sudden death" any more. For all the signs and accompaniments of death are there. Ah, what a wonderful line the late Ilahi Bakhsh Khan wrote:

> Let me once die, and I can breathe again!

No point in writing any more.'

A number of undated letters to Sarur—the last to him which we possess—clearly belong to this time, for there are references to his illness in words almost identical to those of dated letters to other correspondents. These need not be repeated here. Their main subject-matter, as usual in his letters to Sarur, is Persian, and poetry, and other literary themes. In one of them he responds to praise of his poetry with the remark that he must regard it as appreciation higher than it deserves.

'There is a verse of Naziri (God's mercy be upon him) which you may write on a piece of paper, and tie round my neck, and then expel me from the company of poets. This is the verse:

> The brightness of my vision is all rusted
> over now.
> Alas! that He who made my mirror did not
> cherish it!'

In former times, mirrors were made of polished steel. The metaphor recalls the passage which Ghalib wrote about himself and which was quoted in chapter one: 'The love of poetry which I had brought with me from eternity assailed me and won my soul, saying, "To polish the mirror and show in it the face of meaning—this too is a mighty work."'

And the complaint is the familiar, deeply felt one that God, who granted him his poetic powers, did not also grant him to live in an age where true appreciation of his verse would have acted as a constant stimulus to them, so that they would not fail. The letter continues:

'Pretension is one thing, and accomplishment is another. . . . Jalalae Tabatabai (God's mercy be upon him) wrote a letter to Sedaya Hindi. I forget his exact words, but the gist is that one day Maulana Urfi (God's mercy be upon him) and Abul Fazl[1] were disputing together. The Shaikh [Abul Fazl] said to Urfi,

---

[1] The great minister of the Emperor Akbar, 1556-1605.

"I have prosecuted my studies to the furthest limit and brought my knowledge of Persian to perfection". Urfi replied, "How can you match my experience? Ever since I was old enough to understand, every word that I have heard from the old men and old women of my house was spoken in Persian." The Shaikh replied, "I acquired my Persian from Anwari and Khaqani;[2] and you learnt it from old women." Urfi replied, "And Anwari and Khaqani too learnt it from old women".'

Another letter discusses the wording of a sentence in a preface written for a collection of Ghalib's letters to him which Sarur proposed to publish. It ends on a despondent note:

'Today I got another letter from my lord and master. I have not read it yet, but Shah Alam Sahib has written on the back of it, "You have not replied to my letter"—although . . . I have already written to say that I no longer have the strength to write or the quickness of mind to correct verses. Why should I repeat the same thing a dozen times? I conceive two possible ends to my present state: recovery, or death. In the first case I will inform you myself; in the second, all my friends will know of it from others. I write these lines as I lie in bed.'

In the same despondent, even bitter mood, he writes to Tufta on July 23, 1863:

'I wrote to you that I was well, and you believe it and offer thanks to God. I wrote what I had said about the severity of my illness was poetic exaggeration, and I expect you believe that too, although both these things were said ironically. I am sick of lies, and heartily curse all liars. I never tell a lie. But when all my attempts to persuade you I was telling the truth had no effect, then I wrote and told you I was well. And I did so after I had sworn to myself that so long as there was breath in my body, so long as my hand could hold a pen, and so long as I could contemplate correcting your verse, I would send back the very next day every sheaf of papers you sent to me. Briefly, I am near to death. I have boils on both my hands and my leg is swollen. The boils don't heal and the swelling doesn't subside. I can't sit up. I write lying down. Your double page arrived yesterday and today I have corrected it lying here and sent it back. Take care that you go on thinking of me as in good health, and send sheet upon sheet to me. I shall never keep it more than a day. If I am near to death, well, what of that?'

Ghalib's despondency is perhaps due in part to a sense that the quality of Tufta's output did not match its quantity. Two undated letters of about this time indicate a general impatience. In the first he writes: 'It was I who told you to write in the qasida form. Now I forbid you to use it for love poems. Use it for panegyric as need arises, but compose with due thought and care.' Tufta

---

[2] Two celebrated classical Persian poets.

K

apparently asked in whose praise he should write, for Ghalib rejoins: 'That's a good one! "Before I decide on a theme I must look for someone to address it to." If I could have told you in whose praise to write I'd have got a pane-gyric to him out of you long ago and seen that it was presented to him.'

It is significant how even in such distress Ghalib usually felt that he owed it to his friends to go on correcting their verses. Sometimes indeed he tells them that he has had to give up verse-correcting, and perhaps he did indeed resolve to do so. But again and again we find him in fact performing this service for them. Thus, in this period he actually offers his services to his young friend Zaka, a poet of whom he seems to have been very fond. Zaka belonged to Nellore, in South India, where he was born in 1828-29. In his youth he devel-oped such an admiration for Ghalib that it became one of the main objects of his life to meet him. Knowing that there were men in Hyderabad who knew Ghalib, and hoping that they might be able to help him in his quest, he left home without so much as taking leave of his relatives and journeyed to Hydera-bad on foot, reaching there in 1855 or 6. He found employment there and spent the rest of his short life there, for he died in his early forties, only five years after Ghalib's death. Mihr says that he was an excellent humorous and satirical poet. His correspondence with Ghalib, says Mihr, began after he reached Hyderabad. The first letter we possess is dated July 30, 1863. When we consider that it was written only a week after the bitter letter to Tufta quoted above, it is evident how deep was Ghalib's feeling for him: 'I number you as one of my true spiritual brethren,' he writes. 'You are the light of my eyes, and a part of my living heart.' In what follows, the references are not quite clear, but the tone is the same:

'See the trust I have in you: I cannot keep the secret myself, and yet I expect you not to waver in keeping my secret and my confidence.

'The reward of a lyric or an ode is what fate and fortune prescribe, not what the worth of the poetry deserves. Had he in whose praise it was written been a judge of poetry, then one might have suspected one's intermediary of failing to exert himself. But what have the great and rich to do with the taste for poetry, and where do they find the leisure to study poems? . . .

'I do not think myself worthy to correct your verse. . . . It is as a friend, not as an ustad, that I shall write such things as occur to me. But if your mind is made up and you insist that I correct your verses, do not pass on to others what I have written about them until you get the verses back from me [with my written corrections]. If you like to send me the verse you have written hitherto, I will go over that too and return it to you. It will be a pleasure; there was no need to ask my permission.'

A fortnight later, on August 16, 1863, he writes to Sayyah:

'I humbly acknowledge the justice of your complaint, but none of your letters called for a reply, and I have given up correcting verses. For the last year I have been a prey to ailments due to disorders of the blood. There are boils all over my body, and I feel as though I have no strength left. . . . In a year's time I shall be seventy, and I pray for my release. . . .'

In the same letter he encloses a chronogram which he has composed for the birth of a son to Sayyah's patron, Mir Ghulam Baba Khan.

He writes again to Zaka on August 26, 1863. After telling him of his illness he goes on:

'I sent an ode to Nawwab Mukhtar ul Mulk, but he has shown no appreciation. . . . I sent one of my early masnavis in refutation of the Wahhabi sect to Muhi ud Daula. He has not even acknowledged it. Now I am told that Maulvi Ghulam Imam Shahīd, pupil of Qatīl, is beating the drum of "I and no other" and showing off his prowess to men who do not know literary worth when they see it. In a year's time I shall be seventy years old. Apart from a dry fame my art has brought me nothing. Cries of "Well done!" and "Bravo!" have assailed my ears. Well, praise is recompensed with praise; but Mukhtar ul Mulk has not even done that. My eulogy has brought me neither gratitude nor reward. Heaven knows what the Nawwab Sahib thinks I am. As for Muhi ud Daula, all I can say is may God give him his deserts. . . .

'Write and tell me all about Ghulam Imam Shahīd and what his position is there. Someone here tells me that he got no encouragement from Mukhtar ul Mulk, but that Muhi ud Daula had secured him a Court appointment at four hundred rupees a month.'

On September 1, 1863 he writes to Maududi:

'Bountiful master, do you think that Delhi still prospers, and that the Fort thrives and that the Empire continues, that you ask about the writings of Hazrat Shaikh [Kalimullah Jahanabadi] and for news of Sahibzada Shah Qutub ud Din, son of Maulana Fakhr ud Din (God's mercy be upon him)? "The cow ate all this up, and the butcher killed the cow, and the butcher died on the road." [i.e. all this is gone beyond recall.] All these things lasted only so long as the King reigned. Even the house of Kale Sahib (whom God has pardoned) has been razed as though a great broom had swept it away; not a scrap of paper, not a thread of gold, not a wisp of wool remains. The tomb of Shaikh Kalimullah Jahanabadi (God's mercy be upon him) stands desolate. The area once held the population of a good-sized village, for all his descendants lived there. Now it is barren waste; a tomb standing in open ground, with nothing else there. If the people who lived there survived the bullets, God alone knows where they are now. It was they who preserved the Shaikh's writings and some of his relics; when they have gone, of whom am I to ask? What can I do? Your wish is one that cannot be realised.

'Why does my revered Sayyid Sahib put himself to such trouble? If he really wants to send me something, let him not think in formal terms of gifts and presents. I am a beggar who does not beg: if he sends me something I shall not reject it. Let him not bother about how little or how much, but enclose whatever note he pleases and send it in his letter.'

On September 2, 1863, he writes to Alai: 'I have no sense of shame. Instead of dying, I began to get better. My ailments are on the wane and I feel my strength returning.' But it seems that the improvement was not maintained, for in the first of two undated letters to Tufta belonging to about this time he writes again of his illness:

'The swelling in my leg and the boil on my hand are killing me. I tell you— and my servants and the friends who visit me daily can testify to it—that I lie here from morning to night and from night to morning. My letters are written lying down. Many people used to send in their verses for correction, but I have told them all not to. The only verse I correct is the Nawwab of Rampur's and yours.'

The next letter bluntly corrects one of Tufta's recurring misapprehensions:

'God save us! what cursed fool agreed to correct your verses "out of love for poetry"? I tell you I am sick of poetry—or may my God be sick of me! . . . But a good wife determines to stand by her worthless husband through thick and thin; and that is how things are between me and you.'

On November 24, 1863 he writes again. It seems that he had suggested to Tufta a promising patron to eulogise, but that his efforts had brought him nothing. Ghalib writes:

'Light of Ghalib's eyes, . . . Mirza Tufta, God keep you well and happy! My friend is no miser and I am no liar. But in the words of Mir:

> These are the chances of the age we live in.

Anyway, we will devise something, and God willing, something will come of it very soon. I am surprised that your journey brought you no gain.

> Kindness has vanished from the world—
> or else
> In this age there is none to practise it.

Cease singing the praises of the great ones of the world. Compose your verses of love in lyric form, and be happy.'

On the same day he wrote to Qadr Bilgami. He seems once again to be in better health; he writes about the wedding of his nephew's daughter:

'He [my nephew] is the pride of his parents' family, and since his mother and I are of one flesh and blood and bone and community and tribe, I too may feel that pride. He must be saying to himself, "My uncle didn't come to my daughter's wedding; he couldn't bring himself to spend the money." I hold money of less worth than dust and straw, but what could I do? I hadn't the strength to go. If only I'd been as well then as I am now! I'd have been the first to arrive. I would very much like to see him. Let me see when I shall get the chance. I'm well again now after a whole year confined to my bed. [He then describes his illness.] Traces of my illness are still visible. Two toes on each foot are crooked, and swollen on top of that. I cannot wear shoes. And my weakness defies description, except by my verse:

> My soul strives feebly on to break the
> body's bonds.
> I live: it lacks the strength to struggle
> free.

On the 8th of this Rajab—that is, next month, I shall enter my seventieth year:

> Seventy years have passed and strength has
> left my limbs.

So it's stupid to complain of the weakness I feel. May God preserve my faith unwavering.'

On December 3, 1863 he writes to Alai: 'Why have you decided to exemplify the saying, "Like father, like son"? It's true that hypochondria and melancholia are the born slaves of your family, but they haven't been in attendance on you to this day. Why should they come to you now? If they have, you're on no account to let them stay. Drive them on, and see to it that you don't let them stay near you.

'My kind and considerate benefactor, that man of kindness incarnate Munshi Newal Kishor came by the mail. He met me, and your uncle, and your cousin Shihab ud Din Khan. The Creator bestowed upon him the beauty of Venus and the qualities of Jupiter. He is himself the conjunction of two auspicious stars. I hadn't said anything to you, and accepted that ten copies of [my Persian] collected verse cost fifty rupees. But now when I mentioned it to him he agreed to accept the price that had originally been advertised in the newspaper—three rupees, four annas per copy. At this rate ten copies come to thirty-two rupees, eight annas, and thirty-two rupees, eight annas is what you are to pay. In all, sixty-five rupees will have to be sent to the *Avadh Akhbar* Press. I shall be ordering on the 10th or 11th of December—this month. I'll give the thirty-two rupees eight annas to Ali Husain Khan, or I'll send it to Lucknow—whichever you say. Let me have an answer to this letter quickly. . . .'

He then dates the letter and goes on 'Kya ghazab hai hai!' ['Alas, alas! what a calamity!'] and remarks that this gives the date of 1863, and is a chronogram for the death of the Viceroy, Lord Elgin.

On December 8, 1863 he writes to Majruh, apparently for the first time in some months:

'Ah! His Honour Mir Mahdi Majruh of Delhi! Come in, sir! It's many a long day since you last came to see me. Where have you been? And how are you after all this time? And is Mir Sarfaraz Husain well? And Miran Sahib too?' He goes on to comment on verses which Majruh had sent him. Of one Persian verse he says, 'It's of such a verse that they say "The meaning is in the poet's mind!" This line is not from any of the acknowledged masters. Some gentleman who wanted to astound people wrote it and then quoted some master's name and said it was his.'

He goes on to discuss gender. 'There's no regular rule can be applied to determine whether a word is masculine or feminine. A man says what sounds right to him, what his mind accepts.' He admits that he uses *rath* [a kind of carriage] as masculine in the singular but feminine in the plural![1] After giving a number of other examples he concludes, 'My friend, I can't set myself up to issue edicts and decrees in this matter. I write what I think, and people must accept it or not as they please.'

On December 13, 1863 he writes to Shah Karamat Husain explaining some of the conceptions of the mystic love of God:

'Read my verse:

> Till a man bears a wound whose mouth can
> speak for him
> Difficult is the path to hold converse with
> Thee.

The meaning is that you cannot speak to the Divine Beloved with these ordinary lips and mouth. For this you must provide yourself with the mouth of a wound; that is, until your heart is wounded by the sword of love, you cannot attain to this rank.

'The dealings of the Divine Beloved with those who do not truly love Him are called "indifference" and His dealings with His lovers are symbolized by the "glance" [which slays them].' He quotes a Persian quatrain in illustration and continues,

[1] Cf. p. 41-2.

'And now read my verse:

> We went to make complaint of His indifference:
> A single glance has laid us in the dust.

The meaning is that, wearied of His "indifference" we went to complain to Him and to crave His attention; and when He turned His attention to us a single glance annihilated us.'

On the same day, December 13, 1863, he wrote again to Alai:

'I don't remember the day or date, but today is the fourth, or may be, if my memory's failed me, the fifth day since Munshi Newal Kishor left by the mail for Lucknow. He must have reached there yesterday, or else he will today. Today's Sunday, 13th December. One day he was sitting with me, and my young friend Shihab ud Din was there too. I turned to Saqib[1] and said, "If I were a wordly man I would say that I am in service; but since I am a darwesh who keeps to his own humble abode I will say just that I have three sources of sustenance. Sixty-two and a half rupees a month I get from the British government—i.e. seven hundred and fifty rupees a year. Twelve hundred a year come from Rampur, and twenty-four a year from our respected friend here. To elaborate the point, he has for the last two years been sending me his newspaper four times a month, and he doesn't charge me for it. True, I send forty-eight stamps every year to cover the postage. . . ."

'The day before yesterday Maulvi Sadr ud Din Khan Sahib [Azurda] had a stroke. His right hand is useless and his tongue has swollen, so that he finds it difficult to speak, and you can understand very little of what he says. I am crippled, and can't go to see him; I have to ask after him from people who have been to visit him. The day and date I have written above. The identity of the writer you will probably recognize from the handwriting.'

In the original, the word for 'probably' is 'ghalib'.

[1] Shihab ud Din—'Saqib' is his takhallus.

✿ Chapter 13 ✿

1864

Early letters of 1864 show that he felt that most of his sufferings were behind him, at any rate for the moment, though they had left him extremely weak. Thus he writes on January 7, 1864, to Junun:

'I am well, but I am old, and these troubles consumed all the strength that I had left. Now I am a body without soul to quicken it. This month of Rajab 1280 AH sees the beginning of my seventieth year and the onset of ailments and sorrows. "Nothing exists but God and God alone works manifest in all things." '

But only eleven days later, on January 18, 1864 he even feels able to undertake a journey. He writes to Alwar, to Mir Bande Ali Khan, recounting the whole history of his sources of income from the time of his father's death when he was only five years old. He stresses his family connection with Alwar—how his father 'was killed fighting along with Maharaja Bakhtawar Singh' and how the authorities had 'continued my father's stipend to me, granting me a village named Talra in perpetuity, so that you may say that the moment I was weaned of my mother's milk I began eating Alwar's bread.' He describes subsequent developments and concludes:

'I am sixty-nine years old. I have gone deaf. I cannot walk without a staff or sit up without a pillow or a wall to support my back. I am not a worldly man, but a darwesh. I seek ample honour, and a little wealth. God preserve His Highness! He will both give me honour and bestow wealth upon me. And leaving that aside, I long to look upon His Highness's splendour. I wrote a poem hailing his accession to the throne with a chronogram, and sent it along with a petition. Why has His Highness not replied to my petition, and why has he not sent for me? . . . I ask you as a particular favour that you will keep this my letter to you carefully and that when His Highness comes you will show it to him. The moment I hear of his arrival I shall set out for Alwar.'

However, it seems that nothing came of his efforts in this direction.
    On February 2, 1864 he writes to Jauhar:

'Congratulations on your appointment to the tahsildari[1] of Ballabgarh. You

---

[1] The chief revenue office in a tahsil. A tahsil is an area comprising usually a small town and a number of nearby villages.

have moved from Pipli to Nuh, and from Nuh to Ballabgarh; and now one day, God willing, you will come to Delhi.

'I have something to say to you. Hakim Mirza Jan, the worthy son of Hakim Agha Jan, is employed in the area of your tahsil in the medical services of the British authorities. His respected father is a friend of mine of fifty years' standing. He is like a brother to me—and that makes Hakim Mirza Jan my nephew and your cousin. It is incumbent upon you to be of one mind and one heart with him, and be his constant helper. His official appointment is a permanent one. You will not have to take any fresh step—only to try and see to it that things remain favourable to him, and that he continues in the authorities' regard; for Hakim Mirza Jan is an intelligent and conscientious man.'

On February 15, 1864 he writes to Shafaq:

'The past year has been a very trying one for me. I was confined to my bed for twelve to thirteen months. I found it difficult to get up, let alone to move about. There was no fever, no coughing, no diarrhoea, no seizure, no stroke, but something more unpleasant than all these things, namely, overheating of the blood. To put it briefly, between my head and my feet I had twelve boils— and every boil became a wound and every wound a cavity, so that without exaggeration I needed twelve to thirteen plasters and half a pound of ointment a day. For nine to ten months I could neither eat nor sleep, and was in pain both day and night. If I did fall asleep at night, before I had slept an hour the pain in some of my boils would wake me up. I would keep tossing and turning, fall asleep once more, and be awakened once more. Three quarters of the year passed in this way; then things began to improve, and over two to three months I made some sort of recovery. I felt as though my soul had entered my body anew and the angel of death had given up in disgust at my toughness. Now I am well, but weak and lethargic. I haven't got my wits about me, and my memory is gone. It takes me as long to stand up as it does to build a wall the height of a man. I'm filled with gratitude at your enquiry after me: only when you heard I was dead did you ask after me. The oral statement of the man who told you I was dead and my written statements (for example, this one) are half true and half false. If I'm dead, then I'm only half-dead; and if I'm alive, I am only half-alive.

> My soul strives feebly on to break the body's bonds.
> I live: it lacks the strength to struggle free.

If you will send a copy of these lines to my revered friend Maulvi Ghulam Ghaus [Bekhabar] . . ., Chief Clerk to the Lieutenant-Governor of the North-Western Provinces, you will be pleasing him and obliging me.'

On March 7, 1864 he writes to Bekhabar:
K*

'Let me tell you how things stand with me now. After the taking of Delhi Lord Canning sent back the ode I had sent him, with a message from his secretary to the effect that during the days of the Mutiny I had been a courtier of the rebel King, and now the government did not see fit to enter into any relationship with me. There was nothing for it but to keep silent. But I am a shameless man. In Lord Elgin's time, in accordance with my custom, I again sent an ode to him at Simla. Contrary to my expectation I received a reply from the Chief Secretary in accordance with all the old forms. The same paper, sprinkled with gold dust, the same titles of address, the same appreciation of my poem, and the same expression of pleasure. And now that this present great lord has become the Viceroy of the realm of India, I have performed my ancient service. On February 13, 1864 I sent off an ode and a petition. Up to today —March 7th—I have had no reply. . . . Naturally I am anxious. But

> I have not yet lost heart: I wait
> To see what may befall.'

On June 22, 1864 he writes to Amīn ud Din Ahmad Khan:

'Allow me to tell you that your being in Delhi was a source of moral strength to me. Even though we did not meet, at any rate we were in the same city.

'Brother, when I survey the scene I see a number of people, like birds who have lost their nests, flying about here and there. One or two of them occasionally come this way even. Now, sir, tell me· when are you going to keep your promise? When are you going to send Alai to see me? These days one can still travel by night and rest by day. [Mihr explains: "In those days there was no railway [from Delhi] to Loharu. In the hot season it was customary to travel by night and not by day."] Once the rains start, your permission will be of no avail. The traveller will think, "I'm a walker, not a swimmer. How can I get from Loharu to Delhi without a boat? Where will I get a steamship from?"

> O you who do not know what leisure is
> Do what you have to do without delay.'

On June 28, 1864, he writes to Junun:

'A hundred and twenty mangoes have reached me. May God preserve you! I have handed over ten pens and two ounces of ink to your servant. God grant they reach you safely. I am not ill, but I am old and weak and so to speak, only half alive. I have passed sixty-nine years in this world, and performed not one religious act. Alas! A thousand times alas!'

On July 2, 1864, he writes to Miran:

'My dear boy, I got your letter, but it doesn't explain why Mir Sarfaraz Husain was off to Jaipur. Anyway, give my blessings to Mir Mahdi [Majruh] and tell Mir Sarfaraz Husain from me: "You went to Jaipur, and I entrusted you to God's keeping: whose keeping did you entrust *me* to?" '

On July 10, 1864, he writes to Alai. It appears that Alai had contemplated writing an ode directed against someone whom he disliked and incorporating a chronogram of some incident in this connection. Ghalib tells him not to:

'Understand this, my friend: Granted that "to curse Yazid[1] is to worship God"; yet one *speaks* the words, "A curse on Yazid!" No true Muslim yet has written an ode to curse him. Among your natural talents is one for composing chronograms; you have earned merit in heaven by it, and, God willing, will get your reward. Don't now bring censure upon yourself and distress to others. Don't manifest your enmity, and if it is manifest already, don't add permanence to it.' He goes on:

'The late Ali Bakhsh [he had died six months earlier] was four years younger than me. I was born in 1212 AH, and in Rajab of this year shall be entering my sixty-ninth year. He lived to be sixty-six. He had a novel way of speaking and writing. Once he met Muir Sahib[2] in Agra. In the course of conversation he said, "I served with my uncle in Lord Lake's army [in 1803], and took part in the battles against Holkar [the commander of the Maratha forces]. I should be offending against propriety if I were to take off my clothes; otherwise I could show you that my body is a mass of scars from sword-and-lance-wounds." He [Muir] was an alert and intelligent man; he looked at him and said, "Nawwab Sahib, I should guess that in General Lake's time you would be about four or five years old." He replied, "Quite so, your honour."
'May God forgive him and not call him to account for his harmless lies.'

(Ghalib writes of Ali Bakhsh again a year later, in an undated letter to Shākir: 'His honour Mir Qasim Ali Khan Sahib is a truthful man, and I presume that he really did come to my house and found the gate shut. But I have an uneasy feeling, because he was very thick with my late friend Ali Bakhsh Khan, and the departed (God forgive him his sins) was proverbial for his lies and tall stories. So if with this in mind I feel some hesitation in accepting his statement, my hesitation is not entirely unwarranted. Anyway give him my regards.')
An undated letter to Salik belongs perhaps to this time:

'My dear friend, what foolish thoughts beset you? You have mourned a father: now lament an uncle too. God grant you long life, and bring to realization all your plans and fancies. For my part I no longer look even to God to help me, much less to His creation. Nothing goes right for me. I watch myself from the

---

[1] The man responsible for the martyrdom of Husain and his companions at Karbala.
[2] Sir William Muir, who later became Lieutenant-Governor of United Provinces.

sidelines and rejoice at my own distress and degradation. In other words I see myself through the eyes of my enemy. At every blow that falls I say, "Look! Ghalib's taken another beating! Such airs he used to give himself! 'I am a great poet, a great Persian scholar. Today for miles around there is none to match me!' Let us see *now* what he has to say to his creditors. Ghalib's finished; and call him Ghalib if you like; I call him atheist and infidel, and that's the truth! I have made up titles to confer upon him. When kings die they write after their names, 'Whose abode is in Heaven', or 'Who rests in Paradise.' Well, he thought himself King of the Realm of Poetry, and I've devised the forms 'Who dwells in Hell', and 'Whose Station is Damnation' to follow his name.

' "Come along, Star of the Realm!"—one creditor has him by the scruff while another reviles him. And I say to him, "Come, come, My Lord Nawwab Sahib! How is it that you—yes, you a Seljuk, and an Afrasiyabi—are put to such indignity? Well, where is your tongue? Say something! Wine from the shop, and rosewater from the druggist's, and cloth from the drapers', and mangoes from the fruiterer's, and loans from the banker's—and all on credit all the time. He might have stopped to ask himself where he'd get the money to pay it back".'

Another letter to Salik dated July 11, 1864 (and these are the only letters to Salik we possess) is in a similar tone:

"God sends His blessings by stealth." I hear that you are fit and well. We must be thankful that we are alive. "If you have your life, you have everything." They say that to despair of God's help is to be an infidel. Well, I have despaired of Him and am an infidel through and through. Muslims believe that when a man turns infidel, he cannot expect God's forgiveness. So there you are, my friend: I'm lost to this world and the next. But you must do your best to stay a Muslim and not to despair of God. Make the text [of the Quran] your watchword: "Where there is difficulty, there is ease also."

> All that befalls the traveller[1] in the path of God
> Befalls him for his good.

All's well at your home. . . . Yusuf Ali Khan Aziz sends his regards and Baqir and Husain Ali [Ghalib's adopted "grandchildren"] their respectful service. My steward Kallu presents his obeisance. The others lack the status even to do that. Keep on writing to me. Farewell, from him who longs for death, Ghalib.'

On August 24, 1864, he writes to Junun:

'Exalted sir, the ghazal your servant brought has gone where I am going—to

---

[1] In the original, 'salik', which, in a letter to Salik is particularly appropriate.

oblivion. That is, I have lost it. . . .' Most of the rest of the letter is taken up with detailed comments on couplets quoted from his own Urdu verse:

'I could, had I not given you my heart,
            have breathed in peace.
I would, had I not died, have wept and sighed
            a few days more.

'Here we have a very subtle ordering of words. "I could" connects with "have breathed". "I would" links with "have wept". In Arabic involved expression and involved meaning are both faults. In Persian involved meaning is a fault, but involved expression is permissible, and indeed, is considered a poetic merit. Urdu follows the Persian.'

He then shows how the rearrangement of the words in the normal order of prose makes the meaning perfectly clear. After which he takes another couplet, in which the lover tells his mistress:

'To meet you is not easy—all is easy, then.
The difficulty is, it is not difficult.'

'In other words, "If I cannot easily meet you, that makes things easy for me. If it is not easy to meet you, so be it. I cannot meet you, but neither can anyone else [i.e. my rivals]. The difficulty is that at the same time you are not difficult to meet, because you can meet anyone you feel like meeting. I have trained myself to bear separation easily, but I cannot make jealousy easy to bear."

Her fairness and her fair opinion of herself
Have worsted me and given my lustful rival best.

She had such utter confidence in her own powers
She could not see why she should put him to the test.

'Maulvi Sahib, what refinement of thought! It deserves your praise. Fairness of face, and a good opinion of herself—the beloved has both these qualities. . . . She thinks that she never makes a mistaken estimate. "The man struck down by love for me never escapes me," she thinks. "The arrow of my captivating glance never misses its mark." So when she has such confidence in herself, why should she put my rival to the test? Her good opinion of herself has preserved his good name. For the fact was that the beloved was mistaken, and if it had come to the test my rival would have stood revealed not as a true lover, but as a man impelled only by lust.

I do not breathe a word against you, friend,
            but if you meet

The man you gave my letter to, just give him
my regards.

'This theme calls for something by way of preamble. The poet [lover] needed
a messenger [to take a letter to his mistress]. But he was afraid that such a
messenger might himself fall in love with her. A friend of the lover brought a
man to him and said, "This man is a man of honour, a man whom you can trust.
I can guarantee that he won't do any such thing.' Well, he was given a letter
to take to her. As fate would have it, the lover's misgivings proved well-
founded. The messenger looked upon the beloved and at once fell madly in
love with her. The letter, the reply—all were forgotten, and in his frenzy he
rent his clothes and made off to the wilderness. And now the lover, after all
this has happened, says to his friend, "Only God has knowledge of the unseen.
Who knows what is in another's heart? So, my friend, I bear no grudge against
you. But if by any chance you meet my messenger, give him my respects and
say, "Well, sir, what now of your tall claims that you would not fall in love?"'

If it be granted me to live on for a few days more
I have made up my mind to show you what I have in store.

'There is no difficulty here. It means just what it says. Why should the poet
reveal what he intends to do? He hints obscurely that he will do something.
God knows whether he will become a faqir, and make his humble abode in the
city or on its outskirts, or whether he will leave his own country for other
lands.'

About the same time—the letter is dated only '1864'—he writes to Bekhabar:

'I have heard from an outside source that you are writing a pamphlet refuting
my work ... Qāte i Burhan.[1] I didn't believe it, but I was certainly surprised. . . .
'In this city there is a festival called the Flower-men's Festival. It takes place
in the month of Bhadon [August–September], and everyone in the city, from
the nobles to the artisans, goes off to the Qutub [Minar]. There they stay for
two to three weeks. All the shops in the city—Muslim and Hindu alike—stay
closed throughout this time. Our friend Ziya ud Din Khan, and [his son]
Shihab ud Din Khan, and my two boys have all gone to the Qutub. In the
men's quarters these days there's no one but me, and my steward, and one
servant who is ill. When our friend [Ziya ud Din Khan] comes back he'll
write to you again. He's come down the big hills[2] and gone up the little hills.[3]
That's why he hasn't written.'

---

[1] See Ch. 17 below.
[2] The foothills of the Himalayas, where those who can afford to, go to escape the worst of the hot
season.
[3] The Qutub Minar stands on slightly higher ground than Delhi.

Bekhabar evidently replied with indignation to the suggestion that he could write a polemic against Ghalib, for Ghalib's next letter begins:

'Master and guide! One does not get cross at such things! "I heard . . . but I didn't believe it." So far I provide no target for wrath. So what we quarrel about is my surprise. Well the occasion for surprise is that your friend says that . . . you . . . who are my shagird, are writing a reply to my *Qāte i Burhan*. If saints behave like this, then alas for the state of us sinners! What I wrote to you was a report, not a complaint. I wear the dress of a worldly man, but I am a faqir, and a faqir of independent spirit, not one who cries loudly of his need or cheats his fellow men. I am seventy years old, and I tell you without exaggeration that seventy thousand men must have passed before my eyes—and that too counting only the gentlemen; how many of the common people I have seen I cannot compute. I have seen two sincere men, men whose love is true: one, Maulvi Siraj ud Din (God's mercy be upon him), and the other [yourself], Munshi Ghulam Ghaus [Bekhabar] (may Exalted God preserve him). My lamented friend did not possess beauty of form, and his sincere and unfeigned friendship was something specially for me. Praise be to God! my second friend is all mankind's well-wisher, a man (may no evil befall him) of handsome form, and one perfect in love and loyalty, and utterly sincere. In fact, radiance upon radiance. I am not a mere man, but a man who knows men:

> My glance is like a burglar that breaks through
> Into the inmost chamber of the heart.
>
> Rejoice, you pillars of hypocrisy!
> Rejoice! for I have left these fields behind.

I have held you to be a man who possesses in the fullest measure the qualities of kindness and love, and of this much I am certain: Once I looked to two men to mourn for me when I am gone. One I have myself had to weep for, and now—may God preserve him—one friend is left. I pray to Him, "O God, let that day never come when I must bear the wound of parting from him. May I die while he yet lives!" My friend, I love you truly.

'Our friend [Ziya ud Din Khan] is not back from the Qutub yet. . . .'

His next letter (also dated only '1864') tells him:

'There is a gentleman in Calcutta, a deputy-collector[1] named Maulvi Abdul Ghafur, pen-name Nassakh. We have never met, but he has sent me his published diwan . . . I have written him a letter of acknowledgement, and since this is suitable for inclusion in my collection of Urdu prose,[2] I am sending it to

---

[1] The second administrative officer of an Indian district.
[2] Bekhabar was collecting Ghalib's Urdu letters for publication.

you. And tell me, my good sir, is the collection going to be printed or not?[1]
If it's already printed, then please send your humble servant as many copies as
Munshi Mumtaz Ali Khan Sahib's magnanimity impels him to grant as the
author's right.'

The letter to Nassakh is interesting as an example of what he now thought fit
to write in Urdu with publication in mind, but more interesting still for the
brief review of his own poetic experience which it contains. It begins with a
paragraph of elaborate (and, one cannot help feeling, exaggerated) praise of
Nassakh and his verse, ending with the words: 'You are wise in the secrets of
the Urdu tongue, and the pride of the whole realm of India.' He then turns to
himself:

'Your humble servant turned to the practice of Urdu poetry when he first
entered the years of discretion, and again in middle age, as the servant of the
King [Bahadur Shah], for some days plied his pen in this same style. My love
and inclination is for Persian verse and prose. I dwell in India, but bear the
wound of the sword of Isfahan.[2] And as far as my powers allowed I prated
much in the Persian tongue. But now I no longer think of Persian, no longer
speak of Urdu, expecting nothing of this world, and hoping for nothing from
the next. I, and the unending sorrow of disappointment; as I myself say in . . .
one of my odes:

> My eyes are opened now to see what I have done:
> The future holds no hope, the past fills me with shame.

I have lived nine and sixty years in the world. And how much longer can I hope
to live? One Urdu diwan of some thousand to twelve hundred couplets, one
Persian diwan of ten thousand and some hundred couplets, and three small
books of prose—these five things are the outcome of my work. And now what
more should I write? My odes earned no reward, my lyrics no due of praise.
I have consumed my life in idle versifying, and now, as Talib Amuli (God's
mercy be upon him) says:

> I closed my lips from speaking: you would think
> My mouth was once a wound, now long since healed. . . .'

On September 6, 1864, he writes to Tufta:

'Yesterday I sent off a parcel of your verses. I put a one-anna stamp on it and
wrote on it, "This is a parcel, not a letter". The post-office clerk told my servant

---

[1] Literally, 'will it be printed or will it be hidden?'—in the original, 'chapega' (with 'a') or 'chu-
pega' (with 'u')? In the Urdu script the short vowels are generally not written.
[2] i.e. I love Persian poetry. The city of Isfahan is the symbol of his beloved [Persian poetry], the
sword of whose glance wounds her lover's heart.

to post it in the box for letters. He can't read, and did as the clerk told him. The words, "This is a parcel, not a letter" constitute an acceptable certificate: so if the postman there demands the letter-post fee you can refer him to that.'

From the next words it seems that Tufta was contemplating coming to Delhi and had asked Ghalib if he could arrange for him to rent a suitable place for him to stay.

'The house is near mine, and near Hakim Mahmud Khan's, and there is a druggist's shop and other shops nearby. You can rent it for two and a half rupees. But the landlord won't promise to hold it available for more than a week. "After that, if your visitor doesn't come, I'm free to let it to anyone else," he says.

'About Rampur, the short answer is this. I can't write to the Nawwab, nor can I write to you *why* I can't write. Get on the train and come here, and I'll tell you about it.'

On September 17, 1864, he writes to Alai:

'Well, Maulana Alai, the Nawwab Sahib [Alai's father] has given you two months' leave. I'm not making that up. Mirza Ali Muhammad Beg has told me personally that the Nawwab has told you, "That matter is over and done with now; by all means you can go to Delhi. I give you leave to spend anything from two weeks to two months there". So why haven't you come? You have the Lord's blessing, and your lord's [i.e. father's] acceptance of your request; so why this idleness and indifference on your part? If my informant's information is wrong, then you write and tell me what the real state of affairs is.

'Mirza Yusuf Ali Khan Aziz (whom you invited) and Mahdi Husain (whom your father sent for) left for Loharu yesterday, taking Mirza Abdul Qādir Beg's family along with them.'

On October 14, 1864, he writes to Tufta:

'You're quite right when you say that you've sent me a lot of manuscripts which I haven't yet corrected, but don't get the idea that it's only your odes that I've put aside. It's the same with the Nawwab Sahib's [of Rampur] ghazals. You know as well as I do what the rains have been like, and you also know that I don't live in a house of my own, but in a rented one. The rains started in July. Hundred of houses in the city have collapsed, and the rains are of a novel kind. It rains two or three times a day, and every time it does it falls so heavily that the water runs in streams everywhere. The sitting room with the balcony— the place where I rise and sit, and sleep, and wake, and live, and die—hasn't collapsed, it's true, but its roof is like a sieve, and there are bowls and basins and spittoons all over the place [to catch the water leaking from the roof]. I've put the inkwell and books in the small room off the store-room. The landlord doesn't do anything about repairs. It's as though I've been living in Noah's Ark these last three months. But now deliverance has come and both the Nawwab Sahib's ghazals and your odes shall be attended to.

'Mir Badshah came to see me and I learnt from him that all was well with you. Mir Qasim Ali hasn't been to see me. For the last two days Nawwab Mustafa Khan [Shefta] has been here, and I've met him once. He's staying on here for the present. He's ill, and Ahsanullah Khan is treating him. He's already been bled and had leeches applied. Now they're thinking about purging him. Otherwise he's quite all right. I've grown very weak, and am as good as confined to bed. If any stranger comes and courtesy demands that I get up, then I do. Otherwise I lie about all the time, and write letters and correct verses as I lie. Alas, alas!'

From the next letter to Alai, dated November 3, 1864, it is evident that Alai had eventually taken advantage of his father's permission to spend some time away from Loharu, and equally evident that he did not take the opportunity to visit Ghalib:

'No letter from Lahore, and none from Loharu either. I went on waiting—or, rather, hoping, with all the capacity for stupidity which I possess. And now when it's evident that I can no longer expect anything, this gives me a chance to pour out my complaints against you. Yes, I know that in reply to each complaint you'll write a pamphlet as long as the *Tuti Nama*[1] and set out a thousand reasonable reasons. But I'm enjoying myself in anticipation and waiting to see what you have to say.

'You got your grandmother to write,[2] and your aunt to write, and Ghalib to write, and then when you got permission, you didn't come! Does that make nonsense, or doesn't it? Right, my son, write something on this point. . . .

'Give my blessing to the children, and write and tell me how they all are. My regards to Mir Jan Sahib. That'll be the day when you come to Delhi and I hear from your own lips what happened in Lahore. . . .'

In November he had news that the Nawwab of Rampur had fallen ill. Despite occasional differences, he had helped Ghalib a great deal, and Ghalib had a genuine regard for him. He writes on November 8, 1864 in some distress:

'Ever since I heard from elsewhere of Your Highness's indisposition, He Who knows the unseen is witness to the distress which I and my wife and my son Husain Ali have experienced. For a whole day no food was cooked in my house, and all of us fasted through both the morning and the evening meal. In the end this alarming news proved to be false, and we recovered our composure.

---

[1] A long narrative work.
[2] To Alai's father, persuading him to allow Alai to leave Loharu for a while.

But we shall not feel fully at ease until I hear the good tidings that you have recovered and bathed, and I have sent you a chronogram to celebrate the occasion.[1] For the moment all I ask is a reply to this letter, telling me the true position about your ailment. . . .

> May you live on another thousand years
> And every year have fifty thousand days.'

This letter brought a reply on November 12th, and on November 13, 1864 Ghalib wrote again:

'I cannot tell you how I passed the days and nights between the 1st and the 11th of November. It is a long way to Rampur, and I am ill, and my resources are inadequate; but if there had been a mail-coach leaving Delhi for Rampur I would not have hesitated a moment, but would have come to attend upon you. There is no electric telegraph to bring me speedy news of your health. So all I could do in my agitation was send off a letter to you on the 8th of this month. God's kindness and my perfect spiritual guide's (Your Highness's) missive brought me out of the vortex of distress before there was time for a reply to my letter to come. Your kind letter came yesterday, November 12th, and I felt that life had returned to me. . . .'

On November 27, 1864, he wrote again:

'My tongue cannot express and my pen cannot write of the anxiety and care in which I have passed the last week to ten days. Every day until evening my eyes were on the door, watching for the postman to come with a letter from Your Highness. At length God showed his kindness, and my life began anew; for last night, some two hours after dark the postman brought your kind letter. When I read it, a new spirit entered me and my blood coursed through all my veins. To sleep, to go to bed, was out of the question. I sat down by the light and began to write verses of congratulation. Only after I had written seven couplets, including the chronogram of your restoration to health, did I sleep. Now I have written it out in fair and am despatching it.'

The Nawwab seems to have been genuinely appreciative. On January 25, 1865, he writes to Ghalib:

'I received the poem of congratulation on my restoration to health which you sent me, and the joy of recovery increased twofold. What other man can write such verse and such chronograms? It is the truth that Almighty God made you without peer or equal; no matter to what field one turns one's gaze, you are the one, unsurpassed master. . . . Truly such men as you are not to be found. The skies revolve for thousands of years to produce a man of such perfection.

[1] Muslim usage prescribes bathing after recovery from illness, and the occasion is one for celebration. Cf. p. 109.

May God grant you long life and health and prosperity, and long may the world draw benefit from your presence. . . .'

On November 28, 1864,[1] the day after he had sent off his congratulatory poem to the Nawwab, he wrote to Safir Bilgrami:

'Blessing from an old man of seventy. Today as I lay here I have reckoned it up, and found that this is my seventieth year. Alas:

> The years of my life are now ten and three score;
> At the most I can last only three or four more.'

He goes on to praise a story which Safir Bilgrami had written and sent for him to see, after which he notes how often the calligrapher has committed mistakes in copying it out. 'That is the calligrapher's ignorance. May God strike down these perverse calligraphers. They didn't rest until they had ruined my diwan and *Panj Ahang* and *Mihr i Nimroz*. . . .'

On December 3, 1864 he writes to Sayyah, complaining that Sayyah's patron, Mir Ghulam Baba Khan, does not seem to understand what Ghalib wants:

How does it come about that nobody understands what I say?

> There is no man who understands my tongue;
> What words shall I address, then, to my friends?

Remember, the point was that I wanted to get *Qāte i Burhan* reprinted, and to get the Nawwab Sahib [Mir Ghulam Baba Khan] to help me by buying two hundred copies. Well, he has presented me with a watch. I ask you, what good is that to me? For four days I've been contemplating sending it back. Then I thought he would be offended. So in the end I decided to keep it and thought that once the book is printed I'd send off a hundred to a hundred and fifty copies to him. Along with this letter you'll receive a letter to the Nawwab thanking him for the watch. And I may tell you that the key to the watch hasn't come. Presumably by some oversight it got left behind there.'

The letter to the Nawwab reads as follows:

'Revered Nawwab Sahib, graced by all good qualities and bountiful to all men, may Exalted God preserve you in His care. I salute you with the forms which the usage of the Prophet of Islam approves, and prayers for your wealth and prosperity are ever upon my tongue. And then I thank you with every hour and every minute that passes for the gift of the watch. First you are a friend,

---

[1] The letter is dated 1863, but Mihr shows that this must be a mistake for 1864.

then a noble, then a Sayyid, and with all these three things in view I hold your gift very dear and treasure it as I treasure the sight of my eyes. May the God Who adorns the world preserve you and bring you aid and comfort with every hour that passes. It appears that at the time it was despatched the key was, by some oversight, not included. Well, one can be made here. My greetings, and a thousand respects to you. He who seeks his friends' good will, Ghalib.'

On December 9, 1864, he writes to Tufta:

'Last year I was ill, but I was not found wanting in serving my friends. Now I am dead, and a dead man cannot do anything. I've given up calling upon the Delhi authorities—the Commissioner, the Deputy Commissioner and so on—but I *have* to meet the Deputy Commissioner once a month because he has charge of the treasury, and if I didn't meet him he wouldn't issue my pay to my agent. Now the Deputy Commissioner, Mr Decrowther (?) has taken six months' leave and gone to the hills. Mr Rattigan has been appointed in his place. Of course, I had to meet him. He is writing an account of the poets of India in English, and he asked my help. I've borrowed seven books from brother Ziya ud Din Khan and sent them to him. Then he asked me to write out and send him accounts of poets whom I knew well. I sent him accounts of sixteen, limiting myself to men who are still living.'

He then names three of the list—Ziya ud Din Ahmad Khan, Shefta, and Tufta himself—and continues:

'It looks as though after I'd sent this list he must have got his clerk to write to you, and then written to you himself. But I have no information about this: I gather it from what you say in your letter. Now I'll have someone send for his clerk, Maulvi Mazhar ul Haq, and find out all the details. The thing is that the account will be in English, and won't include translations of Urdu and Persian verses. Entries will show only the name of the poet and of his ustad, and the poet's residence, birthplace and takhallus. God grant that you get something out of it; but it looks as though all you're likely to get is the inclusion of your name. Now Mr Rattigan has been made a judge of a small-cause court. Mr Decrowther(?) has returned from the hills and resumed his duties. Mr Rattigan has moved to a place about four miles outside the city. Not to speak of the fact that it's winter, and I'm an old man, it's not easy to get to his place, and besides, I can't see anything worth while coming of it. Anyway, Maulvi Mazhar ul Haq is coming to see me on Sunday, the day after tomorrow. I'll find out from him how things stand, and if a visit or a letter from me seems likely to do you any good, I'll certainly go.'

Five days later, on December 14, 1864 he writes again:

'Come along, Mirza Tufta, and give me a hug. Then sit down and hear what I

have to tell you. On Sunday Maulvi Mazhar ul Haq came and told me everything. The first letter to you was written by his brother, Maulvi Anwār ul Haq,
on Mr Rattigan's instructions. Then Mr Rattigan drafted a letter of his own to
be sent to you. The four volumes you sent him—your two diwans, the *Dagger
of Love* and an account of poets—reached him. He is very pleased, and admires
you greatly. He says, "I should imagine that in all India there is no other poet
so great as he—with fifty thousand couplets to his credit." What you will gain
by his good opinion is a very favourable mention in his book. Beyond that,
let's see. And yes, he has it in his jurisdiction to appoint to posts worth fifteen
to twenty rupees. If you permit me I can speak to him about this.

'I am in a bad way, and I can't make out why you don't believe me:

> To lose one's life is bad, but just as bad
> Is to fall prey to your suspicious mind.

My hearing had already given up the ghost, and now my eyesight has grown
very weak. All my powers, all that a man possesses, are declining. I can't keep my
wits about me at all. My memory's so poor you'd think I'd never had one, and
I'm as though I'd never had any aptitude for the art of poetry. The Nawwab of
Rampur gives me a hundred rupees a month. Last year I sent word to him to
say, "A man must have his wits about him to correct verse, and I do not find
that I have. I ask you to excuse me from performing this service, and to reckon
what I receive from your court as a return for past services. If you will, count
me as your 'sick number',[1] or, if you will, a beggar who lives on your crumbs.
And if your bounty is conditional upon my performance of service, then my
fate depends upon your will." For a whole year he has sent no verse, but I
have received my usual monthly grant up to November. Let's see what happens
as time goes on. So far the Nawwab Sahib in his magnanimity keeps sending
me my allowance. As for you, my friend, practice—touch wood—has made
you perfect. There is nothing that needs correction in your verse. And if you
insist willy nilly on believing that your verse still needs correction, then, my
dear friend, what will you do when I am gone? I am like the lamp dying at
morning, the sun setting behind the mountain's crest. "Verily we are for God,
and verily to Him we shall return." '

[1] Ghalib uses the English words—in a somewhat adapted form. He means that the Nawwab
should continue his allowance, regarding it, if he so chooses, as sick pay.

Chapter 14

1865

But if Ghalib felt that he was 'the lamp dying at morning, the sun setting behind the mountain's crest', the letters for 1865 are none the less as varied and lively as ever. He seems to have kept in moderately good health throughout the year, despite the inevitable weakness of old age. His friend Alai at last visited him in Delhi. His old patron, the Nawwab of Rampur, died in April, and for a while he was uncertain how much he could expect from his successor. But to his satisfaction, the new Nawwab treated him as well as the old. In October he was well enough to travel to Rampur, staying there for the celebrations of the Nawwab's accession and returning only a few days before the end of December.

On January 5, 1865 he writes to Alai. He begins with a complaint that neither the last days of the Muslim month of Rajab nor the first days of Shaban have brought him a visit:

'Well, sir, Mirza Rajab Beg has died, and you did not mourn him. Shaban Beg has been born, the ceremonies of the sixth day have been held, and you did not come to them. . . .

'My son I don't know how I manage to write you these few lines. Shihab ud Din Khan's illness has taken away the zest of life. I tell you, I wish I could die in his place. May God grant him life, and let me not see the day when I must mourn his loss. O God, grant him health! O God, grant him long life! Three children, and another yet unborn—O God, preserve him to watch over them!'

Fortunately, Shihab ud Din survived his illness. In the same month Ghalib writes again:

'God has had mercy on Ziya ud Din's[1] old age and on my helplessness. My dear Shihab ud Din is safe. Piles and dysentery, and fever and migraine—what varied ills beset him! But now at last he is restored to health in all respects. His weakness will leave him in its own good time. And who could call him strong before, that he should think him weak now? An old man was passing along a lane when he stumbled and fell. "Alas for old age!" he said. He looked around, and when he saw that there was no one about he muttered as he went on his way "and youth was no better, either." '

[1] Shihab ud Din's father.

On February 7, 1865, he wrote the only Urdu letter to Shefta which we possess:

'My revered brother, I feel sure that you will have reached the capital of your dominion safe and sound and that in serenity of soul you are keeping the fast [of Ramzan], and that apart from your preoccupation with betel and regret at the absence of Maulvi Altaf Husain [Hali—at this time Shefta's companion] you have nothing to disturb your mind.'

He then goes on to discuss various points of Persian usage.

It seems that Tufta at this time was visiting Lucknow. Ghalib writes to him on February 12, 1865, addressing him in ceremonious style:

'Munshi Sahib, distinguished by fair fortune and prosperity, may Exalted God preserve you! Accept from Ghalib a darwesh's blessing. I thought you were in Qanungos' Muhalla, Sikandarabad, and in fact you are sitting smoking the long-stemmed, Lucknow hookah at the *Avadh Akhbar* Press in Raja Man Singh Mansion in Lucknow, and talking to Munshi Newal Kishor. Well, give him my greetings [and tell him that] today is Sunday and the paper hasn't yet come. I always get it by Thursday, or Friday at the latest.

'Mirza Tufta, what are you saying? What of Mr Rattigan? Where is Mr Rattigan? On Thursday the 19th of January of this year he left for the Panjab. He has been appointed to a post somewhere in Multan district or Peshawar district. I didn't feel strong enough to go and pay him a farewell visit. Anwār ul Haq has got a job . . . at a salary of fifteen rupees [a month].'

The next day, February 13, 1865, he writes to Alai:

'My dear boy, congratulations on the auspicious arrival of your new guest! May Exalted God grant you and the child and its brothers increase of life and wealth! From what you write it is not clear whether the blessed newcomer is a boy or a girl. Saqib[1] thinks it is a boy, and Ghalib thinks it is a girl. Write plainly, and remove our uncertainty. Your letter was addressed to Saqib. But fie upon me! Why do I say letter? It was a long screed and I read it from end to end. . . .

'My friend, this is a field in which I share your inauspicious stars and feel your pain. I am a man devoted to one art. Yet by my faith I swear to you, my verse and prose has not won the praise it merited. I wrote it, and I alone appreciated it. Of all the aspirations my Creator placed in me—to roam in happy poverty and independence, or to give freely from my ample bounty—not even a thousandth part of them was realized. I lacked the bodily strength; else I would have taken a staff in my hand, and hung from it a checkered mat and a tin drinking-vessel and a rope, and taken to the road on foot; now to Shiraz, now sojourning in Egypt, now making my way to Najaf[2] I would have roamed.

[1] Shihab ud Din, Alai's cousin.   [2] The site of the tomb of Ali.

I lacked the means; else I would have played host to a world of men; or if I could not feast a world of men, no matter; at least within the city where I lived none would have gone hungry and unclad. . . .

'The target of God's wrath, rejected of men, old, weak and ailing, poor and afflicted . . . a man who cannot bear to see another beg, and must himself beg his bread from door to door—that man am I.'

Ten days later he is in a happier frame of mind. On February 23, 1865, he writes to Alai again:

'I got your letter yesterday and am sending off a reply to it today. Rajab Beg, Shaban Beg, and Ramzan Beg—these famous months have passed without your coming. I haven't heard of Shawwal Beg as a man's name, but Idi Beg is a possibility. So as the auspicious day of Id approaches, what wonder if . . . you find that you can come? . . .

'Congratulations on the arrival of a daughter. Saqib disputed with me. "I have a nephew," he said. "No," I said, "I have a grand-daughter." Well, I've won, and he's lost. . . .'

On March 11, 1865, he writes a letter of recommendation to Hakim Ghulam Murtaza Khan:

'. . . Think hard, and then grant me that I have never troubled you for anything. Now, in a way, I ask a favour of you. The bearer of this letter, Pandit Jai Narain, presents himself before you. His forebears held high position and distinguished rank in the service of Nawwab Ahmad Bakhsh Khan. Now he has occasion to go seeking employment to Patiala. I adjure you by my life to make all possible efforts to get him appointed to some post, some rank, appropriate to his station. I will regard it as a rank granted to me, and will be deeply grateful.'

On April 1, 1865, he writes to Hakim Ghulam Najaf Khan, who had apparently complained that Ghalib had not written to him:

'My friend, I received your complaint with the utmost respect, but listen to my account and don't go by your own imaginary calculations. First, I had a letter from my dear Zahir [Hakim Ghulam Najaf Khan's son]. I answered it as soon as I had read it and sent it to the post the next day. The gist of it was this: "You are always getting boils and pimples. The reason is that your blood and mine are as one, and I am the special favourite of heating of the blood." Then your letter came. I answered it three days later, to this effect: "My dear grandson Zahir ud Din is a better man than you. He came to see me before he left and wrote to me as soon as he arrived." The post office doesn't issue receipts for letters posted. Both letters were stamped. It's out of the question that my two letters are stranded at the post office here. If the Shaikhupur postmen didn't deliver them, is that my fault? I grant you I wrote only your name and "Shaikhu-pur" as the address. I didn't write the muhalla, and perhaps that's why the letters didn't reach you. Your letter has just this moment come, and I am writing these lines lying down. Now I'll send Inayatullah to your [Delhi] house and get him to find out and bring me the details of your Shaikhupur address.

'Well, sir, Inayatullah is back with a note. I'm addressing the envelope accordingly, but I shan't have time to catch the post, so I'll send it off tomorrow morning.

'Hakim Zahir ud Din Khan, my blessings on you. Sonny, I haven't the energy to write more at present. You must be content with my blessings. I've already sent off an answer to your letter, as I've written above. A curse on all liars. You say: "And yet more curses."

'Nawwab Mustafa Khan [Shefta] arrived here yesterday. He's brought his family with him. The little boys are to be circumcised in the month of Zi Qad and Muhammad Ali Khan married in Zil Hij.

'Five days ago we had hail in Delhi as big as hen's eggs—in some cases even bigger. The new Lieutenant-Governor came and held a durbar. I was honoured and treated with a kindness more than I could have expected. When you come I'll tell you all about it.'

In the collection of letters to Hakim Ghulam Najaf Khan this is followed by an undated note clearly written after he was back in Delhi:

'The rice was poor stuff—it doesn't swell up, and hasn't got long, thin grains. Don't go into a long argument about it, but see that I get old, thin-grained rice. Buy and send me one rupee's worth. And remember, my experience is that new rice gives you constipation, while old rice doesn't.

'Last night Mir Majd ud Din was saying that you have a calligrapher. Well, my friend, I have a book—prose—of about ten to twelve sections I want copied. Find out how many sections your man does per rupee and how much he can write in a day. Send me a note about this right away and then after lunch send the man to see me so that I can give him the paper and the thing I want written. Give my blessing to Zahir ud Din and write and tell me how he is.'

On April 4, 1865, he writes to Safir Bilgrami congratulating him on his translation into Urdu of the romance *Bostan i Khayal* ('The Garden of Fancy'), which he is publishing in two volumes. This work was written in Persian in the eighteenth century and is comparable in length and character to the *Tale of Amir Hamza*, with the difference that the author appears to have been a Shia of the unorthodox Ismaili sect, and the doctrines of this sect find expression in his work. If Safir Bilgrami's "translation" could be contained in two volumes, it must have been a considerable abridgement of the original work, which occupies fifteen.

Ghalib tells Safir Bilgrami: 'You have performed a great service to me in particular and to men of mature taste in general. I have written to Mir Wilayat Ali ordering both volumes. . . .' Mir Wilayat Ali was the manager of the Patna press which had printed the translation. Ghalib had had occasion to write a letter of apology to him a few days earlier (April 1st):

'For your grandfather's sake, please forgive me for my error. Really, I have committed no sin:

> Old age, a hundred ailments, as they say.

I am seventy years old. I have no memory, and absent-mindedness prevails. Yesterday I wrote you a letter ordering the translation of *Bostan i Khayal* by Safir Bilgrami. When I put it in the envelope I forgot to enclose the stamps [in payment], and today when I opened my box I found them there. I was covered in shame and confusion . . . Today I am sending them enclosed in a fresh envelope. God grant that you have already despatched the book. . . .'

On April 13, 1865, he writes to Sayyah to thank him for a photograph:

'. . . . Look here, Munshi Sahib. I know that everyone else approves the invention of photography, but your humble servant doesn't subscribe to this. Just look at the gentleman's picture! It goes as far as his elbows, but his forearms and the rest of him are missing. Let alone talking to him, I can't even shake hands with him! . . .'

On April 21, 1865, he writes again to Safir Bilgrami:

'Light of my eyes and joy of my heart (because I love you), master (because you are a Sayyid), Maulvi Sayyid Farzand Ahmad Safir [Bilgrami], God grant long life to you! I was delighted with your pearls of verse. All your verses are good, but these I write down here went straight to my heart. [He then quotes three couplets.]

> May you live on and on till Judgement Day
> And every day your health and grace increase.'

About the same time—Mihr places the letter, which is undated, between February and May 1865—he writes to Tufta in terms which belie his earlier certificate that Tufta's verse no longer needed correction: 'I'm greatly surprised that after I'd written objecting to the rhymes [of an earlier poem] you've written a ghazal based on those same rhymes. . . . This ghazal's a write-off. Write another and send it to me to correct.'

A letter of May 14, 1865, begins on a similar note: 'Grow old, and learn!

I grant that you write good verse and without effort, but what you call enquiry is nothing but whims and fancies. You go by guesswork, and sometimes your guess corresponds to the facts, and sometimes it doesn't. . . .' It ends with the laconic sentence: 'My money for April, and acknowledgement of my letters of condolence and congratulation, have come from Rampur; for the future, what God wills.' Ghalib might well wonder what the future held in store for him. Nawwab Yusuf Ali Khan had died in April, to be succeeded on the 21st of that month by his son Kalb i Ali Khan. Ghalib's relations with the old Nawwab were of long standing, and apart from exhibiting displeasure when Ghalib ventured to make what could be interpreted as an attempt to recommend others to his bounty, the Nawwab seems always to have treated him with consideration. His successor was largely an unknown quantity, and Ghalib's early letters to him, as we shall see, suggest that he felt some apprehension on this account.

Other undated letters to Tufta are placed by Mihr after this one. In one he evidently apologises for some lapse—perhaps for not returning promptly verses which Tufta had sent for correction: 'My dear friend, the shame I shall feel on the Last Day before God, because I did not worship Him, and before the Prophet, because I offended against the Holy Law, is perhaps less strong than the shame I feel before you.'

In a second he speaks scathingly of some highly-placed person unnamed to whom Tufta had addressed an ode:

'Listen to me, my friend. The man to whom you addressed your ode is as much a stranger to the art of poetry as you and I are to the problems of our respective religions. In fact you and I, in spite of our ignorance of religious matters, at any rate have no aversion for them, while this is a fellow whom poetry makes sick. . . . These people aren't fit to be spoken of, much less to be praised. Ah, Anwari!

> Alas, there is no patron who deserves
> my praise!
> Alas, there is no mistress who inspires
> my verse!'

On May 26, 1865, he writes to Alai's father, Amīn ud Din Ahmad Khan:

'For your entertainment I am sending you a new ghazal I have written. God grant that it please you and you have it taught to a singer.

'Let me tell you the Delhi news. . . . Yesterday, Thursday, 25th May early in the day there was a really fierce dust-storm. Then rain fell heavily, and it turned so cold that Delhi was like a frozen world. The gate to Bara Dariba has been demolished. The rest of Qābil Attar Lane has been destroyed. The mosque in Kashmiri Katra has been levelled to the ground. The width of the street has been doubled. God, God! The domes of the mosques are being demolished, while on the thresholds of the Hindus' temples the flags and banners flutter in the wind. A great monkey,[1] strong as a lion and huge as an elephant, has been born. He roves the city, demolishing buildings as he goes. He has seized the little domes on Faizullah Khan Bangash's mansion and shaken them one by one until he destroyed them to their foundations and brick rang against brick. Monkey, the deeds you do! And in the city too!'

The next words presumably refer to Amīn ud Din's son Alai:

'From the land of the desert [Loharu] the son of a noble, rich in children and poor in wealth, a master of three languages, Arabic, Persian and English, has come to Delhi. He is staying in Ballimaron muhalla and, as need arises, visits the Delhi authorities. For the rest, his doors are kept closed. From time to time—not every morning and every evening—he comes to the humble abode of the faqir Ghalib. . . . The citizens of Delhi are at a loss to know what he lives on. Some say, "He has turned against his father" but I believe that his father has unreasonably withdrawn his favour from him. Let us see how it will end. Ghalib's . . . watchword is, "Wish well to all".'

By mid-June 1865 he was in the awkward position of having to suggest to the new Nawwab of Rampur that there were occasions when money might appropriately be sent him from time to time over and above his monthly allowance. He had recently sent an ode of congratulation, but this had not produced quite the expected response, and he has to write on June 14, 1865:

'Lord and Master, it was the custom of his late Highness whenever I sent him an ode, to acknowledge it with a letter of praise and appreciation, and—I feel ashamed to say this, but there is no other way—to enclose in the envelope as a gift a draft of Rs. 250. The panegyric odes are included in the volume of my collected Persian verse in Your Highness's library, and you may confirm what I have said about the letters from your files. The practice was not a bad one, and if it could be continued that would be good.'

There is no indication in subsequent letters that the Nawwab responded as desired.

The Nawwab had asked him to come to Rampur. On June 18, 1865, he replies:

'I will certainly come to attend upon Your Highness . . . [but] the heat beats down so fiercely that the very wings of the birds are burning. And after fire will come water [the rains]. In both these conditions a man may be excused the toils of travel, especially when he is old and sick. Let the sun once move into Libra, and the seasons of fire and of water be passed, and I will put on the robes of pilgrimage for the journey to the splendid city of Rampur.'

[1] This suggests the Hindu monkey-god Hanuman.

He was evidently pleased with the new Nawwab's initial treatment of him. On July 7, 1865, he writes to Bekhabar:

'May God preserve the ruler of Rampur! I received my money for both April and May as of old, and, God willing, the money for June . . . will come too. Today is Friday, 7th July. As a rule the Nawwab's letter with the draft comes about the 10th or 12th. I have sent off the ode in celebration of his accession, and received the acknowledgement. I no longer keep copies of my verse and prose. My heart is sick of this art. One or two of my friends have a copy of it. I have sent word to them now. If it comes today then tomorrow, and if tomorrow then the next day, I will send it you. At the insistence of brother Amīn ud Din Khan I have written a ghazal in the same metre and rhyme as one of [Amir] Khusrau's. Ala ud din Khan [Alai] has sent him a copy. . . . I am sending off the original to you. It is so hot that I do not know where to turn. And on top of that are my physical ills and spiritual sorrows.'

About this time he had from Majruh what looked like good news from Alwar. In an undated letter he replies:

'I had already heard of the Raja's generosity. Praise be to Exalted God! . . . Now let's see when he returns and whether he sends for me in accordance with his promise. At the time he left for Calcutta he said he would send for me on his return; and of course, if he sends for me I shall go. It looks as though for you and me the time of troubles is drawing to a close and the days of prosperity are dawning. Now I shall have to play the flatterer to Miran Sahib. It will be he who has access to the Raja if my luck holds. Now you must lay the foundations for my prosperity by keeping Miran Sahib well-disposed towards me. My friend, this Miran or Amiran Sahib is His Highness's favourite. He may choose any man from any group he pleases and get him an interview with His Highness, or choose anyone out of the tribe of poets and get him given whatever he pleases. Give him and [Mir Sarfaraz Husain] my blessing.'

On July 17, 1865, he writes again to Majruh and Mir Sarfaraz Husain:

'The delight of my eyes Mir Mahdi [Majruh] and Mir Sarfaraz Husain must be cross with me. They will be grumbling at me and saying to themselves, "Just see, he hasn't written to us." Well,

> I too possess a tongue; if only you
> Would ask me, I would hasten to explain.[1]

So let me explain that you too have not written, so there was no letter to reply to. When Miran Sahib came I asked after you and told him to send you my

[1] Ghalib is here adapting one of his own couplets.

blessings when he wrote. And that is the most I can manage. He came yesterday. I asked him, "Have you heard from Alwar?" He said, "No, not this week". How shall I describe to you the state I am in? I used to chant this verse of mine to myself:

> Back! thronging hosts of black despair,
>   lest you reduce to dust as well
> The one joy left to me—the joy that
>   unavailing struggle brings.

But now this is a song I can no longer sing, because the joy of unavailing struggle has turned to dust. "Verily we are for God and verily to Him we shall return." '

This is the last letter which we possess to Majruh or to any of his circle.

A week later, on July 23, 1865, he writes again to the Nawwab of Rampur:

'Here we need rain, and the wind seems to rain sparks of fire. In the scorching sun men's faces and the rocks of the hills burn. . . . Wherever you turn are hosts of varied sicknesses, and only on men's limbs, which run with sweat, is any trace of moisture . . . to be found. Either the hot wind blows, or the air is completely still. I write these lines because I wonder all the time how Your Highness is faring. The sooner you favour your well-wisher with a reply, the greater will be the boon that you confer on him.'

Three days later, on July 26, 1865, he writes to Amīn ud Din Ahmad Khan:

'I learned from your kind letter that two Persian ghazals I sent had reached you. Did the third one [he here gives the rhyming words] not reach you?—the one I sent at your request. Surely it must have done, and you must have forgotten. Your representative in constant attendance at the court of Asadullah [Ghalib], i.e. Maulana Alai, has, with a view to the pleasure of him who sent him there, kept on at me until I wrote an Urdu ghazai. If you like it, get it taught to a singer. It should go well in the higher ranges of the *jhinjoti* mode. If I live that long I will come in the winter and hear it too.'

In a letter of July 30, 1865, he explains to Sayyah his relationship with Rampur:

'About ten to twelve years ago the late Nawwab of Rampur Yusuf Ali Khan began sending me his verses to correct; and every month he had a draft for a hundred rupees sent me. Judge of his tact and courtesy by the fact that he never demanded receipts for the money. He would enclose his draft with his letter and I would send him a letter in reply. Besides this monthly allowance he would send me other sums from time to time—sometimes two hundred, sometimes two hundred and fifty. During the time of the troubles my income from the Fort ceased and my pension from the British was stopped. This good man continued to send my monthly allowance and occasional extra gifts from time to time; [actually, the monthly allowance began only in July 1859] and that is how I and my dependants managed to survive. The present Nawwab— may God preserve and prosper him for ever and ever—continues to send the draft for my monthly allowance as of old. Let us see whether he continues the practice of the occasional gifts or not.'

In an undated letter to Shākir of about this time he explains one of his couplets:

'My home lies plunged in the black night
of raging grief;
Only a burnt-out candle shows that day
has dawned.

"The black night of raging grief"—that is pitch darkness, impenetrable night. No sign of dawn, as though, in fact, dawn had never come to the world. But there is one indication that day has dawned—the burnt-out candle; because the lamp or the candle that burns through the night goes out as morning dawns. The beauty of the picture lies in the thought that the very thing singled out as the evidence of morning is itself one of the causes of the darkness; and the reader is forced to reflect how dense must be the darkness in that house where the very signs of morning contribute to the darkness . . .

'I have corrected your ghazal and am returning it. You send it as something requiring correction: I receive it as something from which I can learn.'

His next letter to Shākir is dated August 6, 1865:

'On the envelope of your letter you had written, "Sender: Maulvi Abdur Razzaq Jafri ul Haidari" and [elsewhere on the envelope], "Shākir." When I read it, for a long time I thought to myself, "Are these two different people?" After a while I remembered that your name is Maulvi Abdur Razzaq and your takhallus Shākir. Just see how absent-minded I have become!'

He goes on to correct some of Shākir's verses and then to explain at length the meanings of earlier verses of Shākir's as modified by his corrections. This leads him on to speak of his own development as a poet:

'When I began to write poetry I took [the Persian poets] Bedil and Asīr and Shaukat as the models for my Urdu verse. Thus the concluding couplet of one of my ghazals was:

He writes in Urdu, but in Bedil's style—
Who could do that but Asadullah Khan?

Between the ages of fifteen and twenty-five I wrote on highly fanciful themes, and in these ten years got together a big diwan. But in the end, when I learned discretion I rejected this diwan—tore it up completely—leaving only some ten to fifteen couplets in my present diwan by way of samples of my former style.[1]

'Kind sir, your [Persian] prose does not require correction. Your distinctive style of writing is lively and without blemish, and you should maintain it. And if you favour me by wishing to model your prose on mine, study *Panj Ahang* and my other writings attentively and with concentration, and practise writing more and more. . . . You are gifted in high degree with a natural aptitude for writing, and I entertain the strongest hopes that, with your keen intelligence and forceful style, you will soon be writing excellently—a source of pride to me and all your friends, and of envy to your enemies. . . .'

On August 21, 1865, he writes to the Nawwab of Rampur:

'*The Tale of Hamza* is a work of fiction, written by talented men of Iran in the days of Shah Abbas II [1642-1666]. In India they call it *The Tale of Amir Hamza*, and in Persia *The Secrets of Hamza*. It was written something over two hundred years ago, but it is still famous and always will be.'

He goes on to say that he has written an ode in the Nawwab's praise, which he encloses, incorporating characters and incidents from the Hamza story. He hopes the Nawwab will like it.

No doubt he also hoped that the Nawwab's appreciation would find monetary expression. He was therefore all the more delighted when a draft for Rs. 200 reached him on the very day he had posted off the ode. He wrote again next day, on August 22, 1865:

'Your . . . humble pensioner Ghalib is at a loss to know whether he should first thank you for your bounty or first speak of your miraculous insight. . . . These days sundry creditors were dunning me for payment, and in fact were prepared to raise an outcry against me; and your draft for Rs. 200 was like a pitcher of the water of eternal life to me, releasing me from the snare of death. The remarkable thing is that . . . I had sent off an ode at nine in the morning, and at three in the afternoon this miracle occurred. . . .'

His appreciation led him when he heard a few days later that the Nawwab was ill, to offer his friendly advice as to the treatment he should adopt:[2]

'I am not a physician, but I am a man of much experience, with the understanding that seventy years of life brings to a man. I would not speak in these

---

[1] This statement greatly exaggerates what he did—cf. p. 40 above.
[2] The letter is undated, but the Nawwab replied on August 29th.

terms to others, but I cannot help expressing my opinion to Your Highness. God knows what it was, or what your physicians thought it was, that caused your illness, but in my opinion disorders of the stomach and of the heart both contributed to it. Now in order to safeguard your health it is important that you should take water-coconut from time to time. To strengthen the heart you should take the gold-and-ambergris electuary made up according to the prescription of the late Hakim Babar Ali Khan. Its ingredients are gold leaf, white ambergris, essence of *kewra* [a strong-scented flower], and white crys-tallized sugar—made to a special recipe in which the use of too many ingre-dients was deemed inappropriate. (Other electuaries have many more ingre-dients.) Avicenna's stimulant, conserve of pearls, conserve of ox-tongue and ambergris, essence of meats prepared without intoxicating ingredients, com-pounded with stimulants and tonics which are neither too heating nor too cooling. . . . [a word or two is evidently missing here]. From time to time you should drink oxymel[1] and rose-water. Your diet should include plenty of fowl, and lightly-done eggs, but you should exercise care not to eat fowl and eggs at the same sitting. With goat's meat, eggs are permissible, and, indeed, delicious and good to eat. Essence of mint and essence of the small cardamon should always be in your medicine-chest. Increase the use of perfumes. Refrain from sexual intercourse after meals. Sheep's foot gravy should always be on your dinner-table, for you to partake of whenever you feel the inclination.

> May you live on and on till Judgement Day
> And every day your honour and wealth increase.'

He writes again on September 18, 1865 to condole with the Nawwab on the death of his wife:

'I want to write something, but I do not know what to write. I ought to have written a poem of condolence in the Persian language and in eloquent style. But I swear by your feet, I could not bring myself to do so. An ornate style, in verse or prose, is for occasions of rejoicing, when the heart, in the exuber-ance of its joy, blooms like a flower and the mind expands and words are sought for and themes created. But now I am half dead, and my heart is des-pondent and my spirit dejected. . . . How fair is my fortune, that before I had done justice to themes of praise and congratulation I should be called upon to write an elegy! . . . At the very outset of Your Highness's reign you have had to suffer the greatest blow that could be imagined. When the outset of your reign brought you such extreme of pain, it is surely demanded now that for ever and ever, as long as you live no sorrow should befall Your Highness. . . .'

He enclosed a four-line chronogram on the lady's death.

Within a month he was himself on the way to Rampur, to be present at the

---

[1] Vinegar, lime-juice or other acid, mixed with sugar or honey.

celebrations of the Nawwab's accession. He writes of his impending departure in a letter to Alai of October 1, 1865—the first since February, a fact from which we may perhaps deduce that Alai was in Delhi for most of the intervening months. He begins with a verse which shows that Alai and his father were once again on good terms, and continues: 'My friend, you know that I am off to Rampur. All the circumstances are now favourable, and if I live, I shall set off on Friday.' This would have been October 6th, but his departure seems in fact to have been delayed, for he writes in a letter to Shākir dated only 'October, 1865' but evidently written early in the month, that he will be setting out 'either on Tuesday or Wednesday'. He continues:

'The occasion of my going is to mourn the late Nawwab and congratulate the present one. I shall have to stay there two or three months, so from now on address any letters to Rampur. No need to write the address of the house. My name and "Rampur" is enough.'

He goes on to praise a mukhammas (a poem written in stanzas of five lines) which Shākir had sent him to correct:

'I have corrected your mukhammas and am returning it. The truth is that the verses are yours and the delight in them mine. By a fortunate chance, while I was correcting your poem my loyal and loving friend, the wise man of the age and seal of the line of divines profound in learning, Maulvi Mufti Sadr ud Din Khan Sahib Bahadur, Sadr us Sudur of Delhi, whose takhallus is Azurda— may he live for ever and may God raise him to ever greater eminence—was on a visit to me, ennobling my house of sorrow with his presence. He saw your poem, and liked it. He praised your honour's eloquence, drew a senior partner's[1] share of the pleasures your Arabic verses provided, and spoke at length, with fluent tongue and forceful exposition, in praise of the sweetness of your poetry. Then he learnt from me so much of your excellent qualities as my knowledge could provide and my speech express; and this brought him joy and pleasure. I congratulate you. Without ever having seen you, without ever having met you, out of sheer warmth of feeling for you, he commanded me to write to you that he desired the honour of meeting you. Accordingly I do so: be pleased to accept what I write.'

By October 11, 1865, he was well on his way to Rampur, for he wrote on that date from Muradabad to Hakim Ghulam Najaf Khan:

'It's Wednesday, and it must have been about nine in the morning when I got to Muradabad, travelling alone in a palanquin. . . . The two boys, the two carts, the carriage, and the servants are following on behind. They'll be here any

---

[1] In Urdu, 'sharik i ghalib'. This is a play on words, for they can mean both 'senior partner' and 'Ghalib's partner.'

time now. If the night passes uneventfully, and if I live, I shall reach Rampur tomorrow. I'm ill at ease. It's three days since I passed a motion. The boys are well. Tell your teacher [Ghalib's wife]. Give Mirza Shihab ud Din Khan my blessing and Nawwab Ziya ud Din my regards. Read out my letter to both of them—mind you do! Zahir ud Din won't be pleased if I send him my blessing, so tell him I send my respectful service.'

From a letter to another correspondent we know that he reached Rampur on October 13th[1]. Eight days later, on 21st, he wrote again to Hakim Ghulam Najaf Khan:

'I learned from your letter that you are worried about my diet. Well, I swear by God that here I am happy and well. I get my morning meal so early in the day that by about nine o'clock my servants have eaten too. [The servants would not eat until after their master had finished his meal.] The evening meal too comes early. Several kinds of meat and vegetable dishes, pulao, mutanjan [meat boiled in rice with spices and sugar] . . . and at both meals both leavened bread and chapaties, with chutneys and preserves. I am happy, and the boys are happy. Kallu is better again. A water-carrier, a scullion and a sweeper are provided from the Nawwab's establishment, and I have engaged a barber and a washerman. So far I have met the Nawwab twice. The honour he shows me and his consideration and courtesy leave nothing to be desired.

'Zahir ud Din Khan Bahadur, my blessings upon you. Take this letter to your grandmother [Ghalib's wife] and read it to her, and tell her that that thing I told her is not correct. There's nothing in it. All is well with us here.'

Three days later, on October 24, 1865, he writes again:

'You're right, no praise is too high for our friend Fazlullah Khan's[2] sympathy and help; but my fortunes aren't linked with Alwar. Mark my words, I shall get nothing from that quarter—or if, to suppose the impossible, I do, it will be two hundred and fifty rupees, and I owe that much our friend Fazlullah Khan. I shall repay the debt to him. If by any chance, contrary to my firm belief, instructions are given to send me five hundred, and the money arrives, then let me know, hand over two hundred and fifty to friend Fazl [ullah Khan] and write to tell me you have done so. And use the rest as I shall write and tell you.

'Well, my friend, I've . . . built my castle-in-the-air. Now let me tell you what's been happening. The Nawwab Sahib's kindness and consideration increases from day to day. Today is Tuesday, 4th Jamadi us Sani and 24th October. I've received a grant for our food and for the fodder for the horses and the oxen. And I have gained by it, not lost. The celebrations will begin

---

[1] Cf. p. 326 below.

[2] Fazlullah Khan was the brother of the chief minister to the Raja of Alwar, and had evidently been sympathetic to Ghalib's aspirations there.

from December 1st, and will last for one or two weeks. After that I shall leave for Delhi. God willing, I shall see you there again by the end of December.'

The next letter, dated November 2, 1865, is not to Hakim Ghulam Najaf Khan, but to his son Zahir ud Din:

'. . . Tell me, my son, how are you? And how is your brother Mirza Tafazzul Husain? If you see him, give him my blessing and ask after his health. And give your respected father my blessing and tell him that his letter was in answer to mine, so there was nothing in it that demanded an answer from me. And listen, Zahir ud Din my son, go at once to your grandmother [Ghalib's wife] and tell her that both the boys and I are well, and ask her whether Shihab ud Din Khan sent her allowance of fifty rupees for October or not. [Mihr says that Ghalib's wife received a regular monthly allowance from Loharu.] And has Kidar Nath been to the house to issue their pay to Jafar Beg, Wafadar and the others, or not? Well, my son, ask your grandmother these two things and then write to me at once. Mind you don't put it off.'

Two days later, on November 4, 1865, he writes to Rizwan:

'Give my blessing to [your brother] Qurban Ali Beg Khan and write and tell me how he is.

'Today is . . . 4th November. The day before yesterday the Nawwab Sahib went off on tour. He said when he left that he would return in two weeks, spend four days here, and then go to see the exhibition ground at Bareilly.'

Hali says that 'as the Nawwab left, he entrusted Ghalib, in the usual phrase, "to God's keeping". Ghalib replied, "Your Highness, God entrusted me to *your* keeping. And here are you handing me back into His '.' Ghalib's letter continues:

'When he gets back from there he will await the arrival of the Commissioner of Bareilly. He will be here by December 5th. Then there will be the celebrations, lasting for three days. Two or three days after that Ghalib will leave Rampur. God grant that he gets to you alive.'

He then gives him detailed instructions about various things he wants him to do and various matters he wants him to find out about. He concludes:

'Remember, I shall be waiting for an answer on all these points. Today is . . . 4th November. It's certain that eight days is long enough for this letter to reach you and your reply to reach me. I'll wait nine days, and if on the tenth I don't get a letter from you, I'll break off relations with you.'

On November 7, 1865, he writes to Junun. Junun was a Bareilly man, and seems to have hoped that Ghalib might be able to visit him from Rampur and see the exhibition. Ghalib replies:

'. . . What would I be doing visiting Bareilly? I got here on October 13th, and if I live, shall leave for Delhi by the end of December. What would I want with the Bareilly exhibition ground? I have had my fill of even this exhibition ground which men call the world, and I long for the world of light beyond it. . . .'

On November 12, 1865, he writes again to Hakim Ghulam Najaf Khan:

'Two of your letters came one after the other, telling me all the news—that Zahir ud Din had gone to Agra, that my letter addressed to him had been delivered to you and then sent on to Agra, that Zahir ud Din's grandmother [Ghalib's wife] was ill with a cough, that Kidar Nath was annoyed with me, that permission had been sought to reserve the house, and that Fazl i Hasan had been begged to be lenient with me. Why did you open my letter to Zahir ud Din? He's a hot-tempered boy and he'll be cross with you. His grandmother always falls ill with this sort of thing at this time of year. She has a recipe for strong soup. Get that made up and keep an eye on her. Kidar Nath's just a boy. What's he got to be cross about? After all, he's the one who'll go to get the accumulated money [Ghalib's pension] from the treasury. *I'm* the one who's cross with *him*; I paid him his money in full and he hasn't returned my I.O.U. and hasn't distributed the twenty-three rupees, eight annas. What else am I to write about the reserving of the house? I've written to Shihab ud Din Khan. I've written to Shamshad Ali Beg. And now I'm writing to you. I paid the five rupees, eight annas for September before I left. October, November and December comes to sixteen rupees, eight annas. I'll pay that when I get back; in fact, if I can find the opportunity I'll send the money for the three months by draft from here.

'Give my blessing to Ismail Khan Sahib and tell him to get the steps leading up to the entrance repaired and the lavatory . . . set to rights. What luck I have! A curse on the luck that makes our friend Fazl i Hasan act the role of my patron and benefactor! And alas for my wretchedness that what was needed could not be done! To be obliged to these striplings is sheer poison. Fazlullah Khan[1] is a brother to me. I don't mind being under obligation to him. I've asked him a hundred times to do things for me, and I'll ask him a thousand times more. Anyway, what's done is done. But from now on you're not on any account to ask him [Fazl i Hasan] for anything, or to write for anything either. If you have to speak to someone about anything, speak to Fazl[ullah Khan].

'The Nawwab Sahib will be back from his tour either this evening or

[1] Cf. p. 324 above.

tomorrow. Preparations are in hand for celebrations that remind you of Jam-shed's[1] splendour.'

A letter to Tufta of November 28, 1865 praises the Nawwab's generosity:

'Kind friend, dear friend, poetic friend—I learnt from your letter that you had reached Sikandarabad and that my letter had reached you. May you live long and happily! I didn't come here to claim the due reward of my prose and verse; I came to beg. My daily bread comes not from my own pocket, but from the Nawwab's establishment. The date of my departure, my fate and my patron's magnanimity will determine. The Nawwab Sahib is in appearance a soul incarnate and in disposition the expression of God's mercy. He holds the keys of the treasury of bounty, dispensing without delay to each man the sum authorized in the statement he brought with him from the office of eternity. He has remitted well over a hundred thousand rupees a year of the tax on grain. One of his agents had an account of sixty thousand rupees to settle. The Nawwab cancelled this and made him a cash gift of twenty thousand. Munshi Newal Kishor's petition was presented; he listened to the gist of it and it is proposed to make a gift to him on the occasion of his daughter's wedding. I haven't been told how much. Mustafa Khan Sahib [Shefta] is coming . . . to take part in the celebrations, but he hasn't arrived yet .The celebrations begin on December 1st. I hear that a ceremonial robe [from the British authorities] will be presented on December 5th.'

Judging by its content, a letter to Hakim Ghulam Raza Khan dated only '1865' belongs to about this time:

'When I left you, I entrusted you to God's care and set out for Rampur. The weather was good. The hot season was over and the cold had not yet really begun to show its mettle. A moderate climate, with shade and running water everywhere. I had a comfortable journey to Rampur. The present Nawwab is his father's son, as they say—in courtesy and considerateness the equal of the late Nawwab, and in some of his qualities and ways even better.'

He goes on to mention briefly the two instances of his generosity which he had given to Tufta. Then he turns to another theme:

'Listen, my friend. I am a faqir of independent spirit, no worldling, and no deceiver. Flattery is not my way. I describe a man by the qualities I find in him. The Nawwab Sahib sends me a hundred rupees a month without obligation. *You* don't send me anything, so it is not that that persuades me to believe that if I had had a son of my own like you, he would have been my pride and joy and honour. Knowledge, intelligence, kindness, sincerity, rectitude, forbearance

---

[1] The great king of Persian legend.

—you have them all. The fear of God, sobriety, devoutness—you possess them all. All the moral excellencies of which the masters of the ethical sciences have written in their treatises are found in you. May God cherish you and grant you long life and wealth and prosperity beyond compute, and God willing, it will be just as I wish for you.'

The day after the Rampur celebrations ended, on December 6, 1865, he wrote to Alai to describe them:

'The celebrations here are of a magnificence which would have astonished Jamshed. There is a place called Aghapur about three miles outside the city. For eight to ten days there were tents pitched there. The day before yesterday the Commissioner of Bareilly, accompanied by a few other Britishers and their wives, arrived and occupied the tents. There must have been nearly a hundred people gathered there, and all were the state guests of Rampur. Yesterday, Tuesday December 5th, his illustrious highness journeyed there with great pomp. He reached there at two in the afternoon and returned at evening, clad in his ceremonial robe. Wazir Ali Khan, his Steward, threw money from the elephant's howdah as he passed along the route. Over the three miles it can't have been less than two thousand [rupees] that was distributed. Today the exalted sahibs [the British guests] are to be feasted. They will have their lunch and dinner here in Rampur. The illuminations and the firework display will be on a scale that will turn night into day. There will be hosts of dancing-girls and a great assemblage of British officials . . . Some say that the Commissioner and the other exalted sahibs will be leaving tomorrow, some say the day after. Now let me draw you a portrait of the Nawwab. In stature, complexion, appearance, and good qualities he is just like [your uncle] Ziya ud Din Khan. There is a difference in age, and some diversity of features and the style of beard. He is kind, considerate, mild, generous, courteous, religious and abstemious. He is a man of good poetic taste, and knows hundreds of couplets by heart. He does not himself write verse, but he writes [Persian] prose, and writes it well, in the style of Jalalae Tabatabai. He has such an open, pleasant face that the very sight of him banishes all sadness. He speaks so well that to listen to him speaking is to feel that a new soul has entered your body. God grant him eternal prosperity and increase his glory. When all these gatherings are over, I shall seek leave to depart, and when leave is given, shall return to Delhi. Give your father my regards—provided you are permitted to enter his presence and say what you have to say—and write and tell me such news as you have of how the children are faring. It's just before eight, on Wednesday 6th December, 1865. The writer's name is probably [in Urdu, ghalib] known to you.'

The reference to Alai's father shows that once again the relations between father and son were strained.

It would be at about this juncture that he wrote to Sajjad Mirza, the son of
his old friend Husain Mirza:

'Best of the sons of the Prophet, Sajjad Mirza Khan, the blessings of the faqir
Ghalib be upon you! I received your kind letter. . . . Your friend Baqir Mirza
[Baqir Ali Khan] kept crying, "A tahsildari! A tahsildari!"[1] When we got here
we discovered that there are only six tahsils and six police-headquarters in the
whole state. How could they produce a seventh? As for service as a courtier,
you can get this only if you are a Sunni, and if you are well-versed in the
standard branches of learning, and if you have a facile tongue—(and if your
luck favours you). In short, Baqir Ali Khan needed to fulfil three conditions.
The first, he does fulfil; but you, from the beginning to the end of time, can
never do so. [Sajjad Mirza was a Shia.] When the celebrations are over and I am
ready to leave, I will speak [to the Nawwab or his officials] about both the boys
[Baqir Ali Khan and Husain Ali Khan], and about Nāzir ji [Husain Mirza], and
you, and about Muhammad Mirza, son of Saif ud Daula, and Miyan Zaki ud
Din and Miyan Abdus Salam:

And let us see what is the will of God.'

This is the last letter to any member of this family we possess. Mihr writes
briefly of Husain Mirza's history from after the Mutiny as follows:

'When general amnesty was proclaimed he returned [from Lucknow] to Delhi,
but his properties had been confiscated. In those days, besides his relatives in
Lucknow, Nawwab Ziya ud Din Ahmad Khan . . . did everything for him that
the claims of friendship could demand, continuing to help him to the fullest
extent he could. I have heard that for a time he (Husain Mirza) held the post
of tahsildar in Bikaner. When Sir Salar Jang, the Prime Minister of Hyderabad,
came to Delhi, he met, among others, Husain Mirza. Salar Jang expressed his
great regret that they had not met before, and pressed him to come to Hyderabad. And he wished to go there, but in the meanwhile signs of insanity had
begun to appear—an outcome which could be expected, having regard to the
terrible experiences through which he had passed. He remained insane for the
rest of his life, dying on April 26th, 1890. Majruh wrote the chronogram of his
death.'

Ghalib writes again to Alai on December 22, 1865:

'Mirza, it's better to sit face to face than side by side. Come and sit down facing
me. At seven this morning Baqir Ali Khan and Husain Ali Khan, with fourteen

---

[1] The office of chief revenue officer of a tahsil, consisting usually of a small town and the villages
adjacent to it. Ghalib means that Baqir Ali Khan had hoped to be appointed a tahsildar in Rampur
State.

L*

cocks—six large and eight small—left for Delhi. Two of my servants went with them. One and a half—that is, Kallu and the boy Niyaz Ali—are here with me. When they left, the Nawwab presented each of them with a shawl. Mirza Naim Beg, son of Mirza Karim Beg, has been here for the last two weeks. He's staying with his sister. He says, "I'll come with you to Delhi, and go on to Loharu from there." As for my departure, God willing, I shall be off before the week is out.

'You've made a wrong move. You were writing a letter in Urdu on a single theme and suddenly switched into Persian—and that too the Persian of an office clerk. . . . Anyway, I won't produce the letter, but just convey its contents, and that will serve the purpose. . . .

'I've already written the date above. My name I've changed to Maghlub.' [Ghalib means 'vanquisher', maghlub, 'vanquished'.]

On December 26, 1865, he writes again: 'Your two nephews [i.e. Ghalib's 'grandsons'] left [today] for Delhi. I shall take the road . . . the day after tomorrow.'

He then makes a laconic comment in an adapted verse to the effect that where honour and kindness were concerned, they were shown to him in such degree that what was the peak for others was only the starting point for him—and that where wealth and money were concerned he came away empty-handed.

✼ Chapter 15 ✼

1866

From letters to various correspondents we can piece together the details of Ghalib's return journey from Rampur to Delhi. The journey was not a comfortable one, and before he had covered the first stage, from Rampur to Muradabad, he was in trouble. He describes some of his tribulations in a letter to the Nawwab of Rampur on January 10, 1866:

'I have reached Muradabad. The bridge collapsed after my palanquin had crossed it and the cart with the baggage—including the bedding—was left in the open [on the other side], along with the servants, in the freezing cold. They alone know what they went through there in the cold with nothing to eat. I went to stay in a small apartment at the inn, wrapped myself in a blanket, and, hungry and thirsty as I was, lay down to sleep. . . . I got up in the morning feeling worn out and in pain. Two angels sent by Sahibzada Mumtaz Ali Khan Bahadur appeared, and carried me off to Said ud Din Khan Sahib's house. Sahibzada Sahib treated me with an honour and a kindness, and Said ud Din Khan Sahib with a kindness and an honour, beyond my deserts. Then, unexpectedly, Maulvi Muhammad Hasan Khan Bahadur, the Sadr us Sudur, came and took me to his house. I stayed there five days. My friend Nawwab Mustafa Khan Bahadur [Shefta] came to see me there. The next day he took the road for Rampur, the city of delight, and I set out to measure the miles to Delhi, city of affliction, and reached the door of my house of sorrow on Monday 20th Shaban 1282, 8th January, 1866. And this too was only thanks to the assistance of Your Highness's auspicious influence; how else could one such as I have reached Delhi alive?'

Actually the Nawwab had already had news of Ghalib's misfortunes from Shefta after his arrival, and he at once (on January 5th) wrote to Ghalib at Muradabad, expressing his sympathy and concern, and suggesting that he return to Rampur where his illness could be properly treated. But by the time the letter reached Muradabad, Ghalib had already left. A further letter to the Nawwab dated January 21, 1866 again speaks of the difficulties and discomforts of the journey. He writes of

'. . . the cold, the rain, constipation, indisposition, loss of appetite, repeatedly having to go without food, and to stay in strange places, no sun all the way

to Hapur, a freezing wind blowing night and day and piercing you to the soul.
. . . Anyway, from Hapur the Great Sun at length appeared, and we travelled
in sunshine all the way to Delhi.'

Fragments from other letters speak of the last stage of the journey. He passed
the night of January 7th–8th at Ghaziabad, 'about 11 miles from the city
[Delhi]. It was there that I began to feel better. My constipation went, and
improved health brought a return of strength.' He left there on the morning
of the 8th, and 'at 11 o'clock [in the morning]', as he puts it in a letter of
January 10th, 1866 to Bekhabar, 'I descended like a sudden calamity upon my
home'. In another letter he says: 'I found my relations and friends alive and
well. Thanks be to God. I am quite fit now. During the journey I was ill and
in bad shape from start to finish. But the end of the journey was also, so to say,
the end of my troubles'. The tone of a letter of January 13, 1866 to Alai also
suggests that he was again in good form:

'When I was about to leave [for Rampur] your uncle [Ziya ud Din Ahmad
Khan] asked me to get him a pellet-bow, and when I got to Rampur I was able
to get one without any effort. . . . I put it aside. I told the boys, the servants and
everyone else that it was for Nawwab Ziya ud Din. A week before I left, you
asked for one. My friend, I can't tell you how I searched, but I couldn't get one
—not even though I was willing to pay up to ten rupees. I asked the Nawwab
Sahib [of Rampur] for one, but even he had not got one in his stores. Then I
heard of a noble who had one, and hastened to him. I found that he had the
bamboo for the bow—and what a bamboo!—as outstanding among its fellows
as men of our [fresh Turanian] stock among Najaf Khan's [degenerate] Tura-
nians. I had no time to get the whole thing made, for the next day I left Rampur.
Mind you treat this bamboo with proper respect, and have it prepared with
care. King Farrukhsiyar[1] and his brothers are in good spirits. Farrukhsiyar's
mother has given him some halwa sohan[2] . . . to eat.'

Letters of a week or so later, however, suggest that he had perhaps congratulated
himself on his recovery too soon. At all events, he ends his letter of January 21,
1866, to the Nawwab of Rampur: 'I was poorly and out of sorts for a week
[after my return] and am now the same feeble old man as I was before I left
[Delhi last October].' An undated letter to Bekhabar probably belongs to about
this time:

'I was ill, and on top of that there was the intense cold and the winter rains, with
all sunshine banished. The screens were let down, and the house darkened.

---

[1] A jocular reference to Alai's son Amir ud Din Ahmad Khan, nicknamed Farrukh Mirza.
'Farrukhsiyar' literally means 'of auspicious qualities.' It was the name of an eighteenth-century
Mughal Emperor, (1713-1719).
[2] A kind of sweetmeat.

Today the Great Sun has shown his face, and I am sitting in the sunshine
writing to you. But I do not know what to write. The grievous themes of your
letter have distressed my heart. [Then follows a reference to the recent death
of one of Bekhabar's relatives.] I knew that the late Khwaja Sahib was your
uncle, but I had not been fully aware of the close and loving relationship
between you which your letter now tells me of. How can one help feeling so
deeply the parting from one who loved you so well, especially when the parting
is for ever? May Exalted God pardon his sins and give you patience to bear
his loss.

'My good sir, I too am the lamp of early morning. On the 8th Rajab of this
year, I entered my seventy-first year. My strength has gone, my powers have
left me. Sickness overwhelms me . . .

'Today I would have had more to say to you, but my barber has come.
I have not had a trim for the past month. So I am putting this letter in its
wrapping and sending it off to the post while I have my trim.'

All the same, his letters soon show a return to his regular pursuits. He writes
to Sayyah on January 23, 1866, about some unexpected trouble over a large
parcel of books he wanted to send him:

'When I got back from Rampur I found three hundred copies of *Dirafsh i
Kawiani*[1] ready and waiting. I packed up a big bundle of my brother Nawwab
Mir Ghulam Baba Khan Sahib's . . . share of a hundred and fifty copies,[2] and
got it wrapped in canvas and sent off to the post-office. They refused to accept
it, and sent it back. The post-office officials have flatly refused to send it, and
contractors, pamphlet and packet despatchers, and the railway, all with one
accord state in identical words their refusal to despatch it. Get this note read
to his honour and write and tell me what instructions he gives about this. I want
this package to reach him somehow. The sooner you reply to this letter, the
more obliged to you I shall be.'

From a subsequent letter, of February 21, 1866, it appears that the Nawwab
must have given him the obvious advice—to re-pack the books in a number of
smaller parcels.

The same month he writes in an undated letter to Shākir:

'You will have heard that your humble servant got back [from Rampur] on
January 8th—tired out, broken, and ill. I have still not completely recovered.
It is early morning; there is no wind, and the sun is hot. I am sitting writing
these lines propped up against a pillow and with my back to the sun. . . .'

He goes on to defend the following verse of his against the objection of some
critic which Shākir had passed on to him:[3]

[1] The revised, second edition of *Qāte i Burhan*. See ch. 17 below.
[2] Cf. p. 308 above.   [3] Cf. p. 320 above.

My home lies plunged in the black night;
of raging grief
Only a burnt-out candle shows that day
has dawned.

About the same time he writes to Tufta, who had apparently been so upset
by some recent experience that he was contemplating abandoning the world
and becoming a faqir. Ghalib's reply plays on the conventional phrase for such
an action, which literally means 'unclothing oneself'.

'Why do you want to "unclothe yourself"? What have you got to wear anyway, that you should take it off and throw it away? You can abandon clothing,
but that won't release you from the bonds of existence, and you won't get by
without eating and drinking. Take hard times and good and trouble and ease
as they come. Let things come and go as they will:

Resolution alone will serve you, Ghalib;
Troubles press hard on you—and life
is dear.'

On March 1, 1866 he writes to Sayyah:

'I had been thinking for a long time, "Maulana Sayyah hasn't written to me"
when yesterday out of the blue your letter came. I'm answering it today.

'You need not be so apologetic about asking me to get the seal engraved.
I'm not going to do it myself, and what "trouble" and "inconvenience" is
there in getting it done? I like to serve my friends. Give my respects to Mir
Ghulam Baba Khan and send the stone and the design without more ado.
Your instructions shall be carried out and the seal attended to. So put your
mind at rest. What more can I say?

'And yes, Sayyah Sahib, my thoughts are always upon you. Keep on writing
from time to time. I have a feeling that if Mir Ghulam Baba Khan Sahib hadn't
wanted a seal engraved and hadn't spoken to you about it you'd never have
written me this letter. In other words you wrote it on Mir Ghulam Baba Khan's
instructions, and the idea was that I should address my reply to *him*. But then
I thought that you would be upset if I did, and so I wrote to you. My friend,
you have a way of forgetting me, and that is not good. Keep on writing now
and then.'

On March 22, 1866, he writes to Mir Ghulam Baba Khan:

'My nephew[1] Khwaja Badr ud Din Khan has produced *Bostan i Khayal* in
Urdu. I am sending you a notice about it with this letter, and two notices about
a new newspaper about to be published here. If you or any of your friends should

---

[1] The relationship was actually more remote.

wish to buy the book or the paper, they should follow the instructions in the notices. . . .'

On April 23, 1866, he writes indignantly to Sayyah. He had already objected in a letter of February 21st to Sayyah's sending him Rs. 5 to pay for books which Ghalib had expected him to accept as a gift: 'My friend, what are these five rupees' worth of stamps you've sent me? I'm not a bookseller or an agent. Your action offended me, and you shouldn't have done it.' He now returns to the same theme:

'Maulana Saif ul Haq [Sayyah], nowadays every letter you send has a note or a draft or stamps in it. I ask you, *you* tell me, what are these two and a half rupees for? What are they to pay for? That five rupees you sent me before upset me, and now these two and a half crown it all. Anyway, write and tell me about it. Why have you sent it? What is it for? I want an answer to this note quickly. I'll send off the hats after Id.'

On June 17, 1866 he again writes to Sayyah:

'Friend, my greetings to you. Your letter came, and I read both your ghazals and rejoiced. Flattery is not your humble servant's way, and if flattery be allowed to enter into matters where the craft of poetry is concerned, then a man's shagird cannot perfect himself. Remember, you've never yet sent me a ghazal in which I have not made corrections, especially of Urdu usage. These two ghazals are, in word and content, without blemish. No correction was called for anywhere. A hundred thousand praises upon you!'

He makes a similar reference to a guiding principle in an undated letter of about this time to Junun:

'I have examined your ghazals. Your humble servant makes it a rule that where he sees faults or defects in a man's verse he puts them right, and where he finds it free of fault he does not make changes. I swear to you, then, that these ghazals do not call for correction anywhere.'

The letter of June 17, 1866, to Sayyah continues:

'Mir Ghulam Baba Sahib really is just as you say he is. In your travels you must have seen ten thousand men pass before your gaze. And when out of this great legion you single out one for your praise, he must indeed be one in thousands. "That is beyond all doubt."[1] [From the next words it seems that either Sayyah or Mir Ghulam Baba Khan had expressed a wish to send Ghalib a gift and had wanted Ghalib to suggest one.] I don't know what I should ask for. What shall

[1] A quotation from the Quran.

I ask you to send? I'm very fond of mangoes—I like them as much as I like grapes. But how are they to get to me from Surat and Bombay? . . . You would be paying four rupees postage on one rupee's worth of mangoes; and then too it's quite likely that not more than ten in every hundred would get here. No, you really mustn't think of it. There are plenty of good *desi* mangoes of all kinds and varieties to be had here—select and fresh and delicious and fragrant. Plenty of *paiwandi* mangoes too. The Nawwab Sahib often sends me presents of mangoes from his orchards in Rampur. Just see! Today two baskets arrived from a friend at Bareilly—two baskets, each holding a hundred mangoes. Kallu my steward opened them in my presence. Out of two hundred mangoes only eighty-three were sound, and a hundred and seventeen were completely rotten.

'Early this month—June—we had rain for a week. Ever since then it's again been raining fire, and the hot wind is blowing.'

In addition to the pleasure of eating mangoes he also had the pleasure of a flying visit from Tufta about this time: 'Munshi Hargopal Tufta came here by rail, stayed one night, and took himself off the following morning.'

On August 9, 1866, he writes to Mir Ghulam Baba Khan, to whom a son had recently been born:

'Well, reverend sir, did you like the chronogram-name I wrote for your son or not? The name not only gives the date of birth, but brings in both "Sayyid" and "Khan"—Sayyid Mahābat Ali Khan. It would be surprising if you did not like it, and it is more surprising still that neither in your letter nor in that of Miyan Dad Khan [Sayyah] is there anything about it. I do not say that you are willy nilly to give him this name. But at any rate let your humble servant know whether you like it or not.'

A number of other letters which bear only the date '1866' or, in some cases, no date at all, may be taken here. One is to Hakim Ghulam Najaf Khan—the last to him which we possess: 'If you have been making a fool of me and calling me your ustad and your father by way of a joke, well and good. But if you sincerely respect and love me, then do what I ask you and forgive Hira Singh his transgression.' From what follows it appears that Hira Singh had been under Hakim Ghulam Najaf Khan's treatment, but had, without his knowledge, gone to consult other hakims instead. Ghalib continues:

'Be fair, my friend. If he went to Hakim Ahsanullah Khan, he went to a man who is your cousin and from whom you yourself have learned. And if in his anxiety he went to Hakim Mahmud Khan, well, you served your own apprentice-ship under his father, beginning your studies under his direction. In short, if the poor fellow consulted others besides you, it was precisely because of your connection with them that he did so—and that too in a state of anxiety, driven to it by his hysterical fears. Now when he comes to see you it is incumbent on you to be even more attentive to him than before and concentrate all your attention on giving him the treatment that his condition needs.'

Most of the other letters are to Bekhabar. Some make reference to the volume of Ghalib's Urdu letters which Bekhabar was preparing for publication at this time, though it did not ultimately appear until October, 1868. Most are concerned with the correction of verses and discussion of the points that arise from them. But mingled with them are other more personal themes. Thus he writes:

'I don't know what inauspicious star, to use the terms of the Indian astrologers, is casting its influence on me these days, that troubles come pressing in upon me from all sides. I met the Maulvi Sahib once, when he came to Delhi and stayed at Mir Khairati's house. When gentlemen are introduced to one another, this lays the basis for friendship and cordiality, all the more so when they embrace, and talk together, and recite poetry to one another. From the day I met him to the day he left for the Deccan nothing happened between us which could have caused him any displeasure. Since he is your friend and associate, and the bond of love between you and me is established beyond all doubt, you too can bear witness to this, for if—which God forbid—strained relations had arisen between him and me, you would at once have turned your attention to repairing them. Now let me tell you the position with regard to Munshi Habibullah [Zaka]. I have never seen him—or may my eyes burst. Three to four years ago I had a letter out of the blue from Hyderabad, enclosing two ghazals. The purport of the letter was that the writer was employed in the office of Mukhtar ul Mulk, and wished to become my shagird, and that I should kindly correct the two ghazals he enclosed. He is not the first case of this kind. There are many—from Bareilly and Lucknow and Calcutta and Bombay and Surat—who regularly send their Persian and Urdu prose and verse for me to correct; I perform that service for them, and they accept the corrections I make. I have an eye for merit and demerit in verse, and I can assess their quality and the talent for poetry which each of them possesses. As for their habits and ideas, since I do not meet them personally, what can I know of them? But let me come to the point. Munshi Habibullah Zaka's verses continued to come in and I continued to correct them and send them back to him. After the Maulvi Sahib reached Hyderabad, a ghazal of Zaka's arrived one day with a note that it was in the same metre and rhyme as one of Maulvi Ghulam Imam Shahid of Agra. I corrected and returned it as usual, and added a note that Maulana Shahid came not from Agra, but from Lucknow and Allahabad. That was all I said.[1] If that implies any insult, then I grant I insulted him! But I do not know what the Munshi Sahib [Zaka] may have said to the Maulvi Sahib, and what the Maulvi Sahib wrote to you.'

[1] Hardly true! Cf. p. 291 above.

In another letter he writes, apparently in reply to a request for a preface to the forthcoming volume of his letters: 'I have already told you before that I am confined to bed and cannot get up or sit up. I write my letters lying down. How can I write you a preface in this state?' And in the next letter:

'If an old servant who has obeyed your commands all his life fails to carry out an order in his old age, that is no crime. If the collection of my Urdu prose [letters] cannot be printed without a preface by me, then I opt not for impression but for suppression. Sadi—God's mercy be upon him—says

> It is the way of men with freedom in their gift
> To free their slaves when once old age
> has come to them

You come in that category. You are a "man with freedom in your gift". So why don't you act upon this verse?'

He goes on to quote a verse in 'Bengali Urdu' which, he says, 'I brought from Calcutta in 1829 for the amusement of my friends'. In another letter he writes:

'Your letter came yesterday, and I am replying today. First let me quote a sentence of yours, to make me laugh until I gasp for breath and the tears stream down my face: "I don't know how I've got so testy in my old age." Well, my friend, if you've inscribed your name among the aged, I must enter mine on the roll of the dead. I don't think you're more than fifty years old, or if you are, not by more than two or three years. My kinsman Ziya ud Din Khan and you are about the same age: he's a little under fifty, and you're a little over fifty. You each of you need another seventy years or a few less before you reach your natural span of a hundred and twenty.'

An undated letter to Tufta perhaps belongs to about this time. Ghalib seems to have been expecting money from somewhere, though he gives no details:

'Your second letter came the day before yesterday. What secrets have I from you? I'm expecting a windfall, and I've already settled in my own mind that you shall share in it. The time for it is quite near now. God willing, a letter from me with your share of the windfall will reach you very soon.

'Pandit Badri Das, a post office official at Karnal, used to send me his verses for correction when I was alive, although we had never actually met. After my death I sent word to him that from now on he should submit his verses to Munshi Hargopal Tufta. Now I'm writing to you too, to write and inform him of this. I'm still alive. What I've written above about being dead has reference to my giving up correcting people's verses. In other respects I'm alive. Not dead, and not even ill—only old, feeble, poverty-stricken, in debt, deaf, a prey to misfortune, sick of life and hoping for death.'

Two more very short, undated letters are the only others to Tufta which we possess. They form a fitting conclusion to the record of Ghalib's friendship for a man who could clearly be stupid, obstinate and insensitive, and yet who, equally clearly, sincerely loved Ghalib, and was loved by him in return. Both letters acknowledge odes which Tufta had written in Ghalib's praise. The first reads:

'I cannot praise your ode too highly. What ingenuity your verses show! But alas! it is untimely and misplaced. Your praise and the object of your praise are respectively like an apple-tree or a quince-tree that springs up on a rubbish-dump. May God preserve you! You bring your custom to a shop that is failing.'

The second is even shorter: 'I cannot find words to praise you. . . . A hundred thousand praises are the praiser's due: a hundred loathings are the due of him you praise.'

Thus, many of the letters of 1866 show a mental liveliness, a range of interest, and a capacity to react sensitively to all the varied experiences of life which persisted to the end of his days. But his health was declining, and with it—what grieved him no less than this—his capacity to be of service to his friends. Already perhaps at the end of March 1866—the letter is dated only '1866'— he had written to Bekhabar:

'I am counting the months of my seventh decade. I used to have recurrent bouts of colic; now it is with me all the time. . . . I eat less and less, and now my diet, if not non-existent, is something approaching it. . . . I also feel a strange burning in my liver, and though I take only a mouthful at a time, God knows how much water I drink from morning to the time I go to bed.'

On April 8, 1866, he writes to Maududi:

'Do you know the state I am in now? I am extremely weak and feeble. [My hands] have begun to tremble, my eyesight has got much worse, and my senses are not with me. I have done what I could to serve my friends, reading their pages of verse as I lie here and making corrections. But now my eyes cannot see properly and my hands cannot write properly. They say of Shah Sharaf Ali Bu Qalandar that when he reached advanced old age God exempted him from his religious duties and the Prophet excused him the prescribed observances. I expect of my friends that they will exempt me from the service of correcting their verses. The letters they write out of love for me I shall continue to answer to the best of my ability.'

Later letters show that this did not stop his friends from continuing to send verses for correction. Ghalib did not rebuke them, and to the extent that his health allowed, continued to perform this service for them.

On May 12, 1866, he writes to Zaka:

'My kind friend, my benefactor, who admire me although I am worthless and think good of me although I am bad, and who love me and whom I love, do you know anything of my state? I was weak, and now am half-dead. I was deaf, and now am going blind. The journey from Rampur has brought me trembling and failing sight. I cannot write four lines without my fingers crooking and stiffening, and the letters blurring in my sight. I have lived seventy-one years—too long. And now not years, not months, but only days of life remain.

'Your first letter reached me and told me you were ill. A second, with a ghazal, followed on its heels. I read the ghazal. All its couplets were good. . . . The state of my memory is such that I can't remember the metre and rhyme scheme it was written in. All I can remember is that I altered one word in one of the couplets. In short, I looked at the ghazal and sent it off to you, telling you at the same time to write soon with the good news that you were well again.

'Yesterday a registered letter came, like a comet descending. I wondered what it could be. At length I opened it, and found it empty of the good tidings that sickness was gone and health restored, and brimful of unwarranted complaint.

'My friend, a letter addressed to me may get stranded at the place of despatch, but once it reaches the Delhi post-office it is out of the question that it should not reach me. The post-office employees there have it in their power to send it or not to send it to the addressee. . . .

'Well, all I have to add is that you are to write soon to tell me that this letter has reached you and that you are well.'

By August increased financial worries add to the burdens he has to bear. On August 10, 1866 he writes to the Nawwab of Rampur:

'Today is Saturday, 10th August 1866. Your humble servant was watching and waiting for the postman to come bringing a kind letter from you with your draft enclosed. Unexpectedly, he brought instead a letter from my young friend Munshi Sil Chand,[1] asking me why I had not sent a receipt for my allowance for the month of June. After that there was a sentence saying that letters to accompany the July remittances were being prepared and that my own allowance would be sent after a day or two. I was completely puzzled. "Good God," I thought to myself, "I sent off the receipt for June as usual. Why am I being asked for it again?" Then the announcement that the July allowance would be despatched shortly was a virtual sentence of death to me. Good God! On the 10th it is promised, on the 13th or 14th it is despatched; by the 20th it will reach me. And my position is that my English pension goes to my wife, and towards paying off an instalment on my debts, and it is on Your Highness's

---

[1] One of the Nawwab's staff.

bounty that I and my servants and Husain Ali[1] live. My remaining debts amount to something like four hundred or four hundred and fifty rupees, and no one is willing to loan me money any more. In short, I have two submissions to make: first, that I have already sent the receipt for the allowance for June; if it was lost in the post, I could send another; secondly, no matter if this month's (July's) allowance does not reach me until August 20th, but for the future orders may please be given that your humble servant's allowance, which is no more than a gift of alms, be despatched on the 1st or 2nd of the month.

> May you live on and on till Judgement
> Day
> And every day your honour and wealth
> increase.'

On August 13, 1866, he wrote again:

'Let me first explain my situation to you, and then say what else I have to write. Distress and old age have combined to lay me low and rob me of my strength. I swear by Your Highness's feet that my faculties are not in order, nor can I think properly. For years together I have had such troubles to bear that I no longer have the strength to sustain them. God knows what happens and what I understand of it and what I ought to do and what I *do* do. Yesterday towards evening a letter arrived from Your Highness's chief clerk, bringing me the information that the receipt for my June allowance had not reached you. I was sitting there borne down and broken under the weight of debt and destitution. There and then I wrote you a letter, and although it was too late for the post, I sent it off. Today towards evening your [letter] . . . with the draft for the allowance for July came. I gave the draft to my agent and sat down to write this letter. I shall put it in an envelope and keep it by me, and send it to the post first thing in the morning. Should there be anything in the first letter which sounds like impertinence or madness or derangement, let your humble servant's offence be pardoned. And if any word of mine displeased your head clerk, I ask him too to overlook it. The letter with the receipt for the June allowance must have been lost in the post. Or it is not impossible that I myself may have forgotten to send it. Indeed, it is more than probable that I was guilty of this oversight. Please let the employees of your court be informed that I received the June allowance in July and the July allowance in August. I hope that for the future, the draft may be despatched on the second or third of the English month.'

The Nawwab's response was as Ghalib had hoped, if perhaps a little tardy. He wrote on August 25th that there was no need for Ghalib to send another receipt for the June allowance, and that orders had been issued that for the future his

---

[1] The elder boy, Baqir Ali, was by now, it seems, no longer a liability to Ghalib. He ultimately got employment in Alwar.

allowance should be despatched in time to reach him by the first or second of
the month.

About the same time he writes to Rizwan:

'Mirza, weakness is increasingly compelling me to give up the custom of writing
letters. I am not giving letter-writing up: letter-writing is giving *me* up. Don't
think of me as I was when you left me. The Rampur journey robbed me of all
my possessions—my strength and fortitude, my imaginative powers, my lively
disposition. If I don't reply to your letter, that is an occasion for pity, not for
complaint. Listen. Why do you worry if my letters don't come? While I live,
I live oppressed by grief and dejection, feeble and half-dead. When I die you
will hear the news of my death. Well then, until you hear that I have died, you
will know that Ghalib is still alive—broken and infirm, and in illness and pain.
I'm writing these few lines and sending them to your brother [Salik]. But he is
always off on his travels. If, to assume the impossible, he is at home, then
Inayatullah [Ghalib's servant] will hand this to him; and if not, he'll leave it
with Muhammad Mirza.'

He writes a little more cheerfully to Sayyah on September 5, 1866:

'Friend Saif ul Haq, I got your letter. You must forgive the Qazi Sahib. . . .
If I could have discovered any reason why he should be angry with me I would
have apologized and asked his forgiveness for my sin. But since there is no
apparent cause for his displeasure, what am I to do? You must not take offence
at it. Why? Because if I am bad, he has spoken the truth; and if I am good and
he has called me bad, then you should leave him to God.

> Ghalib, do not think ill of them when
> enemies abuse you.
> Does any man exist of whom all men
> speak only good?'

Sayyah had asked him to have his portrait done or his photograph taken. He
replies:

'Sir, at my advanced age what do I want with having my picture done? I am a
recluse. Where am I to find a man to take my photograph? Look, somewhere
there's a picture of me in the King's [Bahadur Shah's] court. If I can get it I'll
send it you.

Good heavens, I was just joking when I wrote that to the Nawwab Sahib. . . .
My friend, I'm deaf; I can't *hear* singing. I'm old; what would I want with
watching dancing? Six *mashas* [about 1/5th oz.] of flour suffice for my food;
what would I eat? There are English wines to be had in Bombay and Surat.
If I could have come to take part in the gathering I'd have had them to drink.'

On September 25, 1866, he writes to Maududi:

'Revered sir, the postman yesterday brought two letters together. One was your letter with a ghazal, and the other a letter from Nawwab Mir Ibrahim Ali Khan, also with a ghazal. Today there were three things of importance I had to tell you, so I am sending off this letter. The first point is, that I am sending back the paper with the ghazal on it. . . . There is a ghazal of Shahīdi in the same rhyme and a different end-rhyme, and it is such that these rhymes should on no account be employed again. You must write another ghazal and on no account include this one in your diwan.'

The second point is of relatively little interest.

'The third point is, when you send me a currency note, do not do what Calcutta people do and send half the note at a time. A letter addressed to me may get stranded at the post-office of the city it is sent from, but once it reaches the post-office in Delhi it is out of the question that it should be lost.'

On October 6, 1866, he writes to Maulvi Numan Ahmad. He had written to him previously on September 5th praising him highly for the skill with which he writes Persian prose in Ghalib's own style. Numan Ahmad must have replied in terms which suggested that he thought Ghalib was flattering him, and Ghalib now responds with some indignation:

'Your humble servant has many faults, and one of them is that he does not tell lies. Because I am a man of noble family that has had ties with the [British] authorities, I often have occasion to meet persons in authority and to have dealings with them from time to time. I have never flattered any of them. I ask you why should I lie to you, respected sir? Why should I flatter you? Nor am I a man so vulgar as to use the words "I swear by God" as a mere expletive. When I . . . swore to you on oath I meant it seriously, and now too I swear to you on oath that you excel other claimants to distinction in this distinctive style of prose. I thought of you as my fellow-artist, a man at one with me, and so laid the grief of my heart before you. And you felt no sympathy with my grief but on the contrary felt displeased with me. Well, this too is the perverseness of my fate that you, respected sir, took it into your head to understand the reverse of what I intended.

'For years I have given up writing letters in Persian. Now the only person I write to in Persian is Prince Bashir ud Din, the grandson of Tipu Sultan. . . . This too I do at his command, for he commands and I obey. I am seventy-two years old, and my faculties have deserted me, and my powers have failed me, and my sight is going and my hands tremble and absent-mindedness prevails. Well, then, your letter came, and I read it; then, deciding that I would answer it another time, I put it . . . aside. Today I sat down to reply, but I cannot find the letter; it is not in my box, nor among my books, nor on the shelf. I did not know what to do, but at length I decided to write the answers to whatever points I could remember.'

He goes on to explain various movements of the heavenly bodies and what they signify for kings and poets.

On October 18, 1866, he writes to Maududi:

'Honoured sir, slave of your noble ancestor[1] that I am, you will be the death of me with your numerous commands, your repeated consignments of verses, and on top of that your asking a hundred times over for confirmation of the receipt of the hundred rupees. Mir Ibrahim Ali Khan Sahib's ghazal, of which one verse was [here he quotes it] I have already corrected and returned—and you keep on pressing me to return it. Your ghazals descend on me in showers. How can I go on reading and correcting them? Other ghazals besides yours get lost. I'm a man of seventy-two, and perpetually ill. I have nothing whatever to eat; once in twenty-four hours I drink meat soup—no bread, no meat, no pulao, no rice. My sight is failing, my hands cannot grip properly, I tremble all the time, my memory is non-existent. If a paper gets lost, it stays lost.

'I have received Mir Alam Ali Khan Sahib's two ghazals, and have put them somewhere, and can't find them. To be brief, I got the [Rs. 100] note which Sayyid Sahib sent me with your letter. I got the money, and spent it as soon as I got it. One of his ghazals—the one of which I have quoted a verse above— I have corrected and sent off. I have no other ghazal of his now. As for Mir Alam Ali Khan Sahib's two ghazals, I remember them coming, and if I can find them I will correct them and return them. Your ghazals are past all counting. I'll look in my box, and search among my books. I want you and the two Sayyid Sahibs to make it a point to send one ghazal with each letter, and not to send another until you have had the first ghazal back with a reply to the letter. Then you can send another letter, with another ghazal enclosed. And each of you should write separately. Read this letter carefully, and get the two Sayyid Sahibs to do the same. I am taking the precaution of sending it unpaid.'

A similar letter to Wafa went off two days later, on October 20, 1866:

'If the feebleness of old age causes delay in serving you, I must be forgiven. If Great God wills, I shall never be found wanting. Of your two ghazals I have corrected one, which I send. The second will reach you within the coming week. Besides the weakness of my limbs and perpetual illness, my senses are deserting me. How can I explain? Two or three days ago I had a letter from my revered master Mir Alam Ali Khan. He writes that he has received two corrected ghazals of Azurda's. Just see what I have done—I have sent someone's ghazals to someone else. And the best of it is that now I cannot even remember what

[1] Ali.

Azurda's name is, and who he is, and where he lives. I have probably sent . . .
[Mir Alam Ali Khan's] ghazals to this good man. God grant that the gentleman,
like Mir Sahib, send Mir Sahib's ghazals to me, so that I can send them on to him.
If he does not, then I will look at the ghazals which have just arrived. These
are the blessings which the age of seventy-one brings a man. Please give my
respected master Mir Sahib this letter to read.'

On November 5, 1866, he writes to the Nawwab of Rampur, who is about to
go to Agra to attend the Governor-General's durbar:

'When I heard of Your Highness's intention to go to Agra I wanted to go there
too. But I could not face a journey by rail. I thought of travelling by stages [by
road, in a palanquin], but then I thought "It is seven stages [i.e. days' journey]
to Agra, and only six to Rampur. If I can go to Agra, why not to Rampur?" I had
fully made up my mind to send my son, your slave, and he too agreed with
alacrity to make the journey. Then all of a sudden he fell ill with a high fever,
and with pains in his shoulder besides. In a full month the fever has not left him,
nor is the pain in his shoulder any better. On Hakim Ahsanullah Khan's advice
he had been bled, but this too brought no relief. Some nights he sleeps a little.
Otherwise he is awake and moaning all night, and keeping everyone else awake
too.

> In that house where a man lies sick,
> there is no peace.

This is the general position. Mir Muhammad Zaki will lay the detailed picture
before you.

> May you live on another thousand years
> And every year have fifty thousand days.'

On November 14, 1866, he writes to Mir Ghulam Baba Khan, who had apparently invited him to Surat to take part in some celebrations:

'Your letter scattered flowers before me, bringing the scenes of spring before
my eyes. An impulse to take the train arose in me; but my legs cannot carry me
and my ears are deaf and my sight is failing and my mental powers are failing,
and my heart is failing, and my stomach is failing. And not only do all these
things fail me; my fortune fails me too. How can I contemplate the journey,
shut up for three or four days and nights together [in the train]? I have to go
to make water every half-hour. Every week or every fortnight I get a sudden
sharp attack of colic. No strength in my body, no spirit in my soul. My coming
to Surat is quite beyond the bounds of possibility. . . .
'My regards to Saif ul Haq Sahib [Sayyah]. A friend of mine who does
pictures has made a sketch of your humble servant and gone off to do a picture

of the [Governor-General's] durbar at Agra. When he comes back he will finish
the picture, and then it shall be sent to you.'

On November 15, 1866, he writes to Nawwab Amīn ud Dīn Ahmad Khan of
Loharu to condole with him on the death of his mother:

'My brother, until today I have been wondering what I should write to you
about [your mother's] death. On such occasions one writes of three things—to
express one's grief, to enjoin patience, and to pray for the forgiveness of the
dead person's sins. But, my brother, to express grief is a mere formality. It is
impossible that another should feel the same grief as you feel. To exhort you
to be patient is to show lack of sympathy. This is a heavy blow, a blow that
revives the grief you felt when the Nawwab Sahib [your father] died. How
should I exhort you to patience at a time like this? And as for prayers for
forgiveness, who am I? and what are my prayers? But since she was my patron
and benefactor, the prayers well up from my heart. Besides, I heard that you
are coming here, and so I did not write. Now that I hear you are not well and
so cannot come I have written these few lines. May Exalted God keep you
safe and well and happy.'

On November 18, 1866, he writes to Sayyah:

'I am ashamed to tell you that your letter with the ode reached me, and that I
put the ode in some book and forgot about it. Now your second letter has
reminded me of the ode. I have looked for it, but I can't find it. It's just as well
that I can remember this much, that I read all the verses right through at the
time and found all of them all right. Have no fear; present the ode and journey
safely to your birthplace. But, my friend, when you get there be sure to write
to me and tell me your address so that I can write to you there. . . .'

On December 4, 1866, he writes to Zaka:

'Life is a burden. On the eighth of this month—that is, of Rajab—I entered my
seventy-third year. My diet is the juice of seven almonds in the morning, mixed
with water sweetened with crystallized sugar, the thick broth of two pounds
of meat at midday, occasionally three fried kababs towards evening, and five
tolas[1] of home-made wine about two and a half hours after sunset, with an
equal amount of essence of. . . .[2]
    'The weakness of my sinews is such that I cannot get up, and if I use both
hands and raise myself on all fours, my calves tremble. I have to go to make
water ten to twelve times during the day and as many times during the night.

---

[1] About an ounce.
[2] The Urdu word in the original means 'milk' but this is clearly a mistake. Ghalib normally mixed
his wine with rose-water.

I have a chamber-pot kept by the bed. I get up, use it, and lie down again. Among the signs that some life remains is the fact that I do not sleep badly at nights. After I have made water, I quickly fall asleep again. My income is a hundred and sixty-two rupees, eight annas [a month] and my expenditure three hundred a month; so tell me, is life difficult or isn't it? Obviously, no man likes to die. So how can I find this death-in-life supportable?'

No wonder that two months earlier, on October 6, 1866, he had written appealing for financial help to the Nawwab of Rampur:

'I am afraid that my young friend Nawwab Mirza Khan[1] has not informed you . . . of my position. Your Highness can bestow wealth and property as much as he pleases on whomever he pleases. I ask from you only relief, and relief means only that I should be able to pay off my remaining debts and should not have any need to borrow again.'

It was some months before the Nawwab responded.

Meanwhile, however, there was one welcome development for which he felt he had the Nawwab to thank. On December 17th he had been summoned to a durbar held by the Lieutenant-Governor of the Punjab, and there, to his surprise, he had for the first time since the Mutiny been accorded the full honours that he had customarily received before it, receiving a robe of honour and other ceremonial gifts.[2] He writes to the Nawwab on December 18, 1866: 'I look upon this bounty as being in reality your gift, and now look forward to a further gift, namely, a prompt reply to this letter.'

[1] The young poet Dagh.
[2] This does not quite square with the earlier account of the restoration of court honours in March 1863. Ghalib now says that though his attendance at court had been restored then, this is the first time that the ceremonial robe was once more presented.

✿❀✿ Chapter 16 ✿❀✿

1867

Money matters again preoccupy him as 1867 opens. He writes on January 8, 1867, to the Nawwab of Rampur:

'My lord and guide, thanks to your charity my debts have now been paid, freeing my pension from deduction and myself from distress. Alike with heart and tongue I sing the praises of your bounty and generosity and pray that your wealth and prosperity may endure for ever. Half of my debt was cleared by your earlier gift, and half by the present one. Now I have to say something which I cannot say and yet cannot help saying. If an allowance of fifty rupees a month each for the two boys[1] be made with effect from January 1867, that is the present month of the present year, and sent month by month along with your humble servant's stipend, then your loyal retainer will never need to incur debt again.'

This request was not to be granted during his lifetime.

On January 11th he writes to Zaka:

'My dear, my very life, Maulvi Munshi Habibullah Khan [Zaka], a broken-spirited Ghalib sends you his greetings; and to the light of his eyes and delight of his heart Munshi Muhammad Miran [Zaka's son] he sends his blessing; and himself he congratulates on the good news that he has a worthy son [—i.e. he regards Zaka's son as his own]. His note to me was in handwriting exactly like yours. Tell me, did you write the letter on his behalf, or did he write it himself? Your boy didn't come with you to Hyderabad. Clearly you have sent for him from his home. Write and tell me all the details. Is he the only fruit of the tree of your desire, or has he any brothers and sisters too? Did he come to Hyderabad by himself, or did you send for your whole family? And yes, the name Muhammad Miran ought to mean that you are Sayyids. The reason I ask you so many questions is that I love you so much; it is not idle curiosity.

'Yusuf Ali Khan is a gentleman, and of a very good family. He used to receive a monthly allowance of thirty rupees from the king of Delhi, but the allowance disappeared when the [Mughal] Empire did. He is a poet—he writes in Urdu. He is a man who is always wanting something and impatient to

---

[1] This perhaps implies that the elder boy, Baqir Ali Khan, was again wholly dependent on Ghalib at this time.

get it. He thinks that everything he wants can be obtained with ease. He reads and writes well enough, but has no more learning than that. His father was my friend, and I look upon him as a son. To the extent that my resources permit, I have made him a monthly allowance, but he is a man with a large family and it does not meet his needs. You will just have to ignore his request and not reply. What else can you do? ...'

He writes to Zaka again on February 15, 1867:

'My brother, I do not know why I feel such faith in you and such love for you. Clearly it has to do with the world of the spirit, for evident causes do not enter into it. ... I am in my seventy-third year. ... My memory has gone so completely that one would think I never had one. My hearing had long been defective; now, like my memory, it is gone altogether. For the last month now my state has been such that when friends come to see me, all our conversation, beyond the formal polite enquiries after each other's health, is done by their writing down what they have to say. My diet is practically non-existent. In the morning, crystallized sugar, and the juice of peeled almonds; at midday, meat broth; towards evening four fried meat kababs; and before I sleep, five tolas[1] of wine mixed with an equal quantity of rosewater. I am old and useless, and a sinner and a profligate and a disgrace. Mir Taqi's verse describes me aptly:

> The whole world knows me, but my tale
> is done.
> In short, do not pursue me; I am gone.

Today I was feeling somewhat better. I had another letter to write, and when I opened my box, the first thing I saw was your letter lying there. I read it again and found that there were some points to which I had not replied.'

Zaka must have asked him to explain how he had come to receive his pension from the British, because Ghalib goes on to give the account of his ancestry and family background which we have quoted at length in Chapter 1, following it with a summary account of the honours he had been accustomed to receive at British durbars. He then turns abruptly to another theme. He has received an anonymous letter from Hyderabad in which the writer attempts to estrange him from Zaka. His response is characteristic:

'I am not a man who thinks perversely or whose understanding is at fault; my judgement is sound and not followed by misgivings. When I have once assessed a man, I never need to revise my assessment. I do not keep secrets from my friends. Someone has sent me an anonymous letter through the post from Hyderabad. He had not sealed it well, and in opening it one line got cut

---

[1] About an ounce.

off from the rest. But the purport is clear all the same. The sender's object was
to create bad feeling between us, to make me displeased with you; but by God's
power my love for you increased and so did my certainty of your heartfelt love
for me. I am enclosing the letter exactly as it is and sending it off to you. On
no account, if you recognize the writing, are you to quarrel with the man who
wrote it. I send it you so you will know that thanks to it, I am aware of your
advancement and increased salary.'

During the same month his Hindu friend Pyare Lal Ashob had published a
small selection of Ghalib's Persian letters, preceded by an Urdu translation of
what he had written about Persian grammar in *Panj Ahang*. Ghalib wrote a
short foreword which makes it clear that the book was prepared for presentation to 'Macleod Sahib, ruler of the land of the Panjab' [i.e. Lieutenant-Gover-
nor], and ends by remarking that

'Urdu was formerly compounded of Arabic, Persian, Hindi and Turkish—
these four languages. Now a fifth language, English, has entered into it. See
the capacity of Urdu! How sweetly this fifth language extends its influence
over it! It has assimilated these languages so well that none of them seems an
excrescence upon it.'

On March 13, 1867, he writes to the Nawwab of Rampur of his failing health:

'[My] condition now is past description. My old ailments have increased, and
three new ones—vertigo, trembling, and failing sight—have come to join
them. I cannot make my own pens; the boys have to make them for me. It is
no more a matter of years; only weeks or months of life remain to me.'

He writes again on April 14, 1867:

'I read in the paper the accounts of the . . . exhibition at Rampur and eat my
heart out because, alas, I am not there. I live on the upper storey and cannot
get down the stairs. And suppose my servants take me in their arms, carry me
downstairs and sit me in the palanquin; the palanquin-bearers are off, and I
survive the journey to Rampur. I reach there; the bearers take the palanquin to
the Benazir Garden and set it down. The palanquin is a cage, and I a captive
bird—and that too one that has lost its wings. I cannot walk. I cannot move
about. To suppose what I have just written is to suppose the impossible. These
things just cannot happen. So I am sending a chronogram [of the exhibition] in
three couplets. . . .'

On April 23, 1867, he writes to Sayyah:

'Two days ago I had a letter from you and one from Chote Sahib [Mir Ghulam

Baba Khan]. Your letter enclosed two notes for Rs. 50 each, and I drew Rs. 100. Today I write to inform you and to send my thanks to the Nawwab Sahib. . . . My friend, you must have seen reports of my condition in various newspapers. I am now completely unfit for anything. God forbid that I should tell a lie: my box is full of verses sent to me for correction from fifty different places. . . . Your own pages are among them. The day I feel a little better I will attend to them all.'

A few weeks later, on June 11, 1867, he again has to write to Sayyah to the same effect:

'My friend, you will get an idea of the state I am in from the fact that I can no longer write letters. I used to write them as I lay here, but now my hands tremble so much and my sight is so weak that I can't do even that. And when this is the state I am in, then tell me, sir, how can I correct verses? And that too in this weather, when the heat is enough to melt the brains in your head and the sunlight is so intense that you cannot bear to look at it. I sleep in the courtyard at night, and in the morning two servants take me up in their arms and bring me through the hall into a small, dark cell where they set me down. I lie all day in this gloomy corner, and then at evening the two servants again take me as usual to my bed in the courtyard. Your ghazals, Mir Ibrahim Ali Khan Baha-dur's ghazals, Mir Alam Ali Khan Bahadur's ghazals, Hakim Mir Ahmad Hasan Sahib's ghazals, and I don't know who else's ghazals are all laid aside in one place. If I live on a few days more and emerge safely from this heat I will attend to them all.

'The position about my portrait is that I have an artist friend who made a sketch of my face and took it away. That was three months ago. To this day he hasn't returned to sketch my body. I made up my mind to submit even to having my photograph taken. I have a friend who does this work. He came to see me at Id, and I asked him to take my likeness. He promised that he would come next day or the day after, and bring with him the things he needed to take it. . . . That was more than four months ago, and he still hasn't come to this day.

'I received Agha Ghulam Husain's short poem. A few couplets in it called for correction. But who was to do it? I was too involved in my own troubles. In the end a loyal shagird of mine, Munshi Hargopal Tufta, came by rail to see me. I pointed out the places where correction was needed, and he altered the verses exactly as I told him. I sent the corrected poem to [the paper] *Akmal ul Mutabe*. Next week you too will see it.'

From a letter dated June 16, 1867, to another correspondent, Prince Bashir ud Din, grandson of the famous Tipu Sultan, it seems that despite all difficulties he had in fact managed to have his photograph taken:

'Your kind letter came today, Tuesday, 16th June 1867, at twelve o'clock. I looked at the envelope and felt that I saw the white gleam of the dawning of my hopes. I was sitting with nothing on near a little grass screen.[1] When I read the letter, it put me in such a state that had I been dressed I would have torn my clothes, and had I not valued my life I would have dashed my brains out. How else should I support the grief I felt? I had a portrait of myself done, and sent it to you. I got . . . Shihab ud Din to address the envelope in English and sent it off unstamped. But I find no acknowledgement in your letter. It seems that the mail has been robbed and my lifeless form torn to pieces. . . .'

It was perhaps in the same month of June 1867[2] he wrote to Amīn ud Din Ahmad Khan—the last letter to him we possess. 'How can I describe what things are like here? In the words of Sadi—God's mercy be upon him—

> There is no water left except the lustre
> That gleams upon the unmatched pearl.

Night and day it rains fire or dust,[3] and one can neither see the sun by day nor the moon by night. Flames leap up from the earth and sparks fall from the sky. I wanted to describe something of the heat, but my reason said, "See here, foolish man! Your pen, like an English match, will burst into flames, and burn up the paper." My brother, the hot wind is a torment, and when from time to time it ceases, that is even harder to endure.

'Anyway, I turn my back now on the warmth of the weather to write of the warmth of a meeting with a youngster exiled from his own country. For that is a warmth which does not burn the soul, but lights up the heart. Two days ago Farrukh Mirza came. [Farrukh Mirza, son of Alai, and grandson of Amīn ud Din Khan.] His father was with him. I said to him, "Well, sir, how are we related? What relation am I to you and what are you to me?" He replied with joined hands [a mark of respect], "Sir, you are my grandfather and I your grandson." Then I asked him, "Has your allowance [from Loharu] come?" He replied, "Respected sir, my daddy's has come, but mine has not." I said, "You'll get it when you go back to Loharu." He replied, "Sir, I tell daddy every day that we should go back to Loharu; why leave Loharu, where he is lord and master, to mingle with the ordinary citizens of Delhi?"

'Glory to God! A mere tot of a boy,[4] and he has such good sense and sound disposition! It is for this beauty of behaviour and goodness of character that I call him Farrukhsiyar.[5] He is a companion beyond compare. Why don't you send for him? But, my brother, you follow in the path of the late Ghulam Husain

---

[1] Cf. p. 232, n. 3.   [2] The month is definite; the year is Mihr's conjecture.

[3] Delhi commonly has dust-storms in the hot season, sometimes so intense as to make the day quite dark.

[4] If Mihr's dating is correct, Farrukh Mirza would be six years old at this time.

[5] Cf. p. 332 above.

Khan, who never let Zain ul Abidin [Arif] and Haidar Hasan and their children draw near him.'

(Mihr explains, 'Ghulam Husain Khan Masrur was married to Ghalib's wife's sister, and was the father of Zain ul Abidin Khan Arif. He abandoned his wife . . . and children, and married another lady. . . .') Ghalib continues:

'A son of such wisdom and extensive learning as Ala ud Din Khan, and a grandson so understanding and who speaks so sweetly and wittily as Farrukh-siyar—these two are God's gift to you—one larger bounty and one smaller. . . . Today is June 22nd. The sun has already passed into Cancer. The summer solstice has passed, and the days grow shorter. Let your wrath and displeasure too diminish day by day.'

On July 3, 1867, he writes to Maududi:

'What you heard to the effect that Ghalib's health has improved slightly, is completely false. I was already feeble, and now I am half-dead. I cannot write letters. I have got one of the boys to write these few lines, taking them down at my dictation, poor fellow. You are a Sayyid and a man to be revered. Pray for me that I may not live past the end of my seventy-third year, and that if I am to live some days more, Exalted God may bestow on me a measure of health so that I may go on serving my friends.'

On August 25, 1867, he writes to Sayyah. He explains to him, as he had to others, why he could not write his own letters, and continues:

'I don't employ a clerk. If a friend or acquaintance calls, I get him to write the replies to letters. My friend, I have only a few more days to sojourn in this world. . . . I have had a detailed account of my condition printed in the news-papers, and asked to be excused answering letters and correcting verses. But no one has acted accordingly. Letters still come in from all sides demanding answers to previous letters and enclosing verses for correction; and I am put to shame. Old, crippled, completely deaf and half blind, I lie here day and night, a chamber-pot under the bed and a commode near it. I don't have occasion to use the commode more than once in every three or four days; and I need the chamber-pot . . . five or six times in every hour.

'The Indian portrait-artist friend I had has left Delhi. There is an Englishman who does portraits, but I haven't the strength to go downstairs from the roof and into the palanquin and to his house, and sit on a chair for an hour or two hours and get my portrait done and still get home alive. I was very sorry to hear how a son had been born to you and had died. My friend, I know exactly what such a loss means. In my seventy-one years I have had seven children,

M

both boys and girls, and none lived to be more than fifteen months. You are still young. May Exalted God give you patience, and another son in his place.'

An undated letter—the last of his letters to Qadr Bilgrami—perhaps belongs to this time:
'Sir, your humble servant has given up writing verse and given up correcting it. The sound of it he can no longer hear, and the sight of it he cannot bear. I am seventy-five [sic] years old. I began writing verse at fifteen, and babbled on for sixty years. My odes have gone unrewarded and my ghazals unpraised. As Anwari says:

> Alas! there is no patron who deserves
> my praise.
> Alas! there is no mistress who inspires
> my verse.

I look to all poets and to all my friends not to write my name in the roll of poets and never to ask my guidance in this art.

> Asadullah Khan, poetically named Ghalib, entitled Najm ud Daula [Star of the Realm]—God grant him His forgiveness.'

A little earlier, in a letter of August 19, 1867, to the Nawwab of Rampur, comes the first mention of a matter that was to bring him much distress in the months to come:

'That slave bought by your gold, Husain Ali Khan, is now engaged to be married, to a girl of his own family—that is, to the grand-daughter of the full-brother of the late Nawwab Ahmad Bakhsh Khan. The month of Rajab has been fixed for the marriage. And it is in your hands, in my old age and penury, to preserve my honour.

> Whom should I tell my need if not to you?
> For I must speak; there is no other way.
> May you live on another thousand years,
> And every year have fifty thousand days.'

It is noticeable that whereas in his letter of January 8, 1867 he had asked (without success) for an allowance to be made to both of his 'boys', he now speaks only of Husain Ali Khan. Perhaps it was at this time, therefore, that Baqir Ali Khan, the elder of the two brothers, had secured employment at the court of the Raja of Alwar. From a letter which Ghalib wrote to him later in the year, on November 16, 1867, we know that he had then been in Alwar for some time, and that his family was, at any rate at that time, not with him. Ghalib writes:

'It is a long time since your letter came, but you did not write your address.

You only wrote "Alwar". So how was I to reply? Now at last Shihab ud Din Khan has told me your address, and so I am writing to you. Jiniya Begam [Baqir Ali Khan's eldest daughter] is well, and often comes to see me. All is well at your home. I sent [your wife] your allowance for October. Mirza Husain Ali Khan presents his respects.'

On September 5, 1867, he writes again to the Nawwab of Rampur:

'I was honoured by the receipt of your kind letter. I found that it contained your command in connection with the marriage of Husain Ali Khan to submit in brief what it was I desired. I obey your command and submit. in brief, I am a beggar that sits in the dust at your palace door, and he is your slave. In more detail, I have neither cash, nor goods, nor possessions, nor property, and my wife has not a single, small item of gold or silver jewellery. None is prepared to give me an advance or a loan. I ask you to grant me money, so that this task may be accomplished and a poor old man not put to shame among his fellows.

'The second matter is, that I receive as alms from your court a hundred rupees a month, and as a pension (in lieu of an estate) from the British government sixty-two rupees, eight annas a month. He Who knows the unseen knows that I live with great difficulty on this income. How am I to support my boy's bride?[1] Let Husain Ali Khan be granted an allowance, but let it be issued not in his name, but in that of his wife, Husn Jahan Begam, daughter of Akbar Ali Khan. And let the receipt for it be sealed with her seal. The amount of the grant for the expenses of the wedding and the amount of the allowance must be left to my lord and master's magnanimity and to this wretched cripple's fortunes.'

The Nawwab replied in a somewhat pompous, half-Persian style on September 18, 1867:

'Since your kind self did not commit to writing the amount of the expenses of the marriage which he proposes, I therefore impel my pen to write in this missive of love, asking that first you inform me of the expenses of the marriage; when these are once ascertained, then an appropriate dispensation for this special occasion will be put into effect, because, as is demanded by our mutual affection and ancient amity, the writer keeps always in view that in matters that are fitting, he act for his kind friend's pleasure.'

Ghalib wrote again on September 23, 1867:

'I was honoured by the receipt of your kind letter. Great is God! Your Highness's sympathy and affection and graciousness to his humble servant have reached such heights that none before him save Sultan Sanjar among the kings of Persia and Shahjahan among the kings of Hindustan can have shown such

---

[1] When a young man is married he generally brings his bride home to live under his parents' roof.

care and solicitude for his servants. Baqir Ali Khan was married to a girl of Nawwab Ziya ud Din's family. He [Ziya ud Din] spent two thousand rupees on food and clothing [to celebrate the wedding] and my wife spent two thousand five hundred rupees, including five hundred in jewellery. The father of Husain Ali Khan's bride, Akbar Ali Khan, is a man of our family, but he is not rich; he is in employment. How can I bring myself to say what you should give? I am a beggar, and it is not customary for a beggar to name the sum he begs. I have stated the position about what was spent on the [earlier] marriage in our family. Two thousand or two thousand five hundred rupees would enable us to celebrate the wedding very well. But let me add at the same time that I have not served you well enough to feel that I have the right to ask so much. I will manage the wedding on whatever you see fit to give.'

A note entered by the Nawwab's chief clerk on the back of the envelope in which Ghalib's letter was received reads: 'Presented. No instructions for a reply yet issued. 28th September, 1867.' Nor does Ghalib again refer to the matter until December. But on December 29, 1867, he writes again:

'Today is Saturday, the first of the blessed month of Ramzan. . . . In the month of fasting kings and nobles distribute alms, and if the marriage of the orphan Husain Ali Khan can fall within this dispensation, and money be sent to this poor old cripple, then preparations can be put in hand this month and the marriage ceremony performed in the month of Shawwal. And since in this blessed month the doors of bounty are opened and the beginning of the English year also falls, the twenty-five rupees' monthly allowance of which you have made auspicious mention can be issued to the said Husain Ali Khan as from January 1868, and I would feel that I have won both worlds.'

❈ Chapter 17 ❈

The Last Years, 1868–69

If Ghalib hoped that the Nawwab of Rampur would enable him to enter 1868 feeling that he had 'won both worlds', the Nawwab, on the other hand, apparently did not feel any compulsion to put him in this happy position. Arshi notes that he replied to Ghalib's letter of December 29, 1867, on January 6, 1868, making no reference to Ghalib's request.

The year therefore opened on a gloomy note, and had Ghalib but known it, there was worse in store. In December 1867 he had brought an action for defamation against one Miyan Amīn ud Din of Patiala, and the outcome was a painful one. But this was the end result of developments which had begun some years previously, and must now be explained.

Hali writes:

'When Ghalib had completed *Dastambu* [in August 1858], in the loneliness and desolation that still prevailed what could he do but make his pen and ink-well his friend and companion, and forget his sorrows . . . by occupying himself in reading and writing? The only two books he had by him at the time were [the Persian dictionary] *Burhan i Qāte* and *Dasatir*. He took up *Burhan i Qāte* and began to glance through it. At first glance he noticed inconsistencies in it, and when he then began to read it more attentively, he found numbers of words which had been wrongly explained . . . and [numerous other] offences against the principles of lexicography. . . . He began to note down the points which were open to objection, and they gradually accumulated to make up a book, which he entitled *Qāte i Burhan*. This he printed and published in 1276 A H. Then, in 1277 A H,[1] he published a second, augmented . . . edition, to which he gave the name of *Dirafsh i Kawiani*.'

Hali then gives a number of examples of Ghalib's objections to the entries in *Burhan i Qāte*, and continues:

'At the time he wrote *Qāte i Burhan* he had no other dictionary . . . by him, and no other materials on which to base his researches into various words. He relied on his memory in all that he wrote, or on his good taste and intuition.

---

[1] These dates are not correct. *Qāte i Burhan* was published in March, 1862 (1278 A H) and *Dirafsh i Kawiani* in 1865 (1282 A H). *Qāte i Burhan* had been written in 1859, as Ghalib's letters show.

Despite this, except for a few places where he has indeed been guilty of lapses, all his charges appear to be sound. . . .

'The book was no sooner published than every Tom, Dick, and Harry girded up his loins to do battle with Ghalib, and against this one book a number of pamphlets . . . were written. The reason for this opposition is clear. Blind acceptance of tradition has become so essential a part of us—not only in religious matters, but in everything else—in every field, in every branch of learning, in every art—that it never occurs to a man that he should enquire into things for himself, nor does he think any one else fit to utter a word against what men of past generations have said. Any book written a century or two centuries ago is regarded as a work of divine revelation, which is to be accepted as such. So no matter how sound and reasonable Ghalib's objections to *Burhan i Qāte* might have been, it was out of the question that they should not arouse fierce opposition. Some think that this opposition arose mainly because Ghalib's mischievous sense of humour frequently leads him to make fun of the compiler of *Burhan i Qāte*, and because he occasionally gets angry and allows himself to use harsh words of him. But this view is not correct. Even if he had not written such words . . ., he still would certainly have aroused opposition, because Indian scholars of the old school, whom nobody pays the slightest attention to these days, no longer get the chance to emerge from their obscure holes and corners except when some eminent and distinguished man writes a book, and they can write a refutation, and so show the world that they too are men to reckon with. . . '

Hali's sarcastic words reflect Ghalib's own attitude in the matter, and whatever the rights and wrongs in specific points of the controversy, there is no doubt that Ghalib's essential position is sound. He asserts his own exceptional proficiency in Persian and claims that this gives him every right to dispute the dogmatic (and, not infrequently, ignorant) assertions of Indian lexicographers of Persian, whether of his own day or of the past, and not accept their findings unquestioningly simply because everyone else does. As we have seen, what he now asserted did not represent any new development. In the Calcutta controversy of nearly forty years earlier he had already made his standpoint clear, and his letters to his shagirds over the years had again and again restated the salient points.[1] Their reactions alone must have shown him that he would often be fighting a lone battle, but this did not deter him. In his letters to his friends he expresses himself bluntly and unequivocally. Thus he writes to Sarur in a letter dated only '1859':

'And let me impress this upon you: you will find that what I have to say about the construction of Persian words and the flights of meaning in Persian verse

---

[1] Cf. especially pp. 47 and 92 ff.

is usually at variance with what the general run of people say; and *I* am in the right.'

He knows that there will be few who share his stand. He writes to Majruh (July 1859) promising to lend him his own authentic text of *Qāte i Burhan*, but goes on,

'But let me tell you, you can be sure that those who read it won't understand it. They'll swear by *Burhan i Qāte* alone. Only a man who has a number of qualifications will take his stand with me. First he must be a man of learning; next, one who knows the art of lexicography; thirdly, a man well-versed in Persian—one who has a real love of the language and who has not only read a great deal of the great poets of the past, but who also knows some of their verse by heart; fourthly, he must be a fair-minded man, not pig-headed; and fifthly, he must be a man of sound taste and intellect, not one of crooked wit and perverse understanding. No man who lacks these five things will pay me the tribute due to my labour.'

He does not expect to find many such men in an age where universal, almost religious, veneration is accorded to the Indian scholars of Persian whom he attacks.

There are passages in his letters in which he explains in, for him, relatively measured terms what in his view is the weakness in their position and in the attitudes of those who support them. Thus he writes to Sarur, in another letter dated only '1859':

'Nizami[1] is now reduced to the state that until the khatri of Faridabad Dilwali Singh, known also by his pen-name Qatīl[2] . . . confirms it, his verse cannot serve as an authority. To Qatīl the works of the classical poets are a closed book. His knowledge of Persian derives from the speech of people who migrated to Lucknow from further west in the time of Sa'adat Ali Khan [ruler of Oudh, 1798-1814].'

Most of these, he continues, though Persian-speaking, were not Persians from Iran; and in any case, the language of speech is one thing and the literary language another—otherwise why would the great writers of Persian prose have sweated blood to write as they did? As for the attitude of their supporters towards them, he writes to Sarur in the letter first quoted:

'First I ask your honour: these gentlemen who write commentaries—are they all angels of God? Is all they write divinely inspired? The meanings they extract are based on conjecture. I do not say that in every case their conjecture is wrong. But neither can anyone say that their every pronouncement is correct.'

---

[1] The classical Persian poet.   [2] Cf. p. 47.

It grieves him that even his own friends and admirers are inclined to reject his opinion automatically if it goes against that of Qatīl or of the later Rampur lexicographer Ghayas ud Din; for even if, for the sake of argument, one accords them a fairly favourable estimate, they have no greater claim than he to be considered authorities. He feels so strongly on this point that he allows himself to speak with some sarcasm even to one whom he normally addresses with great respect. He writes to Sahib i Alam in an undated letter:

'I do not say that you must willy nilly accept what I write, but do not rate me below that son of a khatri [Qatīl] and this schoolmaster [Ghāyas ud Din] . . . Use your intelligence! Think! Abdul Wāse was not a prophet. Qatīl was not Brahma. Waqif was not a great saint. And I am not Yazid or Shimar.[1] If you accept this, well and good. If not, that's your concern.'

He laments that what he lacks is not their qualifications but their good fortune. He writes to Sarur in February, 1859: 'Where shall I get the good fortune of Qatīl of Lucknow and Ghayas ud Din, the mullah schoolmaster of Rampur, that a man like you should hold me in high regard and depend upon my word?'

Ghalib's argument that his judgement and learning are at least as worthy of respect as theirs, was one designed to make his friends pause to reconsider their position. It implies, merely for the sake of this argument, an estimate of Qatīl and others far more favourable than he personally was prepared to grant them. In letters where he gives his own estimate he leaves absolutely no room for ambiguity. He tells Tufta in a letter dated May 14, 1865, that in venerating men like Qatīl people are repeating the error of the children of Israel: 'By the power of enchantment the calf began to speak with a human voice, and the children of Israel worshipped it as God'—an apt hit when one remembers that Qatīl was originally a Hindu, and that to the Hindus the cow is sacred. Where he had told Sarur that of the conjectured meanings given by the lexicographers 'no one could say that their every pronouncement was correct', he tells Rahim Beg that they are 'rarely correct, and mostly incorrect'. He sums up his general view of Qatīl and Ghayas ud Din in the letter to Sahib i Alam already quoted: 'Pure Persian was ruined by that son of a khatri Qatīl . . ., and Ghayas ud Din finished the job.'

He is no less scathing about his own contemporaries. He writes to Shākir towards the end of 1865 about Rahim Beg, who had written a pamphlet against him:

'He is a Meerut man. For the last ten years he has been blind; he cannot read a book, he has to have it read to him; he cannot write, he has to dictate. In fact people from Meerut say that he is not a man of substantial learning, but has to be helped by others. Delhi people say that he never studied under Maulvi Imam Bakhsh Sahbai, but gives it out that he did so as to increase his standing.

[1] The men responsible for the death of Husain, the grandson of the Prophet.

What *I* say is, alas for the poor good-for-nothing who thinks that to have studied under Sahbai is a matter of pride and honour.'

In moments of indignation he can be much more virulent. He tells Tufta in a letter of October 4, 1861 that in his eyes dictionaries like Ghayas ud Din's are on a par with 'the rag a woman wears when she is menstruating', and choice insults like these are not confined to his private letters, for Ghalib replied to his critics in a series of pamphlets, and the controversy was a fierce one, conducted in terms which mid-twentieth-century man too easily forgets were the norm until quite recent times, even if today they seem lacking in decorum and decent restraint. Reasoned, if vehement, argument of the real points at issue formed a part of it, but the participants attacked one another along a much wider front, and name-calling and downright abuse were among the weapons employed on both sides. Ghalib does indeed at one point find an ingenious argument for asserting that, where his opponents are concerned, name-calling is not permissible. In a reply to one of his critics he writes:

'He has used all the choicest epithets of abuse to describe me, not stopping to think that even if Ghalib is no scholar and no poet, yet he has a certain standing as one of noble birth and noble degree, that he is a man to whom honour and distinction are shown, a man of distinguished family, a man known to the nobility and gentry and maharajas of India and numbered by the British government among the nobly-born, one on whom the King [Bahadur Shah] conferred the title of Star of the Realm, one who is addressed in official correspondence as "Khan Sahib, our most kind friend". Is he whom the Government addresses as Khan Sahib to be called "madman" and "ass"? In point of fact such abuse is an insult to the Government. . . .'

All the same Ghalib was not the man to wilt under vigorous attack, no matter how indecorous, and, in general, he cheerfully withstood such blows and repaid them in kind.

However, a stage was reached where one of his adversaries overstepped the mark. Miyan Amīn ud Din, of Patiala, published in 1866 a pamphlet against Ghalib which, Ikram writes, was 'full of obscene abuse and filthy insinuations'. Hali uses similar words of it, but adds that Ghalib's first reaction was to ignore it:

'Somebody pointed out to Ghalib that he had made no rejoinder. Ghalib replied, "If you are kicked by a donkey, do you kick it back?" ' But on further reflection he evidently decided that the terms in which Amīn ud Din had attacked him were intolerable, and he brought an action against him. Ikram describes what happened. 'The case came before the British Assistant Commissioner's court in December 1867. Appearing as witnesses for Ghalib were Lala Pyare Lal Ashob, Hakim Latif Husain, Maulvi Nasīr ud Din and Lala

M*

Hukm Chand, while on the other side were . . . Maulvi Ziya ud Din (Professor of Arabic at Delhi College), Maulvi Sadīd ud Din, and some other scholars. The whole point at issue was whether the sentences which Miyan Amīn ud Din had written about Ghalib in his book and the . . . insinuations he had employed, could properly be called obscene and abusive. Maulvi Ziya ud Din and the other witnesses for the defence, in order to save the accused, testified that these sentences bore meanings which made the charges against the accused impossible to sustain. When Ghalib saw that, thanks to these interpretations, it would be difficult for him to win his case, at the instance of a few of the noble-men of Delhi, he entered on March 23, 1868, a statement that he was satisfied, and withdrew his charge; but it is clear that the whole experience must have been deeply painful to him, not only because of Miyan Amīn ud Din's abusive words about him, but also because of the testimony of eminent gentlemen like Maulana Maulvi Ziya ud Din, who not only interpreted Miyan Amīn ud Din's filthy insinuations without the slightest regard for truth and justice, but in open court spoke of Ghalib as a 'chronic drunkard' and on these grounds contended that such . . . phrases as "the kalal¹ of Agra" could legitimately be used to describe him. . . .'

Hali writes in this connection: 'Some of these maulvis were on visiting terms with Ghalib. Somebody asked him why they had testified against him. Ghalib quoted a couplet of of his Persian verse in reply.' Hali then quotes it. The gist of it is 'I am a noble born and bred, and a man who acts nobly in this world finds himself abandoned by all his fellow-men.' Hali's account continues:

'When Ghalib brought his action some little time elapsed, and then people began to send him anonymous letters . . . cursing him for a wine-drinker and an irreligious man, and so on, and expressing the fiercest hatred and contempt and condemnation. They had a powerful effect on Ghalib. In those days he was all the time extremely depressed and dispirited, and whenever the postman came with the mail his whole expression would change, from apprehension that there would be some such letter in it. It so happened that in those days I had occasion to go to Delhi with the late Mustafa Khan [Shefta]. I did not know about these contemptible anonymous letters, and in my ignorance I one day committed a blunder the very thought of which always fills me with shame. Those were the days when I was drunk with religious self-satisfaction. I thought that in all God's creation only the Muslims, and of the seventy-three Muslim sects only the Sunnis, and of the Sunnis only the Hanafis, and of the Hanafis only those who performed absolutely meticulously the fasts and prayers and other out-ward observances, would be found worthy of salvation and forgiveness—as though the scope of God's mercy were more confined and restricted than Queen Victoria's empire, where men of every religion and creed live peacefully together. The greater the love and affection I felt for a man, the more strongly

¹ A low-class community of men who make and sell wine.

I desired that he should meet his end in the state in which alone, as I thought, he could attain salvation and forgiveness; and since the love and affection I felt for Ghalib were intense, I always lamented his fallen state, thinking, so to say, that in the garden of Rizwan [in Paradise] we should no more be together and that after death we should never see each other again. One day, throwing to the winds all regard for Ghalib's eminence and talent and advanced years, I began to read him a dry-as-dust lecture like an arid preacher. His deafness was by now complete, and one could only converse with him by writing what one had to say. So I wrote a long-winded lecture all about how the five prayers were obligatory and how he must perform them, and laid it before him. It requested him to start saying the five prayers regularly—standing, sitting, by token gestures, in any way at all he found possible; if he could not perform ablution with water before them, then he should use dust [to cleanse himself], but he should in no case fail to perform the prayers. Ghalib deeply resented this initiative on my part, and indeed, with every justification—and the more so because in those days anonymous letter-writers were attacking him in the most unseemly terms for his way of life, expressing their hatred and contempt for him in the sort of downright abuse one hears in the market-place. What Ghalib said in reply to my stupid note is worthy of attention. He said, "I have spent my life in sin and wrong-doing. I have never said a prayer or kept a fast or done any other good deed. Soon I shall breathe no more. Now if in my few remaining days I say my prayers—sitting, or by token gestures—how will that make up for a life-time of sin? I deserve that when I die my friends and kinsmen should blacken my face and tie a rope round my feet and exhibit me in all the streets and by-lanes and markets of Delhi, and then take me outside the city and leave me there for the dogs and kites and crows to eat—if they can bring themselves to eat such a thing. Though my sins are such that I deserve even worse than that, yet without doubt I believe in the oneness of God, and in the moments of quiet and solitude the words 'There is no god but God' and 'Nothing exists but God' and 'God alone works manifest in all things' are ever on my lips." It was perhaps on that same day when this exchange was over and Ghalib was taking his food, that the postman came with a letter . . . Ghalib concluded that it was another anonymous letter . . ., and handed it to me, telling me to open it and read it. When I looked at it I found that . . . it contained nothing but obscene abuse. He asked me, "Who is it from? And what does he say?" I hesitated to tell him, and he snatched it out of my hand saying, "Perhaps it is from one of your spiritual disciples." Then he read it from start to finish. At one point the writer had even abused Ghalib's mother. [Coarse abuse in Urdu concentrates its fire not directly on the man under attack but on the honour of his women-folk, accusing him (in less polite words) of incest with his mother or sister or daughter, according to his age, or accusing his wife of some similar immoral behaviour.] Ghalib smiled and said, "This idiot doesn't even know how to abuse a man. If your man is elderly or middle-aged you abuse his daughter. . . . If he's young, you abuse his wife . . . and if he's only a boy you abuse his mother. This pimp abuses the mother of a man of seventy-two. Who could be a bigger fool than that?" '

Hali goes on to relate how a three-way exchange of poems between Ghalib, Shefta and himself restored friendly relations.

Ghalib's letters of this period are understandably fewer in number than those of earlier years. Many of them show an awareness that death was not far off, but even in these an occasional flash shows that his old qualities did not desert him. He writes to Sayyah on January 25, 1868—the last letter to him which we possess:

'I was delighted to get your letter. Although the hats didn't fit you, they weren't wasted, for my benefactor and your patron [Mir Ghulam Baba Khan] was able to make use of them. I'll send you some more. I am absolutely fed up with the man who was to do my portrait—he promises and promises, but never keeps his promise. . . . Respected sir, who taught you this habit of slandering people? I haven't got any of your ghazals. Give my respects to the Nawwab Sahib and tell him that he is to regard the hats as a gift from me, not from Saif ul Haq [Sayyah].'

Two days later, on January 27, 1868, he writes his last letter to Zaka:

'I got your letter, and enjoyed reading it. You ask after me, but what am I to write? My fingers are not under my control. I have gone blind in one eye. When a friend visits me, I get him to write the replies to letters. People believe that when people give a funeral feast in honour of some dead relation, its smell reaches the soul of the dead man. In just the same way, I only smell my food. Once you could measure it in ounces; now it is measured in scruples. Once I counted my expectation of life in months; now I reckon it in days. My friend, I'm not exaggerating. My state is just as I describe it. "Verily we are for God, and verily to Him we shall return." '

Similar phrasing suggests that a letter to his elder 'grandson' Baqir Ali Khan perhaps belongs to this time:

'Your letter came, and my eyes saw the news of which my ears had already heard, that the matter of your employment was satisfactorily settled. I was very pleased. Put your mind at rest. God willing, you will soon gain advancement, just as the Maharaj [the Raja of Alwar] has assured you. As for your complaint that I don't write to you—my friend, my fingers are now useless, and my eyesight is failing too. I can't write even two lines. Letters come in from all sides and are laid aside until some friend comes to whom I can dictate the replies. Your letter came two days ago, and I had put it aside. Now Mirza Yusuf Ali Khan has come, and I have got him to write this letter. Your grandmother [Ghalib's wife] is well, and so is your brother [Husain Ali Khan]. All is well at [your] home. Your daughter is well. She comes to see me every second or third day— sometimes every day.'

On April 6, 1868, he writes his last letter to his and Sayyah's patron, Mir Ghulam Baba Khan:

'I received your kind letter. You tell me to write and tell you how I am from time to time. Well, formerly I had enough strength left to write a few lines as I lay here, but now even that strength has left me. I cannot afford to employ a scribe. If some relative or friend comes to see me opportunely, then I tell them what I want written and they write it before they leave. It is a fortunate accident that your letter came yesterday, and today a friend of mine has come to see me and I am getting him to write these lines. And please never say that my love for Munshi Miyan Dad Khan [Sayyah] has ceased. My love for him— and through him for you—has so entered my heart and soul that it is as much a part of me as a Muslim's faith is a part of him. It is impossible that such love should ever cease.

'And now I have spoken of my bodily ills and explained the love that subsists between us, what am I to say of the hidden sorrows of my heart? They hang over me like a black cloud or a swarm of approaching locusts. God is all, there is nought but God. Please give my regards to Saif ul Haq Munshi Miyan Dad Khan [Sayyah] and give him this letter to read.'

On June 21, 1868, he writes to provide Alai with written proof that he has designated him as his successor, entitled to guide others in matters of literature as Ghalib himself had done before him:

'I have given you a statement in writing—you will remember in what year I wrote it—designating you my successor, my caliph, where Persian is concerned. Now I am only four[1] years short of eighty, and I estimate that the span of life left to me is not to be measured in years, and perhaps not even in months. I may perhaps live another twelve months, that is a year; but it may be a matter of two to three months, six to seven weeks, ten to twenty days. Now being in my right mind, I give it you in writing in my own hand over my own seal that in the craft of Urdu verse and prose you are my successor. Those who acknowledge me are to acknowledge you as they did me, and accept your authority as they accepted mine.'

Meanwhile his financial problems had been growing more pressing, causing him more and more anxiety. As early as March 9, 1868, he had written again to the Nawwab of Rampur about Husain Ali Khan:

---

[1] Mihr regards this as a miscopying for 'seven'.

'I render you due thanks for my allowance for February 1868. Glory be to God! What miraculous increase this Rs. 100 holds! It feeds a hundred mouths and meets a hundred other of your humble servant's needs.

'Mirza Husain Ali Khan's wedding had been fixed for the month of Rajab. But because Your Highness's bounty did not come, it had to be postponed. Today is the 15th Zi Qad. Thus fifteen days of this month remain and the whole month of Zil Hij. If in this very month of Zi Qad Your Highness be pleased to bestow your bounty, the wedding can be arranged before Zil Hij is over. God grant that my lord and master may bear in mind too that when Ghalib brings the bride to his house, he must needs have the means to feed her. By which I mean that payment of Husain Ali Khan's allowance should commence. Your Highness, I have no one who can present my requests to you from time to time, and I am ashamed to write again and again like this.'

He must have felt as time went on that he must have someone in Rampur to speak for him if he was to get his requests granted. From a letter to the Nawwab dated July 27, 1868, it is clear that he chose the young Nawwab Mirza Khan [Dagh] for this role,[1] while one of August 13, 1868 indicates that he also approached one Muzaffar Husain Khan. In the first of the two letters he writes:

'It is being said in Delhi today that your highness has sent Rs. 500 from Rampur to the widow of the late Mufti Sadr ud Din [Azurda] for his funeral expenses. This leads me, your humble servant, to think that when I die my corpse too shall not want for a shroud and a grave. As Jalal Asīr says:

> I still shall drink your bounty's
> draughts when I am gone.

I have yesterday sent off a letter to Nawwab Mirza Khan [Dagh]. God knows whether he will show it to Your Highness or not. In it I gave details of the position of Mufti Ji's [Azurda's] widow, saying that she was childless and draws Rs. 60 [a month] in rent from house-property. Amīn ur Rahman is her sister's son, not related to the Mufti Ji.

'Now I submit my own position to you. In my last years I have three requests to make of you. First, I have debts of ten to twelve hundred rupees, and I wish them to be paid before I die. My second request is this, that a special grant of your bounty enable me to go through with the marriage of Husain Ali Khan. And the third is that the hundred rupees' allowance which I receive be granted to him for the duration of his life. These two (that is, the last two) wishes may be granted either during my life-time or after my death.'

The second letter (August 13, 1868) indicates that letters from his two intermediaries had assured him that his 'three requests' had been accepted:

---

[1] As he had done once before. Cf. p. 347 above.

'If Merciful God wills, then, in accordance with Your Highness's commands, by the coming of winter—that is, in November or December of the present year of '68, my debts will be cleared and Husain Ali Khan's marriage too will take place.'

In fact, as we shall see, either his intermediaries had misled Ghalib, or the Nawwab had misled them.

On September 7, 1868, Ghalib feels obliged to write again:

'My lord and master, the parents of Husain Ali Khan's betrothed bride are pressing me hard, and life is a misery to me. My brief request is this, that just to win favour in God's sight, Your Highness bestow on me whatever you think fit, and in addition fix an allowance for Husain Ali Khan. But let both these things be done quickly.'

At last, on November 17, 1868, he writes in desperation:

'My affairs have gone from bad to worse, until now they have reached such a pass that I have only Rs. 54 of the hundred rupees left. . . .Altogether I need Rs. 800 to save my honour. Willy nilly, I have given up all thought of Husain Ali Khan's wedding and allowance. I will never mention it to you again, I promise you. Just give me another Rs. 800. How can I think of the marriage? If my honour is saved, it is enough to be thankful for. I have sent a letter to my young friend Nawwab Mirza Khan [Dagh] giving him full details, and he will acquaint you with them. In brief, my life and my honour are in your hands; but let what you grant me be sent quickly.'

To die in debt was a terrible disgrace to a Muslim of noble family, but more than a month later the Nawwab had still sent nothing, though he had apparently promised Dagh that he would do so. Meanwhile Ghalib had made a move to win the sympathy of the Raja of Alwar. His elder 'grandson' Baqir Ali Khan, was at the Alwar Court, and Ghalib wrote to him on December 7, 1868:

'Your letter in answer to mine reached me, but there was nothing in it that called for a reply. I write now to tell you of a new development, namely that last month I had a copy of *Sabad i Chin* [a volume of Ghalib's Persian poems written after the publication of his collected Persian verse], along with a petition, sent to Alwar through . . . Mir Tafazzul Husain Khan. Accordingly, this week I received through him a letter from . . . His Highness . . . the Raja, in which he . . . has addressed me with titles of great honour and written many kind and gracious things about me. You are on the spot. Did you know of this, or not? And if you did, why didn't you write to me? Now I want to ask you whether anyone ever speaks of me in the durbar or not, and if they do, in what forms; and when I am mentioned, what does His Highness say?'

Whether this produced any worth-while result, we do not know. To the
Nawwab of Rampur he wrote again on December 17, 1868:

'Many days have passed since my young friend Nawwab Mirza Khan [Dagh]
wrote to congratulate me upon the good news that Your Highness had agreed
to meet my debts and had asked their amount. I sent word to him that Rs. 800
would meet them all. I write now simply to remind you.'

Arshi notes that the back of the envelope bears a note: 'Presented; no orders
issued.' On January 10, 1869, he wrote his last letter to the Nawwab: 'Your
highness, my creditors have reduced me to desperation. All I can do is to
remind you; beyond that, it is for Your Highness to decide.' Even then it seems
that the Nawwab issued no instructions. The next letter to Ghalib was simply
the regular monthly remittance of Rs. 100. It arrived an hour before Ghalib
died. Thus he died with his debts unpaid, and knowing that no provision had
been made for his wife[1] or for Husain Ali Khan, much less for Husain Ali
Khan's marriage. Husain Ali Khan acknowledged the receipt of the last hundred
rupees with dignity:

'On the 15th February of this year, 1869, corresponding to the 2nd of Zi Qad,
on Monday at the time of the afternoon prayer, my revered and honoured
grandfather, Nawwab Asadullah Khan Ghalib, known as Mirza Nosha Sahib,
departed from this transient world. Your loyal servant cannot express the grief
and sorrow into which this heart-rending loss has plunged him. And my
honoured and respected grandmother has in her old age been reduced by grief
to a state which no words can describe. Your Highness's kind letter, with a
draft for a hundred rupees on account of the allowance for January, '69 brought
honour to our house one hour before my grandfather's death. I submit a
receipt for the draft for Your Highness's information.'

Hali has described his last days:

'A few days before his death he became unconscious. He would remain unconscious for hours at a time, coming to for only a few minutes before relapsing
again. It was perhaps the day before he died that I went to visit him. He had
come to after being unconscious many hours, and was dictating a reply to a
letter from . . . Nawwab Ala ud Din Ahmad Khan [Alai], who had written
from Loharu asking how he was. He replied with a sentence of his own and a
Persian couplet, probably of Sadi's. The sentence was: "Why ask me how I am?
Wait a day or two and then ask my neighbours." And the second line of the
couplet—I cannot remember the first line—was:

[1] Mihr notes: 'The Nawwab . . . granted [Azurda's] widow an allowance of Rs. 200 a month
while to Ghalib's widow he granted nothing.'

> You could not come to see me. Well, God
> keep you!

Before he died he often used to recite the verse:

> My dying breath is ready to depart,
> And now, my friends, God, only God, exists.

At last, on the 2nd of Zi Qad, 1285 and the 15th of February, 1869, at the age of seventy-three years and four months, he departed this world and was buried at the foot of his father-in-law's tomb in the precincts of the shrine of Hazrat Sultan Nizam ud Din. . . . I was present at the funeral, when the funeral prayer was said outside Delhi Gate. Most of the nobles and eminent men of Delhi were there—such as Nawwab Ziya ud Din Ahmad Khan, Nawwab Muhammad Mustafa Khan [Shefta], Hakim Ahsanullah Khan and others. Large numbers of people, both Sunnis and Shias, were present to take part in the funeral procession. Sayyid Safdar Sultan . . . approached . . . Nawwab Ziya ud Din Ahmad Khan and said, "Mirza Sahib [Ghalib] was a Shia. If you permit us we will conduct his funeral in our own style." But the Nawwab Sahib would not agree, and all rites were conducted in accordance with Sunni ritual. No doubt, none was in a better position than the Nawwab Sahib to know exactly what Ghalib's religious beliefs really were, but in my view it would have been better if Shias and Sunnis had both said the funeral prayer—either together or separately—and as Ghalib had during his life-time treated Sunnis and Shias alike, so after his death too both alike should have paid their last tribute to him.'

Hali says that

'. . . chronograms of his death without number continued for a long time to appear in the Urdu newspapers, . . . and elegies on his death were written, in Urdu by Mirza Qurban Ali Beg Salik, Mir Mahdi Husain Majruh and the writer of the present book, and in Persian by Munshi Hargopal Tufta.'

NOTE ON THE LETTERS AND SOME OF GHALIB'S CORRESPONDENTS

Ghalib prided himself on the number of friends he had, and the surviving published letters testify that he had good grounds for his pride. But numerous as the letters are, it is important to realize that we cannot hope to derive from them more than an incomplete and partial picture. Many more letters than we now possess must have been written (and indeed it is not at all improbable that diligent search could yet bring substantial numbers to light). There are obvious gaps in the extant collections, and some of the letters now lost would almost certainly have shed significant light on Ghalib's character and personality. It is almost inconceivable, for instance, that he should not have written many letters to Shefta, the one man who stood by him in his imprisonment of 1847; yet in the whole collection of Urdu letters there is only one addressed to him. Only two Urdu letters to Salik are extant, but their frank and intimate tone argues that there must have been others, and that they would often have been equally revealing. It must also not be forgotten that after Muslims were ultimately permitted once more to take up permanent residence in Delhi in November 1859, a number of friends and acquaintances with whom Ghalib would otherwise have corresponded were now living within visiting distance, and there was no occasion to write letters to them. Finally, we have altogether too little information about most of those to whom he wrote. More adequate attention to the extent and nature of Ghalib's relationship with each of them would have contributed to a more meaningful picture than can be derived from the letters alone. Such information as we have does not generally amount to much.

In the brief notes that follow we have done no more than select a few names of men who between them illustrate something of the varied quality of Ghalib's acquaintance, or about whom there is something else of significance to be said. We have not included any of whom an adequate, connected account occurs in the text of the book—e.g. of Husain Mirza and his kinsmen, whose story is given on pp. 206–208 or of Zaka (cf. p. 290); nor have we, in general, repeated here information given in the text; nor, finally, have we listed names of men about whom available information is so scanty as to be hardly worth while giving. It is unfortunate that this last category includes some—e.g. Majruh—about whom the absence of more information is much to be regretted. Our sources are primarily Mihr's notes in *Khutut i Ghalib* and Mālik Ram's book *Talamiẓa i Ghalib*.

The Loharu family. The members of the family with whom, up to 1857 at any rate, Ghalib had the closest contacts were his wife's cousins Amīn ud Din Ahmad Khan and Ziya ud Din Ahmad Khan; but he himself states that there was a long history of friendly relationships between his family and theirs, and Mihr thinks that Ghalib's grandfather probably migrated to India in the company of their great-uncle Qasim Jan, and was perhaps related to him. In

Ghalib's youth he and Amīn ud Din were clearly good friends, while Ziya ud Din, a scholar and a poet of both Persian and Urdu, had a high regard for Ghalib as a poet and man of letters and was one of those who preserved everything that Ghalib wrote until his library was destroyed by British troops at the re-taking of Delhi in 1857. Ghalib's imprisonment in 1847 and their coolness towards him at this difficult time must have put a strain upon their relationship which was never fully eased, and the few extant letters to Amīn ud Din betray a rather uneasy informality. Ziya ud Din was normally resident in Delhi, and the detailed positive evidence which letters might have given are therefore lacking in his case.

The member of the family to whom Ghalib seems to have felt closest was *Alai*, the son of Amīn ud Din, and a man nearly forty years his junior. Nearly sixty letters to him are extant. Alai is a takhallus. The name was Ala ud Din Ahmad Khan. He seems to have been one of temperament and habits very similar to Ghalib's own, and Ghalib was perhaps the more attached to him because he had had a hand in his education as a child. Alai knew Persian, Turkish and Arabic well, and wrote verse in both Urdu and Persian, but mainly in the latter; and being a man of means, he made literary activities his full-time occupation. Ghalib in his declining years formally certified that he had bestowed his literary mantle upon him, and that Alai should be recognized as literary mentor by all who would have so recognized Ghalib himself. He established a press in Loharu for the publication of works of literature and scholarship, and at one time produced a fortnightly newspaper. He was a keen chess-player, and was secretary of a Chess Society which was founded in Delhi in 1866 on the initiative of a British clergyman, and which included both British and Indian members. When he was thirty-six years old (i.e. in 1869, the year of Ghalib's death) his father handed over the management of the Loharu estates to him, but his extravagance and his indifference to administration brought things to such a pass that not long before his death in 1884 the British authorities intervened, retired him on a pension of 18,000 rupees a year, and installed his eldest son in his place.

Tufta (strictly speaking, Tafta; but we give the name in the current Urdu pronunciation). The takhallus of Ghalib's life-long friend and shagird Munshi Hargopal. He was two or three years younger than Ghalib and belonged to the Hindu Kayasth caste. Among the Kayasths Persian scholarship and culture were traditional, so much so that they could fairly be described as culturally assimilated to the Muslims. Tufta lived in Sikandarabad, a sizeable country town some 40 to 45 miles north of Delhi. His income from landed property and from a hereditary minor administrative post (which, however, he later resigned) was adequate to sustain him, and he devoted himself wholly to writing Persian poetry. He survived Ghalib by just over ten years, dying in September 1879.

Mihr. The takhallus of Hatim Ali Beg. He was descended from a Persian ancestor who came to India with the invader Nadir Shah in 1739 and settled there. His grandfather had been a companion and counsellor of Shuja ud Daula, ruler of Oudh, and Mihr was born in Lucknow, the capital of Oudh, in 1815. As a poet of Urdu he was a shagird of Ghalib's friend, the famous Lucknow poet Nasikh. Unlike many of Ghalib's friends, Mihr gained from the British victory of 1857, for he had actively assisted the British during the revolt and was now well rewarded. After 1857 he moved to Agra. He died in 1879.

Sayyah. The takhallus of Miyan Dad Khan, a man of noble family from Aurangabad, in the Deccan. The family was reduced to poverty in his early youth, but he seems to have lived an extravagant and carefree life whenever he could. It is said that he always got his clothes from Delhi and that he had a passion for perfumes. He was fond of poetry, competent both in Urdu and in Persian, and a good painter and calligrapher. In 1862, having made his way to Bombay, and thence to Surat, he became the courtier-companion of the Surat nobleman Nawwab Mir Ghulam Baba Khan; but he was a great traveller, as is clear from Ghalib's letters to him, and this was why Ghalib gave him the takhallus of Sayyah, which means 'traveller'. In 1878 he was convicted of counterfeiting money and was sentenced to fourteen years imprisonment, but he did not serve the full sentence. His patron Nawwab Mir Ghulam Baba Khan seems to have cared for him well until his death in 1893, but for the next ten to twelve years he experienced great hardship until, shortly before his death, he found someone else to provide for him. He died in 1907.

Sarur. The takhallus of Chaudri Abdul Ghafur, of Marahra, in U.P. Little is known of him. He was the first to compile a collection of Ghalib's letters, completing the work in 1862. But Bekhabar (see below) then undertook a more comprehensive collection, and Ghalib's letters to Sarur now stand as the first part of the collection *Ud i Hindi*. Sarur was a close associate of his fellow-townsman Sahib i Alam, who is one of the few men addressed, or spoken of, with great deference in Ghalib's letters, partly, no doubt, because he was Ghalib's senior (though only by a year), and partly because he was the direct descendant of a much-revered religious figure in Marahra.

Bekhabar. The takhallus of Khwaja Ghulam Ghaus Khan. He came of a Kashmiri family which had migrated first to Lhasa, and then to Nepal, (where Bekhabar was born in 1824) and had finally settled in India at Benares. His uncle became Mir Munshi (Chief Clerk) to the British Lieutenant-Governor of the N.W. Provinces, and Bekhabar accompanied him to Agra, the provincial capital. He ultimately succeeded to his uncle's post, which he held until 1885, when he retired to Allahabad. He died in 1904. Like Ghalib, he had a wide circle of friends, Muslim, Hindu, and British. One of his closest friends was Hatim Ali Beg Mihr (see above). It was Bekhabar who, with Ghalib's help and encouragment, prepared the first published collection of Ghalib's letters, *Ud i Hindi*, which came out four months before Ghalib's death.

BIBLIOGRAPHY

We have used the following books in preparing this volume. (The abbreviations used in the notes and references are shown in brackets after each title.)

A. WORKS OF GHALIB

Kulliyāt i Naṣr i Ghālib, Newal Kishor, Kanpur, 1875. (Nasr i Farsi)

Khutūt i Ghālib, ed. Ghulām Rasūl Mihr, single-volume edition, Lahore, n.d. (1957?) (Khutut)

Makātib i Ghālib, ed. Imtiyāz 'Alī 'Arshī, Rampur, 1937. (Makatib)

Nādirāt i Ghālib, ed. Āfāq Ḥusain Āfāq, Karachi, 1949. (Nadirat)

Mutafariqāt i Ghālib, ed. Mas'ūd Ḥasan Riẓvī, Rampur, 1947. (Mutafariqat)

Adabī Khutūt i Ghālib, ed. Mirzā Muḥammad 'Askarī, 7th impression, Karachi, 1964. (Adabi Khutut)

Urdu translation of *Dastambū* by Makhmūr Sa'īdī, published in the issue of the journal *Taḥrīk*, Delhi, dated April-May, 1961.

Dīwān i Ghālib (Urdu), ed. Imtiyāz 'Alī 'Arshī, Aligarh, 1958. (Diwan)

B. OTHER WORKS

Yādgār i Ghālib, by Altāf Ḥusain Ḥālī, Lucknow, 1932. (Yadgar)

Where necessary, we have checked the text of this edition with others, especially Khalīl ur Raḥmān Dāūdī's edition (Majlis i Taraqqī i Adab, Lahore, 1963). Dāūdī's notes are often perverse, but valuable.

Ghālib, by Ghulām Rasūl Mihr, 4th edn., Lahore, 1946. (Mihr)

Hayāt i Ghālib, by Shaikh Muḥammad Ikrām, Lahore, n.d. (1957?) (Ikram)

Zikr i Ghālib, by Mālik Rām, 4th edn., Delhi, 1964. (Zikr)

Talāmizai Ghālib, by Mālik Rām, Delhi, 1958. (Talamiza)

Āb i Ḥayāt, by Muḥammad Ḥusain Āzād, Lahore, 14th edn., n.d. (1945?). (Azad)

Twilight of the Mughuls, by Percival Spear, Cambridge, 1951. (Spear)

Rambles and Recollections of an Indian Official, by Major-General Sir W. H. Sleeman, K.C.B. Revised annotated edition by Vincent A. Smith, Oxford University Press, 1915. (Sleeman)

The Muslim and Christian Calendars, by G. S. P. Freeman-Grenville, Oxford University Press, 1963.

NOTES AND REFERENCES

INTRODUCTION

p. 9. Studies and translations of Ghalib in English include *Ghalib*, by Sayyid Abdul Latif, Hyderabad (Deccan), 1928; *The Life and Odes of Ghalib*, by Abdulla Anwar Beg, Lahore, 1940; *Interpretations of Ghalib*, by J. L. Kaul, Delhi, 1957; *Ghalib, his life and Persian poetry*, by Arifshah C. Gilani, Karachi, 1957; *Selections from Ghalib*, by H. C. Saraswat, New Delhi, n.d., *Ghalib, the Man and his Verse*, by P. L. Lakhanpal, Delhi, 1960, and *Whispers from Ghalib*, by Sufee A. Q. Niaz, Lahore, 1960.

NOTE ON MUSLIM NAMES

p. 14. Yadgar, p. 12.

p. 14. The eminent historian is Vincent Smith. See his edition of Sleeman, p. 524, n. 2.

p. 16. For Ghalib's dislike of the name Mirza Nosha see p. 176 of the present volume.

CHAPTER 1. FAMILY BACKGROUND: BOYHOOD AND YOUTH IN AGRA

p. 21. Spear, p. 1.

p. 23. Khutut, p. 464.

p. 24 ff. The main source for the factual material in the remainder of the chapter is Ikram. Our judgements do not always agree with his.

p. 24. Yadgar, p. 116, n.

p. 25. In our view the evidence for believing that 'Abdus Ṣamad was a fiction of Ghalib's imagination (as Ghalib himself sometimes asserted) is insufficient to be accepted. The position probably was that 'Abdus Ṣamad helped him to acquire a mastery of Persian, but was never his *ustād* in the more specialised sense of the practised poet who guides a novice in his efforts. Ghalib perhaps sometimes represented him in this light to stop the mouths of those who argued that a poet who had never had an *ustād* could not claim to be an accomplished poet.

p. 27. Yadgar, pp. 12–13.

p. 27, l. 20. The phrase from Ghalib is quoted in Yadgar, p. 13.

p. 27, l. 21. Cf. p. 81 below. The original there translated as 'for centuries' means literally 'for a hundred generations'.

p. 27, l. 37. Ghalib's attitude to Urdu—Cf. (e.g.) p. 80, 81, and 185 below.

p. 28, l. 7. Ghalib's words are quoted in Ikram, p. 34.

p. 28, l. 24. Quoted in Yadgar, p. 8.

CHAPTER 2. DELHI AND CALCUTTA, *c.* 1810–29.

p. 29. Nasr i Farsi, pp. 191–2.

p. 30, l. 3. Spear, p. 6.

p. 30, l. 20. Yadgar, p. 4.

p. 30, l. 38. Ikram, p. 37.

p. 32, l. 11 ff. Sleeman, pp. 523–4, and Vincent A. Smith's prefatory Memoir, p. xxix.

p. 32, l. 33. Yadgar, p. 73.

pp. 33–4. Yadgar, pp. 85 ff.

p. 34, l. 42. Yadgar, p. 105.

p. 35, l. 19. Yadgar, p. 80.

p. 35, l. 24. Yadgar, p. 78.

p. 35, l. 30. For Ghalib's view on *jabr* (predestination) and *ikhtiyār* (free will) cf. for example, p. 70 below.

p. 36. Yadgar, pp. 78, 76, 69, 64.

p. 37. Yadgar, pp. 83, 72–3, 81.

p. 38. Yadgar, pp. 71, 21, 119 ff.

p. 39, l. 2, Yadgar, pp. 122–3.

p. 39, l. 37. Yadgar, p. 121.

p. 40, l. 1. Azad, pp. 504–5.

p. 40, l. 9. Yadgar, p. 121.

p. 40, l. 27. Yadgar, p. 122.

p. 41, l. 1. Nasr i Farsi, p. 196.

p. 41, l. 10. Yadgar, pp. 20–1.

p. 41, l. 17. Khutut, p. 226.

p. 41, l. 26. Yadgar, pp. 125, 65, 31.

p. 42, Yadgar, pp. 75, 76, 78.

p. 42, l. 30. Khutut, p. 228.

p. 43. Nasr i Farsi, p. 197.

p. 44, l. 11. Cf. Ghalib's letter of July 28th, 1862, quoted on p. 272 of the present volume.

p. 44, l. 20. Spear, pp. 182–3. The latter part of this statement may give a false impression; Ahmad Bakhsh originally had to pay the British Rs. 25,000 a year. The account of Ghalib's 'pension' and its history is based partly on Spear and partly (mainly, in fact) on Ikram, but modified in the light of Mālik Rām's comments.

p. 46, l. 2. Yadgar, p. 23. Dāūdī, however, quoting Mihr, says that Sir John Malcolm's role was limited to confirming that the signature and seal on the document of 1806 were in fact Lord Lake's. (See p. 27, n. 2 of his edition of Yadgar.).

p. 46, l. 26 Yadgar, p. 29.

p. 46, l. 29. Mālik Rām points out (Zikr, p. 64), that Ghalib himself gives a different reason for his visit to Lucknow. He says that he fell ill in Kanpur and went to Lucknow because he could not get expert medical attention in Kanpur.

p. 47, l. 15. Khutut, p. 433.

p. 47, l. 27. Yadgar, p. 24.

p. 48, l. 19. Quoted in Ikram, p. 86.

p. 48, l. 29. Quoted in Ikram, p. 85.

p. 49, l. 1. Yadgar, pp. 74–5.

p. 49, l. 16. Diwan, p. 123.

CHAPTER 3. DELHI, 1829–47

p. 51, l. 8. Nasr i Farsi, p. 134.

p. 51, l. 15. Nasr i Farsi, p. 149.

p. 51, l. 26. The letter is quoted in Ikram, p. 97.

p. 52, l. 9. Nasr i Farsi, p. 161.

p. 52, l. 32. Spear, p. 164.

p. 52, l. 39. Ikram, p. 99, n.

p. 54, l. 1. Nasr i Farsi, p. 163.

p. 54, l. 19. Spear, p. 189.

p. 54, l. 28. Nasr i Farsi, p. 103.

p. 56, l. 3. Quoted in Ikram, p. 105.

p. 56, l. 11. Nasr i Farsi, p. 261.

p. 57, l. 14. Nasr i Farsi, p. 169.

p. 57, l. 23. Nasr i Farsi, p. 139.

p. 57, l. 35. Nasr i Farsi, p. 110.

p. 58, l. 13. Nasr i Farsi, p. 159.

p. 59, l. 1. Nasr i Farsi, p. 156.

p. 59, l. 19. See p. 303.

p. 59, l. 22–p. 62. Nasr i Farsi, pp. 135, 137, 140, 147, 150.

p. 62, l. 37. Yadgar, p. 31.

p. 63, l. 31. Quoted in Ikram, p. 73.

p. 64, l. 13. Khutut, p. 186.

p. 64, l. 36. Khutut, p. 366.

p. 66, l. 11. He was charged with keeping a gaming house—cf. Zikr, p. 107.

p. 66, l. 12. Quoted in Ikram, p. 120.

p. 66, l. 19. Yadgar, p. 32.

p. 67 footnote. Cf. Zikr, p. 108.

p. 67, paras. 2 and 3. Talamiza, p. 177 ff.

p. 68, l. 4. Nasr i Farsi, p. 202.

p. 68, l. 14. Mihr, p. 188.

p. 68, l. 27. The full text is given in Mihr, p. 189 ff.

p. 70, l. 23. Yadgar, p. 32.

CHAPTER 4. GHALIB AND THE MUGHAL COURT, 1847–57

p. 71, l. 5. It is possible that Ghalib was already living in the same house before his imprisonment. (Cf. Mihr, pp. 80–1, Nadirat, notes, p. 118, Zikr, p. 254.).

p. 71, l. 9. Yadgar, p. 34.

p. 71, l. 24. Ikram, p. 135.

p. 72, l. 9. Yadgar, pp. 178–9.

p. 72, l. 27. Nadirat, no. 4. Āfāq assumes that this passage is inspired by the memory of 1847, and this assumption seems reasonable.

pp. 73–4. Nasr i Farsi, pp. 268–9, and 273.

p. 74, l. 26. Nadirat, no. 46.

p. 75, l. 1. Nadirat, no. 6.

p. 75, l. 14. Yadgar, p. 174.

p. 75, ll. 20 ff. Nadirat, nos. 14 and 9; no. 26; cf. also no. 46.

p. 76, l. 25. Nadirat, no. 21.

p. 77. Publication of *Mihr i Nīmroz*—cf. Nadirat, p. 152, Nadirat, no. 46. The fate of *Māh i Nimmāh* is discussed by Āfāq in Nadirat, pt. 1, pp. 61–2.

p. 77, ll. 12 ff. Nadirat, nos. 59, 64.

p. 78, l. 31. Nadirat, no. 65.

p. 78, l. 34–p. 79. Azad, pp. 510–12.

p. 80, l. 1. Nasr i Farsi, pp. 225–6.

p. 80, l. 31–p. 81. Azad, pp. 512–13; Diwan, pp. 124–5.

p. 82. Yadgar, p. 126.

p. 83, l. 19. Nadirat, no. 10.

p. 83, l. 28. Nadirat, no. 20.

p. 83, l. 41. Nadirat, no. 27.

p. 84, l. 16. Yadgar, pp. 37–8.

p. 85, l. 9 ff. Yadgar, pp. 88–9.

p. 86, l. 8. Nadirat, no. 51.

p. 86, l. 11. Zakāullah, in a letter to Muḥammad Ḥusain Āzād reproduced in *Nigār* (Rampur), Feb. 1963, p. 11.

p. 86, l. 15. Nadirat, no. 19.

p. 86, l. 30. Nasr i Farsi, p. 238.

p. 87. l. 21 ff. Nasr i. Farsi, pp. 201–2.

p. 88, l. 13. Yadgar, p. 90.

p. 88, l. 29. Nadirat, no. 57.

p. 89, l. 1. Khutut, p. 120.

p. 89, l. 25. Khutut, p. 143 (no. 27).

p. 90, l. 8. Nadirat, no. 58.

p. 90, l. 29. Yadgar, pp. 91–2, and 93.

p. 91, l. 11. Nadirat, no. 28.

p. 91, l. 25. Nadirat, no. 30.

p. 91, l. 29. Nadirat, no. 39.

p. 91, l. 33. Khutut, p. 352.

p. 91, l. 38. Khutut, p. 127.

p. 92, l. 18. Khutut, p. 140 (no. 21).

p. 92, l. 32. Khutut, p. 141 (no. 23).

p. 93, l. 4, Khutut, p. 126 (no. 6).

p. 93, l. 9. Khutut, p. 136.

p. 93, l. 18. Khutut, pp. 139–40.

p. 93, l. 28. Nasr i Farsi, p. 241.

p. 94, l. 1. Nasr i Farsi, p. 232.

p. 94, l. 25. Nasr i Farsi, pp. 215–16.

p. 95, l. 6. Despite this high praise, he sometimes had to explain verses to Ḥaqīr, cf. Nadirat, nos. 22 and 28.

p. 95, l. 13. Khutut, p. 124.

p. 95, l. 20. Khutut, pp. 125–6.

p. 95, l. 32. Khutut, p. 139.

p. 95, l. 39. Khutut, pp. 140, 141.

p. 96, l. 8 ff. Nadirat, nos. 32 and 34.

p. 96, l. 33. Khutut, p. 124.

p. 97, l. 14. Yadgar, p. 97.

p. 97, l. 23. Yadgar, p. 64.

p. 98, l. 1. Nadirat, no. 71.

p. 98, l. 16. Yadgar, p. 75.

p. 98, l. 37. Yadgar, pp. 83–4.

p. 99, l. 26. Ikram, p. 143.

p. 99, l. 34. Khutut, p. 633.

p. 100, l. 2. Yadgar, pp. 81–2.

p. 101, l. 4. Yadgar, p. 72.

p. 101, l. 10. Ikram, pp. 145–6.

p. 101, l. 23. Nadirat, no. 40.

p. 101, l. 25. Ikram, pp. 146–7.

p. 101, l. 35. Yadgar, p. 147.

CHAPTER 5. MORE LETTERS, 1847–56

p. 103, l. 3. Yadgar, p. 179.

p. 103, l. 21. Nasr i Farsi, p. 250. The dating of this letter presents problems which well illustrate the difficulties which editors of Ghalib's text will have to face. The date appears in the published text as "Friday, 1st December AD 1848, 4th Muharram, 1251 AH." However, 1st December 1848 was not a Friday, but a Saturday; it corresponded to 5th Muharram, not the 4th, and to 1265 AH, not 1251 AH. How much of this confusion is due to Ghalib and how much due to his publisher's calligrapher we do not know.

p. 104, l. 16. Yadgar, pp. 103–4.

p. 104, l. 28. Cf. pp. 353–4 below.

p. 104. l. 33. Ikram, p. 139.

p. 104, l. 38. Nadirat, no. 11.

p. 105, l. 14. Talamiza, p. 220.

p. 105, l. 22. Yadgar, p. 39.

p. 105, l. 31 ff. Nadirat, nos. 4, 5.

p. 106, l. 2. Nadirat, no. 22.

p. 106, ll. 11 ff. Nadirat. nos. 39, 41, 45, 46.

p. 107. Nadirat, nos. 46, 47, 48, 49, 50.

p. 108. Nadirat, nos. 59, 67, 68, 5, 19.

p. 109. Nadirat, nos. 31, 32.

p. 110. Nadirat, nos. 33, 34.

p. 111. Nadirat, nos. 46, 12, 41.

p. 112. Nadirat, nos, 42, 33.

p. 113. Nadirat, nos. 35, 29, 40.

p. 113, l. 18. Khutut, p. 133 n.

p. 114. Nadirat, no. 47.

p. 115, l. 7. Khutut, p. 120.

p. 115, l. 19. Nadirat, no. 5, and see Āfāq's note on p. 100.

p. 115, l. 33. Nadirat, no. 15.

p. 116, l. 1. Khutut, p. 123.

p. 116, l. 5. Nadirat, no. 17.

p. 116, l. 28. Khutut, p. 126.

p. 116, l. 41. Nadirat, no. 18.

p. 117. Nadirat, nos. 19, 24.

p. 118, l. 1. Khutut, p. 128. Mihr argues in a footnote (p. 129) that it must be dated May, 1852, though in his main text he writes "10th December, 1852" and says that all previous texts give "1853," which "is clearly wrong."

p. 118, l. 12. Nadirat, notes, pp. 134–5.

p. 118, l. 27. Nadirat, no. 30.

p. 118, l. 31. Khutut, p. 134.

p. 119, l. 5. Khutut, p. 135.

p. 119, l. 10. Nadirat, no. 30.

p. 119, l. 33. Khutut, p. 135.

p. 120, l. 1. Khutut, p. 136.

p. 120, l. 12. Khutut, p. 138.

p. 120, l. 34. Nadirat, no. 36.

p. 121, l. 7. Nadirat, no. 37.

p. 121, l. 19. Khutut, p. 142, no. 25.

p. 121, l. 24. Nadirat, no. 39.

p. 121, l. 32. Nadirat, no. 40.

p. 122, l. 20. Nadirat, no. 41.

p. 122, l. 27. Khutut, p. 143, no. 26.

p. 122, l. 34. Nadirat, no. 46.

p. 123, l. 16. Nadirat, no. 50.

p. 123, l. 32. Khutut, p. 511.

p. 124, l. 4. Khutut, p. 349

p. 124, l. 17. Letter d. October 2nd, 1855—Khutut, p. 351.

p. 124, l. 28. Khutut, p. 354.

p. 124, l. 31. Nadirat, no. 56.

p. 125, Nadirat, nos. 57, 58, 60.

p. 126. Nadirat, nos. 61, 65.

p. 127, l. 8. Khutut, p. 512.

p. 127, l. 33. Khutut, p. 353, no. 5.

p. 128, l. 27. Khutut, p. 584.

p. 129, l. 3 ff. Khutut, p. 587–8.

p. 129, l. 29. Quoted in Ikram, p. 148.

p. 130, l. 1. Khutut, pp. 511–12.

p. 130, l. 8. Nadirat, no. 68.

p. 130, l. 26. Quoted in Ikram, p. 149.

CHAPTER 6. THE REVOLT OF 1857

p. 132, l. 4. Khutut, p. 469.

p. 132, l. 19. Makatib, p. 13.

p. 132, l. 23. Khutut, p. 144.

p. 132, l. 30. Ikram, p. 150.

p. 133, l. 6—135, l. 14. Nasr i Farsi, pp. 397–8. Dastambu occupies pp. 378–411 of Nasr i Farsi. For the remainder of this chapter we give page references only where a new theme commences or where our translation continues after the omission of a passage of substantial length.

p. 135, l. 15. Nasr i Farsi, p. 381.

p. 135, l. 35. Nasr i Farsi, p. 381 (last line) ff.

p. 138, l. 9. Nasr i Farsi, p. 385.

p. 138, l. 24. Nasr i Farsi, p. 386.

p. 140, l. 21. Nasr i Farsi, p. 388. (last line) ff.

p. 143, l. 1. Nasr i Farsi, p. 392.

p. 143, l. 39. Nasr i Farsi, p. 395.

p. 144, l. 36. Nasr i Farsi, p. 396.

p. 145, l. 36. Nasr i Farsi, p. 398.

p. 146, l. 23. Nasr i Farsi, p. 399.

p. 149, l. 8. Khutut, p. 53.

p. 149, l. 22. Yadgar, p. 42.

p. 150, l. 3. Quoted by Ikram, pp. 163–4.

p. 150, l. 23. Khutut, p. 144.

p. 151, l. 35. Spear, pp. 218–19.

p. 152, l. 14. Khutut, p. 370.

p. 152, l. 28. This letter is unaccountably missing from Mihr's Khutut. Mālik Rām's revised edition (1962) of Mahesh Parshād's _Khuṭūṭ i Ghālib_ places it between a letter dated 26th June [1858] and one dated 18th July 1858.

p. 154, l. 7. Makatib, Dībāca, pp. 69–70.

p. 154, l. 18. Khutut, p. 359.

CHAPTER 7. 1858: THE AFTERMATH

p. 156, l. 3. Khutut, p. 144.

p. 156, l. 14. Nasr i Farsi, p. 401.

p. 156, l. 21. Nasr i Farsi, p. 407.

p. 157, l. 33 ff. Nasr i Farsi, pp. 402, 403, 404, 406.

p. 158, l. 6 ff. Nasr i Farsi, pp. 406–7.

p. 158, l. 31. Nasr i Farsi, pp. 408–9.

p. 159, l. 10. Khutut, pp. 370–1.

p. 159, l. 20. Khutut, p. 145.

p. 159, l. 27. Khutut, p. 146.

p. 160, l. 3. Nasr i Farsi, p. 402.

p. 160, l. 21. Khutut, p. 266.

p. 160, n. l, cf. Nasr i Farsi, p. 406.

p. 161, l. 20. Khutut, p. 106.

p. 161, l. 32. Khutut, p. 210.

p. 162, l. 1. Nasr i Farsi, p. 403.

p. 162, l. 19. Nasr i Farsi, p. 402.

p. 162, l. 25. Nasr i Farsi, p. 404.

p. 162, l. 32. Nasr i Farsi, p. 404.

p. 163, l. 2. Nasr i Farsi, p. 405.

p. 163, l. 29. Khutut, p. 211.

p. 164, l. 13. Khutut, p. 371, no. 4.
p. 164, l. 20. Khutut, p. 148, no. 32.
p. 164, l. 27. Khutut, p. 149, no. 35.
p. 164, l. 31. Khutut, p. 267, no. 2.
p. 165, l. 7. Khutut, p. 372.
p. 165, l. 18. Khutut, pp. 106–7.
p. 166, l. 1. Khutut, p. 107.
p. 166, l. 5. Khutut, p. 372.
p. 166, l. 25. Khutut, p. 150.
p. 167, l. 7. Khutut, pp. 267–8.
p. 167, l. 33. Khutut, pp. 468–9.
p. 168, l. 16. Khutut, p. 151.
p. 169, l. 1. Nasr i Farsi, p. 407.
p. 169, l. 14. Khutut, p. 152, no. 39.
p. 169, l. 28. Khutut, p. 152, no. 40.
p. 170, l. 2. Khutut. p. 373, no. 8.
p. 170, l. 7. Khutut, pp. 268–9.
p. 170, l. 15. Khutut, pp. 147–8.
p. 170, l. 36. Nasr i Farsi, p. 409.
p. 171, l. 41. Nasr i Farsi, p. 411.
p. 172, l. 8. Khutut, pp. 268–9.
p. 172, l. 30. Khutut, p. 159.
p. 172, l. 35, Khutut, pp. 216–17.
p. 173, l. 16. Khutut, pp. 153–4.
p. 173, l. 34. Khutut, pp. 154–5.
p. 174, l. 5. Khutut, pp. 156–7.
p. 174, l. 23. Khutut, p. 232.
p. 175, l. 3. Khutut, p. 234.
p. 175, l. 27. Khutut, pp. 157–8.
p. 176, l. 27. Khutut, p. 158.
p. 176, l. 36. Khutut, p. 159.
p. 177, l. 1. Khutut, p. 163.
p. 177, l. 22. Makatib, p. 15.
p. 177, l. 30 ff. Khutut, pp. 166, 168, and 221–2.
p. 178, l. 22. Khutut, p. 262.
p. 178, l. 33. Khutut, p. 212.
p. 179, l. 8. Khutut, p. 236.
p. 180, l. 9. Khutut, p. 214.
p. 180, l. 22. Khutut, p. 215.
p. 180, l. 37. Khutut, p. 242, no. 10.
p. 181, l. 10. Khutut, pp. 168 and 242, no. 11.
p. 181, l. 21. Khutut, p. 244.
p. 182, l. 16. Khutut, p. 242.
p. 182, l. 26. Khutut, p. 219.
p. 182, l. 38. Ikram, p. 159.
p. 183, l. 12. Makatib, p. 16.
p. 183, l. 18. Khutut, p. 169.
p. 183, l. 27. Khutut, pp. 222–3.
p. 184, l. 26. Khutut, pp. 224–6.
p. 184, l. 36. Khutut, p. 245.
p. 185, l. 30. Khutut, p. 171, no. 61.
p. 186, l. 11. Khutut, p. 269.
p. 186, l. 17. Khutut, p. 372.

p. 186, l. 27. Khutut, p. 602.

p. 186, l. 32. Khutut, pp. 55–6.

p. 187, l. 1. Khutut, pp. 47–8.

p. 187, l. 35. Khutut, p. 170.

p. 188, l. 27. Khutut, pp. 469–70.

p. 189, l. 23, Khutut, p. 468, no. 1.

p. 189, l. 29. Khutut, p. 470.

p. 189, l. 36. Khutut, p. 215.

p. 190, l. 1. Khutut, p. 239.

p. 190, l. 11, Khutut, p. 169.

p. 190, l. 15. Khutut, pp. 271–2.

CHAPTER 8. 1859

p. 192, l. 4. Khutut, p. 171, no. 62, where it is mistakenly dated 26th January.

p. 192, l. 8. Khutut, pp. 323–4.

p. 193, l. 3. Khutut, p. 247.

p. 193, l. 10. Khutut, p. 172, no. 63.

p. 193, l. 14. Khutut, pp. 272–4.

p. 194, l. 20. Khutut, pp. 324–5.

p. 195, l. 6. Khutut, pp. 172–3.

p. 195, l. 34. Khutut, p.p 173–4.

p. 196, l. 11. Khutut, p. 174.

p. 196, l. 16. Khutut, p. 274.

p. 197, l. 12. Khutut, p. 275.

p. 197, l. 39. Khutut, p. 276.

p. 199, l. 1. Khutut, p. 277.

p. 199, l. 31. Khutut, p. 278.

p. 199, l. 37. Khutut, pp. 247–8.

p. 200, l. 35. Khutut, pp. 249–50.

p. 201, l. 28. Khutut, p. 513.

p. 202, l. 5. Khutut, p. 279.

p. 203, l. 11. Khutut, p. 226.

p. 204, l. 22. Khutut, pp. 227–8.

p. 204, l. 35. Khutut, pp. 250–1.

p. 206, l. 7. Khutut, p. 175.

p. 206, l. 20. Khutut, p. 176.

p. 207, l. 1. Khutut, pp. 384–7.

p. 208, l. 7. Khutut, p. 387.

p. 209, l. 36. Khutut, p. 396.

p. 211, l. 3. Khutut, pp. 503–4.

p. 211, l. 24. Khutut, pp. 398–9.

p. 212, l. 23. Khutut, p. 252.

p. 212, l. 32. Khutut, p. 399.

p. 213, l. 24. Khutut, p. 389.

p. 213, l. 37. Khutut, p. 280.

p. 214, l. 38. Khutut, p. 281.

p. 215, l. 8. Khutut, p. 400.

p. 216, l. 12, Khutut, p. 515.

p. 216, l. 26, Makatib, p. 20.

p. 216, l. 29. Khutut, pp. 176–7.

p. 217, l. 10. Khutut, pp. 282–3.

p. 217, l. 32. Khutut, p. 390.

p. 218, l. 16. Khutut, pp. 253–4.
p. 218, l. 38. Makatib, p. 21.
p. 219, l. 21. Khutut, p. 283.
p. 220, l. 2. Khutut, p. 391.
p. 220, l. 27. Khutut, p. 254.
p. 221, l. 2. Khutut, p. 403.
p. 223, l. 8. Khutut, p. 405.
p. 223, l. 36. Khutut, p. 284.
p. 224, l. 6. Khutut, p. 285.
p. 224, l. 32. Khutut, p. 286.
p. 225, l. 12. Khutut, p. 392.
p. 225, l. 34. Khutut, p. 179.
p. 226, l. 21. Khutut, p. 393.

CHAPTER 9. 1860

p. 228, l. 2. Khutut, p. 287.
p. 228, l. 17. Khutut, p. 327.
p. 228, l. 27. Makatib, p. 24.
p. 229, l. 4. Makatib, p. 24.
p. 229, l. 14. Khutut, p. 179.
p. 229, l. 23. Khutut, p. 375, no. 11.
p. 229, l. 34. Khutut, p. 180, no. 77.
p. 230, l. 9. Khutut, p. 375, no. 12.
p. 230, l. 29. Khutut, p. 376.
p. 231, l. 18. Khutut, p. 181.
p. 231, l. 24. Khutut, p. 255, no. 30.
p. 231, l. 26. Khutut, p. 407.
p. 231, l. 33. Khutut, p. 288.
p. 232, l. 36. Khutut, p. 181.
p. 233, l. 24. Khutut, p. 182.
p. 233, l. 34. Khutut, p. 487.
p. 234, l. 10. Khutut, p. 182.
p. 234, l. 28. Khutut, p. 57.
p. 234, l. 34. Khutut, p. 183.
p. 235, l. 7. Khutut, p. 491.
p. 235, l. 14. Khutut, p. 408.
p. 235, l. 18. Ikram, p. 181.
p. 235, l. 34. Hali, *Ḥayāt i Jāwed*, Lahore, 1958, pp. 125–6 (footnote).
p. 236, l. 26. Khutut, p. 488.
p. 237, l. 37. Khutut, p. 256.
p. 238, l. 30. Khutut, p. 409.
p. 238, l. 36. Khutut, p. 428.
p. 239, l. 3. Khutut, p. 257, no. 32.
p. 239, l. 13. Khutut, p. 257, no. 33.
p. 239, l. 26. Khutut, p. 105.
p. 240, l. 24. Khutut, p. 409.
p. 241, l. 7. Khutut, p. 290.
p. 241, l. 12. Khutut, p. 428.
p. 241, l. 20. Khutut, p. 429.
p. 241, l. 25. Khutut, p. 57.
p. 242, l. 9. Khutut, p. 183.
p. 242, l. 24. Khutut, p. 358.
p. 243, l. 41. Khutut, p. 360.

p. 244, l. 7. Khutut, p. 361.
p. 244, l. 11. Khutut, p. 361, no. 14.
p. 244, l. 23. Khutut, p. 362.
p. 244, l. 32. Khutut, p. 491.
p. 245, l. 24. Khutut, p. 490.
p. 246, l. 5. Khutut, p. 56.
p. 246, l. 15. Khutut, p. 431.
p. 246, l. 26. Khutut, p. 56.
p. 246, l. 35. Khutut, p. 430.
p. 248, l. 4. Khutut, p. 184.
p. 248, l. 28. Khutut, p. 228.
p. 249, l. 11. Khutut, p. 229.
p. 249, l. 34. Khutut, p. 290.
p. 250, l. 12. Khutut, p. 432.

CHAPTER 10. 1861

p. 251, l. 3. Khutut, p. 291, no. 29.
p. 251, l. 14. Khutut, p. 291, no. 30.
p. 252, l. 7. Khutut, p. 292.
p. 253, l. 4. Khutut, p. 294.
p. 253, l. 14. Khutut, p. 184.
p. 253, l. 29. Khutut, p. 185.
p. 254, l. 3. Khutut, p. 516.
p. 254, l. 10. Khutut, p. 58.
p. 255, l. 2. Khutut, p. 295.
p. 255, l. 12. Khutut, p. 61.
p. 256, l. 17. Khutut, p. 517, no. 7.
p. 256, l. 30. Makatib, p. 29 (footnote).
p. 257, l. 4. Makatib, p. 29.
p. 257, l. 22. Makatib, p. 30.
p. 258, l. 3. Khutut, p. 297.
p. 259 (footnote). Ram Babu Saxena, *European and Indo-European Poets of Urdu and Persian*, Lucknow, 1941, p. 70.
p. 259, l. 7. Khutut, p. 299.
p. 260, l. 6. Khutut, p. 257.
p. 260, l. 30. Khutut, p. 300.
p. 261, l. 21. Khutut, p. 108.
p. 262, l. 4. Khutut, p. 65.
p. 262, l. 35. Khutut, p. 66.
p. 263, l. 21. Khutut, p. 67.
p. 263, l. 32. Khutut, p. 435.
p. 264, l. 14. Khutut, p. 363.
p. 265, l. 1. Makatib, p. 33.
p. 265, l. 9. Khutut, p. 436.
p. 265, l. 17. Khutut, p. 185.
p. 265, l. 20. Khutut, p. 186.
p. 265, l. 22. Khutut, p. 187.
p. 265, l. 24. Khutut, p. 583.
p. 265, l. 28. Khutut, p. 507.

CHAPTER 11. 1862

p. 267, l. 4. Khutut, p. 421.

p. 267, l. 23. Khutut, p. 68.
p. 268, l. 8. Khutut, p. 68.
p. 269, l. 4. Khutut, p. 70.
p. 270, l. 10. Khutut, p. 72.
p. 270, l. 31. Khutut, p. 72.
p. 271, l. 11. Khutut, p. 551.
p. 271, l. 16. Khutut, p. 74.
p. 272, l. 10. Khutut, p. 75.
p. 272, l. 15. Khutut, p. 77.
p. 272, l. 22. Khutut, p. 77.
p. 275, l. 19. Khutut, p. 301.
p. 275, l. 34. Khutut, p. 81.
p. 276, l. 36. Khutut, p. 303.
p. 278, l. 1. Khutut, p. 305.
p. 278, l. 27. Khutut, p. 306.
p. 279, l. 15. Khutut, p. 365.
p. 279, l. 23. Khutut, p. 189.
p. 279, l. 27. Khutut, p. 190.
p. 280, l. 14. Khutut, p. 191.

CHAPTER 12. 1863

p. 281, l. 2. Khutut, p. 437, no. 12.
p. 281, l. 7. Khutut, p. 377.
p. 281, l. 23. Khutut, p. 307.
p. 282, l. 3. Khutut, p. 328.
p. 283, l. 18. Khutut, p. 192.
p. 283, l. 32. Makatib, p. 35.
p. 284, l. 5. Khutut, p. 313.
p. 284, l. 16. Khutut, p. 258.
p. 284, l. 26. Khutut, p. 83.
p. 284, l. 35. Khutut, p. 84.
p. 285, l. 15. Khutut, p. 85.
p. 286, l. 1. Khutut, p. 85.
p. 286, l. 17. Khutut, p. 519.
p. 286, l. 35. Khutut, p. 86.
p. 287, l. 12. Khutut, p. 193, no. 98.
p. 287, l. 35. Khutut, p. 87.
p. 288, l. 16. Khutut, p. 496.
p. 289, l. 10. Khutut, p. 501.
p. 289, l. 20. Khutut, p. 194.
p. 289, l. 37. Khutut, p. 194, no. 100.
p. 289, l. 40. Khutut, p. 196.
p. 290, l. 21. Khutut, p. 451.
p. 290, l. 40. Khutut, p. 453.
p. 291, l. 9. Khutut, p. 454.
p. 291, l. 24. Khutut, p. 422.
p. 292, l. 6. Khutut, p. 88.
p. 292, l. 11 ff. Khutut, p. 197, nos. 104, 105.
p. 292, l. 25. Khutut, p. 197.
p. 293, l. 3. Khutut, p. 555.
p. 293, l. 24. Khutut, p. 88.
p. 294, l. 9. Khutut, p. 308.

CHAPTER 13. 1864

p. 294, l. 26. Khutut, p. 596.
p. 295, l. 8. Khutut, p. 89.
p. 296, l. 4. Khutut, p. 520.
p. 296, l. 10. Khutut, p. 653.
p. 296, l. 30. Khutut, p. 571.
p. 297, l. 13. Khutut, p. 367.
p. 298, l. 1. Khutut, p. 330.
p. 298, l. 17. Khutut, p. 48.
p. 298, l. 31. Khutut, p. 523.
p. 298, l. 37. Khutut, p. 315.
p. 299, l. 7. Khutut, p. 93.
p. 299, l. 27. Khutut, p. 535.
p. 299, l. 34. Khutut, p. 111.
p. 300, l. 22. Khutut, p. 112.
p. 300, l. 37. Khutut, p. 523.
p. 302, l. 24. Khutut, p. 330.
p. 303, l. 3. Khutut, p. 331.
p. 303, l. 33. Khutut, p. 332.
p. 304, l. 7. Khutut, p. 582.
p. 304, l. 33. Khutut, p. 198.
p. 305, l. 16. Khutut, p. 94.
p. 305, l. 28. Khutut, p. 198.
p. 306, l. 18. Khutut, p. 94.
p. 306, l. 34. Makatib, p. 40.
p. 307, l. 9. Makatib, p. 41.
p. 307, l. 20. Makatib, p. 42.
p. 307, l. 32. Makatib, p. 43, n.
p. 308, l. 5. Khutut, p. 598.
p. 308, l. 16. Khutut, p. 438.
p. 308, l. 29. Khutut, p. 413.
p. 309, l. 8. Khutut, p. 199.
p. 309, l. 39. Khutut, p. 200.

CHAPTER 14. 1865

p. 311, l. 13. Khutut, p. 95.
p. 311, l. 23. Khutut, p. 96.
p. 312, l. 2. Khutut, p. 579.
p. 312, l. 10. Khutut, p. 201.
p. 312, l. 23. Khutut, p. 96.
p. 313, l. 9. Khutut, p. 98.
p. 313, l. 19. Khutut, p. 588.
p. 313, l. 28. Khutut, p. 378.
p. 314, l. 23. Khutut, p. 379.
p. 314, l. 33. Khutut, p. 651.
p. 315, l. 6. Khutut, p. 616.
p. 315, l. 16. Khutut, p. 440.
p. 315, l. 22. Khutut, p. 599.
p. 315, l. 31. Khutut, p. 201, no. 113.
p. 315, l. 35. Khutut, p. 202.
p. 316, l. 17. Khutut, p. 204.
p. 316, l. 23. Khutut, p. 205.

N

p. 316, l. 34. Khutut, p. 49.
p. 317, l. 23. Makatib, p. 52.
p. 317, l. 33. Makatib, p. 53.
p. 318, l. 3. Khutut, p. 332.
p. 318, l. 17. Khutut, p. 310.
p. 318, l. 30. Khutut, p. 311.
p. 319, l. 14. Makatib, p. 55.
p. 319, l. 22. Khutut, p. 50.
p. 319, l. 31. Khutut, p. 440.
p. 320, l. 10. Khutut, p. 530, no. 5.
p. 320, l. 25. Khutut, p. 531.
p. 321, l. 15. Makatib, p. 58.
p. 321, l. 26. Makatib, p. 61.
p. 321, l. 35. Makatib, p. 62.
p. 322, l. 26. Makatib, p. 64.
p. 323, l. 2. Khutut, p. 99.
p. 323, l. 10. Khutut, p. 533.
p. 323, l. 35. Khutut, p. 380.
p. 324, l. 10. Khutut, p. 380.
p. 324, l. 25. Khutut, p. 381.
p. 325, l. 5. Khutut, p. 383.
p. 325, l. 17. Khutut, p. 112.
p. 325, l. 22. Yadgar, p. 45.
p. 326, l. 4. Khutut, p. 525.
p. 326. l. 10. Khutut, p. 381.
p. 327, l. 4. Khutut, p. 205.
p. 327, l. 24. Khutut, p. 588.
p. 328, l. 8. Khutut, p. 99.
p. 329, l. 3. Khutut, p. 410, no. 2.
p. 329, l. 20. Khutut, p. 386.
p. 329, l. 34. Khutut, p. 100.
p. 330, l. 14. Khutut, p. 101.

CHAPTER 15. 1866

p. 331, l. 6. Makatib, p. 65.
p. 331, l. 25. Makatib, p. 68, (footnote 2).
p. 331, l. 31. Makatib, p. 68.
p. 332, ll. 5 ff. Khutut, pp. 646, 335, 646.
p. 332, l. 15. Khutut, p. 101.
p. 332, l. 31. Makatib, p. 68.
p. 332, l. 35. Khutut, p. 336.
p. 333, l. 19. Khutut, p. 442.
p. 333, l. 29. Khutut, p. 443.
p. 333, l. 33. Khutut, p. 535.
p. 334, l. 9. Khutut, p. 206.
p. 334, l. 18. Khutut, p. 443.
p. 334, l. 35. Khutut, p. 414.
p. 335, l. 3. Khutut, pp. 444, 443.
p. 335, l. 16. Khutut, p. 444.
p. 335, l. 25. Khutut, p. 525, no. 27.
p. 336, l. 16. Khutut, p. 508.
p. 336, l. 20. Khutut, p. 415.

p. 336, l. 29. Khutut, p. 382.
p. 337, l. 10. Khutut, p. 337, no. 17.
p. 338, l. 2. Khutut, p. 338.
p. 338, l. 5. Khutut, p. 340.
p. 338, l. 16. Khutut, p. 341.
p. 338, l. 27. Khutut, p. 206.
p. 339, l. 7. Khutut, p. 206.
p. 339, l. 11. Khutut, p. 207.
p. 339, l. 20. Khutut, p. 337, no. 16.
p. 339, l. 26. Khutut, p. 424.
p. 340, l. 2. Khutut, p. 460.
p. 340, l. 28. Makatib, p. 75.
p. 341, l. 14. Makatib, p. 76.
p. 341, l. 38. Makatib, p. 76 (footnote).
p. 342, l. 4. Khutut, p. 113.
p. 342, l. 18. Khutut, p. 445.
p. 343, l. 2. Khutut, p. 425.
p. 343, l. 20. Khutut, p. 643.
p. 344, l. 7. Khutut, p. 425.
p. 344, l. 32. Khutut, p. 418.
p. 345, l. 9. Khutut, p. 652.
p. 345, l. 28. Khutut, p. 415.
p. 346, l. 5. Khutut, p. 51.
p. 346, l. 19. Khutut, p. 446.
p. 346, l. 27. Khutut, p. 461.
p. 347, l. 9. Makatib, p. 81.
p. 347, l. 20. Makatib, p. 87.

CHAPTER 16. 1867

p. 348, l. 3. Makatib, p. 89.
p. 348, l. 15. Khutut, p. 462.
p. 349, l. 8. Khutut, p. 463.
p. 350, l. 14. Khutut, p. 641.
p. 350, l. 20. Makatib, p. 91.
p. 350, l. 25. Makatib, p. 92.
p. 350, l. 36. Khutut, p. 448.
p. 351, l. 10. Khutut, p. 449.
p. 352, l. 1. Khutut, p. 567.
p. 352, l. 11. Khutut, p. 51.
p. 353, l. 13. Khutut, p. 426.
p. 353, l. 22. Khutut, p. 450.
p. 354, l. 5. Khutut, p. 557.
p. 354, l. 21. Makatib, p. 95.
p. 354, l. 37. Khutut, p. 114.
p. 355, l. 7. Makatib, p. 96.
p. 355, l. 26. Makatib, p. 97 (footnote 1).
p. 355, l. 34. Makatib, p. 97, no 88.
p. 356, l. 14. Makatib, p. 98 (footnote 1).
p. 356, l. 17. Makatib, p. 100.

CHAPTER 17. THE LAST DAYS, 1868–69

p. 357, l. 3. Makatib, p. 101, note 2.

N*

p. 357, l. 12. Yadgar, p. 45.

p. 357, l. 27. Yadgar, p. 47.

p. 358, l. 38. Khutut, p. 471.

p. 359, l. 6. Khutut, p. 281.

p. 359, l. 24. Khutut, p. 477.

p. 359, l. 35. Khutut, p. 471.

p. 360, l. 8. Khutut, p. 506.

p. 360, l. 14. Khutut, p. 482.

p. 360, l. 22. Khutut, p. 203.

p. 360, l. 29. Khutut, p. 614.

p. 360, l. 31. Khutut, p. 506.

p. 360, l. 36. Khutut, p. 534

p. 361, l. 5. Khutut, p. 188.

p. 361, l. 10. Qāẓī ʿAbdul Vadūd in a review article in the Patna periodical *Maʿāṣir*, part 2, January 1952, quotes some of the more outrageous of Ghalib's own statements.

p. 361, l. 16. Ikram, p. 212.

p. 361, l. 31. Ikram, p. 208.

p. 361, l. 34. Yadgar, pp. 52–3.

p. 361, l. 38. Ikram, p. 209.

p. 362, l. 19. Yadgar, p. 55.

p. 364, l. 10. Khutut, p. 451.

p. 364, l. 19. Khutut, p. 466.

p. 364, l. 30. Khutut, p. 114.

p. 365, l. 6. Khutut, p. 417.

p. 365, l. 25. Khutut, p. 104.

p. 366, l. 1. Makatib, p. 102.

p. 366, l. 19. Khutut, p. 647.

p. 367, l. 1. Makatib, p. 104.

p. 367, l. 8. Makatib, p. 106.

p. 367, l. 14. Makatib, p. 107.

p. 367, l. 28. Khutut, p. 115.

p. 368, l. 3. Makatib, p. 107.

p. 368, l. 7. Makatib, p. 108, note 1.

p. 368, l. 8. Makatib, p. 108.

p. 368, l. 17. Makatib, p. 108, note 2.

p. 368, l. 28 ff. Yadgar, p. 107.

p. 368, (footnote) Khutut, p. 647, n. 2.

p. 369, l. 24. Yadgar, p. 108.

Explanatory Index

Certain names,—e.g. Tafazzul Ḥusain—are listed more than once. This is because identical names do not always indicate identical persons, and in many of Ghālib's references there is insufficient detail to make identification certain. Where any doubt exists, references have been listed separately.